Praise for *Programming Windows Forms in C#*

"Chris may have a strong affinity for semi-colons, but anybody who's programming Windows Forms needs to read this book."
—Brian Randell, Visual Basic Guru and DevelopMentor Instructor

"Chris Sells has done it again. This book has everything a developer needs to know to write serious WinForms applications. Chris leaves no stone unturned in explaining the WinForms programming model and arming developers with the knowledge they need to exploit WinForms to the fullest. And, as if that weren't enough, Chris's writing style makes this book a page-turner for geeks. I couldn't put it down! Until John Grisham gets the .NET religion, you won't find a better WinForms book anywhere."
—Jeff Prosise, co-founder of Wintellect, author of Programming Microsoft .NET

"Chris is clearly 'the' expert on web deployment of WinForms. In this book, Chris explains this material clearly and the power of the technology really shows. Unlike other WinForms books, this manuscript takes a more practical approach to the use of programming tools, such as Visual Studio. Sells's book strikes a nice balance between theory and practice. Windows Forms is an important technology that needs more press. Chris Sells' book is in great position to be the definitive work on the emerging technology."
—Brian Graff, Sr. SW Engineer, PreEmptive Solutions, Inc.

"Chris has written the best WinForms book around. Period."
—Pierre Nallet, DevelopMentor Instructor

"Chris does a nice job of presenting the core elements of WinForms complete with many concise samples and graphic depictions of UI features in action. Even more compelling, however, is how Chris anticipates how most developers will want to use these features, and presents techniques and paradigms of usage that will be invaluable for any serious WinForms developer. This book is destined to become dog-eared in the hands anyone building WinForms applications."
—Fritz Onion, DevelopMentor instructor and author of Essential ASP.NET

"I don't want just a description of the WinForms widgets. I can get that [online or from other books]. What I want is a roadmap for pitfalls to avoid, and innovative solutions for common problems. That is where this book shines."
—Johan Ericcson, SW Engineer, Agilent

"This is the definitive book for every Windows Programmer."
—Fumiaki Yoshimatsu, Sr. Engineer, Intoferia Corporation

"After browsing through countless books that introduce me to Windows Forms basics, it is refreshing to find a book that dives right into some real hard-core programming. This is, without a doubt the best and most useful C#/WinForms book I have ever read. I would suggest this book to be essential reading for very serious .NET WinForms developer who wants to work smarter instead of harder."
—Serge Shimanovsky, Software Developer, Rueters Group PLC

"In this book, Chris Sells discusses how the Windows Forms classes and their supporting infrastructure can be used to write robust and rich smart client applications. If you're an experienced Windows programmer who has previously used MFC or directly utilized the Win32 API to write such applications, you will find Chris's direct delivery very appropriate for transferring your knowledge to the managed classes. If you're a developer with less Windows development experience, you'll find the treatment of core concepts in application UI programming indispensable."
—From the foreword by Mike Blaszczack, Architect, SQL Server Data Warehousing, Microsoft

Microsoft .NET Development Series

John Montgomery, *Series Advisor*
Don Box, *Series Advisor*
Martin Heller, *Series Editor*

The **Microsoft .NET Development Series** is supported and developed by the leaders and experts of Microsoft development technologies including Microsoft architects and DevelopMentor instructors. The books in this series provide a core resource of information and understanding every developer needs in order to write effective applications and managed code. Learn from the leaders how to maximize your use of the .NET Framework and its programming languages.

Titles in the Series

Brad Abrams, *.NET Framework Standard Library Annotated Reference Volume 1*, 0-321-15489-4

Keith Ballinger, *.NET Web Services: Architecture and Implementation*, 0-321-11359-4

Bob Beauchemin, Niels Berglund, Dan Sullivan, *A First Look at SQL Server 2005 for Developers*, 0-321-18059-3

Don Box with Chris Sells, *Essential .NET, Volume 1: The Common Language Runtime*, 0-201-73411-7

Mahesh Chand, *Graphics Programming with GDI+*, 0-321-16077-0

Anders Hejlsberg, Scott Wiltamuth, Peter Golde, *The C# Programming Language*, 0-321-15491-6

Alex Homer, Dave Sussman, Mark Fussell, *A First Look at ADO.NET and System.Xml v. 2.0*, 0-321-22839-1

Alex Homer, Dave Sussman, Rob Howard, *A First Look at ASP.NET v. 2.0*, 0-321-22896-0

James S. Miller and Susann Ragsdale, *The Common Language Infrastructure Annotated Standard*, 0-321-15493-2

Fritz Onion, *Essential ASP.NET with Examples in C#*, 0-201-76040-1

Fritz Onion, *Essential ASP.NET with Examples in Visual Basic .NET*, 0-201-76039-8

Ted Pattison and Dr. Joe Hummel, *Building Applications and Components with Visual Basic .NET*, 0-201-73495-8

Chris Sells, *Windows Forms Programming in C#*, 0-321-11620-8

Chris Sells and Justin Gehtland, *Windows Forms Programming in Visual Basic .NET*, 0-321-12519-3

Paul Vick, *The Visual Basic .NET Programming Language*, 0-321-16951-4

Damien Watkins, Mark Hammond, Brad Abrams, *Programming in the .NET Environment*, 0-201-77018-0

Shawn Wildermuth, *Pragmatic ADO.NET: Data Access for the Internet World*, 0-201-74568-2

Paul Yao and David Durant, *.NET Compact Framework Programming with C#*, 0-321-17403-8

Paul Yao and David Durant, *.NET Compact Framework Programming with Visual Basic .NET*, 0-321-17404-6

For more information go to www.awprofessional.com/msdotnetseries/

Windows Forms
Programming in C#

■ Chris Sells

✦ Addison-Wesley

Boston • San Francisco • New York • Toronto • Montreal
London • Munich • Paris • Madrid
Capetown • Sydney • Tokyo • Singapore • Mexico City

The following articles were originally printed in *MSDN Magazine*, and are reprinted in this book with permission:

".NET Zero Deployment: Security and Versioning Models in the Windows Forms Engine Help You Create and Deploy Smart Clients" by Chris Sells, *MSDN Magazine*, July 2002.

"Visual Studio .NET: Building Windows Forms Controls and Components With Rich Design-Time Features" by Michael Weinhardt and Chris Sells, *MSDN Magazine*, April 2003.

"Visual Studio .NET: Building Windows Forms Controls and Components With Rich Design-Time Features, Part 2" by Michael Weinhardt and Chris Sells, *MSDN Magazine*, May 2003.

The publisher offers discounts on this book when ordered in quantity for special sales. For more information, please contact:

U.S. Corporate and Government Sales
(800) 382-3419
corpsales@pearsontechgroup.com

For sales outside of the U.S., please contact:
International Sales
(317 581-3793)
international@pearsontechgroup.com

Visit Addison-Wesley on the Web:
www.awprofessional.com

Library of Congress Cataloging-in-Publication Data

Sells, Chris.
Windows forms programming in C# / Chris Sells.
    p.   cm
Includes bibliographical references and index.
ISBN 0-321-11620-8 (alk. paper)
1. Microsoft .NET Framework. 2. Computer software—Development. 3. C# (Computer program language) I. Title.

QA76.76.M52S45 2003
005.2'7623—dc21   2003052155

ISBN 0-321-11620-8
Text printed on recycled paper
4 5 6 7 8 9 10 11 12 13—CRS—0807060504
Fourth printing, May 2004

*To my wife, Melissa,
and the Sells brothers:
my sons John and Tom.
They define the heaven that exceeds my grasp.
And to my parents, who made me a reader
from the beginning
and who passed on the secret writer gene,
much to my surprise.*

Contents

Figures

Tables

Foreword

WINDOWS APPLICATION DEVELOPMENT has changed substantially since Windows 1.0 was introduced in 1983. Both the way Windows programmers write software and the architecture of the software they write have changed dramatically. The most recent step in this continuous evolution involves the Microsoft .NET Framework. This new platform influences both the developer's tools and their very definition of "application."

The .NET Framework, its compliant languages, and the tools that support them, let developers trade a bit of performance and some control for improvements in developer productivity, code safety, and overall robustness of the completed application. For many developers, this tradeoff is extremely exciting, as they'll be able to get their work done faster without compromising quality. In fact, some developers find that the quality of their code increases substantially when using languages like C# or VB.NET because the languages themselves are inherently an improvement over older offerings.

In the wake of the release of these new managed toolsets, a common misconception in the software development community is that applications written with the .NET Framework are designed only to be written to be "Web apps"—applications which really live on a central Web server, but show their user interface through a Web browser like Internet Explorer. Web-based applications are very appealing for some solutions. Because some Web browser is probably installed on every machine in the world, no distribution of the Web application is necessary. As long as users know how to reach the application's server and interact with it, they can success-fully use it. Updates to the application are done on the server where the application is actually running and don't need to involve updating every client which has a local copy of the software. No local copy exists!

But not all applications written with the .NET Framework must be Web applications. The .NET Framework provides a set of classes (known collec-tively as "Windows Forms") that are designed to implement "smart client" applications. Smart clients are applications that provide a local user inter-face directly using the Windows user interface features, rather than using HTML as a presentation layer. In fact, it's very common for developers to use Windows Forms to write stand-alone client applications which pro-vide very rich user interfaces, work offline, and still let developers reap the benefits of the .NET Framework.

Smart client applications have several benefits over Web-oriented applications. Being able to get something done while offline is a very important feature, and will remain so until high-bandwidth connections are available everywhere people want to get work done, from airplanes to living rooms. Because their code executes locally, no round-trip must go over the network to the server before the smart client application can respond to the user. That missing round-trip renders smart client applica-tions impervious to network latency as well.

Because of its intimate relationship with the machine where it is run-ning, a smart client application is generally able to provide a much richer user experience. Custom drawing, interesting font settings, and conve-nient controls are some of the visual features which help set apart the smart client application from a Web-based application. Smart client applications also, by their nature, are able to use all of the resources available on the cli-ent computer. Local disk and memory storage is easy to access.

Problems which can benefit from those strengths are great candidates for solutions involving a smart client. Opportunities for those solutions have always been around: For nearly a decade, MFC made it possible for C++ programmers to write client-side applications with very rich user interfaces. MFC's goal was to provide an object-oriented wrapper that added value to C++ programmers. Sometimes, that value was only to make particular APIs more convenient from C++, but the bulk of MFC was aimed at offering a framework that made rich client applications easy to write by integrating features most commonly found in such applications.

Windows Forms developers enjoy a more complete set of lightweight wrappers for the system APIs than MFC developers did. The extensive coverage of the .NET Framework Class Library is born out of necessity as, unlike MFC developers, managed programmers have a few challenges in making direct calls to the raw system APIs.

In this book, Chris Sells discusses how the Windows Forms classes and their supporting infrastructure can be used to write robust and rich smart client applications. If you're an experienced Windows programmer who has previously used MFC or directly utilized the Win32 API to write such applications, you will find Chris's direct delivery very appropriate for transferring your knowledge to the managed classes. If you're a developer with less Windows development experience, you'll find the treatment of core concepts in application UI programming indispensable.

A new language, and a new framework for writing smart client applications, offers a new set of compromises to software engineers. What is software engineering besides choosing a solution which brings an acceptable set of compromises to its users? The more tools a developer has and the better he or she is at applying them appropriately, the more problems that developer will be able to solve. (Best of all, a new set of tools for client applications will give Chris new focus, and he'll quit barraging me with complaints about MFC.) Read on to add Windows Forms to your toolbox.

Mike Blaszczak
Primary MFC Developer
Microsoft Corporation
mikeblas@msn.com

Preface

AS A FAIRLY PUBLIC figure in the Windows developer community, I often get asked if I think that .NET is going to "take off." I always answer the same way: It's not a matter of "if," it's a matter of "when."

Microsoft's .NET Framework has so many benefits that even as a grizzled old C++/Win32 guy, I wasn't able to resist the siren song of a managed development environment. It's ironic that the temporary dip in the economy has caused folks to avoid anything new just when .NET has come along to deliver significant reductions in time to market and cost while simultaneously increasing code quality. The organizations that have already adopted .NET know that it's going to have a long and happy life, especially as it gets pushed further and further into Microsoft's own plans for the future of the Windows platform, both on the server and on the client.

The primary server-side technology in .NET is ASP.NET, which provides the infrastructure needed to build Web sites and Web services. ASP.NET gives developers the reach to deploy Web sites to anyone by aiming at the baseline of features offered by the middle-generation Web browsers. To provide the highest level of functionality possible, ASP.NET does most of the work on the server side, leaving the client-side HTML as a thin wrapper to trigger server-side requests for new pages of data. The server side handles almost everything, from data manipulation to user preferences to the rendering of simple things like menus and toolbars. This model provides the greatest availability across operating systems and browsers.

If, on the other hand, your targeted customers are Windows users, an HTML-based experience limits your users to a lowest-common-denominator approach that is unnecessary. In fact, in an attempt to provide a richer client-side experience, many organizations that know they're targeting Windows users require specific versions of Microsoft's Internet Explorer (IE) Web browser. As soon as that kind of targeting happens, IE becomes less of a browser and more of an HTML-based application runtime. For that purpose, the HTML object model is fairly primitive, often requiring that you do a lot of work to do things that are usually simple (like keeping track of a user's session state). If you're targeting Windows users, the .NET Framework gives you a much richer set of objects for building interactive user interfaces.

This brings me to the subject of this book: Windows Forms (WinForms). WinForms is the face of .NET on the client, providing a forms-based development environment meant to embody the best of the UI object models that have come before it. In addition, it has one feature that no Windows-based development framework has provided to date: the deployment features of HTML-based Web applications. The ability to combine the richness of Windows applications with the deployment of Web applications signals a completely new world for Windows developers, one that makes me more than happy to give up the mess of unmanaged code.

Who Should Read This Book? When writing this book, I had two target audiences in mind. I wanted to provide real-world WinForms coverage for both the programmer who has already programmed in .NET and for the programmer who hasn't. Toward that end, I briefly introduce core .NET topics as they come up. However, the .NET Framework itself is a large area that this book doesn't pretend to cover completely. Instead, when I think more information would be useful, I reference another work that provides the full details. In particular, I find that I've referenced *Essential .NET*, by Don Box, with Chris Sells, a great deal, making it a good companion to this book. In this same category, I also recommend *Pragmatic ADO.NET*, by Shawn Wildermuth, *Advanced .NET Remoting*, by Ingo Rammer, *.NET Web Services*, by Keith Ballinger, and *Applied Microsoft .NET Framework Programming*, by Jeffrey Richter. (For more details on these books, see the Bibliography.)

Two core .NET topics are of special importance to WinForms programmers, and I cover them in more detail in Appendix B: Delegates and Events and in Appendix C: Serialization Basics. The coverage of delegates and events is particularly important if you're new to .NET, although I don't recommend diving into that topic until you've got a WinForms-specific frame of reference (which is provided about one-third of the way through Chapter 1: Hello, Windows Forms).

One other note: Many years ago, I wrote my first five-day training course. The topic was Windows 95 and included a few hours of coverage on the new controls: what they looked like, what their properties, methods, and events were, and how to program against them. Those hours seemed like days both for me and for the students. The details of a particular control are interesting only when you're putting that control to use, and when that time comes, the control-specific documentation and IntelliSense do a marvelous job of giving you the information you need. Toward that end, this book covers none of the standard controls completely. Instead, as each control is interesting in the context of the current topic—such as the DataGrid control in Chapter 13: Data Binding and Data Grids—that control is covered appropriately. Also, Chapter 8: Controls and Chapter 9: Design-Time Integration introduce the broad range of categories of controls that WinForms provides, including the category of nonvisual controls called *components* in .NET.

Finally, to give you a visual to go with all the controls and components and to introduce you to each one's major functionality, Appendix D: Standard WinForms Components and Controls provides a list of the standard controls and components. I wouldn't think of wasting your time by attempting to be more thorough than the reference documentation that comes with the .NET Framework SDK and Visual Studio .NET. Instead, this book focuses on the real-world scenarios that aren't covered in detail elsewhere.

Conventions. If you have decided to take the plunge with this book, I'd like to thank you for your faith and express my hope that I live up to it. To aid you in reading the text, I want to let you in on some conventions I use in my writing.

First and foremost, the wonderful thing about WinForms is how visual it is, and that's why I use a lot of figures to illustrate its features. Some of those pictures really need to be in color to make the point, so be sure to check the color pages at the center of this book for those color plates.

As useful as figures are, I think primarily in code. Code is shown in monospace type:

```
System.Console.WriteLine("Hello, WinForms.");
```

Console application activation is also shown in monospace type:

```
C:\> csc.exe hello.cs
```

When a part of a code snippet or a command line activation is of particular interest, I mark it in bold and often provide a comment:

```
// Notice the use of the .NET System namespace
System.Console.WriteLine("Hello, WinForms.");
```

When I want to direct your attention to a piece of code even more fully, I replace superfluous code with ellipses:

```
class MyForm : System.Windows.Forms.Form {
  ... // fields
  private void MyForm_Load
      (object sender, System.ComponentModel.EventArgs e) {
    MessageBox.Show("Hello from MyForm");
  }
}
```

Furthermore, to make the printed code more readable, I often drop namespaces and protection keywords when they don't provide additional information:

```
// Shortened "System.Windows.Forms.Form" base class
class MyForm : Form {
  ... // fields

  // Removed "private" specifier and "System.ComponentModel" namespace
  void MyForm_Load(object sender, EventArgs e) {
    MessageBox.Show("Hello from MyForm");
  }
}
```

Conversely, when showing .NET attributes, I use their full name:

```
[SerializableAttribute]
class MyCustomType {...}
```

Some languages, such as C#, let you drop the "Attribute" suffix for convenience, but that makes it hard to pin down the details of the attribute class in the online documentation.

Also, I sometimes omit error checking from the printed code for clarity, but I try to leave it in the sample code that comes with this book.

In the prose itself, I often put a word or phrase in italics to indicate a new term that I'm about to define. As an example of this kind of term and its definition, *hegemony* is a preponderant influence or authority, as well as a potent business practice.

Finally, I often mention keyboard shortcuts because I find them convenient. The ones I mention are the default Visual Studio Developer key bindings. If you're not using those key bindings, you'll need to map the keyboard shortcuts to your own settings.

Contact. The up-to-date information for this book, including the source code and the errata, are maintained at http://www.sellsbrothers.com/ writing/wfbook. This site also provides a way for you to send feedback to me about the book, both complimentary and less so.

Acknowledgments. Although this book is already dedicated to my family, I'd also like to acknowledge them here. I work from my home, but in completing the book I often had to spend a great deal of extra time at the end to get the thing out the door. My wife, Melissa, was enormously understanding when I had a deadline and gave me the space I needed to meet it. Also, I tend to leave my office door open because I like my family, and often my boys, John and Tom, will come in to talk to me about their day. Even though they're only nine and seven, respectively, they're uncharacteristically understanding when it comes to letting me focus on my work for "just another five minutes" (although woe is me if I overpromise and underdeliver to those two, I'll tell you). In the family category, I'd also like to thank Beth and Joel Howie, my sister and brother-in-law, for giving me even more space and taking their nephews when the boys were tired of hearing me say "just another five minutes." Of course, I need to thank my parents, who made me a voracious reader and passed along the writing skills I never even knew they had 'til very recently.

Although my family gave me the space to write this book, it would not be what it is without the efforts of some other very helpful folks. Michael Weinhardt was my co-author for the two-part *MSDN Magazine* series "Building Windows Forms Controls and Components with Rich Design-Time Features," which was the predecessor to Chapter 9: Design-Time Integration. He also contributed some of the best figures in this book, including the resource resolution figures in Chapter 10: Resources. Similarly, Shawn "The ADO Guy" Wildermuth helped me a great deal not only with the two database chapters but also with Chapter 8: Controls and Appendix D: Standard WinForms Components and Controls. The book would not have been the same without you two, Mike and Shawn.

In addition, Mike Woodring gave me great feedback on the threading portions of this book. Keith Brown has always been the wind beneath my security wings, giving me tons of guidance on how .NET security really works (and why). Fritz Onion gave me great feedback when this book started as a five-day training course, as did Ian Griffiths. And, lucky for me, I caught Allan Cooper just as he was getting interested in programming again. He read each chapter threatening to stop when he got bored. He gave me fabulous feedback that really left a mark (particularly on the resources chapter).

I'd also like to thank a few guys that didn't know they were helping me with my book, including Ljubomir Spasovski for "Help Authoring in .NET" on dotnetjunkies.com, Bob Powell for the DrawRoundRect method on dotnet247.com, and Joseph Newcomer for his multi-instance article on flounder.com. In this same category, I'd like to thank Jeff Prosise for inspiring this book with the single WinForms chapter in his book *Programming Microsoft .NET*. That one chapter drove me to write this book because I couldn't stand the idea of WinForms summarized in a single chapter. I'd also like to thank Don Box for letting me tag along on his book *Essential .NET*. I didn't write a word of it, but my close involvement with it taught me tons about how .NET really works. That education makes its way into this book.

This book's reviewers deserve special thanks: Bill Woodruff, Brian Graf, Christophe Nasarre, Cristof Falk, Doug Reilly, Fumiaki Yoshimatsu, Johan Ericsson, Mark Rideout, Martin Heller, Pierre Nallet, Richard Blewett, Scott Densmore, Serge Shimanovsky, Suresh Jambu, Tim Tabor, and Zeeshan Amjad. The comments of all my reviewers had a huge impact on the book, and I can't tell you how important you all were to me. I'd especially like to single out Bill, Christophe, Mark, and Martin as being extra thorough, and Christophe (again) for being there after I'd applied reviewer comments to make sure everything still made sense. I can't tell you how much embarrassment you guys saved me. Thanks!

Of course, I have to thank the guys at Microsoft who helped invent this technology and then were there to help the community (and me specifically) in understanding it: Mark Boulter, Chris Anderson, and Jamie Cool.

I'd like to thank *MSDN Magazine*, *MSDN Online*, and *Windows Developer* magazine for allowing me to reuse material from articles that they originally published (as listed in the Bibliography). I'd also like to thank my readers, whose feedback on those initial pieces helped shape the final version of this content, as well as inspiring me to dig even deeper than I had initially.

Last but not least, I'd like to thank the fine folks at Addison-Wesley. In increasingly tight times, they still manage to provide me an environment where I can write what I think best. Special thanks go to Betsy Hardinger: copy editor, frustrated-fiction-author, kindred spirit, and hyphen mentor. In addition to turning my prose into English, she also managed to catch technical inconsistencies that hardcore developers missed. Thanks, Betsy!

These folks, along with a bunch I'm sure I'm missing, have helped shape everything good that comes through in this book. The errors that remain are mine.

Chris Sells
April 2003
www.sellsbrothers.com

■ 1 ■
Hello, Windows Forms

A S EASY TO USE AS Windows Forms (WinForms) is, the sheer amount of functionality that it provides can make it intimidating—especially when combined with the huge number of features that Visual Studio .NET (VS.NET) provides solely for the purpose of building WinForms code. So this chapter takes a quick look at most of what WinForms provides, including forms, controls, application settings, resources, dialogs, drawing, printing, data binding, threading, and even deployment over the Web. We also look at how the VS.NET environment facilitates WinForms development. The remaining chapters will stuff you full, providing the sumptuous details of these topics, but in this chapter you'll get your first taste.

WinForms from Scratch

A typical Windows Forms application has at least one form. Without the form it's just an "application," which is pretty boring. A *form* is simply a window, the unit of the Microsoft user interface we've seen since Windows 1.0.

One form in a WinForms application is typically the *main form*, which means that it is either the parent or the owner[1] of all other forms that may be shown during the lifetime of the application. It's where the main menu

---

1. The distinction between a form's "parent" and "owner" is covered in detail in Chapter 2: Forms.

is shown, along with the toolbar, status bar, and so on. When the main form goes away, the application exits.

The main form of an application can be a simple message box, a dialog box, a Single Document Interface (SDI) window, a Multiple Document Interface (MDI) window, or something more complicated, such as the forms you're used to seeing in applications like Visual Studio .NET. These latter forms may include multiple child windows, tool windows, and floating toolbars.

If your application is enormously simple, you can implement it using the staple of any windowing system, the lowly *message box*:

```
class MyFirstApp {
  static void Main() {
    System.Windows.Forms.MessageBox.Show("Hello, Windows Forms");
  }
}
```

If you're new to C#, Main is the entry point for any C# application. The Main function must be a member of a class, and hence the need for My-FirstApp. However, the .NET runtime doesn't create an instance of the MyFirstApp class when our code is loaded and executed, so our Main function must be marked *static*. In this way, you mark a method as available without creating an instance of the type.

The single line of real code in our first WinForms application calls the static Show method of the System.Windows.Forms.MessageBox class, which is really a long-winded way of saying we're calling a method on the MessageBox class contained within the System.Windows.Forms namespace. *Namespaces* are used extensively in the .NET Framework Class Libraries (FCL) to separate types, such as classes, structures, enumerations, and so on, into logical groupings. This separation is necessary when you've got thousands of Microsoft employees working on the FCL as well as hundreds of third parties extending it and millions of programmers trying to learn it. Without namespaces, you would need all kinds of wacky conventions to keep things uniquely named (as demonstrated by the existing Win32 API).

However, as necessary as namespaces are, they're a little too much typing for me, so I recommend the C# *using* statement, as shown here:

```
using System;
using System.Windows.Forms;

class MyFirstApp {
  static void Main() {
    MessageBox.Show("Hello, Windows Forms");
  }
}
```

When the compiler sees that the MessageBox class is being used, it first looks in the *global namespace*, which is where all types end up that aren't contained by a namespace (for example, the MyFirstApp class is in the global namespace). If the compiler can't find the type in the global namespace, it looks at all the namespaces currently being used—in this case, System and System.Windows.Forms. If the compiler finds a type name being used that exists in two or more namespaces, it produces an error and we're forced to go back to the long notation. But in practice this is rare enough to make the short form the form of choice when you're typing code by hand.

However, even though the MessageBox class is enormously handy for showing your users simple string information or asking them yes/no questions, it's hard to build a real application with MessageBox. For most things, you'll need an instance of the Form class (or a Form-derived class):

```
class MyFirstApp {
  static void Main() {
    Form form = new Form();
    form.Show(); // Not what you want to do
  }
}
```

Although this code will show the form, you'll have to be quick to see it because Show shows the form modelessly. If you're not steeped in user interface lore, a *modeless* form is one that displays but allows other activities (called *modes*) to take place. So, immediately after Show puts our new form on the screen, it returns control to the Main function, which promptly returns, exiting the process and taking our nascent form with it. To show a form *modally*—that is, to not return control to the Main function until the form has closed—the documentation suggests using the ShowDialog function:

```
class MyFirstApp {
  static void Main() {
    Form form = new Form();
    form.ShowDialog(); // Still not what you want to do
  }
}
```

This code would show a blank form and wait for the user to close it before returning control to the Main function, but it's not the code you will generally be writing. Instead, to make it accessible in other parts of your application, you'll be designating one form as the main form. To do this, pass the main form as an argument to the Run method of the Application object, which also resides in the System.Windows.Forms namespace:

```
class MyFirstApp {
  static void Main() {
    Form form = new Form();
    Application.Run(form); // This is what you want to do
  }
}
```

The Application class's static Run method will show the main form, and when it's closed, Run will return, letting our Main function exit and closing the process. To see this in action, you can compile your first WinForms application using the following command line:[2]

```
C:\> csc.exe /t:winexe /r:System.Windows.Forms.dll MyFirstApp.cs
```

---

2. To get a command prompt with the proper PATH environment variable set to access the .NET command line tools, click on Start | Programs | Microsoft Visual Studio .NET | Visual Studio .NET Tools | Visual Studio .NET Command Prompt. If you don't have VS.NET installed, you can set up the PATH using the corvars.bat batch file in your Framework-SDK\Bin directory.

The csc.exe command invokes the compiler on our source file, asking it to produce a Windows application via the /t flag (where the "t" stands for "target"), pulling in the System.Windows.Forms.dll library using the /r flag (where the "r" stands for "reference").

The job of the compiler is to pull together the various source code files into a .NET assembly. An *assembly* is a collection of .NET types, code, or resources (or all three). An assembly can be either an application, in which case it has an .exe extension, or a library, in which case it has a .dll extension. The only real difference between the types of assemblies is whether the assembly has an entry point that can be called by Windows when the assembly is launched (.exe files do, and .dll files do not).

Now that that the compiler has produced MyFirstApp.exe, you can execute it and see an application so boring, it's not even worth a screen shot. When you close the form, MyFirstApp.exe will exit, ending your first Win-Forms experience.

To spice things up a bit, we can set a property on our new form before showing it:

```
class MyFirstApp {
  static void Main() {
    Form form = new Form();
    form.Text = "Hello, WinForms!";
    Application.Run(form);
  }
}
```

Like most objects in the FCL, Form objects have several properties to access, methods to call, and events to handle. In this case, we've set the Text property, which, for a Form, sets the caption. We could do the same thing to set other properties on the form, showing it when we were finished, but that's not the way we generally do things in WinForms. Instead, each custom form is a class that derives from Form and initializes its own properties:

```
class MyFirstForm : Form {
  public MyFirstForm() {
    this.Text = "Hello, WinForms!";
  }
}
```

continues

```
class MyFirstApp {
  static void Main() {
    Form form = new MyFirstForm();
    Application.Run(form);
  }
}
```

Notice that the MyFirstForm class derives from Form and then initializes its own properties in the constructor. This gives us a simpler usage model, as shown in the new Main function, which creates an instance of the MyFirstForm class. You also gain the potential for reuse should MyFirstForm be needed in other parts of your application.

Still, our form is pretty boring. It doesn't even include a way to interact with it except for the system-provided adornments. We can add some interactivity by adding a button:

```
class MyFirstForm : Form {
  public MyFirstForm() {
    this.Text = "Hello, WinForms!";
    Button button = new Button();
    button.Text = "Click Me!";
    this.Controls.Add(button);
  }
}
```

Adding a button to the form is a matter of creating a new Button object, setting the properties that we like, and adding the Button object to the list of controls that the form manages. This code will produce a button on the form that does that nifty 3-D depress thing that buttons do when you press them, but nothing else interesting will happen. That's because we're still not handling the button's click *event*, where an event is a way for a control to notify its container that something has happened. For example, the following code handles the button's Click event:

```
class MyFirstForm : Form {
  public MyFirstForm() {
    this.Text = "Hello, WinForms!";
    Button button = new Button();
    button.Text = "Click Me!";
    button.Click += new EventHandler(button_Click);
    this.Controls.Add(button);
  }
```

```
void button_Click(object sender, EventArgs e) {
  MessageBox.Show("That's a strong, confident click you've got...");
}
}
```

Handling the button's Click event involves two things. The first is creating a handler function with the appropriate signature; we've named this function button_Click. The signature of the vast majority of .NET events is a function that returns nothing and takes two parameters: an object that represents the sender of the event (our button, in this case), and an instance of a System.EventArgs object (or an object that derives from the EventArgs class).

The second thing that's needed to subscribe to an event in C# is shown by the use of the "+=" operator in the MyFirstForm constructor. This notation means that we'd like to add a function to the list of all the other functions that care about a particular event on a particular object, and that requires an instance of an EventHandler delegate object. A *delegate* is a class that translates invocations on an event into calls on the functions that have subscribed to the event. For this particular event, we have the following logical delegate and event definitions elsewhere in the .NET FCL:

```
namespace System {
  public delegate void EventHandler(object sender, EventArgs e);
}

namespace System.Windows.Forms {
  public class Button {
    public event EventHandler Click;
  }
}
```

Notice that the Click event on the Button class is a reference to an EventHandler delegate, and so to add our own method to the list of subscribers, we need to also create an instance of the delegate.[3] Of course, it can quickly become tedious to figure out the delegate signatures of all the events you're interested in or to add controls to a form via code by hand.

---

3. For a more detailed, although less reverent, look at delegates and events, read Appendix B: Delegates and Events. For a much more detailed and reverent look, refer to *Essential .NET* (Addison-Wesley, 2003), by Don Box, with Chris Sells.

Luckily, it's also unnecessary because of the WinForms Wizard and the WinForms Designer provided by Visual Studio .NET.

Windows Forms in Visual Studio .NET

Most WinForms projects start in the New Project dialog box, available via File | New | Project (Ctrl+Shift+N) and shown in Figure 1.1.

To build an application, you'll want the Windows Application project template. To build a library of custom controls or forms for reuse, you'll want the Windows Control Library project template. When you run the Windows Application Wizard, choosing whatever you like for the project name and location, you'll get a blank form in the Designer, as shown in Figure 1.2.

Before we start the drag-and-drop extravaganza that the Designer enables, let's take a look at a slightly abbreviated version of the code generated by the WinForms application Wizard (available by right-clicking on the design surface and choosing View Code or by pressing F7):

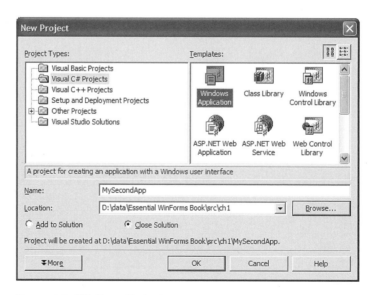

FIGURE 1.1: WinForms Projects

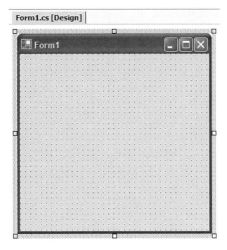

FIGURE 1.2: The WinForms Designer

```
using System;
using System.Windows.Forms;

namespace MySecondApp {
  public class Form1 : System.Windows.Forms.Form {
    public Form1() {
      InitializeComponent();
    }

    #region Windows Form Designer generated code
    /// <summary>
    /// Required method for Designer support - do not modify
    /// the contents of this method with the code editor.
    /// </summary>
    private void InitializeComponent() {
      this.Size = new System.Drawing.Size(300,300);
      this.Text = "Form1";
    }
    #endregion

    static void Main() {
      Application.Run(new Form1());
    }
  }
}
```

Most of this code should be familiar, including the *using* statements at the top, the form class that derives from the Form base class, the static

Main function inside a class providing the entry point to the application, and the call to Application.Run, passing an instance of the main form class. The only thing that's different from what we did ourselves is the call to InitializeComponent in the form's constructor to set the form's properties instead of doing it in the constructor itself. This is done so that the WinForms Designer, which we can use to design our form visually, has a place to put the code to initialize the form and the form's control. For example, dragging a button from the Toolbox onto the form's design surface will change the InitializeComponent implementation to look like this:

```
private void InitializeComponent() {
    this.button1 = new System.Windows.Forms.Button();
    this.SuspendLayout();
    //
    // button1
    //
    this.button1.Location = new System.Drawing.Point(96, 72);
    this.button1.Name = "button1";
    this.button1.TabIndex = 0;
    this.button1.Text = "button1";
    //
    // Form1
    //
    this.AutoScaleBaseSize = new System.Drawing.Size(5, 13);
    this.ClientSize = new System.Drawing.Size(292, 266);
    this.Controls.AddRange(
      new System.Windows.Forms.Control[] {
        this.button1});
    this.Name = "Form1";
    this.Text = "Form1";
    this.ResumeLayout(false);

}
```

Notice again that this code is very similar to what we built ourselves, but this time created for us by the Designer. Unfortunately, for this process to work reliably, the Designer must have complete control over the InitializeComponent method. In fact, notice that the Wizard-generated InitializeComponent code is wrapped in a region, which will hide the code by default, and is marked with a telling comment:

```
/// Required method for Designer support - do not modify
/// the contents of this method with the code editor.
```

It may look like your favorite programming language, but Initialize-Component is actually the serialized form of the object model that the Designer is using to manage the design surface. Although you can make minor changes to this code, such as changing the Text property on the new button, major changes are likely to be ignored—or worse, thrown away. Feel free to experiment with just how far you can go by modifying this serialization format by hand, but don't be surprised when your work is lost. I recommend putting custom form initialization into the form's constructor, after the call to InitializeComponent, giving you confidence that your code will be safe from the Designer.

Of course, we put up with the transgression of the Designer because of the benefits it provides. For example, instead of writing lines of code to set properties on the form or the controls contained therein, all you have to do is to right-click on the object of interest and choose Properties (or press F4) to bring up the Property Browser for the selected object, as shown in Figure 1.3.

Any properties with nondefault values, as indicated by values in bold-face in the browser, will be written into the InitializeComponent method for you. Similarly, to choose an event to handle for the form or the form's controls, you can press the Events lighting bolt at the top of the Property Browser window to open the list shown in Figure 1.4.

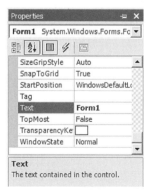

FIGURE 1.3: The Property Browser

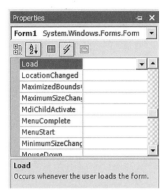

FIGURE 1.4: List of Events

You have a few ways to handle an event from the Property Browser window. One way is to find the event you'd like to handle on the object selected (say, Click) and type the name of the function you'd like to call when this event is fired (say, button_Click). Then press Enter, and VS.NET will take you to the body of an event handler with that name and the correct signature, all ready for you to implement:

```
private void button_Click(object sender, System.EventArgs e) {

}
```

After you've added a handler to a form, that handler will show up in a drop-down list for other events having the same signature. This technique is handy if you'd like the same event for multiple objects to be handled by the same method, such as multiple buttons with the same handler. You can use the sender argument to determine which object fired the event:

```
private void button_Click(object sender, System.EventArgs e) {
  Button button = sender as Button;
  MessageBox.Show(button.Text + " was clicked");
}
```

If, as is often the case, you'd like each event that you handle for each object to be unique or you just don't care what the name of the handler is, you can simply double-click on the name of the event in the Property Browser; an event handler name will be generated for you, based on the name of the control and the name of the event. For example, if you double-clicked on the Load event for the Form1 form, the event handler name would be Form1_Load.

Furthermore, if you're handling the *default event* of an object, you can handle it simply by double-clicking on the object itself. This will generate an event handler name just as if you'd double-clicked on that event name in the Property Browser event list. The default event of an object is meant to be intuitively the most handled event for a particular type. For example, I'm sure you won't be surprised to learn that the default event for a button is Click and that the default event for a Form is Load. Unfortunately, neither the Designer nor the Property Browser gives any indication what the default event will be for a particular type, but experimentation should reveal few surprises.

Arranging Controls

The beauty of the Designer is that it lets you lay out your controls lovingly within your form, making sure everything lines up nicely, as shown in Figure 1.5.

But then someone resizes it, as shown in Figure 1.6.

The user isn't resizing the form to get more gray space but to make the controls bigger so that they will hold more data. For that to happen, the controls need to resize to take up the newly available space. You can do this manually by handling the form's Resize event and writing the code. Or you can do it with anchoring.

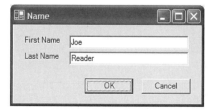

FIGURE 1.5: Nicely Laid-Out Form at Ideal Size

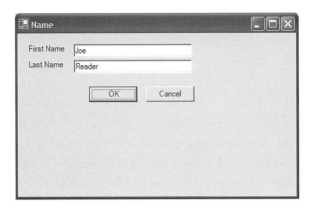

FIGURE 1.6: Nicely Laid-Out Form Resized

Anchoring is one of the ways that WinForms provides for automatic layout control of your forms and the controls contained therein. By default, all controls are anchored to the upper-left, so that as the form is resized and moved, all controls are kept at their position relative to the upper-left corner of the form. However, in this case, we'd clearly like to have the text box controls widen or narrow as the form is resized. We implement this by setting each text box's Anchor property. In the Property Browser for the control, we choose the Anchor property, which displays an editor like the one in Figure 1.7.

To change the text boxes so that they anchor to the right edge as well as the top and left edges is a matter of clicking on the anchor rectangle on the right and changing the Anchor property to Top, Left, Right. This will cause the text boxes to resize as the form resizes, as shown in Figure 1.8.

The default anchoring is top-left, but those edges need not be a part of the anchoring settings at all. For example, notice that Figure 1.8 anchors the

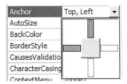

FIGURE 1.7: Setting the Anchor Property

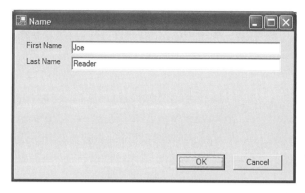

FIGURE 1.8: Anchoring Text Boxes Top, Left, Right and Buttons Bottom, Right

OK and Cancel buttons to the bottom-right, as is customary with Windows dialogs.

If instead of building a dialog-style form, you'd like to build a window-style form, anchoring is not your best bet. For example, suppose you're building an Explorer-style application, with a menu bar and toolbar on the top, a status bar on the bottom, and a tree view and a list view taking up the rest of the space as determined by a splitter between them. In that kind of application, anchoring won't do. Instead, you'll want docking.

Docking allows you to "stick" any control on the edge of its container, the way a status bar is stuck to the bottom of a form. By default, most controls have the Dock property set to None (the default for the StatusBar control is Bottom). You can change the Dock property in the Property Browser by picking a single edge to dock to or to take up whatever space is left, as shown in Figure 1.9.

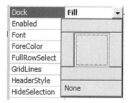

FIGURE 1.9: Setting the Dock Property

As an example, the form in Figure 1.10 shows the Dock properties for a status bar, a tree view, and a list view, the latter two being split with a splitter control. You can arrange all this without writing a line of code.

Anchoring, docking, and splitting are not the only ways to arrange controls on a form. WinForms also lets you group controls and handle custom layout for special situations. In addition, WinForms supports arranging windows within a parent, which we call MDI. These techniques are all covered in detail in Chapter 2: Forms.

Controls

Often, after arranging a set of controls just right, you need that group of controls elsewhere. In that case, you can copy and paste the controls between forms, making sure that all the settings are maintained, or you can encapsulate the controls into a *user control* for a more robust form of reuse. User controls are containers for other controls and are best created in a Windows Control Library project.

To add a Windows Control Library project to an existing solution, you use the Add New Project item from the menu you get when you right-click on your WinForms application's solution in Solution Explorer. You'll also want to make sure that you're creating the new project in the same location as your existing solution, because VS.NET 2002 defaults to placing new projects one folder too far up the hierarchy in most cases. Figure 1.11 shows how to add a new project called MyFirstControlLibrary to an existing solution called MySecondApp.

After you've created a control library project, you'll be presented with a user control design surface very like that of a form. The only real difference

FIGURE 1.10: Docking and Splitting

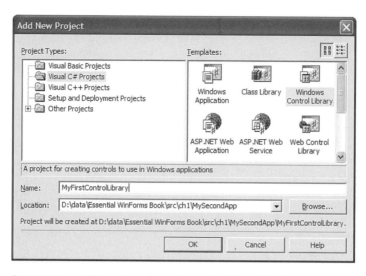

FIGURE 1.11: Adding a New Project to an Existing Solution

is that there's no border or caption, which will be provided by the form host of your new control. The code generated by the Wizard looks very much like the code generated for a new form except that the base class is UserControl instead of Form:

```
using System;
using System.Windows.Forms;

namespace MyFirstControlLibrary {
  public class UserControl1 : System.Windows.Forms.UserControl {
    public UserControl1() {
      InitializeComponent();
    }

    private void InitializeComponent() {
    }
  }
}
```

In the Designer, you can drop and arrange any controls on the user control that you like, setting their properties and handling events just as on a form. Figure 1.12 shows a sample user control as seen in the Designer.

When you're happy with your control, build the project and select it from the Toolbox where it has automatically been added by VS.NET to either the

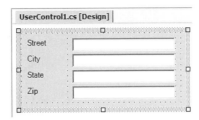

FIGURE 1.12: A User Control Shown in the Designer

Windows tab if you're using VS.NET 2002 or the "My User Controls" tab if VB.NET 2003. Drag and drop it onto the forms choice, setting properties and handling events via the Property Browser just as with any of the built-in controls. Figure 1.13 shows the user control from Figure 1.12 hosted on a form.

User controls aren't the only kind of custom controls. If you're interested in drawing the contents of your controls yourself, scrolling your controls, or getting more details about user controls, you'll want to read Chapter 8: Controls.

Application Settings

As some applications get more sophisticated, users expect more from all their applications. For example, some applications let users set fonts and colors and all kinds of crazy things (guaranteeing that you'll never be able

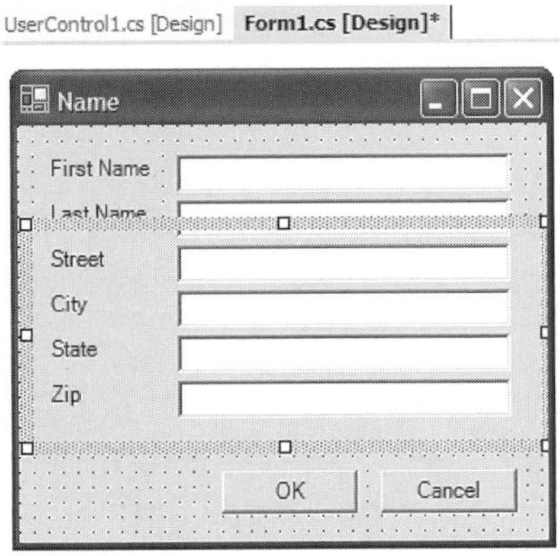

FIGURE 1.13: Hosting a User Control

to successfully test every combination). In addition to the other fancy user interface (UI) features that it provides, WinForms supports the idea of reading a control's properties from an application's configuration file, also called a *.config file*.

.NET allows every application to have a .config file associated with it. For example, when .NET loads MySecondApp.exe, it will look for a corresponding MySecondApp.exe.config file in the same folder as the application.

A .config file can have standard settings for things such as security, remoting, loading, and versioning. In addition to standard .NET settings, a configuration file can have custom settings strictly for the application's use. For example, the following is a .config file containing settings specifying a custom key-value pair:

```
<configuration>
  <appSettings>
    <add key="MainFormOpacity" value=".5" />
  </appSettings>
</configuration>
```

Notice that the .config file is in XML format. This means that savvy users can open the .config file in Notepad to change the setting. For this setting to be used to set the main form's opacity property, the setting needs to be read:

```
using System.Configuration;

public class MainForm : System.Windows.Forms.Form {
  public MainForm() {
    InitializeComponent();

    // After InitializeComponent call
    AppSettingsReader appSettings = new AppSettingsReader();
    object o = appSettings.GetValue("MainFormOpacity", typeof(double));
    this.Opacity = (double)o;
  }
  ...
}
```

Instead of opening the .config file directly, this code uses the AppSettingsReader class from the System.Configuration class. This class provides access to the key-value pairs in the <appSettings> section of the .config file associated with the application. We use the reader to get the value of the MainFormOpacity key and use that to set the property on the form.

If this is the kind of thing you'd like to provide in your application's forms for a wide variety of properties, it will be a chore to manually pull each value from the AppSettingsReader. For this reason, each control on each form, as well as the form itself, has a set of dynamic properties available in the Property Browser. The *dynamic properties* are those automatically read from the application's .config file. For example, to tell the Designer to generate code to pull in the opacity setting for the main form, you click the Advanced property's "…" button under the Dynamic Properties for the form, bringing up the list of potential properties to be made dynamic, as shown in Figure 1.14.

Any property checked in this dialog will be read from the .config file. Notice the key mapping provided by the dialog after we've chosen to make Opacity dynamic. This mapping is the key that will be used in the .config file.

After you've chosen a dynamic property, three things happen. First, a file called app.config is added to your project. This file will be automatically copied into the output directory of your project as it is built and will

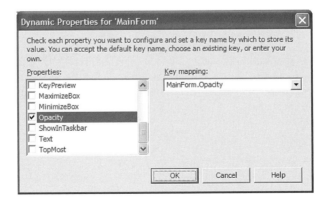

FIGURE 1.14: Dynamic Properties for MainForm

be renamed to match the name of your application, saving you from having to manually keep .config files up-to-date in Release and Debug directories.

The second thing that happens is that the contents of app.config will be populated with whatever value is set in the Property Browser for that property. For example, the following app.config file will be generated for MainForm.Opacity (assuming a default opacity value of 1):

```
<?xml version="1.0" encoding="Windows-1252"?>
<configuration>
  <appSettings>
    <!--    User application and configured property settings go here.-->
    <!--    Example: <add key="settingName" value="settingValue"/> -->
    <add key="MainForm.Opacity" value="1" />
  </appSettings>
</configuration>
```

The final thing that happens for each dynamic property is that the InitializeComponent function is augmented with code to pull in the properties at run time, saving you the need to write that code yourself:

```
public MainForm() {
    InitializeComponent();
}

private void InitializeComponent() {
  System.Configuration.AppSettingsReader configurationAppSettings =
    new System.Configuration.AppSettingsReader();
  ...
  this.Opacity =
    ((System.Double)(configurationAppSettings.GetValue(
      "MainForm.Opacity", typeof(System.Double))));
  ...
}
```

As useful as the .config file is, it's not for everything. In fact, its usefulness is limited to read-only machinewide application settings because the AppSettingsReader has no matching AppSettingsWriter. Instead, machinewide or per-user application settings that can be changed, such as the position of the main form between sessions, should be kept either in a file in an operating system–provided *special folder* or, even better, in a .NET-specific place called *isolated storage*. Both of these are covered in detail, along with a discussion of application lifetime and environment, in Chapter 11: Applications and Settings.

Resources

The .config file, dynamic properties, files in special folders, and isolated storage all provide data used to control an application's look and feel, as well as its behavior, while remaining separate from the code itself. One other major place for this kind of data for applications and controls is resources. A *resource* is a named piece of data bound into the EXE or DLL at build time. For example, you could set the background image of a form in your application by loading a bitmap from a file:

```
public MainForm() {
  InitializeComponent();
  this.BackgroundImage =
    new Bitmap(@"C:\WINDOWS\Web\Wallpaper\Azul.jpg");
}
```

The problem with this code, of course, is that not all installations of Windows will have Azul.jpg, and even those that have it may not have it in the same place. Even if you shipped this picture with your application, a space-conscious user might decide to remove it, causing your application to fault. The only safe way to make sure that the picture, or any file, stays with code is to embed it as a resource.

Resources can be conveniently embedded in two ways. One way is to right-click on your project in Solution Explorer, choose Add Existing Item, and open the file you'd like to embed as a resource. The file will be copied into your project's directory but is not yet embedded. To embed the file, right-click on it and choose Properties, changing Build Action from Content (the default) to Embedded Resource. To load the resource, many of the .NET classes, such as Bitmap, provide constructors that take resource identifiers:

```
public MainForm() {
  InitializeComponent();
  this.BackgroundImage =
    new Bitmap(this.GetType(), "Azul.jpg");
}
```

When embedded as a resource, the name of the resource will be composed of the project's default namespace[4] and the name of the file where the resource came from—in this example, MySecondApp.Azul.jpg. When the picture is loaded at run time, the first argument is a type that shares the same namespace as that of the embedded resource, and the second argument is the rest of the name.

Luckily, if the resource-naming scheme is less than intuitive for you or you'd really like to see what the background image is going to look like in the Designer, you can set the value of many properties in your forms by using the Property Browser directly, skipping the need to write the resource-loading code at all. For example, to set the background image for a form, you merely press the "…" button in the Property Browser next to the BackgroundImage property and choose the file from the file system; the data will be read directly into a bundle of resources maintained for that form. This action causes the image to be shown in the Designer and the code to be generated that loads the resource at run time:

```
namespace MySecondApp {
  public class MainForm : System.Windows.Forms.Form {
    public MainForm() {
      InitializeComponent();
    }

    private void InitializeComponent() {
      System.Resources.ResourceManager resources =
        new System.Resources.ResourceManager(typeof(MainForm));
      ...
      this.BackgroundImage =
        (Bitmap)resources.GetObject("$this.BackgroundImage");
      ...
    }
  ...
}
```

In this case, instead of using the Bitmap constructor directly, the generated code is using the ResourceManager class. This class will load the bundle of resources specific to this form, whether those resources happen to be in the executing application or in a library assembly with a set of localized resources specific to the current user's culture settings. In this way, you can localize your forms without changing the code or even recompiling. For

---

4. You can get the default namespace of a C# project by right-clicking on a project in the Solution Explorer and choosing Properties | Common Properties | General | Default Namespace.

more details about resources, including localization and internationalization concerns, see Chapter 10: Resources.

Dialogs

You've already seen how to create and show forms, but there is a special usage of forms that show as dialogs. Although it's not always the case, *dialogs* are typically modal and exist to take information from a user before a task can be completed—in other words, a dialog is a form that has a "dialog" with the user. For example, the Options dialog in Figure 1.15 was created by right-clicking on a project in Solutions Explorer and choosing Add Windows Form. Implementing the form was a matter of exposing the favorite color setting as a property, dropping the controls onto the form's design surface, and setting the ControlBox property to false so that it looks like a dialog.

You can use this form as a modal dialog by calling the ShowDialog method:

```
void viewOptionsMenuItem_Click(object sender, EventArgs e) {
  MyOptionsDialog dlg = new MyOptionsDialog();
  dlg.FavoriteColor = this.color;
  if( dlg.ShowDialog() == DialogResult.OK ) {
    this.color = dlg.FavoriteColor;
  }
}
```

Notice that an instance of the custom class, MyOptionsDialog, is created, but before it's shown, the initial values are passed in via a property. When the modal ShowDialog method returns, it provides a member of the

FIGURE 1.15: A Dialog Box (See Plate 1)

DialogResult enumeration, either OK or Cancel in this case. Although it's possible to implement the OK and Cancel buttons' Click events inside the MyOptionsDialog class, there's a much easier way to make OK and Cancel act as they should: You set each button's DialogResult property appropriately, and set the MyOptionsDialog form properties AcceptButton and CancelButton to refer to the appropriate buttons. In addition to closing the dialog and returning the result to the caller of ShowDialog, setting these properties enables the Enter and ESC keys and highlights the OK button as the default button on the form.

You may still feel the need to handle the OK click event to validate the data typed into the dialog. Although you can do that, WinForms provides built-in support for validation. By using an ErrorProvider component, along with the Validating event, you can validate the contents of each control when the user moves focus from that control. For example, if we want the user to specify a color with some green in it, we can drop an ErrorProvider component onto the MyOptionsDialog form and handle the Validating event for the Change button whenever it loses focus:

```
void changeColorButton_Validating(object sender, CancelEventArgs e) {
  byte greenness = changeColorButton.BackColor.G;
  string err = "";
  if( greenness < Color.LightGreen.G ) {
    err = "I'm sorry, we were going for leafy, leafy...";
    e.Cancel = true;
  }
  errorProvider1.SetError(changeColorButton, err);
}
```

In the Validating handler, notice that we set the CancelEventArgs Cancel property to true. This cancels the loss of focus from the control that caused the validating event and stops the dialog from closing. Also notice the call to ErrorProvider.SetError. When this string is empty, the error provider's error indicator for that control is hidden. When this string contains something, the error provider shows an icon to the right of the control and provides a tooltip with the error string, as shown in Figure 1.16.

The Validating event handler is called whenever focus is moved from a control whose CausesValidation property is set to true (the default) to another control whose CausesValidation property is set to true. To let the

FIGURE 1.16: ErrorProvider Providing an Error (See Plate 2)

user cancel your dialog without entering valid data, make sure to set the Cancel button's CausesValidation property to false, or else you'll have pretty frustrated users.

ErrorProvider and the Validating event provide most of what's needed for basic validation, but more complicated validation scenarios require some custom coding. Similarly, because not all dialogs are modal, you'll need other ways of communicating user settings between your dialog and the rest of your application. For a discussion of these issues, as well as a list of the standard dialogs and how to use them, you'll want to read Chapter 3: Dialogs.

Drawing and Printing

As nifty as all the built-in controls are and as nicely as you can arrange them on forms using the Designer, user controls, and dialogs, sometimes you need to take things into your own hands and render the state of your form or control yourself. For example, if you need to compose a fancy About box, as shown in Figure 1.17, you'll need to handle the form's Paint event and do the drawing yourself.

The following is the Paint event-handling code to fill the inside of the About box:

```
using System.Drawing.Drawing2D;
...
void AboutDialog_Paint(object sender, PaintEventArgs e) {
  Graphics g = e.Graphics;
  g.SmoothingMode = SmoothingMode.AntiAlias;
```

FIGURE 1.17: Custom Drawing (See Plate 3)

```csharp
Rectangle rect = this.ClientRectangle;
int cx = rect.Width;
int cy = rect.Height;
float scale = (float)cy/(float)cx;

using( LinearGradientBrush brush =
          new LinearGradientBrush( this.ClientRectangle,
                                   Color.Empty,
                                   Color.Empty,
                                   45) ) {
  ColorBlend blend = new ColorBlend();
  blend.Colors =
    new Color[] { Color.Red, Color.Green, Color.Blue };
  blend.Positions = new float[] { 0, .5f, 1 };
  brush.InterpolationColors = blend;
  using( Pen pen = new Pen(brush) ) {
    for( int x = 0; x < cx; x += 7 ) {
      g.DrawLine(pen, 0, x * scale, cx - x, 0);
      g.DrawLine(pen, 0, (cx - x) * scale, cx - x, cx * scale);
      g.DrawLine(pen, cx - x, 0 * scale, cx, (cx - x) * scale);
      g.DrawLine(pen, cx - x, cx * scale, cx, x * scale);
    }
  }

  StringFormat format = new StringFormat();
  format.Alignment = StringAlignment.Center;
  format.LineAlignment = StringAlignment.Center;
  string s = "Ain't graphics cool?";
  g.DrawString(s, this.Font, brush, rect, format);
  }
}
```

Notice the use of the Graphics object from the PaintEventArgs passed to the event handler. This provides an abstraction around the specific device we're drawing on. If we'd like to print instead, it's a matter of getting at another Graphics object that models the printer. We can do that using the PrintDocument component and handling the events that it fires when the user requests a document to be printed. For example, we can drag the PrintDocument component from the Toolbox onto our AboutDialog form and use it to implement a Print button:

```
void printButton_Click(object sender, EventArgs e) {
  PrintDialog dlg = new PrintDialog();
  dlg.Document = printDocument1;
  if( dlg.ShowDialog() == DialogResult.OK ) {
    printDocument1.Print();
  }
}
```

Notice that before we ask the PrintDocument component to print, we use the standard PrintDialog component to ask the user which printer to use. If the user presses the OK button, we ask the document to print. Of course, it can't print on its own. Instead, it will fire the PrintPage event, asking us to draw each page:

```
using System.Drawing.Printing;
...
void printDocument1_PrintPage(object sender, PrintPageEventArgs e) {
  Graphics g = e.Graphics;
  ...
}
```

If you'd like to print more than one page, set the HasMorePages property of the PrintPageEventArgs class until all pages have been printed. If you'd like to be notified at the beginning and end of each print request as a whole, you'll want to handle the BeginPrint and EndPrint events. If you'd like to change settings, such as margins, paper size, landscape versus portrait mode, and so on, you'll want to handle the QueryPageSettings event.

After you have the PrintDocument events handled, WinForms makes adding print preview as easy as using the PrintPreview dialog:

```
void printPreviewButton_Click(object sender, EventArgs e) {
  printPreviewDialog1.Document = printDocument1;
  printPreviewDialog1.ShowDialog();
}
```

For more details of the printing and the drawing primitives used to render state onto a Graphics object, you'll want to read Chapter 4: Drawing Basics and Chapter 7: Printing.

Data Binding

Database-centric applications are fully supported in WinForms. To get started, you can use Server Explorer to add connections to whatever databases you'd like. For example, Figure 1.18 shows Server Explorer and the tables in a database maintained on a popular Windows developer resource site.

Dragging a table from Server Explorer onto a Designer surface creates two components: a *connection* to connect to the database, and an *adapter* to shuttle data back and forth across the connection. Right-clicking on the adapter in the Designer and choosing Generate Dataset allows you to create a new *data set*, a DataSet-derived class specially generated to hold data for the table you originally dragged from Server Explorer. The default Generate Dataset options will also create an instance of the new data set for you to associate with controls.

FIGURE 1.18: A Database Connection in Server Explorer

Associating a source of data, such as a data set, with one or more controls is known as *data binding*. Binding a control to a data source provides for bidirectional communication between the control and the data source so that when the data is modified in one place, it's propagated to the other. Several data bound controls are provided with WinForms, including ListBox and ComboBox, but of all of them, the DataGrid control is the most flexible. Figure 1.19 shows a form with a data grid bound to the data set that's already been created.

When there's a data set on the form, it's easy to bind the data grid to it. You set the data grid's DataSource property in the Property Browser and fill the data set when the form is loaded. To do this, you use the data adapter:

```
void DownloadsForm_Load(object sender, EventArgs e) {
  sqlDataAdapter1.Fill(downloadsDataSet1);
}
```

This is only a scratch on the surface of what can be done with data binding in general and the data grid specifically. For more information, read Chapter 12: Data Sets and Designer Support, and Chapter 13: Data Binding and Data Grids.

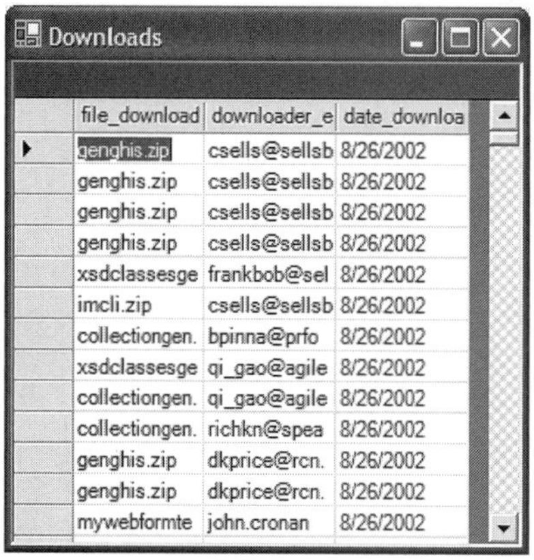

FIGURE 1.19: A DataGrid Bound to a Data Set

Multithreaded User Interfaces

Because the Designer provides so much functionality via drag and drop and the Property Browser, it won't be long before you get to the meat of your programming chores. And when that happens, you're bound to run into a task that takes long enough to annoy your users if you make them wait while it completes—for example, printing or calculating the last digit of pi.

It's especially annoying if your application freezes while an operation takes place on the UI thread, showing a blank square where the main form used to be and leaving your users time to consider your competitors. To build applications that remain responsive in the face of long-running operations, you need threads. And even though WinForms doesn't provide threading support, .NET provides many threading options that WinForms integrates well with, once you're familiar with how to do it appropriately. To explore your threading options, read Chapter 14: Multithreaded User Interfaces.

Deployment

When you've got your application just how you like it, all arranged and responsive and fancy, you'll want to share it. You have several options. You can create an archive of your files and send them as an e-mail to your friends and family, from which they can extract the files into the folder of their choice and run your application. Or, if you like, you can use the VS.NET Setup Project template to create a project that produces a Microsoft Setup Information (MSI) file containing your application's files. Recipients can use this MSI file to install the application into the folder of their choice.

Of course, the problem with both of these techniques is that as soon as you share your application, that's when you find the crushing bug that, when the moon is full and the sun is in the house of Orion, causes bad, bad things to happen. When problems come up, you need to remember who received your application so that you can let them know to install the new version before the existing version formats C: or resets your boss's Mine-sweeper high scores. Of course, all of this explains why your IT department mandates that all internal applications be Web applications.

The Web application deployment model is so simple, there is no deployment. Instead, whenever users surf to the Web application in the morning, they get the version that the IT department uploaded to the server the night before. That deployment model has never been available out of the box for Windows applications. Until now.

At this point, you should stop reading and try the following:

1. Using the Windows Application project template, create a project called DeploymentFun.

2. Drag and drop some controls from the Toolbox, and compile your application.

3. In the shell explorer, navigate to your DeploymentFun\bin folder and right-click on the Debug folder, choosing Properties.

4. Choose Web Sharing and turn it on, using DeploymentFun as the name of the share.

5. Using Start | Run, enter the following URL:

   http://localhost/DeploymentFun/DeploymentFun.exe

You've just used the *no-touch deployment* feature of .NET to deploy your WinForms application like a Web application, except that it's a real Windows application complete with full user control over the frame, the toolbar, the menu bar, the status bar, shortcut keys, and so on. Any libraries that are required to make your application run, such as custom or third-party controls, will be downloaded from the same virtual directory that the application came from. And, just like a Web application, by default your WinForms application is running in a security sandbox. In the case of no-touch deployment applications, the sandbox is provided by .NET *Code Access Security*, which dictates that the permissions of your code are limited according to where the code came from, such as across the intranet. This is in contrast to classic Windows security, where code is awarded permissions based on who launched the application, an approach that doesn't work very well when everyone seems to run as Administrator.

For the details of deploying WinForms applications and controls over the Web—including hosting WinForms controls on a Web page, application deployment, versioning, caching, and most importantly, security—turn to Chapter 15: Web Deployment.

Moving from MFC

Because C# is a member of the C family of languages, you may be a former C++ programmer, and even a former Microsoft Foundation Classes (MFC) programmer. MFC was a wonderful framework for building document-centric applications. Even today, MFC provides some features that WinForms still doesn't have, such as command handling and document management. Of course, WinForms also has plenty of features that MFC never had, including anchoring and Web deployment. If you'd like an overview of the differences between WinForms and MFC and a discussion of how to deal with the lack of some features, you should read Appendix A: Moving from MFC.

Where Are We?

WinForms provides a great deal of functionality, as this chapter has shown. Not only does it give you the basics needed to build applications, forms, controls, resources, and dialogs, but it also provides advanced features such as anchoring, docking, user controls, print preview, data binding, and Web deployment, along with wizards to get you started and a Form Designer to let you visually develop your look and feel. And, where WinForms stops, the rest of the .NET Framework steps in to provide drawing, object serialization, threading, security, and tons of other bits of functionality in thousands of classes and components. One book can't cover all of those, but I'll show you what you need to know to write real WinForms applications and controls in the rest of this one.

■ 2 ■
Forms

IN A TECHNOLOGY named "Windows Forms," you can expect the form to play a critical role. This chapter explores the basics, including the display of forms, the lifetime of a form, form size and location, non-client form adornments, menus, and child controls, as well as advanced topics such as form transparency, nonrectangular forms, control layout, MDI forms, and visual inheritance. And if that's not enough, Chapter 3 is all about using forms as dialogs.

Some of the material in this chapter—notably child control topics such as anchoring and docking—applies equally well to user controls as it does to forms. Although some material is common to both topics, topics that are more commonly associated with forms are covered in this chapter, and topics more commonly associated with controls are covered in Chapter 8: Controls.

Showing Forms

Any form—that is, any class that derives from the Form base class—can be shown in one of two ways. Here, it is shown modelessly:

```
void button1_Click(object sender, System.EventArgs e) {
  AnotherForm form = new AnotherForm();
  form.Show(); // Show form modelessly
}
```

Here, a form is shown modally:

```
void button1_Click(object sender, System.EventArgs e) {
  AnotherForm form = new AnotherForm();
  form.ShowDialog(); // show form modally
}
```

Form.Show shows the new form modelessly and returns immediately without creating any relationship between the currently active form and the new form. This means that the existing form can be closed, leaving the new form behind.[1] Form.ShowDialog, on the other hand, shows the form modally and does not return control until the created form has been closed, either by using the explicit Close method or by setting the DialogResult property (more on this in Chapter 3: Dialogs).

Owner and Owned Forms

As the ShowDialog method shows the new form, it uses the currently active form as the new form's logical owner.[2] An *owner* is a window that contributes to the behavior of the *owned* form. For example, if an owner has a modal child, then activating the owner, such as by using the Alt+Tab task-switching keystroke, activates the owned form. In the modeless case, when the owner form is minimized or restored, so is the owned form. Also, an owned form is always shown on top of an owner form, even if the owner is currently active, as if the user has clicked on the owner, as shown in Figure 2.1.

When a form is activated modelessly via the Show method, by default the new form does not have an owner. Setting the owner of a modeless form is a matter of setting the new form's Owner property:

```
void button1_Click(object sender, System.EventArgs e) {
  AnotherForm form = new AnotherForm();
  form.Owner = this; // Establish owner/owned relationship
  form.Show();
}
```

---

1. However, if the main form is closed, Application.Run will close all other forms and return.
2. The form shown using ShowDialog will have an Owner property set to null if no owner is provided explicitly. However, the user interaction behavior for modal forms is the same whether or not the Owner property is set.

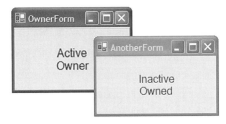

FIGURE 2.1: Owner-Owned Relationship

In the modal case, in spite of the implicit owner-owned relationship that WinForms creates, the modal form will have a null Owner property unless the Owner property is set explicitly. You can do this by setting the Owner property just before the call to ShowDialog or by passing the owner form as an argument to the ShowDialog override that takes an IWin32Window[3] parameter:

```
void button1_Click(object sender, System.EventArgs e) {
  AnotherForm form = new AnotherForm();
  form.ShowDialog(this); // Passing the owner as an argument
}
```

An owner form can enumerate the list of forms it owns using the OwnedForms collection:

```
void button1_Click(object sender, System.EventArgs e) {
  AnotherForm form = new AnotherForm();
  form.Owner = this;
  form.Show();

  foreach( Form ownedForm in this.OwnedForms ) {
    MessageBox.Show(ownedForm.Text);
  }
}
```

You may have noticed that in addition to an optional owner, a form can have an optional parent, as exposed via the Parent property. As it turns out,

---

3. IWin32Window is an interface exposed by UI objects in WinForms that expose a Win32 HWND via the IWin32Window.Handle property.

normal forms have a Parent property that is always null. The one exception to this rule is MDI child forms, which I discuss later. Unlike the owner-owned relationship, the parent-child relationship dictates clipping—that is, a child's edge is clipped to the edge of the parent, as shown in Figure 2.2.

The parent-child relationship is reserved for parent forms (or parent container controls) and child controls (with the exception of MDI, which is discussed later).

Form Lifetime

Although the user can't see a form until either Show or ShowDialog is called, a form exists as soon as the object is created. A new form object wakes up in the object's *constructor*, which the runtime calls when an object is first created. It's during the constructor that InitializeComponent is called and therefore when all the child controls are created and initialized.

It's a bad idea to put custom code into the InitializeComponent function because the Designer is likely to throw it away. However, if you'd like to add other controls or change anything set by the InitializeComponent method, you can do that in the constructor. If the initial form implementation was generated by one of the VS.NET wizards, you'll even have a

FIGURE 2.2: A Child ListBox Control Clipped to the Client Area of Its Parent Form

helpful comment indicating where the Designer thinks that you should add your initialization code:

```
public Form1() {
  // Required for Windows Form Designer support
  InitializeComponent();

  // TODO: Add any constructor code after InitializeComponent call

  // Adding a control
  Button anotherButton = new Button();
  this.Controls.Add(anotherButton);

  // Changing a property
  this.Text = "Something Not Known At Design Time";
}
```

When Form.Show or Form.ShowDialog is called, that's the form's cue to show itself as well as all its child controls. You can be notified that this has happened when the code handles the Load event:

```
void InitializeComponent() {
  . . .
  this.Load += new System.EventHandler(this.Form1_Load);
  . . .
}

void Form1_Load(object sender, System.EventArgs e) {
  MessageBox.Show("Welcome to Form1!");
}
```

The Load event is useful for doing any final initialization right before a form is shown. Also, the Load event is a good place to change the Visible property and the ShowInTaskbar property if you'd like the form to start as hidden:[4]

```
void Form1_Load(object sender, EventArgs e) {
  // Don't show this form
```

continues

---

4. Starting a form as hidden is useful for forms that need to be running but that shouldn't show themselves right away. An example is a form with a notify icon in the taskbar.

```
  this.Visible = false;
  this.ShowInTaskbar = false;
}
```

When a form is shown, it will become the *active* form. It's the active form that receives keyboard input. An inactive form is made active when users click on it or otherwise indicate to Windows that they would like it to be active, such as by using Alt+Tab to switch to it. You can make an inactive form active programmatically by using the Form.Activate method.[5] When a form is made active, including when the form is first loaded, it receives the Activated event:

```
void InitializeComponent() {
  . . .
  this.Activated += new System.EventHandler(this.Form1_Activated);
  . . .
}

void Form1_Activated(object sender, System.EventArgs e) {
  this.game.Resume();
}
```

If an application has a form that is the currently active window as far as the operating system is concerned, you can discover that using the Form.ActiveForm static method. If Form.ActiveForm is null, it means that none of your application's forms is currently active. To track when a form deactivates, handle the Deactivate event:

```
void InitializeComponent() {
  . . .
  this.Deactivate += new System.EventHandler(this.Form1_Deactivate);
```

---

5. Older implementations of Win32 allowed an application to set itself active on top of the currently active window, something that could be pretty annoying. Modern implementations of Win32 allow an application to set a window as active only if another window in that application is currently active. Some of these implementations flash a background application's button on the shell's taskbar to indicate that the application would like your attention.

```
    ...
}

void Form1_Deactivate(object sender, System.EventArgs e) {
  this.game.Pause();
}
```

If, in addition to controlling whether or not a form is active, you'd like to control its visibility, either you can use the Hide and Show methods, which set the Visible property, or you can set the Visible property directly:

```
void hideButton_Click(object sender, System.EventArgs e) {
  this.Hide(); // Set Visible property indirectly
  this.Visible = false; // Set Visible property directly
}
```

As you might expect, there is an event that you can handle as your form flickers in and out of visual reality. It's called VisibleChanged. The Activated, Deactivate, and VisibleChanged events are all handy for restarting and pausing activities that require user interaction or attention, such as in a game. To stop an activity altogether, you'll want to handle the Closing or the Closed event. The Closing event can be canceled if users change their minds:

```
void Form1_Closing(object sender, CancelEventArgs e) {
  DialogResult res = MessageBox.Show(
    "Abort your game?", "Game In Progress", MessageBoxButtons.YesNo);
  e.Cancel = (res == DialogResult.No);
}

void Form1_Closed(object sender, EventArgs e) {
  MessageBox.Show("Your game was aborted");
}
```

Notice that during the Closing event the handler can set the Cancel-EventArgs.Cancel property to true, canceling the closing of the form. This is also the best place to serialize a form's visible properties, such as size and location, before Windows closes the form. On the other hand, the Closed event is merely a notification that the form has already gone away.

Form Size and Location

During its lifetime, the form is likely to take up space at some location. The initial location for the form is governed by the StartPosition property, which can have one of several values from the FormStartPosition enumeration:

```
enum FormStartPosition {
  CenterParent,
  CenterScreen,
  Manual,
  WindowsDefaultBounds,
  WindowsDefaultLocation, //  default
}
```

These values have the following behavior:

- **WindowsDefaultLocation.** The form's starting position will be determined by Windows, which will pick a location staggered from the upper-left corner of the screen toward the lower right in an attempt to make sure that new windows neither cover each other nor fall off the screen. The form will be shown with whatever the Size property was set to in the Designer.

- **WindowsDefaultBounds.** Windows will be asked to determine a default size as well as location.

- **CenterScreen.** The form will be centered on the *desktop*, that area not taken up by the shell taskbar and the like.

- **CenterParent.** The form will be centered over the owner (or the currently active form, if there's no owner) when ShowDialog is used. If Show is used, the behavior is that of WindowsDefaultLocation.

- **Manual.** Allows you to set the initial location and the size of the form without any Windows intervention.

The size and location of the form are exposed via the Size and Location properties, of type Size and Point, respectively (both from the System.Drawing namespace). As a shortcut, the properties of the size of a form are exposed directly via the Height and Width form properties, and those of the location are exposed via the Left, Right, Top, and Bottom properties. Figure 2.3 shows the basic size and location properties on a form.

When the upper-left corner of a form changes, that's a *move*, which can be handled in the Move or LocationChanged event handler. When the width or height of a form changes, that's a *resize*, which can be handled in the Resize or SizeChanged event handler.[6] Sometimes one gesture of the mouse can cause all move and size events to happen. For example, resizing a form by dragging the top-left corner would change the location and the size of the form.

The location of the form is in absolute screen coordinates. If you're interested in the location of the form relative to the desktop—so that, for example, your form's caption never appears underneath the shell's

FIGURE 2.3: The DesktopLocation, Location, ClientSize, and Size Properties (See Plate 4)

---

6. Why are there two events for move and two more for resize? The XxxChanged events are so named to be consistent with data binding. The Move and Resize events are more familiar to Visual Basic programmers and are kept for their benefit. Both events are functionally equivalent.

taskbar—then even if it's on the top edge, as shown in Figure 2.3, you can use the DesktopLocation property. Here's an example:

```
void Form3_Load(object sender, EventArgs e) {
  // Could end up under the shell's taskbar
  this.Location = new Point(1, 1);

  // Will always be in the desktop
  this.DesktopLocation = new Point(1, 1);

  // A simpler form of the preceding line
  this.SetDesktopLocation(1, 1);
}
```

Locations are expressed via the Point structure from the System.Drawing namespace, the interesting parts of which are shown here:

```
struct Point {
  // Fields
  public static readonly Point Empty;

  // Constructors
  public Point(int x, int y);

  // Properties
  public bool IsEmpty { get; }
  public int X { get; set; }
  public int Y { get; set; }

  // Methods
  public static Point Ceiling(PointF value);
  public void Offset(int dx, int dy);
  public static Point Round(PointF value);
  public virtual string ToString();
  public static Point Truncate(PointF value);
}
```

The PointF structure is very similar to the Point structure, but PointF is used in drawing applications when more precise floating point measurements are required. Sometimes you'll need to convert from a Point to a PointF object to be able to call some methods or set some properties. You can do so without any extra effort:

```
// Can convert directly from Point to PointF
Point pt1 = new Point(10, 20);
PointF pt2 = pt1; // Yields PointF(10.0f, 20.0f)
```

However, because floating point numbers contain extra precision that will be lost in the conversion, you'll need to be explicit about how to convert from a PointF to a Point object using the static Truncate, Round, and Ceiling methods of the Point class:

```
// Need to be explicit when converting from a PointF to a Point
PointF pt1 = new PointF(1.2f, 1.8f);
Point pt2 = Point.Truncate(pt1); // Yields Point(1, 1);
Point pt3 = Point.Round(pt1); // Yields Point(1, 2);
Point pt4 = Point.Ceiling(pt1); // Yields Point(2, 2);
```

The size of a window is reflected in the Size property, also from System.Drawing (Size also has a SizeF counterpart and provides the same capabilities for conversion):

```
struct Size {
  // Fields
  public static readonly Size Empty;

  // Constructors
  public Size(int width, int height);

  // Properties
  public int Height { get; set; }
  public bool IsEmpty { get; }
  public int Width { get; set; }

  // Methods
  public static Size Ceiling(SizeF value);
  public virtual bool Equals(object obj);
  public static Size Round(SizeF value);
  public virtual string ToString();
  public static Size Truncate(SizeF value);
}
```

Although the Size property represents the size of the entire window, a form isn't responsible for rendering all of its contents. The form can have edges, a caption, and scrollbars, all of which are drawn by Windows. The part that the form is responsible for is the ClientSize, as shown in

Figure 2.3. It's useful to save the ClientSize property between application sessions because it's independent of the current adornment settings the user has established. Similarly, resizing the form to make sure there's enough space to render your form's state is often related to the client area of the form and not to the size of the form as a whole:

```
void Form2_Load(object sender, EventArgs e) {
   this.ClientSize = new Size(100, 100); // Calls SetClientSizeCore
   this.SetClientSizeCore(100, 100);
}
```

A Rectangle combines a Point and a Size and also has a RectangleF counterpart. The Bounds property gives a rectangle of the form relative to the screen, whereas the DesktopBounds property is a rectangle relative to the desktop for top-level windows (and not for child windows). The ClientRectangle property is a rectangle relative to the form itself, describing the client area of the form. Of the three, ClientRectangle tends to be the most used, if for no other reason than to describe which area to use when drawing:

```
void Form1_Paint(object sender, PaintEventArgs e) {
   Graphics g = e.Graphics;
   g.FillEllipse(Brushes.Yellow, this.ClientRectangle);
   g.DrawEllipse(Pens.DarkBlue, this.ClientRectangle);
}
```

Also, it's sometimes necessary to convert a point that's relative to the screen to one that's relative to the client or vice versa. For example, the HelpRequest event, generated when the user clicks on the Help button and then clicks on a control, is sent to the handler in screen coordinates. However, to determine which control was clicked on requires the mouse position in client coordinates. You can convert between the two coordinate systems by using PointToScreen and PointToClient:

```
void Form1_HelpRequested(object sender, HelpEventArgs e) {
   // Convert screen coordinates to client coordinates
   Point pt = this.PointToClient(e.MousePos);

   // Look for control user clicked on
   foreach( Control control in this.Controls ) {
```

```
    if( control.Bounds.Contains(pt) ) {
      Control controlNeedingHelp = control;
      ...
      break;
    }
  }
}
```

To translate an entire rectangle between screen and client coordinates, you can also use RectangleToScreen and RectangleToClient.

Restricting Form Size

Often our careful control layouts or rendering requirements dictate a certain minimum amount of space. Less often, our forms can't be made to take advantage of more than a certain amount of space (although anchoring and docking, described later, should help with that). Either way, it's possible to set a form's minimum or maximum size via the MinimumSize and MaximumSize properties, respectively. The following example sets a fixed height of 200, a minimum width of 300, and a maximum width so large as to be unlimited:

```
void Form2_Load(object sender, EventArgs e) {
  // min width is 300, min height is 200
  this.MinimumSize = new Size(300, 200);

  // max width is unlimited, max height is 200
  this.MaximumSize = new Size(int.MaxValue, 200);
}
```

Notice that the code uses the maximum value of an integer to specify that there is no effective maximum width on the form. You may be tempted to use zero for this value instead, but if either the Width or the Height property of the Size used to set the minimum or maximum is nonzero, then both values are used. This would set the maximum size of your form to zero instead of "no maximum."

One other setting that governs a form's size and location is WindowState, which can be one of the values from the FormWindowState enumeration:

```
enum FormWindowState {
  Maximized,
  Minimized,
```

continues

```
    Normal, // Form.WindowState default value
}
```

By default, the WindowState is set to Normal, which means that it's not maximized to take up the entire desktop, nor is it minimized so that none of the form shows at all and only a button is shown in the taskbar. Your program can get or set this property at will to manage the state of your form. However, if you're saving the size and location of your form between application sessions, you may decide to reset the WindowState to Normal so that the size being saved represents the size in the normal state and not the minimized or maximized size:

```
void Form2_Closing(object sender, CancelEventArgs e) {
    // Capture the properties before the form is gone
    FormWindowState state = this.WindowState;
    this.WindowState = FormWindowState.Normal;
    Point location = this.Location;
    Size size = this.ClientSize;

    // ... save state, location and size properties between sessions ...
    // ... restore properties in Load event ...
}
```

For a description of how and where to keep application settings between sessions, read Chapter 11: Applications and Settings.

Z-Order

Another location property that you may let your users influence or keep between sessions is the TopLevel property. So far I've discussed location in terms of x and y. However, as the user switches between windows, Windows also juggles the *z-order*, which dictates which windows are drawn on top of one another.

Furthermore, z-order is split into two tiers. Normal windows are drawn lowest z-order to highest, front to back. Above all the normal windows are the *topmost* windows, which are also drawn relative to each other, lowest z-order to highest, but no matter the z-order, are always drawn on top of any normal window. For an example of a topmost window, pressing Ctrl+Shift+ESC under many versions of Windows will bring up Task Manager. By default, it's a topmost window and always draws on top of normal windows, whether or not it is the active window. You can change this behavior (I always do) by unchecking the Options | Always On Top setting. If Task Manager were implemented using WinForms, it would implement this feature by toggling the TopMost property on its main form.

Form Adornments

In addition to size and location, forms have a number of properties that manage various other aspects of their appearance as well as corresponding behavior. The following settings govern the *non-client* adornments of a form: those parts of a form outside the client area that are drawn by Windows.

- **FormBorderStyle** sets whether the form has a border, whether it can be resized, and whether it has a normal-size or small caption. Good forms and dialogs leave the default value of Sizable. Annoying dialogs change this property to one of the nonsizable options. Generally, programmers choose nonsizable options because of fear of control-layout issues, but WinForms handles that nicely, as I discuss later in this chapter.

  In addition, there are two tool window styles—one fixed and one sizable—for use in building floating toolbar-style windows.

- **ControlBox** is a Boolean determining whether or not the icon on the upper left of the form as well as the close button on the upper right are shown. If this property is set to false, neither left-clicking on the upper-left corner of the form nor right-clicking on the caption will show the System menu. Similarly, when ControlBox is false, the MaximizeBox and MinimizeBox properties will be ignored, and those buttons will not be shown. This property defaults to true but is often set to false for modal dialogs.

- The **MaximizeBox** and **MinimizeBox** properties determine whether the maximize and minimize buttons are shown on the form's caption. These properties default to true but are often set to false for modal dialogs.

- The **HelpButton** property shows the question mark button next to the close button in the upper right, but only if ControlBox is set to true and MaximizeBox and MinimizeBox are both set to false. This property defaults to false but is often set to true for modal dialogs. When the user clicks on the help button and then somewhere else on the form, the HelpRequested event is fired for the form to provide the user with help. Whether the HelpButton property is true or false, the HelpRequested event is always fired when the user presses F1.
- The **Icon** property determines the image used as the icon for the form.
- The **SizeGripStyle** property allows values from the SizeGripStyle enumeration: Auto, Hide, or Show. A *size grip* is the adornment on the lower-right corner of a window that indicates that it can be resized. The default is Auto and indicates the size grip in the lower-right corner "if needed," depending on the form's FormBorderStyle property. The Auto setting judges the size grip needed if the form is sizable and is shown modally. Also, if the form has a StatusBar control, the form's SizeGripStyle is ignored in favor of the SizingGrip Boolean property on the status bar control itself.
- **ShowInTaskbar** is a Boolean governing whether the form's Text property should appear in a button on the shell taskbar. This property defaults to true but is often set to false for modal forms.

Although most of the properties are independent of each other, not all of these combinations will work together. For example, when the FormBorderStyle is set to either of the tool window settings, no maximize or minimize box is shown, regardless of the value of the MaximizeBox and MinimizeBox properties. Experimentation will reveal what works and what doesn't.

Form Transparency

In addition to the properties that specify how the non-client area of a form are rendered by Windows, the Form class provides a set of properties that allow you to change the appearance of the form as a whole, including making it partially transparent or removing pieces of the form altogether.

The property that governs transparency of the entire form is called Opacity and defaults to 1.0, or 100% opaque. A value between 0.0 and 1.0 denotes a degree of opacity using the alpha-blending[7] support in more modern versions of Windows, where any number less than 1.0 results in a form that is partially transparent. Opacity is mostly a parlor trick, but it's kind of fun for making top-level windows less annoying than they would normally be, as shown here:

```
void InitializeComponent() {
  ...
  this.Opacity = 0.5;
  this.Text = "Opacity = 0.5";
  this.TopMost = true;
  ...
}

void OpacityForm_Activated(object sender, EventArgs e) {
  timer1.Enabled = true;
}

void timer1_Tick(object sender, EventArgs e) {
  if( this.Opacity < 1.0 ) this.Opacity += 0.1;
  this.Text = "Opacity = " + this.Opacity.ToString();
}

void OpacityForm_Deactivate(object sender, EventArgs e) {
  timer1.Enabled = false;
  this.Opacity = 0.5;
  this.Text = "Opacity = " + this.Opacity.ToString();
}
```

This example shows code from a top-level form whose Opacity property starts at 50%. When the form is activated, it starts a timer that increases the Opacity by 10% on each tick, giving a nice "fade in" effect, as shown in Figure 2.4. When the form is deactivated, it is set to 50% opaque again, making it available for viewing and clicking but hopefully not obscuring too much.

---

7. Alpha-blending is the blending of partially transparent elements together based on an alpha value denoting their level of transparency.

FIGURE 2.4: Opacity (See Plate 5)

Nonrectangular Forms

Opacity affects the transparency of the entire form. It's also possible to change the shape of the form by making parts of the form completely transparent. One way to do this is with the TransparencyKey property, which designates a color to use in marking transparent pixels. When a pixel on the form is supposed to be drawn with the transparent key color, that pixel will instead be removed from the form, in two senses: The pixel will not be drawn, and clicking on that spot on the form will actually result in a click on what's showing through from underneath.

For example, setting the TransparencyKey property to the same as the BackColor property of the form will cause a form to lose its background (as well as anything else drawn with that color), as shown in Figure 2.5.

The novelty of the form shown in Figure 2.5 seems limited until you combine it with FormBorderStyle.None, which removes the non-client area altogether, as shown in Figure 2.6.

The combination of a transparent color to erase the form's background and the removal of the form border yields a nonrectangular window, which is all the rage with the kids these days. The transparency key color is used to create a *region* that describes the visible area of the form to Windows.

As easy as setting TransparencyKey is, you need to be careful with it. For example, you need to choose a color that you know won't appear in the

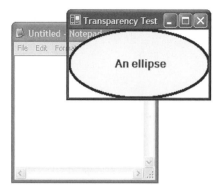

FIGURE 2.5: Form Shown in Front of Notepad with TransparencyKey Set to BackColor

FIGURE 2.6: TransparencyKey Combined with FormBorderStyle.None

parts of your form that you need to show, or else they'll be made transparent, too. Also, when using the TransparencyKey, you must calculate the region each time the form is drawn. And most importantly, Transparency-Key requires certain capabilities of the video driver that are often missing, causing it to fail completely.

So instead of using TransparencyKey, you may want to set the form's Region property directly. This approach is slightly less convenient but much more robust. Regions are covered in detail in Chapter 6: Advanced Drawing, but here's an example of using an ellipse as the form's region:

```
using System.Drawing.Drawing2D;

void SetEllipseRegion() {
  // Assume: this.FormBorderStyle = FormBorderStyle.None
```

continues

```
  Rectangle rect = this.ClientRectangle;
  using( GraphicsPath path = new GraphicsPath() ) {
    path.AddEllipse(rect);
    this.Region = new Region(path);
  }
}

void TransparentForm_Load(object sender, EventArgs e) {
  SetEllipseRegion();
}

void TransparentForm_SizeChanged(object sender, EventArgs e) {
  SetEllipseRegion();
}
```

Notice that our code sets the region both when the form is loaded and whenever the form is resized. However, as careful as we are to handle resizing, with the caption and the edges on the form missing, there's no way for the user to actually move or resize the form. When that's the case, you're on the hook to implement moving and resizing yourself. Here's an example of using the mouse events to move the form around when the user clicks in the client area of the form:

```
Point downPoint = Point.Empty;

void TransparentForm_MouseDown(object sender, MouseEventArgs e) {
  if( e.Button != MouseButtons.Left ) return;
  downPoint = new Point(e.X, e.Y);
}

void TransparentForm_MouseMove(object sender, MouseEventArgs e) {
  if( downPoint == Point.Empty ) return;
  Point location =
    new Point(
      this.Left + e.X - downPoint.X, this.Top + e.Y - downPoint.Y);
  this.Location = location;
}

void TransparentForm_MouseUp(object sender, MouseEventArgs e) {
  if( e.Button != MouseButtons.Left ) return;
  downPoint = Point.Empty;
}
```

When the user clicks on the client area of the form, the MouseDown event is fired, and we handle this event by caching the point on the screen where the user clicked. When the user moves the mouse, the MouseMove event is fired, and we use that to move the form based on the difference between the current mouse location and the point where the user first clicked. Finally, when the user releases the mouse button, the MouseUp event fires, which we use to stop the move. You'd need something similar to implement resizing. The details of mouse events, as well as keyboard events, are covered in Chapter 8: Controls.

Form Menus

As interesting as forms themselves are—with their lifetime, adornments, transparency settings, and input options—they're all the more interesting with controls on them. But before we get into managing a form's controls in general, we need to take a quick look at menus, which have special support in WinForms. Not only does VS.NET have a special Menu Designer (as shown in Figure 2.7), but also, unlike every other control, a Form can show only one main menu at a time, as stored in the Form.Menu property (which is of type MainMenu).

Although you are limited to a single main menu showing on a form at a time, you can switch menus at run time to your heart's content by setting the Form.Menu property:

```
void showMenu1Button_Click(object sender, EventArgs e) {
  this.Menu = this.mainMenu1;
}

void showMenu2Button_Click(object sender, EventArgs e) {
  this.Menu = this.mainMenu2;
}
```

continues

FIGURE 2.7: The VS.NET Menu Designer

```
void showNoMenuButton_Click(object sender, EventArgs e) {
  this.Menu = null;
}
```

In fact, if you drag multiple MainMenu components from the Toolbox onto the form, you can select each one and edit it separately, but you'll need to set the form's Menu property to pick which one to start with. No matter which menu you choose to designate as the form's main menu (or even if you choose none at all), menus themselves are only containers for items modeled via the MenuItem class.

In fact, menus and menu items are both containers. The MainMenu class has a MenuItems collection that contains zero or more MenuItem objects. This makes up the list of items across the top of the menu, such as File, Edit, and Help. Each of these MenuItem objects in turn has its own MenuItems collection, which contains the next level of items—for example, File | Save, File | Recent Files, File | Exit. Anything below that level shows up as a cascading menu of items, such as File | Recent Files | foo.txt.

The Menu Designer takes the menu structure you lay out and generates the code to populate the menu items in InitializeComponent. For example, using the Designer to create the File | Exit and Help | About menu items as shown in Figure 2.7 results in code that looks like this (and really makes you appreciate the Designer):

```
private void InitializeComponent() {
  this.mainMenu1 = new System.Windows.Forms.MainMenu();
  this.fileMenuItem = new System.Windows.Forms.MenuItem();
  this.fileExitMenuItem = new System.Windows.Forms.MenuItem();
  this.helpMenuItem = new System.Windows.Forms.MenuItem();
  this.helpAboutMenuItem = new System.Windows.Forms.MenuItem();
  ...

  // mainMenu1
  this.mainMenu1.MenuItems.AddRange(
    new System.Windows.Forms.MenuItem[] {
      this.fileMenuItem,
      this.helpMenuItem});

  // fileMenuItem
  this.fileMenuItem.Index = 0;
  this.fileMenuItem.MenuItems.AddRange(
    new System.Windows.Forms.MenuItem[] {
```

```
      this.fileExitMenuItem});
  this.fileMenuItem.Text = "&File";

  // fileExitMenuItem
  this.fileExitMenuItem.Index = 0;
  this.fileExitMenuItem.Text = "&Exit";

  // helpMenuItem
  this.helpMenuItem.Index = 1;
  this.helpMenuItem.MenuItems.AddRange(
    new System.Windows.Forms.MenuItem[] {
      this.helpAboutMenuItem});
  this.helpMenuItem.Text = "&Help";

  // helpAboutMenuItem
  this.helpAboutMenuItem.Index = 0;
  this.helpAboutMenuItem.Text = "&About...";

  // Form1
  ...
  this.Menu = this.mainMenu1;
  ...
}
```

The MenuItem class has the following design-time properties and events:

```
class MenuItem : Menu, IComponent,  IDisposable {
  // Properties
  public bool Checked { get; set; }
  public bool DefaultItem { get; set; }
  public bool Enabled { get; set; }
  public bool MdiList { get; set; }
  public int MergeOrder { get; set; }
  public MenuMerge MergeType { get; set; }
  public bool OwnerDraw { get; set; }
  public bool RadioCheck { get; set; }
  public Shortcut Shortcut { get; set; }
  public bool ShowShortcut { get; set; }
  public string Text { get; set; }
  public bool Visible { get; set; }

  // Events
  public event EventHandler Click;
  public event DrawItemEventHandler DrawItem;
  public event MeasureItemEventHandler MeasureItem;
  public event EventHandler Popup;
  public event EventHandler Select;
}
```

The major things you'll want to focus on are the Checked and Radio-Check properties (which mark an item as chosen), the Enabled and Visible properties (which determine whether the item can be chosen or whether it will be shown), the Shortcut property (which allows you to assign a keyboard shortcut to a menu item, such as Ctrl+S for Save), and the Text property, which is what's shown to the user. A Text property that includes an "&" (ampersand) will underline the next character; for example, "&Save" will show as "Save", thereby providing a visual cue for keyboard menu navigation via the Alt key. Typing "-" (hyphen) as the Text in the Menu Designer will create a separator between groups of related menu items. The menu merging and MdiList properties are MDI-related, and I discuss them later in this chapter.

Of course, the Click event handler is the big celebrity in the menu item list of events because it gets fired when the user clicks on a menu item:

```
void fileExitMenuItem_Click(object sender, EventArgs e) {
  this.Close();
}

void helpAboutMenuItem_Click(object sender, EventArgs e) {
  MessageBox.Show("Ain't menus cool?", "About...");
}
```

Context Menus

Just as a form can show at most one main menu, a form (or a control) can show at most one context menu, as managed via the ContextMenu property. Unlike the MainMenu property, which is of type MainMenu, the ContextMenu property is of type ContextMenu, and you'll need to make sure to drag the correct class from the Toolbox. A ContextMenu is also a collection of menu items, but unlike MainMenu objects, ContextMenu objects have no concept of items "across the top." Context menus are always vertical at every level, and this is reflected in the Context Menu Designer, as shown in Figure 2.8.

In the case of context menus, the Designer always shows "Context Menu" at the top level, and items can only fall under that. However, everything else is the same: Each ContextMenu object has a MenuItems collection filled with MenuItem objects, all with the same properties and events.

FIGURE 2.8: Context Menu Designer

The one remaining difference between MainMenu objects and Context-Menu objects is that controls also have a ContextMenu property, whereas only a form has a MainMenu property.

Although many controls have their own context menus—for example, a TextBox has things such as Copy and Paste in its context menu—you can replace a control's built-in context menu by setting the ContextMenu property of the control. As a rule, most of the operations available from any control's context menu are also available as methods on the control. This means that you can replace the context menu on a control but still provide the operations that the control's menu would provide, implementing those options by sending the command to the control itself:

```
void copyMenuItem_Click(object sender, EventArgs e) {
  textBox1.Copy();
}
```

Child Controls

Unlike main and context menus, controls[8] dragged from the Toolbox onto the surface provided by the Designer are added to the form's Controls collection. You can use that collection yourself to add controls dynamically at run time (as I showed earlier in this chapter), or you can add arrays of controls the way the Designer-generated InitializeComponent does:

---

8. Technically speaking, both MainMenu and ContextMenu are *components*, as are all the rest of the items that you can drag and drop from the Toolbox that show up on the tray along the bottom of the design surface. For a list of the standard WinForms components, see Appendix D: Standard WinForms Components and Controls.

```
void InitializeComponent() {
  this.SuspendLayout();
  // ...child control creation and initialization...
  this.Controls.AddRange(
    new System.Windows.Forms.Control[] {
      this.statusBar1,
      this.textBox1});
  this.ResumeLayout(false);
}
```

Notice the calls to SuspendLayout and ResumeLayout. SuspendLayout is an optimization to keep the form from updating itself visually until ResumeLayout is called. By bracketing several tasks—the child control creation and initialization as well as the addition of the controls to the control collection—in SuspendLayout and ResumeLayout, we don't have to worry about the form trying to draw itself until everything is set up. This is something that you can do if you need to make a nontrivial set of changes to the form's properties or controls yourself.

Control Z-Order

In addition to Add and AddRange, you can remove controls from the form's collection using Remove and RemoveRange (another good place to use SuspendLayout and ResumeLayout). When the controls have been in the collection long enough to be drawn, the order in the collection establishes the z-order among the controls on the form. Figure 2.9 shows an

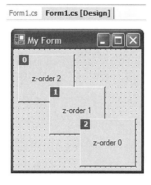

FIGURE 2.9: Z-Order and Tab Order

example of a form with three buttons that have been added to the controls collection in z-order order:

```
this.Controls.AddRange(
  new System.Windows.Forms.Control[] {
    this.zOrder0Button,
    this.zOrder1Button,
    this.zOrder2Button});
```

If you need to change the z-order at design time, you can right-click on a control and choose Bring To Front, which brings the control to z-order zero, or Send To Back, which sets the z-order to the last item in the collection. Similarly, you can move a control at run time using the Control.BringToFront and Control.SendToBack methods.

Control Tab Order

Directing your attention again to Figure 2.9, notice the little numbers in the upper-left corner. Those numbers indicate the tab order of the controls on the form and are put there by the View | Tab Order menu item in VS.NET. *Tab order* is the order in which the controls will receive focus as the user presses the Tab key. Tab order is exposed on each control by the TabIndex property. Also notice that tab order has no relation to z-order; our button with a z-order of 0 has a tab order of 2.

Themed Controls

Modern versions of Windows (Windows XP and later) support controls that are drawn with a theme. A *theme* can be whatever the Windows shell team adds in the future, but one of the main aspects of a theme is that a user can adjust the way the basic controls are drawn. For example, when buttons aren't themed, they look like those in Figure 2.10.

FIGURE 2.10: Unthemed Buttons in Windows XP

However, when the Windows XP theme is applied in the Display control panel, buttons (and other standard controls) take on a futuristic look, as shown in Figure 2.11.

By default, a WinForms application always gets the Windows standard controls without themed rendering. Under version 1.0, enabling themed rendering required a .manifest file.[9] Enabling themed controls under WinForms v1.1 no longer requires a .manifest file. Instead, there's a method on the System.Windows.Forms.Application class that you call before showing any UI:

```
static void Main() {
    Application.EnableVisualStyles();
    Application.Run(new Form1());
}
```

The EnableVisualStyles method eliminates the need to add a .manifest file to your application, but that's not the whole job; you'll also need to set the FlatStyle on each control on your form from the default value of FlatStyle.Standard to FlatStyle.System. Figure 2.12 shows the difference when the application is running under Windows XP.

FIGURE 2.11: Themed Buttons in Windows XP

FIGURE 2.12: WinForms FlatStyles

---

9. You can read about adding theme support to WinForms 1.0 applications in "Using Windows XP Themes with Windows Forms," http://www.gotdotnet.com/team/ windowsforms/Themes.aspx

As a shortcut to setting the FlatStyle property on the subset of controls that support it (buttons, group boxes, and labels), you can consider a hunk of code such as the following:[10]

```
public MyThemedForm() {
  // Required for Windows Form Designer support
  InitializeComponent();

  // Set the FlatStyle for all controls
  SetFlatStyleSystem(this);
}

void SetFlatStyleSystem(Control parent) {
  foreach( Control control in parent.Controls ) {
    // Only these controls have a FlatStyle property
    ButtonBase button = control as ButtonBase;
    GroupBox group = control as GroupBox;
    Label label = control as Label;
    if( button != null ) button.FlatStyle = FlatStyle.System;
    else if( group != null ) group.FlatStyle = FlatStyle.System;
    else if( label != null ) label.FlatStyle = FlatStyle.System;

    // Set contained controls FlatStyle, too
    SetFlatStyleSystem(control);
  }
}
```

Only the standard Windows controls support a themed appearance by default. If you build your own custom controls that draw themselves, they'll have to handle their own themed rendering (how to build and draw custom controls is discussed in Chapter 8: Controls).

Hosting COM Controls

As wonderful and varied as WinForms controls are, especially considering the burgeoning third-party WinForms control market, Component Object Model (COM) controls[11] have been around a lot longer, and you may still need to use some of them in your WinForms applications. WinForms

---

10. To be more thorough about getting controls and contained controls on a form, see the GetAllControls method in Chapter 3: Dialogs.
11. COM controls are also known as OLE controls and ActiveX controls.

provides built-in support for hosting COM controls, and VS.NET makes it easy to take advantage of that support.

The first step is to get your COM control of choice to show up on the Toolbox so that you can drag it onto your forms. To get a COM control to show up in the Toolbox, right-click on the Toolbox and choose Customize Toolbox, which will bring up the Customize Toolbox dialog, as shown in Figure 2.13.

All the items under the COM Components tab are COM controls registered on your machine. Checking any of them and pressing OK will add the control to the Toolbox, as shown in Figure 2.14.

After a COM control has been added to the Toolbox, you can drop an instance onto a form, set the properties, and handle the events. Any COM control added to your WinForms project will cause a pair of interop assemblies to be generated by VS.NET[12] and added to the project. It's this code

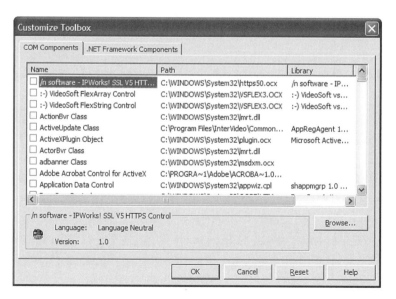

FIGURE 2.13: Customize Toolbox Dialog

---

12. The aximp.exe command line tool generates COM control interop assemblies in the same way that VS.NET does.

FIGURE 2.14: COM Component Added to the Toolbox

that you're referencing and that forwards your calls to the underlying COM control.[13]

Also, COM controls need COM initialized in a UI-friendly manner, so make sure that the STAThreadAttribute adorns your Main method:

```
[STAThreadAttribute]
static void Main() {
  Application.Run(new Form1());
}
```

When you create a new Windows Forms application in VS.NET, this attribute is applied by default, so to hurt yourself you must actively remove it.

Layout

After all this talk of collecting and ordering controls, you may be wondering how to arrange them, especially in the face of the needs of different

---

13. For more information about COM interop, see *Essential .NET, Volume I: The Common Language Runtime* (Addison-Wesley, 2003), by Don Box, with Chris Sells.

users with respect to system font size and the size of the data being entered.

Form Auto-Scaling

For example, if you lay out a form with system font size set to Normal (96 dots per inch, or dpi) in the Display control panel, what happens when your users are using Large (120 dpi) or one of the custom settings? You'd certainly prefer that a form such as that in Figure 2.15 show correctly at all font sizes.

If you're the curious type, you might even attempt to simulate this form for Large fonts by changing the form's font size from 8.2 points (the default) to 10 points, preserving approximately the same proportion as between 96 dpi and 120 dpi. Unfortunately, this wouldn't leave you feeling confident because this change yields a form that looks like the one in Figure 2.16.

Notice that increasing the font size increases the height of the TextBox control, but not the size of the form overall, to maintain the same proportional sizing and spacing. However, if you perform the actual test by changing from Normal to Large fonts in the Advanced settings of the Display control panel (which will likely require a restart of Windows), you may be pleased to notice that showing your form at this new font size looks like Figure 2.17 without the need to recompile your application.

FIGURE 2.15: A Sample Form at Normal Size Fonts

FIGURE 2.16: Increasing the Form's Font Size at Normal Size Fonts

FIGURE 2.17: The Sample Form at Large Size Fonts

The secret to making this work is a form property called AutoScale. When a form is first loaded, if AutoScale is set to true (the default), it uses another property called AutoScaleBaseSize. This property is actually set by the Designer and specifies the average width and height of characters in the form's font. The default font—8.25-point MS Sans Serif under Windows XP Normal fonts—has an average width and height of 5×13. This information will be encoded into the InitializeComponent function:

```
this.AutoScaleBaseSize = new Size(5, 13);
```

Under Large fonts, the default font will be 7.8-point MS Sans Serif, but the average width and height of the font has now increased to 6×15 (that's why they call it "Large" fonts). At load time, the form calls Form.Get-AutoScaleSize and notices the difference between the scale it was designed with and the current scale, and the form adjusts its height and width and those of its controls along with the positions of the controls. This keeps the "feel" of the form roughly the same, no matter what the system font settings are.

In our sample, the form's client area width increased from 296 to 378 (~27%) as the width of the font went from 5 to 6 (~20%). Similarly, the height increased from 54 to 66 (~22%) as the height of the font went from 13 to 16 (~23%). Rounding errors make the scaling imperfect, and it seems that WinForms uses a little fudge factor to make sure that things are big enough. But in general, the auto-scaling should yield forms that look pretty good given the amount of work you had to do to achieve the effect (~0%).

Anchoring

Scaling for system font settings is not all the work that needs to be done to make your form adjust itself to your users' whims. For example, to enter a long string into a text box, users may attempt to widen the form, as shown in Figure 2.18.

Unfortunately, the user isn't likely to be happy with this. The form gets bigger, but the contained controls do not. Ideally, we'd like the text box to expand as the form expands, something that can be achieved manually:

```
int delta = 0;

void Form1_Load(object sender, EventArgs e) {
  delta = ClientRectangle.Width - textBox1.Width;
}

void Form1_SizeChanged(object sender, EventArgs e) {
  textBox1.Width = ClientRectangle.Width - delta;
}
```

During the form's Load event, this code captures the delta between the width of the text box and the width of the client rectangle so that when the form's size is changed, we can reset the width of the text box to maintain the difference in width as a constant. Keeping this difference constant means keeping the distance between the right edge of the text box a fixed number of pixels from the right edge of the form.

Keeping an edge of a control a constant distance away from its container edge is called *anchoring*. By default, all controls are anchored to the top and left edges of their containers. We're accustomed to Windows moving our child controls to keep this anchoring intact as the container's left or top edge changes. However, Windows does only so much. It doesn't resize our controls to anchor them to other edges. Fortunately, WinForms does, without requiring you to write the manual anchoring code just shown.

FIGURE 2.18: All Controls Anchored Top, Left

You can change the edges that a control is anchored to by changing the Anchor property to any bitwise combination of the values in the AnchorStyles enumeration:

```
enum AnchorStyles {
  None,
  Left, // default
  Top, // default
  Bottom,
  Right,
}
```

Getting our text box to resize as the form is resized is a matter of changing the Anchor property to include the right edge as well as the left and the top edges. Using the Property Browser, you even get a fancy drop-down editor, as shown in Figure 2.19.

Even though Windows provides built-in support for anchoring to the top and left edges, anchoring does not have to include the left or top edges at all. For example, it's common to anchor a modal dialog's OK and Cancel buttons to only the bottom and right edges so that these buttons stay at the bottom-right corner as the dialog is resized, but aren't resized themselves. Resizing of a control happens if you have two opposing edges selected. If you don't have either of the opposing edges selected, neither left nor right, then the control will not be resized in that dimension but will maintain the same proportion of space between the opposing edges. The middle square in Figures 2.20 and 2.21 shows this behavior as well as several other anchoring combinations.

Docking

As powerful as anchoring is, it doesn't do everything. For example, if you wanted to build a text editor, you'd probably like to have a menu, a toolbar,

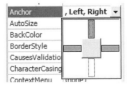

FIGURE 2.19: Setting the Anchor Property in the Property Browser

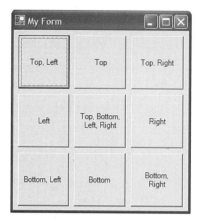

FIGURE 2.20: Anchoring Settings before Widening

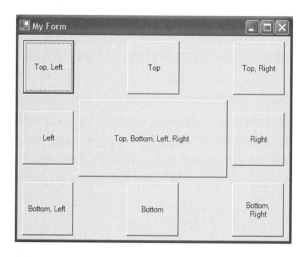

FIGURE 2.21: Anchoring Settings after Widening

and a status bar along with a text box that takes up the rest of the client area not occupied by the menu, the toolbar, and the status bar. Anchoring would be tricky in this case, because some controls need more or less space depending on the run-time environment they find themselves in (recall what happened to the text box when we increased the font size earlier). Because anchoring depends on keeping a control a fixed number of pixels away from a form's edge, we'd have to do some programming at run-time to figure out how high the status bar was, for example, and then set that as the distance to anchor the text box away from the edge. Instead, it would be much easier to tell the form that the text box should simply take whatever space remains in the client area. For that, we have docking.

Docking is a way to specify a specific edge that we'd like to have a control "stick" itself to. For example, Figure 2.22 shows a form with three controls, all docked. The menu is docked to the top edge, the status bar is docked to the bottom edge, and the text box is docked to fill the rest.

You implement the docking behavior by setting each control's Dock property to one of the values in the DockStyle enumeration (exposed nicely in the Property Browser, as shown in Figure 2.23):

```
enum DockStyle {
  None, // default
  Left,
  Top,
  Right,
  Bottom,
  Fill,
}
```

Docking and Z-Order
As the form resizes, the docking settings keep the controls along their designated edges (or the rest of the space, as determined by the Fill DockStyle).

FIGURE 2.22: A Docking Example

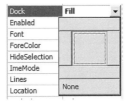

FIGURE 2.23: Setting the Dock Property in the Property Browser

It's even possible to have multiple controls docked to the same edge, as shown in Figure 2.24.

Although I don't recommend docking two status bars to the same edge, it's certainly possible. Docking is done in reverse z-order priority. In other words, for statusBar1 to be closest to the bottom edge, it must be further down in the z-order than statusBar2. The following AddRange call gives statusBar1 edge priority over statusBar2:

```
this.Controls.AddRange(
  new System.Windows.Forms.Control[] {
    this.statusBar2, // z-order 0, lowest bottom edge priority
    this.textBox1, // z-order 1
    this.statusBar1}); // z-order 2, highest bottom edge priority
```

Given the drag-and-drop Designer model, which inserts each new control with a z-order of 0, it makes sense that docking priority is the reverse of z-order. However, as you add new controls on the form and need to adjust the z-order, you may find a conflict between controls along a certain edge and those set to fill. In that case, the fill control needs to have the lowest edge priority on the form or else it will dock all the way to an edge set to be used by another control. Figure 2.25 shows an example.

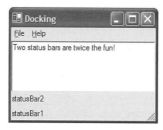

FIGURE 2.24: Two Status Bars Docked to the Bottom Edge

FIGURE 2.25: TextBox Whose DockStyle.Fill Has Higher Docking Priority than StatusBar

Notice that the text box has a scroll bar, but the bottom part of it is cut off by the status bar along the bottom edge. This indicates that the status bar has a lower docking priority than the text box. However, docking priority isn't set directly in the Designer. Instead, you set the z-order. In our example, right-clicking on the text box in the Designer and choosing Bring To Front will push the text box to the top of the z-order but to the bottom of the docking priority, letting the status bar own the bottom edge and removing it from the client area that the text box is allowed to fill. As a rule, whenever you see a visual anomaly like this on your form, you can generally resolve the problem by bringing to the front the control set to Dock-Style.Fill.

Splitting

Often, when docking is used, you'd like the user to have the ability to resize some of the controls independently of the size of the form itself. For example, Windows Explorer splits the space between the toolbar and the status bar, with a tree view on the left and a list view on the right. To resize these controls, Explorer provides a *splitter*, which is a bar separating two controls. The user can drag the bar to change the proportion of the space shared between the controls. Figure 2.26 shows a simple example of a Splitter control between a TreeView control docking to the left edge and a List-View control docked to fill.

Splitter controls are available in the Toolbox. The splitter manages the size of the preceding control in the z-order (or the empty space, if there is

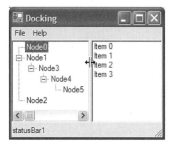

FIGURE 2.26: An Example of Splitting (with Pointer Indicating a Potential Drag)

no preceding control). For example, the relative z-orders of the tree view, splitter, and list view shown in Figure 2.26 are set this way:

```
this.Controls.AddRange(
  new System.Windows.Forms.Control[] {
    this.listView1, // z-order 0, size set directly by splitter
    this.splitter1, // z-order 1, splitter
    this.treeView1, // z-order 2, size set indirectly by splitter
    this.statusBar1});
```

You can split controls vertically by setting the Dock property to Dock-Style.Left (the default) or split them horizontally by setting the Dock property to DockStyle.Top. An example of horizontal splitting is shown in Figure 2.27, where the group box has a z-order of zero, followed by a splitter with the Dock property set to DockStyle.Top.

Grouping

To achieve advanced layout effects, it's often necessary to break the problem into groups. For example, imagine a form showing a list of people on the left and a list of details about the current selection on the right, as shown in Figure 2.28.

You can't tell by looking at this single picture, but as the group boxes in Figure 2.28 change size, the controls inside the group boxes also change size. This happens because of two attributes of group boxes. The first is that group boxes are *container controls*, meaning that they act as a parent for child controls, just as a form does. The list box on the left is a child of the group box on the left and not directly a child of the form. Similarly, the

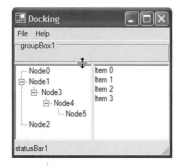

FIGURE 2.27: Horizontal Splitting

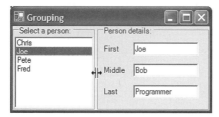

FIGURE 2.28: Grouping, Docking, and Anchoring

label and text box controls on the right are children of the group box on the right.

The second important attribute of container controls is that they share the same layout characteristics of forms, in that child controls can be anchored or docked. As a result, the anchoring and docking settings of a control are relative, not to the edges of the form, but rather to the edges of the container. For example, the list box in Figure 2.28 is actually set to DockStyle.Fill to take up the entire client area of the group box. Similarly, the anchoring properties of the text boxes on the right are anchored top, left, and right; therefore, as the group box changes width or changes position relative to the parent form, the text boxes act as you would expect relative to the group box.

The GroupBox control is one of three container controls WinForms provides; the other two are the Panel control and TabControl. The Panel control is just like a group box except that there is no label and no frame. A panel is handy if you'd like something that looks and acts like a *subform*, or a form within a form. TabControl is a container of one or more TabPage controls, each of which is a container control with a tab at the top, as shown in Figure 2.29.

FIGURE 2.29: A TabControl with Two TabPage Controls

Custom Layout

The combination of anchoring, docking, splitting, and grouping solves a large majority of common layout problems. However, it doesn't solve them all. For example, these techniques don't let you automatically spread controls proportionally across a client area in a table or gridlike manner, as shown in Figure 2.30.

The following Layout event handler arranges the nine button controls of Figure 2.30 proportionally as the form is resized. (This is also a very good use of the SuspendLayout and ResumeLayout methods to suspend layout, and of the SetClientSizeCore method to set the client area based on an even multiple of the width and the height.)

```
void GridForm_Layout(object sender, LayoutEventArgs e) {
  // Suspend layout until we're finished moving things
  this.SuspendLayout();

  // Arrange the buttons in a grid on the form
  Button[] buttons = new Button[] { button1, ..., };
  int cx = ClientRectangle.Width/3;
  int cy = ClientRectangle.Height/3;
  for( int row = 0; row != 3; ++row ) {
    for( int col = 0; col != 3; ++col ) {
      Button button = buttons[col * 3 + row];
      button.SetBounds(cx * row, cy * col, cx, cy);
    }
  }

  // Set form client size to be multiple of width/height
  SetClientSizeCore(cx * 3, cy * 3);
```

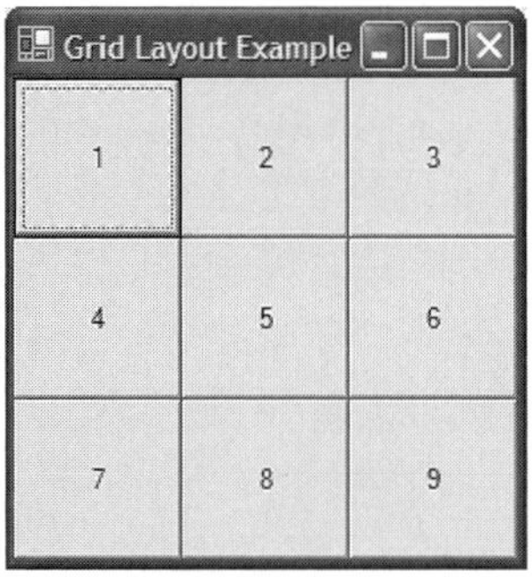

FIGURE 2.30: Custom Layout Example

```
  // Resume the layout
  this.ResumeLayout();
}
```

Although you can use the Layout event to handle all the layout needs of a form, it's much easier to use anchoring, docking, and grouping wherever possible and fall back on the Layout event only to handle special cases.

Multiple Document Interface

Just as controls can be grouped into containers, windows themselves can be grouped into containers in a style of application called Multiple Document Interface (MDI). MDI was invented as a way to contain a set of related windows in a single frame, as shown in Figure 2.31.

An MDI form has two pieces: a parent and a child. You designate the parent form by setting the IsMdiContainer property to true, and you designate the child form by setting the MdiParent property before showing the form:

```
void InitializeComponent() {
  ...
  this.IsMdiContainer = true;
  ...
}
```

continues

FIGURE 2.31: Sample MDI Form

```
void cmdFileNewChild_Click(object sender, EventArgs e) {
  Form child = new ChildForm();
  child.MdiParent = this;
  child.Show();
}
```

Just as the parent has a property indicating that it's an MDI parent, the child has a property, IsMdiChild, that tells it that it's being shown as an MDI child. And just as a form is a collection of controls, an MDI parent form has a collection of MDI children called MdiChildren. When a child is activated, either by direct user input or by the Activate method, the MDI parent receives the MdiChildActivate event. To see or change which of the MDI children is currently active, each MDI parent form provides an ActiveMdiChild property.

An MDI parent is expected to have two sets of special menu items: one to arrange the children inside the parent frame, and a second one to list the active children and select among them. Figure 2.32 shows a typical menu of this sort.

In Figure 2.32, the top-level Window menu has four items for arranging the child forms inside the MDI parent. By setting the Window menu's MdiList property to true, you display a separator and all the Text properties of all the MDI child forms at the end of the menu, allowing the user to pick one to activate. If the Window menu were empty—for example, if you wanted to list the child windows in a submenu—no separator would be added.

FIGURE 2.32: An MDI Child Management Menu

To implement the items that arrange the children inside the parent, the Form class provides the LayoutMdi method, which takes one of the four MdiLayout enumeration values:

```
void windowArrangeIconsMenuItem_Click(object sender, EventArgs e) {
  this.LayoutMdi(MdiLayout.ArrangeIcons);
}

void windowCascadeMenuItem_Click(object sender, EventArgs e) {
  this.LayoutMdi(MdiLayout.Cascade);
}

void windowTileChildrenVertMenuItem_Click(object sender, EventArgs e) {
  this.LayoutMdi(MdiLayout.TileVertical);
}

void windowTileChildrenHorizMenuItem_Click(object sender, EventArgs e) {
  this.LayoutMdi(MdiLayout.TileHorizontal);
}
```

To implement the Windows cascading menu to show MDI child forms and have the selected child brought to the front, you set the Windows menu item MdiList property to true.

Menu Merging

WinForms makes MDI so easy that it almost takes all the satisfaction out of things until we get to menu merging, which gives us something to sink our teeth into. The basic idea of *menu merging* is that there is only one main menu shown in a form, even if that form contains MDI children. Instead of letting each MDI child have its own menu, you merge the menu items of the child with the menu items of the parent, simplifying things for the user.

Why don't you simply put everything into the parent's main menu to start with? The reason is that lots of menu items, such as File | Close, don't make sense without a child, so showing them isn't helpful. Similarly, the set of operations can well change between MDI children, so the merged menu should consist only of the items from the parent that always make sense, such as File | Exit, and the items from the currently active child.

For example, Figure 2.33 shows an MDI parent File menu when there are no children, and Figure 2.34 shows the same File menu when there is a child.

FIGURE 2.33: MDI Parent File Menu with No MDI Children

FIGURE 2.34: MDI Parent File Menu with an MDI Child

In the Designer, both the parent and the child forms have a main menu, as shown in Figure 2.35.

Notice that the child's menu items don't contain all the items shown in Figure 2.34 when the child is active at run time. Instead, the child has only

FIGURE 2.35: The Parent and Child Menus in the Designer

the new items that are to be added to the parent menu. For the merging to work, we need to set two properties on the menu items to be merged—at the top level, such as File, as well as at the lower levels, such as File | New.

Merging is governed on a per-item basis via MergeType and Merge-Order. The MergeType property is one of the following MenuMerge enumeration values:

```
enum MenuMerge {
  MergeItems,
  Add,
  Remove,
  Replace,
}
```

MergeOrder dictates how things are ordered at the top level and in the submenus. The top-level menu is arranged by merge order left to right, lowest to highest. In our example, notice that the parent File and Window menus are separated by the child Edit menu. To do this, you set the merge order for File, Edit, and Window to 0, 1, and 2, respectively. But don't be confused by the numbers I used. I could have easily used 0, 100, and 404 to achieve the same menu item placement. The actual numbers don't matter—only the order.

Because the parent as well as the child menus have a File menu at merge order 0, we have several options. One is to set the merge types to Add, giving us two File menus when a child is created. That's useful when the menus have different names, as with our Edit and Window menus, but it doesn't work when they have the same name.

Another option is to set the merge type to Remove on the parent menu, removing the parent's File menu when the child menu items are merged. Remove is handy when a menu item isn't useful after two menus are merged, but not in this case because the child needs a File menu.

A third option is to use Replace and let the child's File menu completely replace that of the parent, but this removes all the menu items owned by the parent File menu that are child-independent.

In our example, the option we want is MergeItems, which merges second-level items using the same algorithm used to merge items at the top level—that is, as specified by the MergeOrder and MergeType properties.

Tables 2.1 and 2.2 show the menu merge settings used by the example to create a merged top-level menu and a merged File menu.

If you find that you can't get the items you want in the merged menu or if you have dynamic menu items, you can access the parent's menu using the parent's public MergedMenu property. In this way, you can either modify WinForms' automatic action, or you can replace it with something of your own making.

And as if that weren't enough, because you can still put controls on an MDI parent form, you can actually mix docking with MDI to achieve layouts such as the one shown in Figure 2.36.

Notice that the MDI children automatically arrange themselves in the client area not occupied with docked controls, making these kinds of layouts possible.

Visual Inheritance

After all the settings and behavior and layout details you've learned to pack into forms in this chapter, you may decide that you'd like to keep

TABLE 2.1: Parent Menu Merge Settings

Parent MenuItem	MergeType	MergeOrder
File	MergeItems	0
File | New Child	Add	0
File | Exit	Add	2
Window	Add	2

TABLE 2.2: Child Menu Merge Settings

Child MenuItem	MergeType	MergeOrder
File	MergeItems	0
File | Save	Add	1
File | Close	Add	1
Edit	Add	1

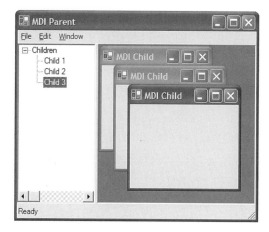

FIGURE 2.36: Mixing Docking and MDI

some of your hard work in a Form-derived base class for easy reuse by further derivations, and you can certainly do that. If you follow the convention that forms initialize their own properties and the properties of their child controls in a function called InitializeComponent, the Designer provides direct support for your *visual inheritance*: the reuse of a form base class via inheritance.

The goal of visual inheritance is to allow a base class to capture common UI elements, which are then shared and augmented by deriving classes. For example, imagine a BaseForm class that derives from Form and provides a menu bar, a status bar, and an icon, as shown hosted in the Designer in Figure 2.37.

FIGURE 2.37: Base Class Used in Visual Inheritance

BaseForm can now serve as a base class for all forms that contain at least this functionality,[14] such as the EditorForm shown in Figure 2.38.

The EditorForm class was created by deriving from BaseForm, overriding the Text property, adding the TextBox control to the form, and overriding the Text property of the status bar from the base class. I could have done this work by hand, but instead I created the EditorForm. I right-clicked on the project in Solution Explorer and chose Add | Add Inherited Form. Then I set the form's name and chose BaseForm from the list of forms in the project displayed in the Inheritance Picker dialog, as shown in Figure 2.39.

The initial EditorForm looked just like BaseForm except for the little arrow over the status bar (as shown in the lower-left corner of Figure 2.38).

FIGURE 2.38: EditorForm Derived from BaseForm

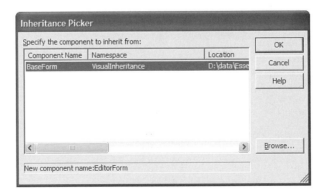

FIGURE 2.39: The Inheritance Picker Dialog

---

14. Make sure that your project is compiled before you use the Designer on inherited forms.

This arrow indicates a control inherited from the base. After inheriting the new form class from the existing form class, I used the Toolbox to add the new controls and used the Property Browser to change the form's Text property.

However, to change the Text property of the status bar, I first had to change the access modifier. By default the Designer adds all fields as private, which means that they're accessible only from that class, the BaseForm class in our example. If you want to use the Designer to set a property on one of the controls in the base class from the deriving class, by default you can't until you change the access modifier in the field declaration in the base class:

```
private StatusBar statusBar;
```

You change the private keyword to protected to allow access by deriving classes:

```
protected StatusBar statusBar;
```

If you're really into Cooperesque[15] visual design, you can change this keyword by selecting the status bar on BaseForm using the Designer and changing the Modifiers field.

The purpose of this exercise in reuse is that when a new feature is needed across the set of forms that derive from BaseForm or when a bug is found, you can make the changes to the base form, and deriving forms automatically benefit. For example, BaseForm could add an Edit menu, and that would propagate to the EditorForm on the next compile.

As nifty as visual inheritance is, it's not without its limitations. For example, although you can completely replace the main menu of a base form in a deriving form, you can't add or subtract menu items or replace menu item event handlers from the base. However, as a template mechanism to avoid duplicating controls and code, visual inheritance is definitely worth your consideration.

---

15. Alan Cooper invented the drag-and-drop visual design mechanism for Visual Basic.

Where Are We?

We've explored how to show forms, control their lifetime, size, and location, dictate their non-client adornments, manage main and context menus and child controls, make whole forms partially transparent and parts of forms completely transparent, arrange controls using anchoring, docking, splitting, and grouping, arrange MDI children in MDI parent forms, and package forms for reuse via visual inheritance. You might think that you know all there is to know about forms. However, you would be mistaken. Chapter 3 is all about using forms as dialogs.

■ 3 ■
Dialogs

A DIALOG IS DEFINED by its usage. If a form is the application's main window, it's a window, not a dialog. However, if a form pops up in response to a user request for service, such as a request to open a file, and stops all other user interactions with the application, it's a dialog (a modal dialog, specifically).

However, things get a little murky when we consider modeless dialogs. They don't stop the user from interacting with the rest of the application, but they do provide a means of interaction outside the main window.

What makes things a bit murkier is the WinForms terminology. Standard dialogs are exposed by the XxxDialog family of components, such as the FileOpenDialog. Most of these components support only modal activation using ShowDialog, but a couple of them support modeless activation using Show. In contrast, custom dialogs are classes that derive from the Form base class and can be shown modally or modelessly based on whether they're activated using ShowDialog or Show.

No matter how a dialog is defined, this chapter covers things you'd normally think of as dialog-related issues, including standard dialogs, custom forms to be used as dialogs, modal and modeless activation and lifetime, transferring data in and out, validating user-entered data, and providing help. To aid you in making the transition to the unification of dialog-like functionality with forms, I don't use the term "dialog" except when referring to the standard dialog components.

Standard Dialogs

WinForms ships with several standard dialogs (sometimes known as "common dialogs") provided as components from the System.Windows. Forms namespace. A *component* is like a control in that you can drag it from the Toolbox onto a design surface and set its properties using the Property Browser. However, unlike a control, a component doesn't render in a region. Instead, it shows up on the tray along the bottom of the design surface so that you can choose it, and it isn't shown at run time at all. For the details of components, read Chapter 9: Design-Time Integration.

Because all the standard dialogs are components, they can be created in two ways: manually or by using the Designer. For example, creating and showing an instance of the ColorDialog component manually looks like this:

```
void colorDialogButton_Click(object sender, EventArgs e) {
  ColorDialog dlg = new ColorDialog();
  dlg.Color = Color.Red;
  DialogResult res = dlg.ShowDialog();
  if( res == DialogResult.OK ) {
    MessageBox.Show("You picked " + dlg.Color.ToString());
  }
}
```

However, if you drag a ColorDialog component from the Toolbox, you can show it without explicitly writing the creation code, because the Designer will generate it for you in the InitializeComponent function:

```
void InitializeComponent() {
  ...
  this.colorDialog1 = new ColorDialog();
  ...
}

void colorDialogButton_Click(object sender, EventArgs e) {
  colorDialog1.Color = Color.Red;
  DialogResult res = colorDialog1.ShowDialog();
  if( res == DialogResult.OK ) {
    MessageBox.Show("You picked " + colorDialog1.Color.ToString());
  }
}
```

I tend to prefer the latter approach because I like to set properties visually, but either one works just fine. The following standard dialogs come with WinForms:

- **ColorDialog** allows the user to pick a color exposed by the Color property of type System.Drawing.Color.
- **FolderBrowserDialog** allows the user to pick a folder exposed by the SelectedPath property of type string. This component is available only in .NET 1.1 and later.
- **FontDialog** allows the user to choose a font and its properties, such as bold, italics, and so on. The user-configured font object of type System.Drawing.Font is available from the Font property of the component.
- **OpenFileDialog** and **SaveFileDialog** allow the user to pick a file to open or save, as appropriate for the dialog. The chosen file name is available from the FileName property of type string.
- **PageSetupDialog**, **PrintDialog,** and **PrintPreviewDialog** are related to printing, which is discussed in Chapter 7: Printing.

All but one of the standard dialogs, including the FolderBrowserDialog that .NET 1.0 forgot, are wrappers around existing common dialogs in Windows. Because these dialogs don't support modeless operation, neither do the WinForms components. However, the PrintPreviewDialog component, which provides a new dialog just for WinForms and is not available from Windows, supports both modal and modeless operation using ShowDialog and Show, respectively.

Styles

Chapter 2: Forms introduces the important dialog-related properties: ControlBox, FormBorderStyle, HelpButton, MaximizeBox, MinimizeBox, and ShowInTaskbar. By default, a new form shows the control box, is sizable, doesn't show the help button, can be minimized and maximized, and is shown in the shell's taskbar. For a main window, these are fine settings and will yield a form that looks like the one in Figure 3.1.

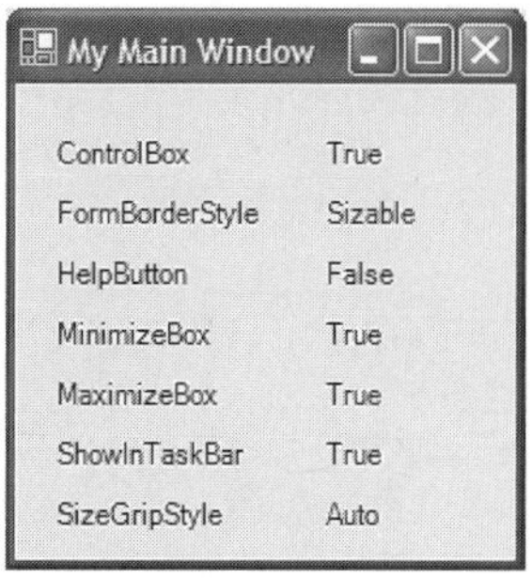

<figure>
<table>
<tr><td>ControlBox</td><td>True</td></tr>
<tr><td>FormBorderStyle</td><td>Sizable</td></tr>
<tr><td>HelpButton</td><td>False</td></tr>
<tr><td>MinimizeBox</td><td>True</td></tr>
<tr><td>MaximizeBox</td><td>True</td></tr>
<tr><td>ShowInTaskBar</td><td>True</td></tr>
<tr><td>SizeGripStyle</td><td>Auto</td></tr>
</table>
</figure>

FIGURE 3.1: Typical Main Window Form Settings

A typical modal form, on the other hand, is more likely to hide the minimize and maximize boxes, to show the help button, and to choose not to show up in the taskbar (the parent will already be there), as shown in Figure 3.2.

You may find it interesting that even though the SizeGripStyle hasn't changed from its default of Auto between the main window and the modal form examples, by default the size grip is shown only when the form is shown modally. Similarly, although the ControlBox property remains true when the border style is changed to FixedDialog, the control box will not be shown, as you can see in Figure 3.3. Clearly, WinForms has its own ideas about what to show along the edge of your form, sometimes disregarding your preferences.

Typical modeless form settings are just like the sizable modal form settings (shown in Figure 3.2) except that calling Show instead of ShowDialog causes the size grip to go away.

<figure>
<table>
<tr><td>ControlBox</td><td>True</td></tr>
<tr><td>FormBorderStyle</td><td>Sizable</td></tr>
<tr><td>HelpButton</td><td>True</td></tr>
<tr><td>MinimizeBox</td><td>False</td></tr>
<tr><td>MaximizeBox</td><td>False</td></tr>
<tr><td>ShowInTaskBar</td><td>False</td></tr>
<tr><td>SizeGripStyle</td><td>Auto</td></tr>
</table>
</figure>

FIGURE 3.2: Typical Modal Form Settings

FIGURE 3.3: Typical Modal Form Settings

These examples should serve most of your needs, although it's certainly possible to vary form properties to get a few more variations. For example, you can use the border styles FixedToolWindow and SizableToolWindow to show the caption in miniature (handy for floating toolbar or toolbox windows).

Setting Modal Versus Modeless Behavior Dynamically

If you'd like your form to change its settings based on whether or not it's being shown modally, you can check a form's Modal property:

```
void LoanApplicationDialog_Load(object sender, EventArgs e) {
  if( this.Modal ) {
    // Show as a fixed-sized modal form
    this.FormBorderStyle = FormBorderStyle.FixedDialog;
  }
  else {
    // Show as a sizable modeless form
    this.FormBorderStyle = FormBorderStyle.Sizable;
  }
}
```

Depending on whether the form was shown using ShowDialog or Show, the Modal property will be true or false, respectively. However, because the way a form is shown isn't known until after it's been created, the Modal property isn't accurate in the constructor and will always be false at that time. You will be able to get the form's actual Modal property value only in the Load event or later.

Data Exchange

No matter what kind of form you've got, after you've created it, you need to get data into it and out of it. Although it is possible for a form to update an application's data directly when the user presses OK or Apply, this is generally considered bad practice for anything except the main form of your application. The problem is that changes in one part of the application might adversely affect your code. For this reason, forms should be as stand-alone as possible. This means that forms will have a set of properties that they manage, letting the client of the form populate the initial values of the properties and pulling out the final values as appropriate, just as you saw earlier in the typical usage of ColorDialog.

Because most properties managed by a form are actually properties on the controls that make up the form, you may be tempted to make the control fields in your form public, letting the client of the form do this:

```
LoanApplicationDialog dlg = new LoanApplicationDialog();
dlg.applicantNameTextBox.Text = "Joe Borrower"; // DON'T!
DialogResult res = dlg.ShowDialog();
if( res == DialogResult.OK ) { /* user pressed OK */ }
```

The problem with this approach is the same problem you'll encounter when making any field public: If LoanApplicationDialog wants to change the way the applicant's name is displayed, such as from a TextBox control to a Label control, all users of the LoanApplicationDialog class must now be updated. To avoid this problem, the general practice is to expose public custom form properties that get and set the form's child control properties:[1]

```
public string ApplicantName {
  get {
    return applicantNameTextBox.Text;
  }

  set {
    applicantNameTextBox.Text = value;
  }
}
```

---

1. Because the dialog's constructor calls InitializeComponent, which creates the dialog's child controls, the client of the dialog is free to get and set properties as soon as the dialog object is created.

The client uses properties in the same way a field is used. However, unlike a field, getting or setting a property executes code that you're free to change without requiring a code change in the form client. Furthermore, properties result in a simpler usage model for the form client, because they no longer need to concern themselves with the implementation details best left to the form:

```
LoanApplicationDialog dlg = new LoanApplicationDialog();
dlg.ApplicantName = "Joe Borrower";
DialogResult res = dlg.ShowDialog();
```

Handling OK and Cancel

Before data can be retrieved from the property of a modal form, Show-Dialog must first return, and this means that the form must be closed. One way to do that is by calling the Form.Close function inside each button's Click event handler:

```
void okButton_Click(object sender, EventArgs e) {
  this.Close();
}

void cancelButton_Click(object sender, EventArgs e) {
  this.Close();
}
```

Unfortunately, calling Close will return DialogResult.Cancel from the ShowDialog method by default. For other buttons, we'd like to be able to return other members of the DialogResult enumeration:

```
enum DialogResult {
  Abort,
  Cancel, // result of calling Form.Close()
  Ignore,
  No,
  None, // default
  OK,
  Retry,
  Yes,
}
```

The Abort, Ignore, No, and Retry values are used mostly by Message-Box.Show,[2] but you should feel free to use them for your own custom forms. The one we want to return from ShowDialog when the OK button is pressed is, of course, OK. Checking the return value from ShowDialog is a shortcut for checking the DialogResult property of the form itself, something you can do instead:

```
dlg.ShowDialog();
DialogResult res = dlg.DialogResult;
if( res == DialogResult.OK ) { /* user pressed OK */ }
dlg.ShowDialog()
```

By default, the DialogResult property of any form is None. To return something other than Cancel from ShowDialog, you set the form's Dialog-Result property before closing the form:

```
void okButton_Click(object sender, EventArgs e) {
  this.DialogResult = DialogResult.OK;
  this.Close();
}

void cancelButton_Click(object sender, EventArgs e) {
  // Close will set the DialogResult to Cancel, so setting
  // it explicitly is just good manners
  this.DialogResult = DialogResult.Cancel;
  this.Close();
}
```

When you set the form's DialogResult to something other than None, a modal form interprets that to mean that it should close. Calling Close in this case isn't even necessary, reducing our code to the following for modal forms:

```
void okButton_Click(object sender, EventArgs e) {
  this.DialogResult = DialogResult.OK;
}

void cancelButton_Click(object sender, EventArgs e) {
  this.DialogResult = DialogResult.Cancel;
}
```

---

2. In contrast with Form.Show, MessageBox.Show is modal, not modeless, introducing an inconsistency between the two methods with the same name.

With this code in place, clicking on the OK or Cancel button dismisses a form such as the one shown in Figure 3.4. This action returns the correct result and, using properties, exposes whatever information the user entered during the lifetime of the form.

Unfortunately, we don't have quite all the behavior we need from our OK and Cancel buttons. In Figure 3.4 notice that the OK button is not drawn as the default button. The *default button* is the one invoked when the Enter key is pressed, and it's typically drawn with a thicker border than nondefault buttons. In addition, although you can't see this in a picture, the Cancel button isn't invoked when the ESC key is pressed. Enabling this behavior is a matter of designating in the form itself which buttons should be invoked when Enter and ESC are pressed. You do this by setting the form's AcceptButton and CancelButton properties:

```
void InitializeComponent() {
  ...
  this.AcceptButton = this.okButton;
  this.CancelButton = this.cancelButton;
  ...
}

void okButton_Click(object sender, EventArgs e) {
  this.DialogResult = DialogResult.OK;
}

void cancelButton_Click(object sender, EventArgs e) {
  this.DialogResult = DialogResult.Cancel;
}
```

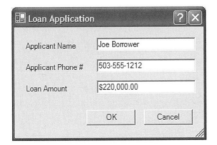

FIGURE 3.4: A Sample Form Used as a Dialog (See Plate 6)

Notice that we used the Designer to set these two properties. This is handy because the Property Browser shows a drop-down list of all the buttons currently on the form to choose from. As it turns out, after you've set the form's CancelButton property, you don't need to set the DialogResult property in the Cancel button's Click event handler, making the Cancel button's Click event handler itself unnecessary. This works because when you set the form's CancelButton property, the Designer sets the Dialog-Result property on the Cancel button itself. Because it's normally a button that dismisses a form, the Button class provides a DialogResult property to designate the result that pressing this button will have on the form. By default, the value of this property is DialogResult.None, but the Designer sets to Cancel the DialogResult property of the button designated as the CancelButton on the form.

However, the Designer does not set the form's AcceptButton Dialog-Result property in the same manner.[3] Luckily, if you set the DialogResult property of the OK button to DialogResult.OK yourself, you can dismiss the form without having the OK or Cancel button click event handler at all:

```
void InitializeComponent() {
    ...
    this.okButton.DialogResult = DialogResult.OK;
    ...
    this.cancelButton.DialogResult = DialogResult.Cancel;
    ...
    this.AcceptButton = this.okButton;
    this.CancelButton = this.cancelButton;
    ...
}

// okButton_Click handler not needed
// cancelButton_Click handler not needed
```

So even though it's possible to implement the client event handlers for the OK and Cancel buttons, often you can get away with simply setting the form's AcceptButton and CancelButton properties and setting the

---

3. There's an open debate in the WinForms community as to which is a bug: that the Designer sets the DialogResult of the CancelButton, or that the Designer doesn't set the DialogResult of the AcceptButton. As for me, I think it's a bug that the Designer doesn't do the same thing for both buttons.

DialogResult property of the OK button. This technique gives you all the data exchange behavior you'll need in a modal form (except data validation, which I cover later in this chapter).

Modeless Form Data

Modeless forms require a different strategy from modal forms to communicate user-updated data to the form's client. For one thing, setting the DialogResult property of a modeless form doesn't automatically dismiss it as it does for a modal form. For another thing, because Show returns immediately, the client usage model is different. Finally, modeless forms acting as dialogs usually have Apply and Close buttons, so data entered into the form can be used before the modeless form even goes away.

What's needed is a way to notify a client of a modeless form when the Accept button is pressed. Luckily, standard .NET events[4] can be used for this purpose:

```
class PropertiesDialog : Form {
  ...

  // Event to fire when Accept is pressed
  public event EventHandler Accept;

  void acceptButton_Click(object sender, EventArgs e) {
    // Fire event when Accept is pressed
    if( Accept != null ) Accept(this, EventArgs.Empty);
  }

  void closeButton_Click(object sender, EventArgs e) {
    this.Close();
  }
}
```

In this example, notice that PropertiesDialog exposes a public event called Accept using the standard EventHandler delegate signature. When the Accept button is pressed, the modeless form fires the Accept event to

---

4. For more information about .NET delegates and events, see Appendix B: Delegates and Events.

notify any interested parties that the Accept button has been pressed. The client of the form can subscribe to the event when the form is created:

```
// Client creates, connects to, and shows modeless form
void showProperties_Click(object sender, EventArgs e) {
  PropertiesDialog dlg = new PropertiesDialog();
  dlg.Accept += new EventHandler(Properties_Accept);
  dlg.Show();
}

// Client handles event from form to access accepted values
void Properties_Accept(object sender, EventArgs e) {
  PropertiesDialog dlg = (PropertiesDialog)sender;
  MessageBox.Show(dlg.SomeProperty);
}
```

When the form is created but before it's shown, notice that the client subscribes to the Accept event. When the Accept button is pressed, the notification shows up in the client's event handler. By convention, the form passes itself when it fires the event so that the receiver of the event can use a simple cast operation to get back the reference to the form. The only thing left to do is to make the modeless form's Close button call the form's Close method, and you've got yourself a modeless form.

Data Validation

You should never trust your users. I don't mean you can't trust them to pay (a separate issue that I won't go into here); I mean you can't trust the data that your users enter. They may not give you all the data that you need, or they may not give you data in the correct format. List boxes, radio buttons, and all the other controls that give users choices do so to make sure that they provide data in the correct format. However, sometimes you need to validate free-form data entry, such as what a user types into a text box. For that, you handle a control's Validating event:

```
void applicantNameTextBox_Validating(object sender, CancelEventArgs e) {
  // Check for existence of application name
  if( applicantNameTextBox.Text.Length == 0 ) {
    MessageBox.Show("Please enter a name", "Error");
```

```
      e.Cancel = true;
  }
}
```

The Validating event is called when the focus is moved from one control on the form that has the CausesValidation property set to true to another control that has the CausesValidation property set to true—for example, from a TextBox control to the OK button. The Validating event gives the handler the chance to cancel the moving of the focus by setting the CancelEventArgs.Cancel property to true. In this example, if the user doesn't enter a name into the text box, then the Validating event handler notifies the user of the transgression and cancels the event, keeping the focus on the text box containing invalid data.

If the Validating event is not canceled, the form will be notified via the Validated event:

```
void applicantNameTextBox_Validated(object sender, EventArgs e) {
  MessageBox.Show("Nice name, " + applicantNameTextBox.Text, "Thanks!");
}
```

Each control has CausesValidation set to true by default. To allow the user to cancel the form without entering valid data, you must set the CausesValidation property to false for your Cancel or Close button:

```
void InitializeComponent() {
  ...
  this.cancelButton.CausesValidation = false;
  ...
}
```

Regular Expressions and Validation

One handy tool for data validation that's not specific to WinForms but is provided by .NET is the Regex class from the System.Text.RegularExpressions namespace. The Regex class provides a regular expression interpreter. A *regular expression* is a general-purpose way to describe the format of string data so that, among other things, a string can be checked to make sure that it fits a required format.

The regular expression language is beyond the scope of this book,[5] but let's look at an example. A string to check that the format of a phone number fits the U.S. format, including area code, parentheses, spaces, and dashes, would look like the following:

```
^\(\d{3}\) \d{3}-\d{4}$
```

This regular expression breaks down as follows:

- The leading "^" means to start checking the string from the beginning. Without this, any leading characters that don't match the regular expression will be ignored, something that could lead to improperly formatted phone numbers.
- The "\(" means to match against a literal "(" character. The "\" prefix is necessary to escape the "(", which otherwise would be treated specially by the Regex class.
- The "\d{3}" means to match three digits.
- The "\) " means to match a ")" character, followed by a space character.
- The "\d{3}-\d{4}" means to match three more digits, followed by a "-" character, followed by four more digits.
- The trailing "$" means to match the string all the way to the end so that no other characters can come after the phone number.

This regular expression can be used in a Validating event handler to check for a U.S. phone number:

```
void applicantPhoneNoTextBox_Validating(
  object sender, CancelEventArgs e) {
```

5. For an overview of regular expression in .NET, read "Regular Expressions in .NET," by Michael Weinhardt and Chris Sells, *Windows Developer*, 11/02, http://www.wd-mag.com/documents/s=7547/win0212d/

```
Regex re = new Regex(@"^\(\d{3}\) \d{3}-\d{4}$");
if( !re.IsMatch(applicantPhoneNoTextBox.Text) ) {
  MessageBox.Show(
    "Please enter a US phone number: (xxx) xxx-xxxx",
    "Error");
  e.Cancel = true;
  }
}
```

If the string entered into the phone number text box does not match the regular expression in its entirety, the IsMatch method of the Regex class will return false, letting the handler indicate to the user that the data is not in the correct format. Taken together, regular expressions and validation provide a powerful tool to check a wide range of input strings provided by the user.

Data Format Notification

As much as I lean on the message box in my test development, I prefer not to use it for actual applications. For one thing, users are likely to forget the acceptable format for a phone number after the message box goes away. One alternative is to use a status bar, but status bars tend to be ignored because they're at the bottom of the screen, far away from what the user is looking at.[6] A better way is to use the ErrorProvider component, which shows the user that there's a problem and provides a tooltip with extra information, as shown in Figure 3.5.

When the user attempts to change focus from the empty text box, we use an instance of the ErrorProvider component to set an error associated with that text box, causing the icon to be displayed to the right of the text box and making the tooltip available for more information. To implement this behavior, you drag an ErrorProvider component onto the form and handle the Validating event:

```
void applicantNameTextBox_Validating(object sender, CancelEventArgs e) {
  string error = null;
```

continues

---

6. According to legend, Microsoft did a usability study awarding people $50 if they would look under their chair, putting the notification for this award in the status bar. The $50 went unclaimed during the testing.

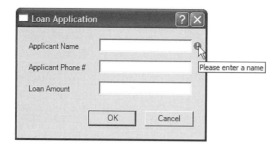

FIGURE 3.5: Sample Use of the ErrorProvider Component

```
if( applicantNameTextBox.Text.Length == 0 ) {
  error = "Please enter a name";
  e.Cancel = true;
}
errorProvider1.SetError((Control)sender, error);
}
```

Notice the call to ErrorProvider.SetError. The first argument is the control the error is associated with, which we get from the sender argument to
the Validating event. The second argument is the error string, which is
used as the tooltip. If there is no problem, the error is null, which causes the
error indicator for that control to go away, showing that there's no error.

Thorough Validation

As useful as the Validating event is, especially when combined with the
ErrorProvider component, there is one validation issue you'll have to deal
with separately. Because the Validating event is triggered only when focus
is moved from one control to another, if a control has invalid data but never
receives focus, it will never be validated. For example, the form in Figure
3.5 has three text boxes. Even if you were to handle the Validating event for
all three text boxes, the user could still enter valid data into the first one
(assuming it gets focus first) and press the OK button, causing the form to
close and return DialogResult.OK. The problem is that the other two text

boxes will never get focus, will never receive the Validating event, and therefore will never get a chance to cancel the acceptance of the form.

One way to deal with this problem is to make sure that all controls start with valid data, requiring the user to set focus to invalidate the data and triggering the validation events when focus is lost. However, there are lots of cases when you can't fill in valid initial data. What's a good default for a phone number? Or e-mail address? Or mother's maiden name? For these cases, you'll need to write the code manually to validate the form in the OK button's Click event handler:

```
void okButton_Click(object sender, EventArgs e) {
  // Validate each direct child control manually
  foreach( Control control in this.Controls() ) {
    control.Focus();
    if( !this.Validate() ) {
      this.DialogResult = DialogResult.None;
      break;
    }
  }
}
```

This code walks the list of controls in the form's control collection, setting each one in turn to have the focus. By itself, this will not trigger the Validating event, unfortunately, so we also must trigger that event by also calling the form's Validate method. The Form.Validate method does not validate all the controls in the form. Instead, it validates only the control that just lost focus. If validation fails on any one control, we change the form's DialogResult property (preset to DialogResult.OK by the OK button's DialogResult property), and that stops the form from closing.

If you've got controls that contain other controls, such as controls contained by group boxes, you must be a little more thorough about checking each control for child controls to make sure that they're validated, too:

```
// Retrieve all controls and all child controls etc.
// Make sure to send controls back at lowest depth first
// so that most child controls are checked for things before
```

continues

```
// container controls, e.g., a TextBox is checked before a
// GroupBox control
Control[] GetAllControls() {
  ArrayList allControls = new ArrayList();
  Queue queue = new Queue();
  queue.Enqueue(this.Controls);

  while( queue.Count > 0 ) {
    Control.ControlCollection
      controls = (Control.ControlCollection)queue.Dequeue();
    if( controls == null || controls.Count == 0 ) continue;

    foreach( Control control in controls ) {
      allControls.Add(control);
      queue.Enqueue(control.Controls);
    }
  }

  return (Control[])allControls.ToArray(typeof(Control));
}

void okButton_Click(object sender, EventArgs e) {
  // Validate each control manually
  foreach( Control control in GetAllControls() ) {
    // Validate this control
    control.Focus();
    if( !this.Validate() ) {
      this.DialogResult = DialogResult.None;
      break;
    }
  }
}
```

The GetAllControls method gets all of a form's controls, as well as all the controls' child controls, all those controls' children, and so on. This function is handy whenever you need to dig through the complete set of controls on a form, not just when you're validating. You'll see it used a few more times in this chapter.

The OK or Apply button's Click event handler is also a good place to do any other kind of validation that can't be done using the validation events, such as checking multiple related fields at the same time. If for any reason you don't want the form to close, set the form's DialogResult to None, and it won't.

Implementing Help

As useful as the ErrorProvider user interface is (at least compared with the status bar), it would be nice to provide help to our users that didn't take the form of a reprimand. It would also be useful to give them help without making them try something that fails. WinForms supports these goals in several ways.

Tooltips

One simple way is to provide each control with a tooltip so that when the user hovers the mouse pointer over the control, relevant instructions appear, as shown in Figure 3.6.

You can use the ToolTip component to add tooltips to any control in a form. After there is a ToolTip component on the form, each control sprouts a new property that shows up as "ToolTip on toolTip1" in the Property Browser. Any new property that an object adds to another object on a form is called an *extender property,* because the object doing the extending is providing additional functionality to the extended object.[7] Setting the ToolTip extender property for a control gives it a tooltip as provided by the ToolTip component.

Using the ErrorProvider for General Information

The problem with tooltips displayed in this way is that the user may not know that they're available (when was the last time you hovered your

FIGURE 3.6: Using Tooltips

---

7. Extender properties are covered in detail in Chapter 9: Design-Time Integration.

pointer over a text box looking for help?). Luckily, ErrorProvider is really good at providing a visual indicator, so it could be used with a different icon[8] to show something like Figure 3.7.

If you like this kind of thing, it can be implemented using two error providers: one with a friendly information icon, and a second one with a mean error icon (as set using the ErrorProvider's Icon property). The *information provider* is used when the form is first loaded as well as when there's no error. Otherwise, the error provider is used, as shown here:

```
void LoanApplicationDialog_Load(object sender, EventArgs e) {
  // Use tooltips to populate the "information provider"
  foreach( Control control in GetAllControls() ) {
    string toolTip = toolTip1.GetToolTip(control);
    if( toolTip.Length == 0 ) continue;
    infoProvider.SetError(control, toolTip);
  }
}

void applicantNameTextBox_Validating(object sender, CancelEventArgs e) {
  string toolTip = toolTip1.GetToolTip((Control)sender);
  if( ((TextBox)sender).Text.Length == 0 ) {
    // Show the error when there is no text in the text box
    errorProvider.SetError((Control)sender, toolTip);
    infoProvider.SetError((Control)sender, null);
    e.Cancel = true;
  }
```

FIGURE 3.7: Combining the ToolTip Component with the ErrorProvider Component

---

8. I got the sample icon from Common7\Graphics\icons\Computer\W95MBX04.ICO in my VS.NET installation directory. Feel free to use whatever icon makes you happy.

```
else {
  // Show the info when there is text in the text box
  errorProvider.SetError((Control)sender, null);
  infoProvider.SetError((Control)sender, toolTip);
  }
}
```

Just as the ToolTip component adds the ToolTip extender property to each control on the form, the ErrorProvider adds an Error property to each control. Setting a control's Error property in the Property Browser is the equivalent of calling SetError for that control. However, the Error property is not a good place to store a message, because clearing the message is the only way to hide the ErrorProvider for a particular control. Instead, given that the ToolTip property never needs clearing, the example uses it whenever a message should be displayed: when the mouse is hovered over a control, when the information provider is showing, or when the error provider is showing. This has the added benefit of keeping hard-coded strings out of the code and in a place that can easily be made localizable, as discussed in Chapter 10: Resources.

Handling the Help Button and F1

Although the little icons on the forms are useful, you may not want to use this kind of nonstandard interface to provide help messages in your forms. The standard way to provide this kind of information is to use the help button (the question mark) in the upper-right corner of the form, which is enabled by setting the HelpButton property of the form to true. When that button is pressed, the cursor changes, and when the user clicks on a control, the HelpRequested event is fired to the form:

```
void LoanApplicationDialog_HelpRequested(
  object sender, HelpEventArgs e) {
  // Convert screen coordinates to client coordinates
  Point pt = this.PointToClient(e.MousePos);

  // Look manually for control user clicked on
  // NOTE: GetChildAtPoint doesn't deal well with
  // contained controls, such as controls in a group box
  Control controlNeedingHelp = null;
  foreach( Control control in GetAllControls() ) {
    if( control.Bounds.Contains(pt) ) {
```

continues

```
      controlNeedingHelp = control;
      break;
    }
  }

  // Show help
  string help = toolTip1.GetToolTip(controlNeedingHelp);
  if( help.Length == 0 ) return;
  MessageBox.Show(help, "Help");
  e.Handled = true;
}
```

Notice that the HelpRequested handler uses both of the HelpEventArgs properties:

```
class HelpEventArgs : EventArgs {
  public bool Handled { get; set; }
  public Point MousePos { get; }
}
```

MousePos is the screen coordinates where the user clicked, and Handled lets us stop the HelpRequested event from going any further if we handle it. In the example, we're converting MousePos, provided in screen coordinates, to client coordinates and walking the list of controls looking for the one the user clicked on. If we find it, we put the control's tooltip into a message box and stop the event from propagating elsewhere.

The help button is useful to most users, but keyboard-oriented Windows users will be more familiar with the F1 key, which is meant to communicate to the application that help is requested on whatever is currently active, which is normally the control with focus. Pressing F1 also results in the HelpRequested event being fired. However, you'll notice that the HelpEventArgs class provides no indication of how the event was fired. So if we want to do something such as open an HTML file when F1 is pressed, we must check whether it was a mouse button that triggered the event:

```
void LoanApplicationDialog_HelpRequested(object sender, HelpEventArgs e)
{
  // If no mouse button was clicked, F1 got us here
  if( Control.MouseButtons == MouseButtons.None ) {
    // open a help file...
  }
```

```
  // Help button got us here
  else {
    // show the message box...
  }
}
```

Because we know that a mouse click triggers the HelpRequested event when it comes from the help button, we need to know whether any mouse buttons were pressed when the HelpRequested event was fired. To do this, we check the Control.MouseButtons property, which provides the state of the mouse buttons during the current event. If no buttons were pressed to fire this event, the user got to the handler using the F1 key; otherwise, the user got here using the help button.

Using HTML Help

When you implement F1, it is not hard to launch an URL to show an HTML page. However, when using the help button, users are accustomed to seeing help messages in shadowed tooltips, known as *pop-up help*, as shown in Figure 3.8.

Implementing pop-up help isn't supported by the ToolTip component because it doesn't show shadows and doesn't provide a programmatic way to request that a tooltip to be shown. However, the Help class supports both of these features with the ShowPopup method:

FIGURE 3.8: Using HelpProvider to Implement the Help Button

```
void LoanApplicationDialog_HelpRequested(object sender, HelpEventArgs e)
{
  if( Control.MouseButtons == MouseButtons.None ) {
    // open a help file...
  }
  // Help button got us here
  else {
    // Look for control user clicked on
    Point pt = this.PointToClient(e.MousePos);
    foreach( Control control in GetAllControls() ) {
      if( control.Bounds.Contains(pt) ) {
        // Show help
        string help = toolTip1.GetToolTip(control);
        if( help.Length == 0 ) return;
        Help.ShowPopup(this, help, e.MousePos);
        e.Handled = true;
        break;
      }
    }
  }
}
```

The Help class is a wrapper around the HTML Help functions provided by Windows and provides the following interesting methods:

```
class Help {
  public static void ShowHelp(Control parent, string url);

  public static void ShowHelp(
    Control parent, string url, HelpNavigator command, object param);

  public static void ShowHelp(
    Control parent, string url, string keyword);

  public static void ShowHelp(
    Control parent, string url, HelpNavigator navigator);

  public static void ShowHelpIndex(Control parent, string url);

  public static void
    ShowPopup(Control parent, string caption, Point location);
}
```

The ShowPopup method that we used in the preceding example takes a control to act as a parent, the string to show, and a point, in screen coordinates, on which to center the resulting tooltip. To implement the F1 key by opening an HTML file, you can opt to use one of the ShowHelp functions:

```
void LoanApplicationDialog_HelpRequested(object sender, HelpEventArgs e)
{
  // F1
  if( Control.MouseButtons == MouseButtons.None ) {
    string file = Path.GetFullPath("loanApplicationDialog.htm");
    Help.ShowHelp(this, file);
    e.Handled = true;
  }
  ...
}
```

Notice that we're using the Path.GetFullPath method (from the System. IO namespace) to turn a relative path name into a full path name. The URL argument to the ShowHelp methods can be a full file path or a full URL, but ShowHelp doesn't seem to like relative path names. Using this technique, F1 will take users to a page of HTML describing the form as a whole. However, users pressing F1 would probably prefer help that is specific to the control that's currently active; in other words, if they press F1 while in the Loan Amount field, they'd like to see help about the Loan Amount field. For that to happen against a file in the local file system requires moving from HTML to Microsoft's compiled HTML Help format.

Compiled HTML Help

When it was clear that HTML files were more flexible than the WinHelp help file format, Microsoft decided to make the switch from WinHelp to something HTML-based. However, WinHelp had a number of advantages over raw HTML, including tools for indexing, searching, and having multiple pages in a single file. The result of merging the flexibility of HTML with the convenience of WinHelp yielded HTML Help, which consists of a set of functions, a set of tools, and a file format that compiles all pages into a single file with a .chm extension. The details of how to build HTML Help files are beyond the scope of this book, so I recommend downloading the HTML Help Workshop from the Microsoft Developer Network site[9] to experiment with it yourself.

The instructions for creating a minimal HTML Help file with the HTML Help Workshop are as follows:

1. Run the HTML Help Workshop.
2. Create a new project. This is the list of files that goes into creating a .chm file.
3. Create a new HTML file. Add some text to the <body> tag and save the file. This file will become a topic page.
4. Make sure that the Project tab is selected, and click on the Add/Remove Topic Files button. Add the HTML file you created and saved in step 3. This action adds the topic file to the project.
5. Click on the Contents tab and choose Create a New Contents File. This enables the table of contents.
6. Make sure that the Contents tab is selected, and click on the Insert a Page button. Add the HTML file from the previous steps, and make sure that the Entry Title field has a value before pressing OK. This adds an entry to the table of contents.
7. Click on the Index tab and choose Create a New Index File. This enables the index. Feel free to add a keyword or two to populate the index.
8. Click on the Project tab again, and click on the Change Project Options button. Choose the Compiler tab. Enable the Compile Full-Text Searching Information option. This enables search.
9. Compile and view.

When you've got an HTML Help file, you can integrate it into your form using the Help class by passing the name of the .chm file to the ShowHelp function. Furthermore, if you'd like to scroll to a particular

---

9. http://msdn.microsoft.com

subtopic inside a topic, you can do so by first using the HTML <a> tag to name a subtopic:

```
<!-- loanapplicationdialog.htm -->
<html>
  <head>
    <title>loan application dialog</title>
  </head>
  <body>
    <h1><a name="name">Applicant Name</a></h1>
    Please enter a name.
    <h1><a name="phoneno">Applicant Phone #</a></h1>
    Please enter a phone number.
    <h1><a name="loanamount">Applicant Loan Amount</a></h1>
    Please enter a loan amount.
  </body>
</html>
```

When you've done that, you can map the name of the subtopic to the control when F1 is pressed:

```
void LoanApplicationDialog_HelpRequested(object sender, HelpEventArgs e)
{
  // F1
  if( Control.MouseButtons == MouseButtons.None ) {
    string subtopic = null;
    if( this.ActiveControl == this.applicantNameTextBox) {
      subtopic = "name";
    }
    else if( this.ActiveControl == this.applicantPhoneNoTextBox ) {
      subtopic = "phoneNo";
    }
    else if( this.ActiveControl == this.applicantLoanAmountTextBox ) {
      subtopic = "loanAmount";
    }

    Help.ShowHelp(this, "dialogs.chm",
        "loanApplicationDialog.htm#" + subtopic);
    e.Handled = true;
  }
  ...
}
```

Now when F1 is pressed and focus is on a specific control, the topic is brought up in the help viewer window, and the specific subtopic is scrolled into view, as shown in Figure 3.9.

FIGURE 3.9: Showing the loanAmount Subtopic

However, now that we're back to mapping between controls and strings (subtopics, in this case), this is a perfect use for a component that provides extender properties. The extender properties would allow you to set the help information for each control using the Property Browser, keeping that information out of the code. The component that provides extender properties to manage this information is HelpProvider.

Using the HelpProvider Component

HelpProvider actually implements both topic navigation support for the F1 key and pop-up help for the help button. HelpProvider is a wrapper around the Help class for a specific file, so it works well only for HTML Help. After dropping a HelpProvider component onto your form, you should set its HelpNamespace property to the name of the file it should manage, such as dialogs.chm.

HelpProvider adds the following properties to each control on a form:

```
string HelpKeyword // Defaults to ""
HelpNavigator HelpNavigator; // Defaults to AssociateIndex
string HelpString; // Defaults to ""
bool ShowHelp; // Defaults to true
```

When F1 is pressed, an empty HelpKeyword results in the HelpString being shown using pop-up help. Otherwise, F1 causes the HelpKeyword to be passed to ShowHelp and used based on the HelpNavigator property, which can be one of the following:

```
enum HelpNavigator {
  AssociateIndex,
  Find,
  Index, // What ShowHelpIndex does
  KeywordIndex,
  TableOfContents,
  Topic, // The default for ShowHelp
}
```

For example, if HelpNavigator is Topic, then HelpKeyword is the name of the topic to show—say, loanApplicationDialog.htm. ShowHelp is a Boolean that determines whether the HelpProvider should handle the HelpRequested event for the control. Setting ShowHelp to false allows you to handle the HelpRequested event manually, as we've been doing so far.

So after dropping a HelpProvider component onto our sample form, we don't have to handle the HelpRequested event at all. Instead, given the HelpNamespace property set to dialogs.chm, we can set the HelpProvider properties on each control in the form (as shown in Table 3.1). This action causes F1 and the help button to be handled automatically.

TABLE 3.1: Sample HelpProvider Settings

Control	HelpKeyword	HelpNavigator	HelpString	ShowHelp
applicantName TextBox	loanApplication Dialog.htm #name	Topic	"Please enter a name"	True
applicantPhone NoTextBox	loanApplication Dialog.htm #phoneNo	Topic	"Please enter a phone number"	True
applicantLoan Amount	loanApplication Dialog.htm #loanAmount	Topic	"Please enter a loan amount"	True

Showing Help Contents, Index, and Search

Dialogs don't often have menus—let alone Help menus with Contents, Index, and Search menu items—but while we're on the topic of integrating help with forms, I thought it would be a good idea to mention how to implement these help menu items. You can do this most easily by using the Help class:

```
void helpContentsMenuItem_Click(object sender, EventArgs e) {
  Help.ShowHelp(this, "dialogs.chm", HelpNavigator.TableOfContents);
}

void helpIndexMenuItem_Click(object sender, EventArgs e) {
  Help.ShowHelpIndex(this, "dialogs.chm");
}

void helpSearchMenuItem_Click(object sender, EventArgs e) {
  Help.ShowHelp(this, "dialogs.chm", HelpNavigator.Find, "");
}
```

Where Are We?

This chapter dealt with topics that are often dialog-related: getting data in and out, validating data, and letting users know about the required data format (including providing access to online help). But none of these topics is specific to "dialogs" (which is a slippery term to get hold of anyway). However, in this chapter and Chapter 2: Forms, we've covered almost everything a programmer needs to know about forms. If there are things that you haven't seen that interest you, such as drag and drop and form localization, you'll want to read on, especially Chapter 8: Controls (for drag and drop) and Chapter 10: Resources (for form localization).

■ 4 ■
Drawing Basics

A S HANDY AS FORMS ARE, especially when laden with controls, sometimes the built-in controls[1] aren't sufficient to render the state of your
application. In that case, you need to draw the state yourself. The drawing
may be to the screen, to a file, or to a printer, but wherever you're drawing
to, you'll be dealing with the same primitives—colors, brushes, pens, and
fonts—and the same kinds of things to draw: shapes, images, and strings.
This chapter starts by examining the basics of drawing to the screen and
the building blocks of drawing.

Note that all the drawing techniques discussed in this chapter and in
the next two chapters relate equally as well to controls as they do to forms.
For information about building custom controls, see Chapter 8: Controls.

One more thing worth noting before we begin is that the System.Draw-
ing namespace is implemented on top of GDI+ (Graphics Device Inter-
face+), the successor to GDI. The original GDI has been a mainstay in
Windows since there was a Windows, providing an abstraction over
screens and printers to make writing GUI-style applications easy.[2] GDI+ is
a Win32 DLL (gdiplus.dll) that ships with Windows XP and is available for

---

1. The standard controls that come with WinForms are listed in Appendix D: Standard Win-
   Forms Components and Controls.
2. GDI programming certainly isn't easy when compared with System.Drawing programming, but it's orders of magnitude easier than supporting printers and video display
   adapters by hand, which was what DOS programmers had to do to put bread on the table.

older versions of Windows. GDI+ is also an unmanaged C++ class library that wraps gdiplus.dll. Because the System.Drawing classes share many of the same names with the GDI+ C++ classes, you may very well stumble onto the unmanaged classes when looking for the .NET classes in the online documentation. The concepts are the same, but the coding details are very different between unmanaged C++ and managed anything else, so keep an eye out.

Drawing to the Screen

No matter what kind of drawing you're doing, the underlying abstraction that you're dealing with is the Graphics class from the System.Drawing namespace. The Graphics class provides the abstract surface on which you're drawing, whether the results of your drawing operations are displayed on the screen, stored in a file, or spooled to the printer. The Graphics class is too large to show here, but we'll come back to it again and again throughout the chapter.

One way to obtain a graphics object is to use CreateGraphics to create a new one associated with a form:

```
bool drawEllipse = false;

void drawEllipseButton_Click(object sender, EventArgs e) {
  // Toggle whether or not to draw the ellipse
  drawEllipse = !drawEllipse;

  Graphics g = this.CreateGraphics();
  try {
    if( drawEllipse ) {
      // Draw the ellipse
      g.FillEllipse(Brushes.DarkBlue, this.ClientRectangle);
    }
    else {
      // Erase the previously drawn ellipse
      g.FillEllipse(SystemBrushes.Control, this.ClientRectangle);
    }
  }
  finally {
    g.Dispose();
  }
}
```

After we have a graphics object, we can use it to draw on the form. Because we're using the button to toggle whether or not to draw the ellipse, we either draw an ellipse in dark blue or use the system color as the background of the form. All that's fine, but you may wonder what the try-catch block is for.

Because the graphics object holds an underlying resource managed by Windows, we're responsible for releasing the resource when we're finished, even in the face of an exception, and that is what the try-finally block is for. The Graphics class, like many classes in .NET, implements the IDisposable interface. When an object implements the IDisposable interface, that's a signal for the client of that object to call the IDisposable Dispose method when the client is finished with the object. This lets the object know that it's time to clean up any resources it's holding, such as a file or a database connection. In this case, the Graphic class's implementation of IDisposable Dispose can release the underlying graphics object that it's maintaining.

To simplify things in C#, the try-catch block can be replaced with a *using* block:

```
void drawEllipseButton_Click(object sender, EventArgs e) {
  using( Graphics g = this.CreateGraphics() ) {
    g.FillEllipse(Brushes.DarkBlue, this.ClientRectangle);
  } // g.Dispose called automatically here
}
```

The C# using block wraps the code it contains in a try block and always calls the IDisposable Dispose method at the end of the block for objects created as part of the using clause. This is a convenient shortcut for C# programmers. It's a good practice to get into and something you'll see used extensively in the rest of this book.

Handling the Paint Event

After we've got the Graphics resources managed properly, we have another issue: When the form is resized or covered and uncovered, the ellipse is not automatically redrawn. To deal with this, Windows asks a form (and all child controls) to redraw newly uncovered content via the Paint event, which provides a PaintEventArgs argument:

```
class PaintEventArgs {
  public Rectangle ClipRectangle { get; }
  public Graphics Graphics { get; }
}


bool drawEllipse = false;

void drawEllipseButton_Click(object sender, EventArgs e) {
    drawEllipse = !drawEllipse;
}

void DrawingForm_Paint(object sender, PaintEventArgs e) {
  if( !drawEllipse ) return;
  Graphics g = e.Graphics;
  g.FillEllipse(Brushes.DarkBlue, this.ClientRectangle);
}
```

By the time the Paint event is fired, the background of the form has already been drawn,[3] so any ellipse that was drawn during the last Paint event will be gone; this means that we must draw the ellipse only if the flag is set to true. However, even if we set the flag to draw the ellipse, Windows doesn't know that the state of the flag has changed, so the Paint event won't be triggered and the form won't get a chance to draw the ellipse. To avoid the need to draw the ellipse in the button's Click event as well as the form's Paint event, we must request a Paint event and let Windows know that the form needs to be redrawn.

Triggering the Paint Event

To request a Paint event, we use the Invalidate method:

```
void drawEllipseButton_Click(object sender, EventArgs e) {
  drawEllipse = !drawEllipse;

  this.Invalidate(true); // Ask Windows for a Paint event
                         // for the form and its children
}
```

Now, when the user toggles the flag, we call Invalidate to let Windows know that a part of the form needs to be redrawn. However, because drawing is one of the more expensive operations, Windows will first handle all

---

3. A form or control can draw its own background by overriding the OnPaintBackground method.

other events—such as mouse movements, keyboard entry, and so on—before firing the Paint event, just in case multiple areas of the form need to be redrawn at the same time.

To avoid this delay, use the Update method, which forces Windows to handle the Paint event immediately. Because invalidating and updating the entire client area of a form are so common, forms also have a Refresh method that combines the two:

```
void drawEllipseButton_Click(object sender, EventArgs e) {
  drawEllipse = !drawEllipse;

  // Can do one or the other
  this.Invalidate(true); // Ask Windows for a Paint event
                         // for the form and its children
  this.Update(); // Force the Paint event to happen now

  // Or can do both at once
  this.Refresh(); // Invalidate(true) + Update
}
```

However, if you can wait, it's best to let Windows handle the Paint event in its own sweet time. It's delayed for a reason: It's the slowest thing that the system does. Forcing all paints to happen immediately eliminates an important optimization.

If you've been following along with this simple example, you'll be pleased to see that pressing the button toggles whether or not the ellipse is shown on the form and that covering and uncovering the form draws as expected. However, if you resize the form, you'll be disappointed, as shown in Figures 4.1 and 4.2.

Notice that in Figure 4.2, it seems as if the ellipse is being drawn several times, but incompletely, as the form is resized. What's happening is that as the form is being expanded, Windows is drawing only the newly exposed

FIGURE 4.1: Ellipse Form before Resizing

FIGURE 4.2: Ellipse Form after Resizing

rectangle, assuming that the existing rectangle doesn't need to be redrawn. Although we're redrawing the entire ellipse during each Paint event, Windows is ignoring everything outside the *clip region*—that part of the form that needs redrawing—and that leads to the strange drawing behavior. Luckily, you can set a *style* to request that Windows redraw the entire form during a resize:

```
public DrawingForm() {
  // Required for Windows Form Designer support
  InitializeComponent();

  // Trigger a Paint event when the form is resized
  this.SetStyle(ControlStyles.ResizeRedraw, true);
}
```

Forms (and controls) have several drawing styles (you'll see more in Chapter 6: Advanced Drawing). The ResizeRedraw style causes Windows to redraw the entire client area whenever the form is resized. Of course, this is less efficient, and that's why Windows defaults to the original behavior.

Colors

So far, I've been drawing the ellipse in my form using a built-in dark blue brush. A *brush*, as you'll see, is for filling the interior of a shape, whereas a *pen* is used to draw the edge of a shape. Either way, suppose I'm not quite happy with the dark blue brush. Instead, I'd like a brush of one of the more than 16 million colors that doesn't come prebuilt for me, and this means that I first need to specify the color in which I'm interested. Color is modeled in .NET via the Color structure:

```
struct Color {
  // No color
  public static readonly Color Empty;

  // Built-in colors
  public static Color AliceBlue { get; }
  // ...
  public static Color YellowGreen { get; }

  // Properties
  public byte A { get; }
  public byte B { get; }
  public byte G { get; }
  public bool IsEmpty { get; }
  public bool IsKnownColor { get; }
  public bool IsNamedColor { get; }
  public bool IsSystemColor { get; }
  public string Name { get; }
  public byte R { get; }

  // Methods
  public static Color FromArgb(int alpha, Color baseColor);
  public static Color FromArgb(int alpha, int red, int green, int blue);
  public static Color FromArgb(int argb);
  public static Color FromArgb(int red, int green, int blue);
  public static Color FromKnownColor(KnownColor color);
  public static Color FromName(string name);
  public float GetBrightness();
  public float GetHue();
  public float GetSaturation();
  public int ToArgb();
  public KnownColor ToKnownColor();
}
```

Fundamentally, a Color object represents four values: the amount of red, green, and blue color and the amount of opacity. The red, green, and blue elements are often referred to together as RGB (red-green-blue), and each ranges from 0 to 255, with 0 being the smallest amount of color and 255 being the greatest amount of color. The degree of opacity is specified by an *alpha* value, which is sometimes seen together with RGB as ARGB (Alpha-RGB). The alpha value ranges from 0 to 255, where 0 is completely transparent and 255 is completely opaque.

Instead of using a constructor, you create a Color object by using the FromArgb method, passing brightness settings of red, green, and blue:

```
Color red =    Color.FromArgb(255, 0, 0); // 255 red, 0 blue, 0 green
Color green = Color.FromArgb(0, 255, 0); // 0 red, 255 blue, 0 green
Color blue =   Color.FromArgb(0, 0, 255); // 0 red, 0 blue, 255 green
Color white = Color.FromArgb(255, 255, 255); // white
Color black = Color.FromArgb(0, 0, 0); // black
```

If you'd like to specify the degree of transparency as well, you pass an alpha value:

```
Color blue25PercentOpaque = Color.FromArgb(255*1/4, 0, 0, 255);
Color blue75PercentOpaque = Color.FromArgb(255*3/4, 0, 0, 255);
```

The three 8-bit color values and the 8-bit alpha value make up the four parts of a single value that defines the 32-bit color that modern video display adaptors can handle. If you prefer to pass the four values combined into the single 32-bit value, you can do that with another of the overloads, although it's fairly awkward and therefore usually avoided:

```
// A = 191, R = 0, G = 0, B = 255
Color blue75PercentOpache = Color.FromArgb(-1090518785);
```

Known Colors

Often, the color you're interested in already has a well-known name, and this means that it will already be available from the static fields of Color that define known colors, from the KnownColor enumeration, and by name:

```
Color blue1 = Color.BlueViolet;
Color blue2 = Color.FromKnownColor(KnownColor.BlueViolet);
Color blue3 = Color.FromName("BlueViolet");
```

In addition to 141 colors with names such as AliceBlue and OldLace, the KnownColor enumeration has 26 values describing the current colors assigned to various parts of the Windows UI, such as the color of the border on the active window and the color of the default background of a control. These colors are handy when you're doing custom drawing and you'd like to match the rest of the system. The system color values of the KnownColor enumeration are shown here:

```
enum KnownColor {
  // Nonsystem colors elided...
  ActiveBorder,
  ActiveCaption,
  ActiveCaptionText,
  AppWorkspace,
  Control,
  ControlDark,
  ControlDarkDark,
  ControlLight,
  ControlLightLight,
  ControlText,
  Desktop,
  GrayText
  Highlight,
  HighlightText,
  HotTrack,
  InactiveBorder,
  InactiveCaption,
  InactiveCaptionText,
  Info,
  InfoText,
  Menu,
  MenuText,
  ScrollBar,
  Window,
  WindowFrame,
  WindowText,
}
```

If you'd like to use one of the system colors without creating your own instance of the Color class, you can access them already created for you and exposed as properties of the SystemColors class:

```
sealed class SystemColors {
  // Properties
  public static Color ActiveBorder { get; }
  public static Color ActiveCaption { get; }
```

```
    public static Color ActiveCaptionText { get; }
    public static Color AppWorkspace { get; }
    public static Color Control { get; }
    public static Color ControlDark { get; }
    public static Color ControlDarkDark { get; }
    public static Color ControlLight { get; }
    public static Color ControlLightLight { get; }
    public static Color ControlText { get; }
    public static Color Desktop { get; }
    public static Color GrayText { get; }
    public static Color Highlight { get; }
    public static Color HighlightText { get; }
    public static Color HotTrack { get; }
    public static Color InactiveBorder { get; }
    public static Color InactiveCaption { get; }
    public static Color InactiveCaptionText { get; }
    public static Color Info { get; }
    public static Color InfoText { get; }
    public static Color Menu { get; }
    public static Color MenuText { get; }
    public static Color ScrollBar { get; }
    public static Color Window { get; }
    public static Color WindowFrame { get; }
    public static Color WindowText { get; }
}
```

The following two lines yield Color objects with the same color values, and you can use whichever one you like:

```
Color color1 = Color.FromKnownColor(KnownColor.GrayText);
Color color2 = SystemColors.GrayText;
```

Color Translation

If you have a color in one of three other formats—HTML, OLE, or Win32—or you'd like to translate to one of these formats, you can use ColorTranslator, as shown here for HTML:

```
Color htmlBlue = ColorTranslator.FromHtml("#0000ff");
string htmlBlueToo = ColorTranslator.ToHtml(htmlBlue);
```

When you have a Color, you can get its alpha, red, blue, and green values as well as the color's name, whether it's a known color or a system color. You can also use these values to fill and frame shapes, which require brushes and pens, respectively.

Brushes

The System.Drawing.Brush class serves as a base class for several kinds of brushes, depending on your needs. Figure 4.3 shows the five derived brush classes provided in the System.Drawing and System.Drawing.Drawing2D namespaces.

Figure 4.3 was created with the following code:

```
void BrushesForm_Paint(object sender, PaintEventArgs e) {
  Graphics g = e.Graphics;
  int x = 0;
  int y = 0;
  int width = this.ClientRectangle.Width;
  int height = this.ClientRectangle.Height/5;
  Brush whiteBrush = System.Drawing.Brushes.White;
  Brush blackBrush = System.Drawing.Brushes.Black;

  using( Brush brush = new SolidBrush(Color.DarkBlue) ) {
    g.FillRectangle(brush, x, y, width, height);
    g.DrawString(brush.ToString(), this.Font, whiteBrush, x, y);
    y += height;
  }

  string file = @"c:\windows\Santa Fe Stucco.bmp";
  using( Brush brush =
         new TextureBrush(new Bitmap(file)) ) {
```

continues

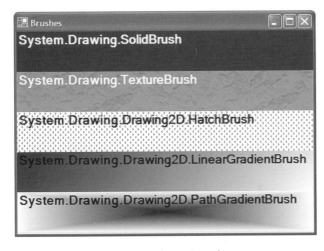

FIGURE 4.3: Sample Brushes (See Plate 6)

```
   g.FillRectangle(brush, x, y, width, height);
   g.DrawString(brush.ToString(), this.Font, whiteBrush, x, y);
   y += height;
}

using( Brush brush =
        new HatchBrush(
           HatchStyle.Divot, Color.DarkBlue, Color.White) ) {
  g.FillRectangle(brush, x, y, width, height);
  g.DrawString(brush.ToString(), this.Font, blackBrush, x, y);
  y += height;
}

using( Brush brush =
        new LinearGradientBrush(
           new Rectangle(x, y, width, height),
           Color.DarkBlue,
           Color.White,
           45.0f) ) {
  g.FillRectangle(brush, x, y, width, height);
  g.DrawString(brush.ToString(), this.Font, blackBrush, x, y);
  y += height;
}

Point[] points = new Point[] {  new Point(x, y),
                                new Point(x + width, y),
                                new Point(x + width, y + height),
                                new Point(x, y + height) };
using( Brush brush = new PathGradientBrush(points) ) {
  g.FillRectangle(brush, x, y, width, height);
  g.DrawString(brush.ToString(), this.Font, blackBrush, x, y);
  y += height;
  }
}
```

Solid Brushes

A SolidBrush is constructed with a color used to fill in the shape being
drawn. As a convenience, because solid color brushes are heavily used, the
Brushes class contains 141 Brush properties, one for each of the named colors in the KnownColor enumeration. These properties are handy because
they're resources cached and managed by .NET itself, making them a bit
easier to use than brushes you have to create yourself:[4]

---

4. In fact, if you attempt to dispose of one of the .NET-provided resources, such as pens,
   brushes, and so on, you'll eventually get an exception, either when you dispose of it in the
   first place or later when you try to use it again after it's been disposed of.

```
// Managed by .NET
Brush whiteBrush = System.Drawing.Brushes.White;

// Managed by your program
using( Brush myWhiteBrush = new SolidBrush(Color.White) ) {...}
```

Similarly, 21 of the 26 system colors from the KnownColor enumeration are provided in the SystemBrushes class.[5] This is handy if you want to use one of the system colors to create a brush but prefer to let WinForms handle the underlying resource. The brushes that aren't available by name from the SystemBrushes properties are still available using the FromSystemColor method, which returns a brush that's still managed by .NET:

```
// Calling Dispose on this brush will cause an exception
Brush brush = SystemBrushes.FromSystemColor(SystemColors.InfoText);
```

Texture Brushes

A TextureBrush is constructed with an image. By default, the image is used repeatedly to tile the space inside the shape being drawn. You can change this behavior by choosing a member of the WrapMode enumeration:

```
enum WrapMode {
  Clamp, // draw only once
  Tile, // default
  TileFlipX, // flip image horizontally along X axis
  TileFlipY, // flip image vertically along Y axis
  TileFlipXY, // flip image along X and Y axes
}
```

Figure 4.4 shows the various modes.

Hatch Brushes

A HatchBrush is used to fill space using one of several built-in two-color patterns, where the two colors are used to draw the foreground and the background of the pattern. Figure 4.5 shows the 56 hatches in the HatchStyle enumeration using black as the foreground color and white as the background color.

---

5. GrayText, InactiveCaptionText, InfoText, MenuText, and WindowFrame are more commonly used for pens, not brushes, and that is why they're not represented in the class SystemBrushes but are represented in the SystemPens class.

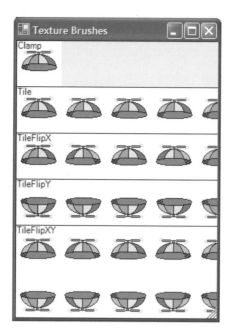

FIGURE 4.4: Various TextureBrush WrapMode Values (See Plate 7)

BackwardDiagonal	Cross	DarkDownwardDiagonal	DarkHorizontal
DarkUpwardDiagonal	DarkVertical	DashedDownwardDiagonal	DashedHorizontal
DashedUpwardDiagonal	DashedVertical	DiagonalBrick	DiagonalCross
Divot	DottedDiamond	DottedGrid	ForwardDiagonal
Horizontal	HorizontalBrick	LargeCheckerBoard	LargeConfetti
LargeGrid	LightDownwardDiagonal	LightHorizontal	LightUpwardDiagonal
LightVertical	Max	Min	NarrowHorizontal
NarrowVertical	OutlinedDiamond	Percent05	Percent10
Percent20	Percent25	Percent30	Percent40
Percent50	Percent60	Percent70	Percent75
Percent80	Percent90	Plaid	Shingle
SmallCheckerBoard	SmallConfetti	SmallGrid	SolidDiamond
Sphere	Trellis	Vertical	Wave
Weave	WideDownwardDiagonal	WideUpwardDiagonal	ZigZag

FIGURE 4.5: Available Hatch Brush Styles Shown with Black Foreground and
White Background

Linear Gradient Brushes

A LinearGradientBrush is used to draw a smooth blending between two end points and between two colors. The gradations are drawn at a specified angle, as defined either by passing a float or by passing one of four LinearGradientMode values:

```
enum LinearGradientMode {
  Horizontal, // 0 degrees
  Vertical, // 90 degrees
  ForwardDiagonal, // 45 degrees
  BackwardDiagonal, // 135 degrees
}
```

The angle is used to set up a *blend*, which governs the transition between colors over the area of the brush along the angle of the line. You can set this blend either directly or indirectly. In the direct technique, you use a Blend property, which determines positions and factors of fall-out between the two colors. To set the blend indirectly, you use a *focus* point for the end color and a fall-out rate toward the start color, as shown in Figure 4.6.

Notice that the normal linear gradient brush transitions between the start and end colors, whereas the triangle version transitions from the start color to the end color at some specified focus (in this example, it is set right in the middle). Furthermore, the bell shape transitions toward the end color using a normal bell curve distribution. The following is the code that draws the first three brushes (notice the use of the SetBlendTriangular-Shape and SetSigmaBellShape methods to adjust the blend):

```
using(
  LinearGradientBrush brush =
```

continues

FIGURE 4.6: Normal, Triangle, and Bell Linear Gradient Brushes (See Plate 8)

```
new LinearGradientBrush(
this.ClientRectangle,
Color.White,
Color.Black,
LinearGradientMode.Horizontal) ) {

  // Normal: focus set at the end
  g.FillRectangle(brush, x, y, width, height);
  g.DrawString("Normal", this.Font, blackBrush, x, y);
  y += height;

  // Triangle
  brush.SetBlendTriangularShape(0.5f); // Set focus in the middle
  g.FillRectangle(brush, x, y, width, height);
  g.DrawString("Triangle", this.Font, blackBrush, x, y);
  y += height;

  // Bell
  brush.SetSigmaBellShape(0.5f); // Set focus in the middle
  g.FillRectangle(brush, x, y, width, height);
  g.DrawString("Bell", this.Font, blackBrush, x, y);
  y += height;

  ...
}
```

At the bottom of Figure 4.6, we're still transitioning from white to black, but we're transitioning through red in the middle. This is because we took over the blending with an instance of a ColorBlend object that lets us set custom colors and positions:

```
// Custom colors
ColorBlend blend = new ColorBlend();
blend.Colors = new Color[] { Color.White, Color.Red, Color.Black, };
blend.Positions = new float[] { 0.0f, 0.5f, 1.0f };
brush.InterpolationColors = blend;
g.FillRectangle(brush, x, y, width, height);
```

Path Gradient Brushes

In the unlikely event that your linear gradient brush is not defined for the entire shape you're drawing, the brush will be tiled just like a texture brush, as governed by the WrapMode. If you want to get even fancier than linear gradients along a single angle, you can use the PathGradientBrush, as shown in Figure 4.7.

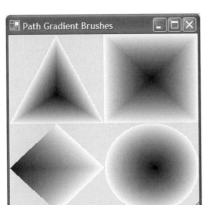

FIGURE 4.7: Four Sample Uses of the PathGradientBrush Class (See Plate 9)

The PathGradientBrush is defined by a set of points that define the surrounding edges of the path, a center point, and a set of colors for each point. By default, the color for each edge point is white, and for the center point is black. The gradient color transitions happen along each edge defined by the points toward the center. The triangle brush was created this way:

```
Point[] triPoints = new Point[] { new Point(width/2, 0),
                                  new Point(0, height),
                                  new Point(width, height), };
using( PathGradientBrush brush = new PathGradientBrush(triPoints) ) {
  int x = 0;
  int y = 0;
  g.FillRectangle(brush, x, y, width, height);
}
```

Notice that we defined the three surrounding points in the Point array but didn't define the center point explicitly. The center point is calculated based on the surrounding points; but it doesn't need to be in the midpoint between all points, as shown by the diamond brush and the following code:

```
Point[] diamondPoints = new Point[] { ... };
using( PathGradientBrush brush =
        new PathGradientBrush(diamondPoints) ) {
  brush.WrapMode = WrapMode.Tile;
```

continues

```
brush.CenterPoint = new Point(0, height/2);
int x = 0;
int y = height;
g.FillRectangle(brush, x, y, width, height);
}
```

Notice that we use the CenterPoint property to set the gradient end-point to be along the left edge of the diamond. The center of a path gradient brush doesn't even have to be inside the polygon described by the points, if you don't want it to be.

Notice also the use of the WrapMode property. By default, this is set to Clamp, which causes the brush to draw only once in the upper-left corner. The points on the brush are relative to the client area, not to where they're being used to fill, so we must set the WrapMode if we want the brush to draw anywhere but in the upper-left corner. Another way to handle this is to apply a transform on the graphics object before drawing, a technique described in Chapter 6: Advanced Drawing.

Although it's possible to describe a circle with a lot of points, it's far easier to use a GraphicsPath object instead. A GraphicsPath is really a data structure that contains zero or more shapes (the GraphicsPath class is discussed in more detail later in this chapter). It's useful for describing an area for drawing, just as we're doing with the set of points describing our brush. The points are used by the PathGradientBrush to create a GraphicsPath internally (hence the name of this brush), but we can create and use a GraphicsPath directly:

```
using( GraphicsPath circle = new GraphicsPath() ) {
  circle.AddEllipse(0, 0, width, height);
  using( PathGradientBrush brush = new PathGradientBrush(circle) ) {
    brush.WrapMode = WrapMode.Tile;
    brush.SurroundColors = new Color[] { Color.White }; // default
    brush.CenterColor = Color.Black; // defaults to white
    int x = width;
    int y = height;
    g.FillRectangle(brush, x, y, width, height);
  }
}
```

After we create an empty GraphicsPath object, notice the addition of an ellipse to the path before we use it to create a brush. The center of whatever set of shapes is in the path is used as the brush's center point, just as you'd expect, but the center color defaults to white when we use a GraphicsPath; that's why the code manually sets the CenterColor property to black.

Notice also the use of the SurroundColors property, which is an array of colors, one for each point on the gradient path. If there are more points than colors (as is clearly the case when we're providing only a single color for all the points around the edge of a circle), the last color in the array is used for all remaining points. For example, this code draws a red gradient from the first point of the triangle but uses blue for the other two points, as shown in Figure 4.8:

```
using( PathGradientBrush brush = new PathGradientBrush(triPoints) ) {
  brush.SurroundColors = new Color[] { Color.Red, Color.Blue };
  int x = 0;
  int y = 0;
  g.FillRectangle(brush, x, y, width, height);
}
```

Like linear gradient brushes, path gradient brushes allow you to adjust the blend as well as the colors used to transition between start and end points.

Pens

Whereas the Brush classes are used to fill shapes, the Pen class is used to frame shapes. The interesting members are shown here:

```
sealed class Pen : MarshalByRefObject, ICloneable,  IDisposable {
  // Constructors
  public Pen(Brush brush);
  public Pen(Brush brush, float width);
```

continues

FIGURE 4.8: A PathGradientBrush with One Red Surrounding Point and Two Blue Ones (See Plate 10)

```
  public Pen(Color color);
  public Pen(Color color, float width);

  // Properties
  public PenAlignment Alignment { get; set; }
  public Brush Brush { get; set; }
  public Color Color { get; set; }
  public float[] CompoundArray { get; set; }
  public CustomLineCap CustomEndCap { get; set; }
  public CustomLineCap CustomStartCap { get; set; }
  public DashCap DashCap { get; set; }
  public float DashOffset { get; set; }
  public float[] DashPattern { get; set; }
  public DashStyle DashStyle { get; set; }
  public LineCap EndCap { get; set; }
  public LineJoin LineJoin { get; set; }
  public float MiterLimit { get; set; }
  public PenType PenType { get; }
  public LineCap StartCap { get; set; }
  public float Width { get; set; }

  // Transformation members elided...

  // Methods
  public void SetLineCap(...);
}
```

Pens have several interesting properties, including a width, a color or a brush, start and end cap styles, and a dash pattern for the line itself. One note of interest is that the width of a pen is specified in the units of the underlying Graphics being drawn on (more information about Graphics units is available in Chapter 6: Advanced Drawing). However, no matter what the underlying units, a pen width of 0 always translates into a width of 1 physical unit on the underlying Graphic surface. This lets you specify the smallest visible pen width without worrying about the units of a particular surface.

You'll notice that the Pen class is *sealed*. This means that it can't be used as a base class for further penlike functionality. Instead, each pen has a type that governs its behavior, as determined by the PenType enumeration:

```
enum PenType {
  SolidColor, // Created from a color or a SolidBrush
  TextureFill, // Created from a TextureBrush
  HatchFill, // Created from a HatchBrush
  LinearGradient, // Created from a LinearGradientBrush
```

```
PathGradient, // Created from a PathGradientBrush
}
```

If you're interested in common, solid-color pens, the 141 named pens are provided as static Pen properties on the Pens class, and 15 system pens are provided as static Pen properties on the SystemPens class, providing the same usage as the corresponding Brushes and SystemBrushes classes. As with SystemBrushes, the FromSystemColor method of the SystemPens class returns a pen in one of the system colors that's managed by .NET.

Line Caps

In addition to their brushlike behavior, pens have behavior at ends and joints and along their length that brushes don't have. For example, each end can have a different style, as determined by the LineCap enumeration shown in Figure 4.9.

All these lines were generated with a black pen of width 12 passed to the Graphics.DrawLine method. The white line of width 1 in the middle is drawn using a separate call to Graphics.DrawLine to show the two end points that define the line. Each black pen is defined with the EndCap property set to a value from the LineCap enumeration:

```
using( Pen pen = new Pen(Color.Black, 12) ) {
  pen.EndCap = LineCap.Flat; // default
  g.DrawLine(pen, x, y + height*2/3, x + width*2/3, y + height*2/3);
  g.DrawLine(whitePen, x, y + height*2/3, x + width*2/3, y + height*2/3);
  ...
}
```

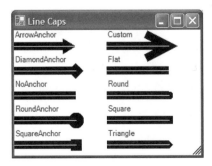

FIGURE 4.9: Examples from the LineCap Enumeration

The default line cap style is flat, which is what all the StartCap properties are set to. You'll notice some familiar line cap styles, including flat, round, square, and triangle, which have no anchor, as well as arrow, diamond, round, and square, which have anchors. An *anchor* indicates that part of the line cap extends beyond the width of the pen. The difference between square and flat, on the other hand, dictates whether the line cap extends beyond the end of the line (as square does, but flat does not).

You can manage these kinds of drawing behaviors independently by using the LineCap.Custom enumeration value and setting the CustomStartCap or CustomEndCap field to a class that derives from the CustomLineCap class (from the System.Drawing.Drawing2D namespace). The custom line cap in Figure 4.9 shows a pen created using an instance of the AdjustableArrowCap class, the only custom end cap class that .NET provides:

```
using( Pen pen = new Pen(Color.Black, 12) ) {
  pen.EndCap = LineCap.Custom;
  // width and height of 3 and unfilled arrow head
  pen.CustomEndCap = new AdjustableArrowCap(3f, 3f, false);
  . . .
}
```

Dashes

In addition to the ends having special styles, a line can have a dash style, as defined by the DashStyle enumeration, shown in Figure 4.10.

Each of the lines was created by setting the DashStyle property of the pen. The DashStyle.Custom value is used to set custom dash and space

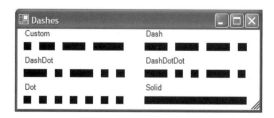

FIGURE 4.10: Examples Using the DashStyle Enumeration

lengths, where each length is a multiplier of the width. For example, the following code draws the increasing length dashes shown in Figure 4.10 with a constant space length:

```
using( Pen pen = new Pen(Color.Black, 12) ) {
  pen.DashStyle = DashStyle.Custom;
  // Set increasing dashes and constant spaces
  pen.DashPattern =
    new float[] { 1f, 1f, 2f, 1f, 3f, 1f, 4f, 1f, };
  g.DrawLine(
    pen, x + 10, y + height*2/3, x + width - 20, y + height*2/3);
}
```

If you'd like to exercise more control over your custom dash settings, you can set the DashCap property on the pen to any of the values in the DashCap enumeration, which is a subset of the values in the LineCap enumeration with only Flat (the default), Round, and Triangle.

To exercise more control over the line itself, in addition to dash settings, you can define *compound* pens using the CompoundArray property. This allows you to provide lines and spaces in parallel to the lines being drawn instead of perpendicularly, as dash settings do. For example, Figure 4.11 was drawn with a pen set up this way:

```
using( Pen pen = new Pen(Color.Black, 20) ) {
  // Set percentages of width where line starts, then space starts,
  // then line starts again, etc. in alternating pattern
  pen.CompoundArray =
    new float[] { 0.0f, 0.25f, 0.45f, 0.55f, 0.75f, 1.0f, };
  g.DrawRectangle(pen, new Rectangle(...));
}
```

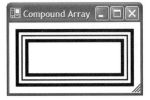

FIGURE 4.11: A Single Rectangle Drawn with a Pen Using a Compound Array

Alignments

Most of the examples, including Figure 4.11, have shown pens of width greater than 1. When you draw a line of width greater than 1, the question is, where do the extra pixels go—above the line being drawn, below it, or somewhere else? The default pen alignment is *centered*, which means that half the width goes inside the shape being drawn and the other half goes outside. The alignment can also be *inset*, which means that the entire width of the pen is inside the shape being drawn, as shown in Figure 4.12.

In Figure 4.12, both ellipses are drawn using a rectangle of the same dimensions (as shown by the red line), but the different alignments determine where the width of the line is drawn. There are actually several values in the PenAlignment enumeration, but only Center and Inset are currently supported, and Inset is used only for closed shapes (an open figure has no "inside").

Joins

One final consideration you'll have when drawing figures that have angles is what to do with the line at the angle. In Figure 4.13, the four values in the PenJoin enumeration have been set in the Pen class's LineJoin property before the rectangles were drawn (again, a white line of width 1 is used to show the shape being drawn).

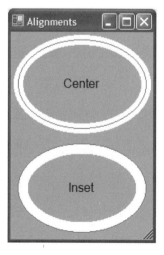

FIGURE 4.12: Pen Alignment Options (See Plate 11)

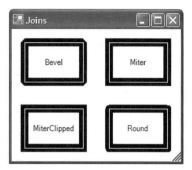

FIGURE 4.13: Sample PenJoin Values

Notice in Figure 4.13 that each corner provides a different join. The one exception is MiterClipped, which changes between Bevel and Miter dynamically based on the angle of the corner and the limit set by the Miter-Limit property.

Creating Pens from Brushes

So far in this section on pens, all the examples have used solid-color pens. However, you can also create a pen from a brush. For example, Figure 4.14 shows an image you first encountered in Chapter 1: Hello, Windows Forms.

The pen used to draw the lines in Figure 4.14 was created from a Linear-GradientBrush:

```
using( LinearGradientBrush brush =
        new LinearGradientBrush( this.ClientRectangle,
                                 Color.Empty, // ignored
                                 Color.Empty, // ignored
                                 45) ) {
```

continues

FIGURE 4.14: Creating a Pen from a LinearGradientBrush

```
blend.Colors = new Color[] { Color.Red, Color.Green, Color.Blue };
blend.Positions = new float[] { 0, .5f, 1 };
brush.InterpolationColors = blend;
using( Pen pen = new Pen(brush) ) {
    ...
}
}
```

The ability to create a pen from a brush lets you use any effect you can create using the multitude of brushes provided by System.Drawing.

Shapes

Now that you know how to frame and fill shapes with pens and brushes, you might be interested in the shapes that are available. Figure 4.15 shows them.

All the shapes in Figure 4.15 were edged using a DrawXxx function from the Graphics object for the form—for example, DrawArc and Draw-Bezier. The shapes that can be filled were drawn using a FillXxx function, such as FillClosedCurve and FillEllipse. Not all of the shapes could be filled because not all of them are closed shapes; for example, there is no FillCurve. However, all the open shapes (except the Bezier) have closed-shape equivalents; for example, a filled arc is called a pie.

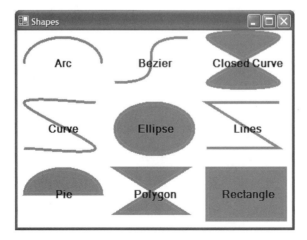

FIGURE 4.15: The Basic Shapes (See Plate 12)

Also, notice the use of the Lines shape. This shape could be drawn using multiple calls to the DrawLine function, but three of the shapes—line, rectangle, and Bezier—have helpers that draw more of them at once. In addition to being convenient, these helpers handle the appropriate mitering at intersections that you'd otherwise have to do by hand. For example, the Graphics object provides all the following functions for drawing rectangles: DrawRectangle, DrawRectangles, FillRectangle, and FillRectangles.

Curves

Most of the shapes are specified as you'd expect. You specify the rectangle and the ellipse using an x, y, width, and height, or a Rectangle object. You specify the arc and the pie as with a rectangle, but you also include a start and a length of *sweep*, both specified in degrees (the shown arc and pie start at 180 degrees and sweep for 180 degrees). The lines and polygon are specified with an array of points, as are the curves, but the curves are a little different.

The curve (also known as a *cardinal spline*) acts just like a set of lines, except as a point is approached, there's a curve instead of a sharp point. In addition to a set of points, the curve is specified using a *tension*, which is a value that determines how "curvy" the curve is around the points. A tension of 0 indicates no curve, and a tension of 0.5 is the default. The tension can get as high as allowed by the floating point type. Figure 4.16 shows some common variations.

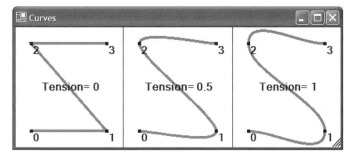

FIGURE 4.16: Curves Drawn with Various Values of Tension

Figure 4.16 shows the same set of points (as indicated by the black dots and index number) drawn using the DrawCurve function with three different values of tension. As the tension increases, so does the amount of curve at each point.

Unlike normal curves, Bezier curves are specified with exactly four points: one start point, followed by two *control* points, followed by an end point. If the DrawBeziers function is used to draw multiple curves, the end point of the preceding curve becomes the start point of the next. Figure 4.17 shows three Bezier curves drawn using the same set of points, but in different orders.

In each case, the Bezier is drawn between the start point and the end point, but the two control points are used to determine the shape of the curve by exerting more "control" over the curve as they get farther away.

Smoothing Modes

When drawing shapes, you may want the smooth rendering you've seen in the really cool applications. The shapes in Figures 4.15, 4.16, and 4.17 were all drawn without any kind of "smoothing," as evidenced by the jagged edges. The jagged edges are caused by the swift transition between the color of the shape being drawn and the color of the background. A technique known as *antialiasing* uses a smoother transition between the shape color and the background color, in much the same way that a gradient brush provides a smooth transition from one color to another. To turn on

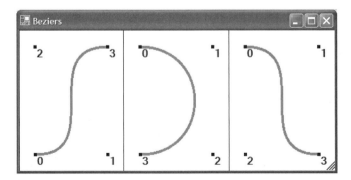

FIGURE 4.17: Three Bezier Curves Drawn Using the Same Set of Points in Different Orders

antialiasing for shapes subsequently drawn on the Graphics object, you set the SmoothingMode property:

```
g.SmoothingMode = SmoothingMode.AntiAlias;
```

The default value of the SmoothingMode property is Smoothing-Mode.None. In addition to the AntiAlias value, SmoothingMode has three other values: Default, HighSpeed, and HighQuality. These are merely aliases for None, None, and AntiAlias, depending on your system settings. Figure 4.18 shows the difference between using and not using antialiasing.

Notice that setting the SmoothingMode has no effect on the text drawn on the Graphics object. You set the rendering effects of text using the Text-RenderingHint property, which I discuss in Chapter 5: Drawing Text.

Saving and Restoring Graphics Settings

Setting the SmoothingMode in the preceding section is the first time we've changed a property on the Graphics object that affects subsequent operations. You can also set other properties that affect subsequent operations, and we'll cover those topics as appropriate. When you change a property of a Graphics object in a method other than the Paint event handler itself, it's a good idea to reset it on the Graphics object before the method returns:

```
void DrawSomething(Graphics g) {
  // Save old smoothing mode
  SmoothingMode oldMode = g.SmoothingMode;

  // Make things draw smoothly
  g.SmoothingMode = SmoothingMode.AntiAlias;
```

continues

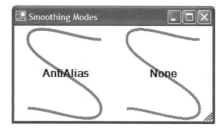

FIGURE 4.18: The Effect of Changing the SmoothingMode from AntiAlias to None

```
  // Draw things...

  // Restore smoothing mode
  g.SmoothingMode = oldMode;
}
```

This can quickly become painful when there are multiple properties to restore. Luckily, you can save yourself the trouble by taking a snapshot of a Graphics object state in a GraphicsState object from the System.Drawing. Drawing2D namespace:

```
void DrawSomething(Graphics g) {
  // Save old graphics state
  GraphicsState oldState = g.Save();

  // Made things draw smoothly
  g.SmoothingMode = SmoothingMode.AntiAlias;

  // Draw things...

  // Restore old graphics state
  g.Restore(oldState);
}
```

The Save method on the Graphics class returns the current state of the properties in the Graphics object. The call to Restore takes a GraphicsState object and sets the Graphics object to the state cached in that object. The code shows a pair of calls to Save and Restore, but it's not necessary to keep them in balance, something that's handy for switching a lot between a couple of states.

Paths

In addition to using the basic shapes, you can compose and draw shapes together using a path. A *path*, modeled via the GraphicsPath class, is very much like a Graphics object, in that it's a logical container of zero or more shapes (called *figures* or *subpaths*). The difference (in addition to the fact that a Graphics object is backed by a surface such as a screen or a printer) is that the figures can be started and ended arbitrarily. This means that you can compose one or more complicated figures from a set of basic shapes. You collect figures into a path so that you can frame or fill them as a unit using a single brush or pen, which is applied when the path is drawn. For example, Figure 4.19 shows a rounded rectangle (a shape that the Graphics object can't draw for you directly).

Imagine a method called GetRoundedRectPath that takes a rectangle and a radius of an arc describing the curve. Calling the function returns a path, which can be filled and framed using the Graphics methods FillPath and FramePath:

```
Graphics g = e.Graphics;
int width = this.ClientRectangle.Width;
int height = this.ClientRectangle.Height;
Rectangle rect = new Rectangle(10, 10, width - 20, height - 20);
using( GraphicsPath path = GetRoundedRectPath(rect, width/10) ) {
  g.FillPath(Brushes.Yellow, path);
  g.DrawPath(Pens.Black, path);
}
```

Even though the rounded rectangle path is composed of eight shapes (four arcs and four lines), the entire path is filled with one brush and framed with one pen. Here is the implementation of the method that composes the rounded rectangle:

```
GraphicsPath GetRoundedRectPath(Rectangle rect, int radius) {
  int diameter = 2 * radius;
  Rectangle arcRect =
    new Rectangle(rect.Location, new Size(diameter, diameter));
  GraphicsPath path = new GraphicsPath();

  // top left
  path.AddArc(arcRect, 180, 90);

  // top right
  arcRect.X = rect.Right - diameter;
  path.AddArc(arcRect, 270, 90);
```

continues

FIGURE 4.19: A Rounded Rectangle Composed of Arc Figures in a GraphicsPath Object (See Plate 13)

```
    // bottom right
    arcRect.Y = rect.Bottom - diameter;
    path.AddArc(arcRect, 0, 90);

    // bottom left
    arcRect.X = rect.Left;
    path.AddArc(arcRect, 90, 90);

    path.CloseFigure();
    return path;
}
```

This function adds four arcs to the path—one at each of the corners of the rectangle. Each shape added to the path will be filled or framed as appropriate when the path is drawn or filled. In fact, notice that no pen or brush is used to add each shape. The pen or brush is provided when the path is drawn, not when the shapes are added.

Also, notice that none of the lines is added explicitly. The first three lines are added implicitly by the path itself. As each new unclosed shape is added, the starting point of the new shape is joined to the ending point of the last unclosed shape, creating a connected figure. After the last arc is added, we call the CloseFigure method to join the ending point of that arc to the starting point of the first arc. If CloseFigure had not been called, we'd still have a closed figure when the path was filled and framed, but the line connecting the top-left arc with the bottom-left arc would be missing. On the other hand, adding a closed shape, such as a rectangle or an ellipse, will close itself, so there's no need to call CloseFigure.

If, after calling CloseFigure, we were to add another shape, then another figure would be started for us implicitly. If you'd like to start a new figure without closing the current figure, you can do so by calling StartFigure. Figure 4.20 shows what would happen if StartFigure were called after

FIGURE 4.20: Starting a New Figure in a Path Without Closing the Current Figure (See Plate 14)

the second arc at the top right is added to the path. Notice that there would be two figures in the path, the first one unclosed because the second figure was started without closing the first.

Paths can add any of the shapes that the Graphics class can draw or fill. In fact, paths are handy because they can be used to create closed figures that aren't normally closed. For example, the following function returns a closed Bezier, another shape that the Graphics class doesn't provide directly:

```
GraphicsPath GetClosedBezierPath(Rectangle rect, Point[] points) {
  GraphicsPath path = new GraphicsPath();
  path.AddBeziers(points);
  path.CloseFigure();
  return path;
}
```

Fill Modes

When you compose a path of multiple figures that overlap, by default the overlap will be subtractive. For example, the following code produces the donut in Figure 4.21:

```
GraphicsPath GetDonutPath(Rectangle rect, int holeRadius) {
  GraphicsPath path = new GraphicsPath();
  path.AddEllipse(rect);
  Point centerPoint = new Point(...);
  Rectangle holeRect = new Rectangle(...);
  path.StartFigure(); // not needed because an ellipse will close itself
  path.AddEllipse(holeRect);
  return path;
}
```

However, notice that when the donut is resized, as in Figure 4.22, only the overlapping parts subtract from each other.

FIGURE 4.21: Figures That Overlap Completely Act Subtractively

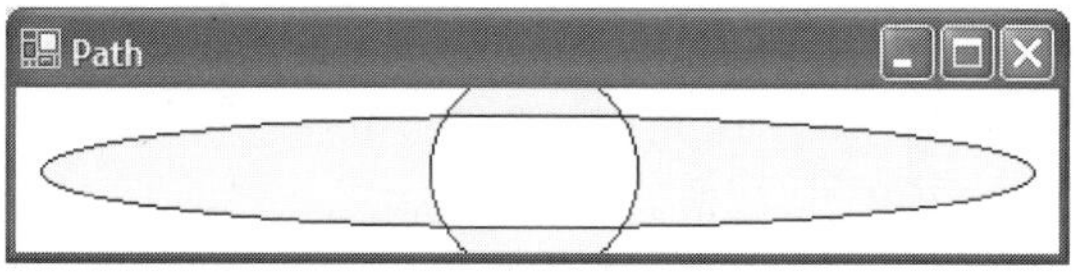

FIGURE 4.22: Overlapping Figures and the Alternate FillMode (See Plate 15)

This behavior is governed by the FillMode property on the Path, of type FillMode. The FillMode enumeration has two values: Alternate and Winding. Alternate, the default, changes how shapes are filled by noticing when lines cross. Switching to Winding mode, in this case, would fill both circles, because Winding mode changes how shapes are filled based on a complicated scheme of line segment direction that wouldn't be invoked in our case. You can also set the FillMode on a polygon and a closed curve, but the default Alternate FillMode is the overwhelming favorite and is seldom changed.

Images

As useful as curves and lines are, most modern applications also include the need to load and display professionally produced, prepackaged images. Also, some applications themselves produce images that can be saved to a file for later display. Both kinds of applications are supported by the two kinds of images in .NET: bitmaps and metafiles.

A *bitmap* is a set of pixels at certain color values stored in a variety of standard *raster* formats such as Graphics Interchange Format (GIF) (.gif files) and Joint Picture Experts Group (JPEG) (.jpg files), as well as Windows-specific formats such as Windows bitmap (.bmp files) and Windows icon (.ico files). A *metafile* is a set of shapes that make up a *vector* format, such as a GraphicsPath, but can also be loaded from Windows metafile (.wmf) and enhanced Windows metafile (.emf) formats.

Loading and Drawing Images

Bitmaps as well as metafiles can be loaded from files in the file system as well as files embedded as resources.[6] However, you must use the appropriate class. The Bitmap class (from the System.Drawing namespace) handles only raster formats, and the Metafile class (from the System.Drawing.Imaging namespace) handles only vector formats. Both the Bitmap class and the Metafile class derive from a common base class, the Image class. Image objects are what you deal with most of the time, whether it's drawing them into a Graphics object or setting a Form object's Background property.

The easiest way to load the image is to pass a file name to the appropriate class's constructor. After an image has been loaded, it can be drawn using the Graphics.DrawImage method:

```
using( Metafile wmf = new Metafile(@"2DARROW3.WMF") ) {
  // Draw the full image, unscaled and
  // clipped only to the Graphics object
  g.DrawImage(wmf, new PointF(0, 0));
}

using( Bitmap bmp = new Bitmap(@"Soap Bubbles.bmp") ) {
  g.DrawImage(bmp, new PointF(100, 100));
}

using( Bitmap ico = new Bitmap(@"POINT10.ICO") ) {
  g.DrawImage(ico, new PointF(200, 200));
}
```

Drawing an image using a point will cause the image to be rendered at its native size and clipped only by the Graphics object. You can be explicit about this desire by calling DrawImageUnscaled, but it acts no differently than passing only a point to DrawImage.

Scaling, Clipping, Panning, and Skewing

Drawing an image unscaled, although useful, is somewhat boring. Often, you'd like to perform operations on the image as it's drawn to achieve effects. For example, to *scale* an image as it's drawn to fit into a rectangle, you pass a rectangle instead of a point to DrawImage:

```
// Scale the image to the rectangle
Rectangle destRect = ...;
g.DrawImage(bmp, destRect);
```

---

6. For details of loading images from resources, see Chapter 10: Resources.

Going the other way, if you'd like to clip an image but leave it unscaled, you can use the DrawImage method, which takes both a source and a destination rectangle of the same size (Figure 4.23 shows the difference):

```
// Clip the image to the destination rectangle
Rectangle srcRect = ...;
Rectangle destRect = srcRect;
g.DrawImage(bmp, destRect, srcRect, g.PageUnit);
```

The code that does the clipping specifies a source rectangle to take from the image and a destination rectangle on the graphics object. Because both rectangles were the same size, there was no scaling, but this technique allows any chunk of the image to be drawn (and scaled) to any rectangle on the graphics object. This technique also allows for *panning*. You simply take a chunk out of the rectangle that's not at the upper left (as shown in Figure 4.24):

```
Bitmap bmp = new Bitmap(@"C:\WINDOWS\Soap Bubbles.bmp");
Size offset = new Size(0, 0); // Adjusted by buttons

void panel1_Paint(object sender, PaintEventArgs e) {
  Graphics g = e.Graphics;
  Rectangle destRect = this.panel1.ClientRectangle;
  Rectangle srcRect =
    new Rectangle(
      offset.Width, offset.Height, destRect.Width, destRect.Height);
  g.DrawImage(bmp, destRect, srcRect, g.PageUnit);
}
```

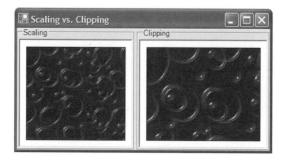

FIGURE 4.23: Scaling an Image Versus Clipping an Image

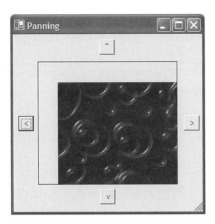

FIGURE 4.24: A Form That Pans an Image in Four Directions

Not only can you scale an image (or part of an image) to a rectangle, but you can also scale an image (or part of an image) to an arbitrary parallelogram. Several of the DrawImages overloads take an array of three PointF objects that describe three points on a parallelogram, which in turn acts as the destination (the fourth point is extrapolated to make sure that it's a real parallelogram). Scaling to a nonrectangular parallelogram is called *skewing* because of the skewed look of the results. For example, here's a way to skew an entire image (as shown in Figure 4.25):

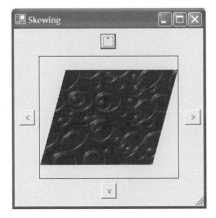

FIGURE 4.25: An Example of Skewing an Image

```
Bitmap bmp = new Bitmap(@"C:\WINDOWS\Soap Bubbles.bmp");
Size offset = new Size(0, 0); // Adjusted by buttons

void panel1_Paint(object sender, PaintEventArgs e) {
  Graphics g = e.Graphics;
  Rectangle rect = this.panel1.ClientRectangle;
  Point[] points = new Point[3];
  points[0] =
    new Point(rect.Left + offset.Width, rect.Top + offset.Height);
  points[1] = new Point(rect.Right, rect.Top + offset.Height);
  points[2] = new Point(rect.Left, rect.Bottom - offset.Height);
  g.DrawImage(bmp, points);
}
```

Rotating and Flipping

Two other kinds of transformation that you can apply to an image are rotating and flipping. *Rotating* an image allows it to be turned in increments of 90 degrees—that is, 90, 180, or 270. *Flipping* an image allows an image to be flipped along either the X or the Y axis. You can perform these two transforms together using the values from the RotateFlipType enumeration, as shown in Figure 4.26.

Notice in Figure 4.26 that the RotateNoneFlipNone type is the original image. All the others are rotated or flipped or both. To rotate only, you pick a type that includes FlipNone. To flip only, you pick a type that includes

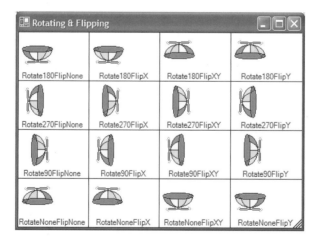

FIGURE 4.26: The Rotating and Flipping Types from the RotateFlipType Enumeration (See Plate 16)

RotateNone. The values from the RotateFlipType enumeration affect an
image itself using the RotateFlip method:

```
// Rotate 90 degrees
bitmap1.RotateFlip(RotateFlipType.Rotate90FlipNone);

// Flip along the X axis
bitmap2.RotateFlip(RotateFlipType.RotateNoneFlipX);
```

The effects of rotation and flipping are cumulative. For example, rotating an image 90 degrees twice will rotate it a total of 180 degrees.

Recoloring

Rotating and flipping aren't merely effects applied when drawing; rather,
these operations affect the contents of the image. You can also transform
the contents using an ImageAttributes object that contains information
about what kind of transformations to make. For example, one of the
things you can do with an ImageAttributes class is to map colors:

```
void panel2_Paint(object sender, PaintEventArgs e) {
  Graphics g = e.Graphics;
  using( Bitmap bmp = new Bitmap(@"INTL_NO.BMP") ) {
    // Set the image attribute's color mappings
    ColorMap[] colorMap = new ColorMap[1];
    colorMap[0] = new ColorMap();
    colorMap[0].OldColor = Color.Lime;
    colorMap[0].NewColor = Color.White;
    ImageAttributes attr = new ImageAttributes();
    attr.SetRemapTable(colorMap);

    // Draw using the color map
    Rectangle rect = new Rectangle(0, 0, bmp.Width, bmp.Height);
    rect.Offset(...); // Center the image
    g.DrawImage
      (bmp, rect, 0, 0, rect.Width, rect.Height, g.PageUnit, attr);
  }

}
```

This code first sets up an array of ColorMap objects, each of which contains the old color to transform from and the new color to transform to. The
color map is passed to a new ImageAttribute class via the SetRemapTable.
The ImageAttribute object is then passed to the DrawImage function,

which does the color mapping as the image is drawn. Figure 4.27 shows an example.

Notice that in addition to mapping the colors, the sample code uses the Width and Height properties of the Bitmap class. The Bitmap class, as well as the Image base class and the Metafile class, provides a great deal of information about the image.

Another useful piece of information is the color information at each pixel. For example, instead of hard-coding lime as the color, we could use the pixel information of the bitmap itself to pick the color to replace:

```
ColorMap[] colorMap = new ColorMap[1];
colorMap[0] = new ColorMap();
colorMap[0].OldColor = bmp.GetPixel(0, bmp.Height - 1);
colorMap[0].NewColor = Color.White;
```

In this case, we're mapping whatever color is at the bottom left as the pixel to replace. In addition to replacing colors, the ImageAttributes object can contain information about remapping palettes, setting gamma correction values, mapping color to grayscale, and other color-related options as well as the wrap mode (as with brushes).

Transparency

Of course, simply mapping to white or any other color isn't useful if the image needs to be drawn on top of something else that you'd like to show through. For this case, there's a special color called Transparent that allows the mapped color to disappear instead of being replaced with another color:

FIGURE 4.27: An Example of Mapping Color.Lime to Color.White (See Plate 17)

```
ColorMap[] colorMap = new ColorMap[1];
colorMap[0] = new ColorMap();
colorMap[0].OldColor = bmp.GetPixel(0, bmp.Height - 1);
colorMap[0].NewColor = Color.Transparent;
```

Figure 4.28 shows the effects of using Color.Transparent.

Again, I used the bottom-left pixel as the color to replace, which is the convention used by other parts of .NET. In fact, if you're going to always draw a bitmap with a transparent color and if the color to be made transparent is in the bitmap itself in the bottom-left pixel, you can save yourself the trouble of building a color map and instead use the MakeTransparent method:

```
// Make the bottom-left pixel the transparent color
bmp.MakeTransparent();
g.DrawImage(bmp, rect);
```

If the pixel you'd like to use as the transparency color isn't in the bottom left of the bitmap, you can also use the MakeTransparent overload, which takes a color as an argument. Calling MakeTransparent actually replaces the pixels of the transparency color with the Color.Transparent value. Some raster formats, such as the GIF and Windows icon formats, allow you to specify a transparency color value as one of their legal values. However, even if the raster format itself doesn't support a transparency color, all Bitmap objects, regardless of the raster format, support the MakeTransparent method.

Animation

Just as some raster formats support transparency as a native color, some also support animation. One in particular is the GIF format. The way that

FIGURE 4.28: Using Color.Transparent in a Color Map (See Plate 18)

images expose support for animation is by supporting more than one image in a single file. GIFs support animation by supporting more than one image in a time dimension, but other formats (such as TIFF files) can support different resolutions or multiple images as pages. You can count how many pages are in each "dimension" by calling the GetFrameCount method with FrameDimension objects exposed by properties from the FrameDimension class:

```
// Will throw exceptions if image format doesn't support
// multiple images along requested dimension
int timeFrames = gif.GetFrameCount(FrameDimension.Time);
int pageFrames = gif.GetFrameCount(FrameDimension.Page);
int resolutionFrames = gif.GetFrameCount(FrameDimension.Resolution);
```

To select which frame to be displayed when the image is drawn is merely a matter of selecting the "active" frame along a dimension:

```
int frame = 4; // Needs to be between 0 and frame count -1
gif.SelectActiveFrame(FrameDimension.Time, frame);
g.DrawImage(gif, this.ClientRectangle);
```

In addition to the multiple frames, the GIF format encodes timing information for each frame. However, that's where things get tricky. Because different image formats support different information, the Image class exposes "extra" information via its GetPropertyItem method. The GetPropertyItem method takes a numeric ID and returns a generic PropertyItem object. The IDs themselves are defined only in a GDI+ header file and the PropertyItem object's Value property. The Value property exposes the actual data as an array of bytes that needs to be interpreted, making usage from .NET difficult. For example, here's how to get the timings for a GIF file:

```
// Get bytes describing each frame's time delay
int PropertyTagFrameDelay = 0x5100; // From GdiPlusImaging.h
PropertyItem prop = gif.GetPropertyItem(PropertyTagFrameDelay);
byte[] bytes = prop.Value;

// Convert bytes into an array of time delays
int frames = gif.GetFrameCount(FrameDimension.Time);
int[] delays = new int[frames];
for( int frame = 0; frame != frames; ++frame ) {
```

```
  // Convert each 4-byte chunk into an integer
  delays[frame] = BitConverter.ToInt32(bytes, frame * 4);
}
```

After you have the time delays, you can start a timer and use the Select-ActiveFrame method to do the animation. If you do it that way, make sure to convert the delays to milliseconds (1/1000ths of a second), which is what .NET timers like, from centiseconds (1/100ths of a second), which is what GIF time delays are specified in. Or just use the ImageAnimator helper class, which can do all this for you:

```
// Load animated GIF
Bitmap gif = new Bitmap(@"C:\SAMPLE_ANIMATION_COPY.GIF");

void AnimationForm_Load(object sender, EventArgs e) {
  // Check whether image supports animation
  if( ImageAnimator.CanAnimate(gif) ) {
    // Subscribe to event indicating the next frame should be shown
    ImageAnimator.Animate(gif, new EventHandler(gif_FrameChanged));
  }
}

void gif_FrameChanged(object sender, EventArgs e) {
  if( this.InvokeRequired ) {
    // Transition from worker thread to UI thread
    this.BeginInvoke(
      new EventHandler(gif_FrameChanged),
      new object[] { sender, e });
  }
  else {
    // Trigger Paint event to draw next frame
    this.Invalidate();
  }
}

void AnimationForm_Paint(object sender, PaintEventArgs e) {
  // Update image's active frame
  ImageAnimator.UpdateFrames(gif);

  // Draw image's current frame
  Graphics g = e.Graphics;
  g.DrawImage(gif, this.ClientRectangle);
}
```

The ImageAnimator knows how to pull the timing information out of an image and call you back when it's time to show a new one, and that is what calling ImageAnimator.Animate does. When the event is fired, invalidating the rectangle being used to draw the animated GIF triggers the Paint event. The Paint event sets the next active frame using the ImageAnimator.UpdateFrames method and draws the active frame. Figures 4.29, 4.30, and 4.31 show an image being animated.

The only thing that's a bit tricky is that the animated event is called back on a worker thread, not on the main UI thread. Because it's not legal to make any method calls on UI objects, such as the form, from a thread other than the creator thread, we used the BeginInvoke method to transition back from the worker thread to the UI thread to make the call. This technique is discussed in gory detail in Chapter 14: Multithreaded User Interfaces.

Drawing to Images

Certain kinds of applications need to create images on-the-fly, often requiring the capability to save them to a file. The key is to create an image with

FIGURE 4.29: Sample Animation, First Frame

FIGURE 4.30: Sample Animation, Middle Frame

FIGURE 4.31: Sample Animation, Last Frame

the appropriate starting parameters, which for a Bitmap means the height, width, and pixel depth. The image is then used as the "backing store" of a Graphics object. If you're interested in getting the pixel depth from the screen itself, you can use a Graphics object when creating a Bitmap:

```
// Get current Graphics object for display
Graphics displayGraphics = this.CreateGraphics();

// Create Bitmap to draw into based on existing Graphics object
Image image = new Bitmap(rect.Width, rect.Height, displayGraphics);
```

After you have an image, you can use the Graphics FromImage method to wrap a Graphics object around it:

```
Graphics imageGraphics = Graphics.FromImage(image);
```

After you've got a Graphics object, you can draw on it as you would normally. One thing to watch out for, however, is that a Bitmap starts with all pixels set to the Transparent color. That may well be exactly what you want, but if it's not, then a quick FillRectangle across the entire area of the Bitmap will set things right.

After you've done the drawing on the Graphics object that represents the image, you can draw that image to the screen or a printer, or you can save it to a file, using the Save method of the Image class:

```
image.Save(@"c:\image.png");
```

Unless otherwise specified, the file is saved in PNG format, regardless of the extension on the file name. If you prefer to save it in another format, you can pass an instance of the ImageFormat class as an argument to the Save method. You create an instance of the ImageFormat class using the GUID (Globally Unique ID) of the format, but the ImageFormat class comes with several properties prebuilt for supported formats:

```
sealed class ImageFormat {

  // Constructors
  public ImageFormat(Guid guid);

  // Properties
  public Guid Guid { get; }
```

continues

```
public static ImageFormat Bmp { get; }
public static ImageFormat Emf { get; }
public static ImageFormat Exif { get; }
public static ImageFormat Gif { get; }
public static ImageFormat Icon { get; }
public static ImageFormat Jpeg { get; }
public static ImageFormat MemoryBmp { get; }
public static ImageFormat Png { get; }
public static ImageFormat Tiff { get; }
public static ImageFormat Wmf { get; }
}
```

As an example of creating images on-the-fly and saving them to a file, the following code builds the bitmap shown in Figure 4.32:

```
void saveButton_Click(object sender, EventArgs e) {
  Rectangle rect = new Rectangle(0, 0, 100, 100);

  // Get current graphics object for display
  using( Graphics displayGraphics = this.CreateGraphics() )

  // Create bitmap to draw into based on existing Graphics object
  using( Image image =
          new Bitmap(rect.Width, rect.Height, displayGraphics) )

  // Wrap Graphics object around image to draw into
  using( Graphics imageGraphics = Graphics.FromImage(image) ) {

    imageGraphics.FillRectangle(Brushes.Black, rect);
    StringFormat format = new StringFormat();
    format.Alignment = StringAlignment.Center;
    format.LineAlignment = StringAlignment.Center;
    imageGraphics.DrawString("Drawing to an image", ...);

    // Save created image to a file
    image.Save(@"c:\temp\image.png");
  }
}
```

FIGURE 4.32: Example of Drawing to an Image

Icons

Before I wrap up the images section, I want to mention two kinds of images for which .NET provides special care: icons and cursors. You can load a Windows icon (.ico) file into a Bitmap object, as with any of the other raster formats, but you can also load it into an Icon object. The Icon class is largely a direct wrapper class around the Win32 HICON type and is provided mainly for interoperability. Unlike the Bitmap or Metafile classes, the Icon class doesn't derive from the base Image class:

```
sealed class Icon :
  MarshalByRefObject, ISerializable, ICloneable, IDisposable {

  // Constructors
  public Icon(string fileName);
  public Icon(Icon original, Size size);
  public Icon(Icon original, int width, int height);
  public Icon(Stream stream);
  public Icon(Stream stream, int width, int height);
  public Icon(Type type, string resource);

  // Properties
  public IntPtr Handle { get; }
  public int Height { get; }
  public Size Size { get; }
  public int Width { get; }

  // Methods
  public static Icon FromHandle(IntPtr handle);
  public void Save(Stream outputStream);
  public Bitmap ToBitmap();
}
```

When setting the Icon property of a Form, for example, you'll use the Icon class, not the Bitmap class. Icons support construction from files and resources as well as from raw streams (if you want to create an icon from data in memory) and expose their Height and Width. For interoperability with Win32, Icons also support the Handle property and the FromHandle method. If you've got an Icon and you'd like to treat it as a Bitmap, you can call the ToBitmap method and the data will be copied to a new Bitmap object. After you've loaded an icon, you can draw it to a Graphics object using the DrawIcon or DrawIconUnstretched method:

```
Icon ico = new Icon("POINT10.ICO");
g.DrawIcon(ico, this.ClientRectangle); // Stretch
g.DrawIconUnstretched(ico, this.ClientRectangle); // Don't stretch
```

Several icons used by the system come prepackaged for you as properties of the SystemIcons class for your own use, as shown in Figure 4.33.

Cursors

The other Win32 graphics type that WinForms provides for is the Cursor type, which, like Icon, doesn't derive from the Image base class:

```
sealed class Cursor : IDisposable, ISerializable {
  // Constructors
  public Cursor(string fileName);
  public Cursor(IntPtr handle);
  public Cursor(Stream stream);
  public Cursor(Type type, string resource);

  // Properties
  public static Rectangle Clip { get; set; }
  public static Cursor Current { get; set; }
  public IntPtr Handle { get; }
  public static Point Position { get; set; }
  public Size Size { get; }

  // Methods
  public IntPtr CopyHandle();
  public void Draw(Graphics g, Rectangle targetRect);
  public void DrawStretched(Graphics g, Rectangle targetRect);
```

FIGURE 4.33: Icon Properties from the SystemIcons Class as Shown under Windows XP

```
  public static void Hide();
  public static void Show();
}
```

A Cursor is a graphic that represents the position of the mouse on the screen. It can take on several values based on the needs of the window currently under the cursor. For example, by default, the cursor is an arrow to indicate that it should be used to point. However, when the cursor passes over a text editing window, it often turns into an I-beam to provide for better positioning between characters.

A cursor can be loaded from a file (*.cur) or from one of the system-provided cursors in the Cursors class, as shown in Figure 4.34.

You can draw a cursor manually using the Draw or DrawStretched method of the Cursor class, but most of the time, you draw a cursor by setting it as the current cursor using the static Current property of the Cursor class. Setting the current cursor will remain in effect only during the current event handler and only when the cursor is over windows of that application. Changing the cursor won't stop another window in another application from changing it to something it finds appropriate. For

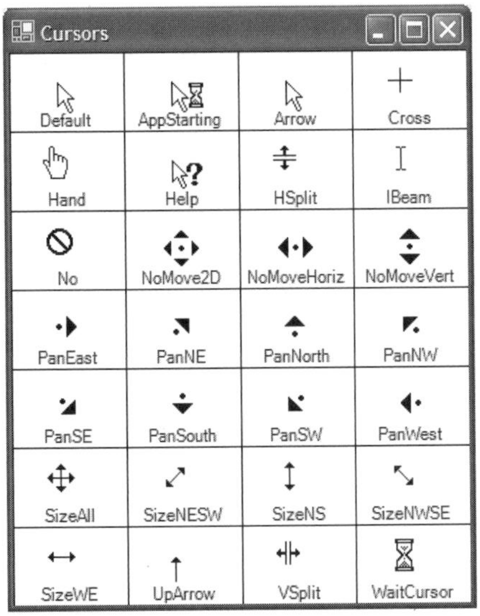

FIGURE 4.34: System Cursors from the Cursors Class

example, the following changes the application's cursor to the WaitCursor during a long operation:

```
void Form1_Click(object sender, EventArgs e) {
  try {
    // Change the cursor to indicate that we're waiting
    Cursor.Current = Cursors.WaitCursor;

    // Do something that takes a long time
    ...
  }
  finally {
    // Restore current cursor
    Cursor.Current = this.Cursor;
  }
} // Cursor restored after this event handler anyway...
```

Notice the use of the form's Cursor property to restore the current cursor after the long operation completes. Every form and every control has a Cursor property. This cursor becomes the default when the mouse passes over the window. For example, the following code sets a form's default cursor to the Cross:

```
void InitializeComponent() {
  ...
  this.Cursor = System.Windows.Forms.Cursors.Cross;
  ...
}
```

Notice the use of InitializeComponent to set the Form's cursor, indicating that this is yet another property that can be set in the Property Browser, which shows a drop-down list of all the system-provided cursors to choose from.

Where Are We?

In this chapter, we've discussed the basics of drawing, including colors, brushes, pens, shapes, paths, and images. Of course, that's not all you'll need to know about drawing in your WinForms applications and controls. Chapter 5 is dedicated to fonts and drawing strings.

5

Drawing Text

P ROBABLY THE MOST USEFUL thing to draw in any application is text. Sometimes you'll draw text yourself, and sometimes it will be drawn for you by the controls you're using. No matter who does the drawing, you often can specify the font used to draw the text, and that's what the first part of this chapter is about. The second part deals with drawing text yourself into a Graphics object or a GraphicsPath.

Fonts

A *font* is an instance of the Font class, which includes a font family, a size, and a font style. And, as you might expect, a *font family* is an instance of the FontFamily class, which is a group of typefaces that differ only in style. A *typeface* is a named collection of drawing strokes that make up the outlines of the characters, such as those you're reading right now. It's the typeface name that you're used to seeing in the "Font" menu of most programs. The *font style* constitutes the variations within a typeface, such as bold, italics, and underline. So a typeface would be "Arial," a font family would include "Arial Regular" and "Arial Bold," and a font would be "12-point Arial Bold."

Fonts can be measured in several sizes, including pixels, points, ems, and design units. A *pixel* is a point of light on a screen or a point of ink on a printer. Pixels are often packed into inches for measurement. For example, the resolution of video display adapters and printers is typically specified in *dots per inch* (dpi), where a dot is the same as a pixel. Pixels are device-dependent, so a pixel on a 72-dpi display bears no size relationship to a pixel on a 300-dpi printer.

A point, on the other hand, is 1/72nd of an inch no matter what device it's drawn on, and the Graphics object will scale appropriately as text is drawn. Converting between points and pixels requires knowing the dpi of the device you're drawing on, which is conveniently available via the Graphics.DpiY property:[1]

```
using( Graphics g = this.CreateGraphics() ) {
  // A 12-point font will be 16 pixels high on a 96-dpi monitor
  float dpi = g.DpiY;
  float points = 12f;
  float pixels = (points * dpi)/72f;
  ...
}
```

The *em* unit of measure is so named because metal typesetters used capital M as the guide against which all other letters were measured. M was used because it took up the most vertical and horizontal space. The number of points that a font is specified represents "one em" for that font.

Finally, *design units* are a font designer's way to specify a font family's dimensions no matter what the resolution of the rendering device or the size of the rendered font. For example, Arial has a height of 2,048 design units. The design units are used to scale a font family to a point size when individual strokes of the font are rendered (more on this later).

The Font class itself is shown here:

```
sealed class Font :
  MarshalByRefObject, ICloneable, ISerializable, IDisposable {

  // Constructors
  public Font(...); // Several overloads

  // Properties
  public bool Bold { get; }
```

---

1. There's also a Graphics.DpiX property, but that's used for measuring width. Points specify the height of a font.

```
public FontFamily FontFamily { get; }
public byte GdiCharSet { get; }
public bool GdiVerticalFont { get; }
public int Height { get; }
public bool Italic { get; }
public string Name { get; }
public float Size { get; }
public float SizeInPoints { get; }
public bool Strikeout { get; }
public FontStyle Style { get; }
public bool Underline { get; }
public GraphicsUnit Unit { get; }

// Methods
public static Font FromHdc(IntPtr hdc);
public static Font FromHfont(IntPtr hfont);
public static Font FromLogFont(object lf);
public static Font FromLogFont(object lf, IntPtr hdc);
public float GetHeight();
public float GetHeight(float dpi);
public float GetHeight(System.Drawing.Graphics graphics);
public IntPtr ToHfont();
public void ToLogFont(object logFont);
public void ToLogFont(object logFont, Graphics graphics);
}
```

Creating Fonts

You can create a Font object by specifying, at a minimum, the typeface and the size in points:

```
using( Font font = new Font("Arial", 12) ) { ... }
```

If you specify a font that's not available, you'll get an instance of the MS Sans Serif font in whatever size you specify. If you'd like to specify the font in a unit other than points, you can do so using an overload of the Font constructor that takes a value from the GraphicsUnit enumeration:

```
enum GraphicsUnit {
  Display, // 1/75th of an inch (1/100th of an inch for printers)
  Document, // 1/300th of an inch
  Inch, // 1 inch
  Millimeter, // 1 millimeter
  Pixel, // 1 device-dependent pixel
  Point, // 1/72nd of an inch
  World, // discussed in Chapter 6: Advanced Drawing
}
```

Except for GraphicsUnit.Pixel and GraphicsUnit.World, all the units are really just variations of a point, because they're all specified in device-independent units. Using these units, all the following specify 12-point Arial:[2]

```
// Can't use GraphicsUnit.Display for creating fonts,
// because Display varies based on where shapes are drawn
Font font1 = new Font("Arial", 12,         GraphicsUnit.Point);
Font font2 = new Font("Arial", 16,         GraphicsUnit.Pixel);
Font font3 = new Font("Arial", 0.1666667f, GraphicsUnit.Inch);
Font font4 = new Font("Arial", 50,         GraphicsUnit.Document);
Font font5 = new Font("Arial", 4.233334f,  GraphicsUnit.Millimeter);
```

If you'd like to specify a style other than regular, you can do so by passing a combination of the values from the FontStyle enumeration:

```
enum FontStyle {
  Bold,
  Italic,
  Regular, // default
  Strikeout,
  Underline,
}
```

For example, the following will create Arial Bold Italic:

```
Font font =
  new Font("Arial", 12, FontStyle.Bold | FontStyle.Italic);
```

If the font family you're specifying with the typeface argument to the Font constructor doesn't support the styles you specify, a run-time exception will be thrown.

If you've got a font but you don't like the style, you can create a Font based on another Font. This is handy when you'd like to base a new font on an existing font but need to make a minor adjustment:

```
Font font =
  new Font(this.Font, FontStyle.Bold | FontStyle.Italic);
```

---

2. A dpi of 96 is assumed, which yields 16 pixels for a 12-point font.

Font Families

When creating a font, you use the typeface name to retrieve a font family from the list of fonts currently installed on the system. The typeface name is passed to the constructor of the FontFamily class. The FontFamily class is shown here:

```
sealed class FontFamily : MarshalByRefObject, IDisposable {
  // Constructors
  public FontFamily(GenericFontFamilies genericFamily);
  public FontFamily(string name);
  public FontFamily(string name, FontCollection fontCollection);

  // Properties
  public static FontFamily[] Families { get; }
  public static FontFamily GenericMonospace { get; }
  public static FontFamily GenericSansSerif { get; }
  public static FontFamily GenericSerif { get; }
  public string Name { get; }

  // Methods
  public int GetCellAscent(FontStyle style);
  public int GetCellDescent(FontStyle style);
  public int GetEmHeight(FontStyle style);
  public static FontFamily[] GetFamilies(Graphics graphics);
  public int GetLineSpacing(FontStyle style);
  public string GetName(int language);
  public bool IsStyleAvailable(FontStyle style);
}
```

Creating a Font from a FontFamily looks like this:

```
FontFamily family = new FontFamily("Arial");
Font font = new Font(family, 12, FontStyle.Bold | FontStyle.Italic);
```

Creating a Font from a FontFamily object is useful if you'd like to pick a font family based on general characteristics instead of a specific typeface name. A FontFamily can be constructed with one of the GenericFontFamilies enumeration values:

```
enum GenericFontFamilies {
  Monospace, // Courier New
  SansSerif, // Microsoft Sans Serif
  Serif, // Times New Roman
}
```

Constructing a FontFamily using a value from GenericFontFamilies is useful if you'd like to avoid the risk that a more specific font won't be available on the system. In fact, the FontFamily class even provides properties that you can use directly for each of these FontFamilies:

```
// The hard way
Font font1 = new Font(new FontFamily(GenericFontFamilies.Serif), 12);

// The easy way
Font font2 = new Font(FontFamily.GenericMonospace, 12);
```

If, instead of hard-coding a font family (even a generic one), you'd like to let users pick their favorite, you need to present them a UI that lets them pick from the font families they have installed. The FontFamily class provides the Families property for determining the currently installed font families:

```
foreach( FontFamily family in FontFamily.Families ) {
  // Can filter based on available styles
  if( !family.IsStyleAvailable(FontStyle.Bold) ) continue;

  familiesListBox.Items.Add(family.Name);
}
```

You can also construct a Font object from an HDC, an HFONT, or a LOGFONT, all of which are features that support interoperability with Win32.

Font Characteristics

After you've got a Font object, you can interrogate it for all kinds of properties, such as its family, its name (which will be the same as the family name), and a couple of GDI properties for Win32 interoperability. Most importantly, you'll probably want to know about a font's style, using either the Style property of type FontStyle or using individual properties:

```
// The hard way
bool bold1 = (this.Font.Style & FontStyle.Bold) == FontStyle.Bold;

// The easy way
bool bold2 = this.Font.Bold;
```

Another important characteristic of a Font is its dimensions. The width of a character in a specific font varies from character to character, unless you've used a *monospace* font such as Courier New, in which all characters are padded as necessary so that they're the same width. The Graphics object provides the MeasureString method for measuring the maximum size of a string of characters of a specific font:

```
using( Graphics g = this.CreateGraphics() ) {

  SizeF size = g.MeasureString("Howdy", this.Font);
  float length = size.Width;
  ...
}
```

When it's called this way, the size returned from MeasureString assumes that the string is clipped to a single line; this means that the width will vary with the width of the string, but the height will be a constant.[3] Because the Graphics object can wrap multiline strings to a rectangle, you can also measure the rectangle needed for a multiline string. You do this by calling the MeasureString method and specifying a maximum layout rectangle for the string to live in:

```
SizeF layoutArea = this.ClientRectangle.Size;
// New line character '\n' will force text to next line
string s = "a string that will\ntake at least two lines";
SizeF size = g.MeasureString(s, this.Font, layoutArea);
```

The Width property returned in the SizeF object is the width of the longest wrapped line, and the Height is the number of lines needed to show the string multiplied by the height of the font (up to the maximum height specified in the layout area). The height used as the multiplier isn't the height of the font as specified. For example, 12 points would be 16 pixels at 96 dpi, but that's not the value that's used. Instead, the height is approximately 115% of that, or about 18.4 pixels for a 12-point font at 96 dpi. This expanded value is exposed from the Font.GetHeight method and is meant to maximize readability when lines of text are drawn one after another. For example, if you wanted to handle wrapping yourself, you could lay out

---

3. Although individual character heights vary, the vertical space reserved for them does not.

text one line at a time, incrementing the y value by the result of Font. GetHeight:

```
foreach( string line in multiline.Split('\n') ) {
  float width = manualPanel.ClientRectangle.Width;
  float height = manualPanel.ClientRectangle.Height - y;
  RectangleF layoutRect = new RectangleF(0, y, width, height);

  // Turn off auto-wrapping (we're doing it manually)
  StringFormat format = new StringFormat(StringFormatFlags.NoWrap);
  g.DrawString(line, this.Font, Brushes.Black, layoutRect, format);

  . . .

  // Get ready for the next line
  y += this.Font.GetHeight(g);
}
```

In this code, we split the string into multiple lines for embedded new line characters, just as DrawString does when it does the wrapping for us. We also set up a StringFormat (more about that later) that turns off wrapping; otherwise, DrawString will wrap at word boundaries for us. After we draw the string at our chosen rectangle, we increment y by the result of Font.GetHeight so that the next line of text is far enough below the text we just drew to make it pleasing to read. Figure 5.1 shows what DrawString would do with a multiline string automatically, and what our manual code does.

In addition to the strings, Figure 5.1 shows the rectangles obtained by measuring each string: one rectangle when DrawString wraps the text for us, one rectangle per line when we do it ourselves. Notice also that the rectangle produced by MeasureString is a bit bigger than it needs to be to draw

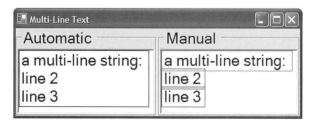

FIGURE 5.1: Automatic Word-Wrap Performed by DrawString Compared with Manual Word-Wrap Using Font.GetHeight (See Plate 19)

the text. This is especially evident in the overlapping rectangles shown on the manual side. MeasureString is guaranteed to produce a size that's big enough to hold the string but sometimes will produce a size that's larger than it needs to be to meet that guarantee.

Font Height

While we're on the subject of font height, it turns out that there are a lot of ways to measure the height of a font. The Font class provides not only the GetHeight method[4] but also the Size property, which is the base size provided in the units passed to the Font object's constructor (the GraphicsUnit value specified at construction time is available via the Font's Unit property). As I mentioned, the height of a font is determined from the base size. The height of the font is further broken down into three parts called *cell ascent*, *cell descent*, and *leading* (so named because typesetting used to be done with lead). Two of these three measures are available in design units from the FontFamily class (available via the Font's FontFamily property) and are shown in Figure 5.2. Together, these three values make up the line spacing, which is also provided as a property on the FontFamily and is used to calculate the font's height and leading (leading isn't available directly).

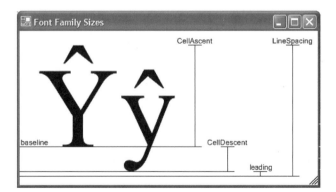

FIGURE 5.2: The Parts of a Font Family's Height

---

4. The Font also provides a Height property, but it should be avoided in favor of the Get-Height method. The GetHeight method scales to a specified Graphics object, whereas the Height property scales only to the current video adapter's dpi, making it pretty worthless for anything except the nontransformed video adapter.

The line spacing is expressed in design units but is used at run time to determine the result of calling Font.GetHeight. The magic of the conversion between design units and pixels is managed by one more measure available from the FontFamily class: the em height. The *em height* is a logical value but is equivalent to the font's size in points, so scaling between design units and pixels is performed using the proportion between the font's size and the font family's em height. For example, the scaling factor between Arial's em height (2,048) and its 12-point pixel height (16 at 96 dpi) is 128. Dividing Arial's line spacing (2,355) by 128 yields 18.39844, which is the same as the result of calling GetHeight on 12-point Arial at 96 dpi. Table 5.1 shows the various measures of font and font family height.

TABLE 5.1: Font and FontFamily Sizes (Sample Font Is Arial 12 Point at 96 dpi)

Measure	Units	Example	Description
FontFamily.GetEmHeight	Design Units	2,048	Base size, equivalent to Size
FontFamily.GetCellAscent	Design Units	1,854	Height above base line
FontFamily.GetCellDescent	Design Units	434	Height below base line
FontFamily.GetLineSpacing	Design Units	2,355	CellAscent + CellDescent + Leading, normally about 115% of EmHeight
Leading	Design Units	67	Extra space below bottom of CellDescent for readability, not exposed by any property
Font.Size	GraphicsUnit passed to Font ctor (defaults to Point)	16 pixels	Base size, equivalent to EmHeight

TABLE 5.1: Font and FontFamily Sizes (Sample Font Is Arial 12 Point at 96 dpi) (continued)

Measure	Units	Example	Description
Font.SizeInPoints	Points	12 points	Base size in points, equivalent to Size and EmHeight
Font.GetHeight	Pixels	18.39844	Equivalent to LineSpacing scaled to either Graphics object or dpi
Font.Height	Pixels	19	Equivalent to LineSpacing scaled to system dpi and rounded to next-highest integer value
Scaling Factor	Design Unit or Pixels	128	Used to convert design units to physical or logical values for rendering

Strings

Of course, deciding on a font is only half the fun. The real action is drawing strings after the font's been picked. For that, you use the DrawString method of the Graphics object:

```
using( Font font = new Font("Arial", 12) ) {
  // This will wrap at new line characters
  g.DrawString("line 1\nline 2", font, Brushes.Black, 10, 10);
}
```

The DrawString method takes, at a minimum, a string, a font, a brush to fill in the font characters, and a point. DrawString starts the drawing at the point and keeps going until it hits the edges of the region in the Graphics object. This includes translating new line characters as appropriate but does not include wrapping at word boundaries. To get the wrapping, you specify a layout rectangle:

```
using( Font font = new Font("Arial", 12) ) {
  // This will automatically wrap long lines and
  // it will wrap at new line characters
  g.DrawString("a long string...", font, Brushes.Black,
    this.ClientRectangle);
}
```

Formatting

If you'd like to turn off wrapping or set other formatting options, you can do so with an instance of the StringFormat class:

```
sealed class StringFormat :
  MarshalByRefObject, ICloneable, IDisposable {
  // Constructors
  public StringFormat(...); // various overloads

  // Properties
  public StringAlignment Alignment { get; set; }
  public int DigitSubstitutionLanguage { get; }
  public StringDigitSubstitute DigitSubstitutionMethod { get; }
  public StringFormatFlags FormatFlags { get; set; }
  public static StringFormat GenericDefault { get; }
  public static StringFormat GenericTypographic { get; }
  public HotkeyPrefix HotkeyPrefix { get; set; }
  public StringAlignment LineAlignment { get; set; }
  public StringTrimming Trimming { get; set; }

  // Methods
  public float[] GetTabStops(ref Single firstTabOffset);
  public void
    SetDigitSubstitution(
      int language, StringDigitSubstitute substitute);
  public void SetMeasurableCharacterRanges(CharacterRange[] ranges);
  public void SetTabStops(float firstTabOffset, float[] tabStops);
}
```

A StringFormat object lets you set all kinds of interesting text characteristics, such as the tab stops and the alignment (vertically and horizontally) as well as whether to wrap:

```
// Turn off auto-wrapping
StringFormat format = new StringFormat(StringFormatFlags.NoWrap);
g.DrawString("...", font, brush, rect, format);
```

The StringFormatFlags enumeration provides a number of options:

```
enum StringFormatFlags {
  0, // No flags (default)
  DirectionRightToLeft, // Draw text right-to-left
  DirectionVertical, // Draw text up-to-down
  DisplayFormatControl, // Show format control character glyphs
  FitBlackBox, // Keep all glyphs inside layout rectangle
  LineLimit, // Show only whole lines
  MeasureTrailingSpaces, // MeasureString includes trailing spaces
  NoClip, // Don't clip text partially outside layout rectangle
  NoFontFallback, // Don't fall back for characters missing from Font
  NoWrap, // Don't interpret \n or \t (implied when no rect provided)
}
```

Note that a *glyph* is a symbol that conveys some kind of information. For example, the X in the upper-right corner of a window is a glyph that indicates that the window can be closed.

You can combine and set one or more StringFormatFlags on a String-Format object by using either the StringFormat constructor or the Format-Flags property. For example, the following draws text down-to-up and disables automatic wrapping:

```
StringFormat format = new StringFormat();
format.FormatFlags =
  StringFormatFlags.DirectionVertical | StringFormatFlags.NoWrap;
g.DrawString("...", font, brush, rect, format);
```

When text doesn't fit into the allotted space, you have a few options. If the string is too tall, you have three choices. You can clip to the layout rectangle, letting partial lines show, which is the default. You can show only complete lines if they fit inside the layout rectangle, which is the behavior you get with StringFormatFlags.LineLimit. Finally, you can decide to show complete lines even if they lie outside the layout rectangle, which is what you get with StringFormatFlags.NoClip. Combining LineLimit with NoClip is not useful, because the behavior is the same as LineLimit. The three options are shown in Figure 5.3.

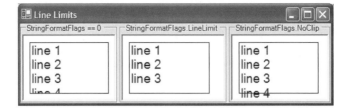

FIGURE 5.3: The Effect of the LineLimit StringFormatFlags Value

String Trimming

If, on the other hand, the string is too long, you can decide what happens by setting the Trimming property of the StringFormat object to one of the StringTrimming enumeration values:

```
enum StringTrimming {
  None, // No trimming (acts like Word for single lines)
  Character, // Trim to nearest character (the default)
  EllipsisCharacter, // Trim to nearest character and show ellipsis
  Word, // Trim to nearest word
  EllipsisWord, // Trim to nearest word and show ellipsis
  EllipsisPath, // Trim file path by putting ellipsis in the middle
}
```

Figure 5.4 shows the results of applying the StringTrimming values when you draw a string.

Tab Stops

Something else of interest in Figure 5.4 is the use of tabs to line up the string, instead of forcing the text to be in a monospaced font and lining up

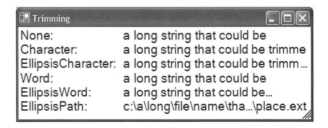

FIGURE 5.4: Examples of the StringTrimming Enumeration

the text with spaces. Tabs are set using the SetTabStops method of the StringFormat class:

```
StringFormat format = new StringFormat();
SizeF size =
  g.MeasureString(
    StringTrimming.EllipsisCharacter.ToString(), this.Font);
format.SetTabStops(0, new float[] { size.Width + 10 });
```

This call to SetTabStops sets a single tab stop to be the width of the longest string, plus a pleasing amount of leading. When tab stops are specified and when StringFormatFlags.NoWrap is absent from the StringFormat object, then the tab character causes the characters that follow to be drawn starting at the tab stop offset (unless the string has already passed that point). If the StringFormat object has not been given any tab stops, then the tab character will not be interpreted. If DrawString is called without any StringFormat object at all, it will build one internally that defaults to four times the size of the font; for example, a 12-point font will have tab stops every 48 points.

There are several ways to specify tab stops logically. For example, imagine that you'd like a tab stop at every 48 units, as DrawString does by default when no StringFormat is provided. You might also imagine that you'd like to specify only a certain number of tab stops at specific locations. Finally, you might imagine that you'd like to have an array of tab stops, but use an offset determined at run time to calculate the actual tab stops. All these techniques are supported, but you must use a single SetTabStops method, and that makes things somewhat unintuitive.

The array of floating point values passed to set the tab stops represents the spaces between successive tab stops. The first value in this array is added to the first argument to SetTabStops to get the first tab stop, and each successive value is added to the preceding value to get the next tab stop. Finally, when more tabs are found than tab stops, the last value of the array is added repeatedly to get successive tab stops. Table 5.2 shows various arguments passed to SetTabStops and the resultant offsets for each stop.

You may have noticed the GetTabStops method on the StringFormat class, but unfortunately it hands back only the same tab stop settings handed

TABLE 5.2: Sample Arguments to SetTabStop and Resultant Tab Stops

Arguments to SetTabStop	Resultant Tab Stops	Description
0, { 100 }	100, 200, 300, ...	Tab stops every 100 units
0, { 100, 0 }	100, 100, 100, ...	One tab stop at 100 units
0, { 50, 75, 100 }	50, 125, 225, 325, 425, ...	A tab stop at 50, 125, and 225 and then one every 100 units
0, { 50, 75, 100, 0 }	50, 125, 225, 225, 225, ...	A tab stop at 50, 125, and 225 units
50, { 100 }	150, 250, 350, ...	One tab stop at 150 units and then one every 100 units
50, { 100, 0 }	150, 150, 150, ...	One tab stop at 150 units
50, { 50, 75, 100 }	100, 175, 275, 375, 475, ...	A tab stop at 100, 175, and 275 and then one every 100 units
50, { 50, 75, 100, 0 }	100, 175, 275, 275, 275, ...	A tab stop at 100, 175, and 275 units

to SetTabStops in the first place. It would have been handy to get back the resultant tab stops so that you could make sure you've set them correctly.

Hotkey Prefixes

In addition to new lines and tab characters, DrawString can substitute other characters, including ampersands and digits. Substitution of ampersands is a convenience for specifying Windows hotkeys for menu items and form fields. For example, by default the string "&File" will be output as "&File" (but without the quotation marks). However, you can specify that the ampersand be dropped or that the next character be underlined, as governed by the HotkeyPrefix enumeration from the System.Drawing.Text namespace:

```
enum HotkeyPrefix {
  Hide,  // Drop all & characters
  None,  // Show all & characters (default)
  Show,  // Drop & characters and underline next character
}
```

For example, the following translates "&File" into "<u>F</u>ile" (no quotation marks) as the string is drawn:

```
StringFormat format = new StringFormat();
format.HotkeyPrefix = HotkeyPrefix.Show;
g.DrawString("&File", font, brush, rect, format);
```

Digit Substitution

One other substitution that DrawString can perform is for digits. Most languages have adopted the Arabic digits (0, 1, 2, 3, …) when representing numbers, but some also have traditional representations. Which representation to show is governed by the method and language as determined by a call to the SetDigitSubstitution method on the StringFormat class:

```
CultureInfo culture = new CultureInfo("th-TH"); // Thailand Thai
StringFormat format = new StringFormat();
format.SetDigitSubstitution(
  culture.LCID, StringDigitSubstitute.Traditional);
g.DrawString("0 1 2...", font, brush, rect, format);
```

The substitution method is governed by the StringDigitSubstitute (and can be discovered with the DigitSubstitutionMethod on the StringFormat class), as shown in Figure 5.5.

The integer language identifier comes from the LCID (language and culture ID) of an instance of the CultureInfo class. It can be constructed with a two-part name: a two-letter country code followed by a two-letter

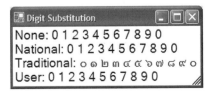

FIGURE 5.5: StringDigitSubstitute Values as Applied to Thailand Thai

language code,[5] separated by a hyphen. The methods applied to the national and traditional languages of Thailand are shown in Figure 5.5.

Alignment

In addition to substitution, tabs, wrapping, and clipping, you can use StringFormat to set text alignment (both horizontally and vertically) by setting the Alignment and LineAlignment properties, respectively, using one of the StringAlignment enumeration values:

```
enum StringAlignment {
  Center,
  Near, // Depends on right-to-left setting
  Far, // Depends on right-to-left setting
}
```

Notice that instead of Left and Right alignment, the StringAlignment enumeration values are Near and Far and depend on whether the Right-ToLeft string format flag is specified. The following centers text in a rectangle both horizontally and vertically:

```
format.Alignment = StringAlignment.Center; // Center horizontally
format.LineAlignment = StringAlignment.Center; // Center vertically
```

Two combinations on a StringFormat object are so commonly needed that they're set up for you and are exposed via the GenericDefault and GenericTypographic properties of the StringFormat class. The Generic-Default StringFormat object is what you get when you create a new String-Format object, so it saves you the trouble if that's all you're after. The GenericTypographic StringFormat object is useful for showing text as text, not as part of drawing a UI element. The properties you get from each are shown in Table 5.3.

Antialiasing

All the strings I've shown in the sample figures in this section have been nice and smooth. That's because I'm using Windows XP with ClearType turned on. If I turn that off, I go back to the old, blocky way of looking at

---

5. The country code and language codes are defined by ISO standards.

TABLE 5.3: The Settings of the Built-in StringFormat Classes

GenericDefault	GenericTypographic
StringFormatFlags = 0	StringFormatFlags = LineLimit, NoClip
Alignment = Near	Alignment = Near
LineAlignment = Near	LineAlignment = Near
DigitSubstitutionMethod = User	DigitSubstitutionMethod = User
HotkeyPrefix = None	HotkeyPrefix = None
No tab stops	No tab stops
Trimming = Character	Trimming = None

things. However, when I'm drawing strings, I don't have to settle for what the user specifies. I can set the TextRenderingHint property of the Graphics object before I draw a string to one of the TextRenderingHint enumeration values, as shown in Figure 5.6.

In this case, SystemDefault shows what text looks like without any smoothing effects. The SingleBitPerPixel setting does just what it says, although it's clearly not useful for anything that needs to look decent. The AntiAlias and ClearType settings are two different algorithms for smoothing that are meant to make the text look good: one for any monitor, and one specifically for LCD displays. The grid fit versions of the algorithms use extra hints to improve the appearance, as you can see from the examples.

FIGURE 5.6: Examples of the TextRenderingHint Enumeration

Of course, as the quality improves, the rendering time also increases, and that's why you can set the option as appropriate for your application. Furthermore, when drawing using one of the antialiasing algorithms, you can adjust the TextContrast property of a Graphics object. The contrast ranges from 0 to 12, where 0 is the most contrast and 12 is the least, with 4 being the default. The contrast makes fonts at smaller point sizes stand out more against the background.

Strings and Paths

One more string-drawing trick that might interest you is the ability to add strings to graphics paths. Because everything that's added to a path has both an outline and an interior that can be drawn separately, you can add strings to a path to achieve outline effects, as shown in Figure 5.7:

```
// Need to pass in DPI = 100 for GraphicsUnit == Display
GraphicsPath GetStringPath(
  string s,
  float dpi,
  RectangleF rect,
  Font font,
  StringFormat format) {

  GraphicsPath path = new GraphicsPath();
  // Convert font size into appropriate coordinates
  float emSize = dpi * font.SizeInPoints / 72;
  path.AddString(
    s, font.FontFamily, (int)font.Style, emSize, rect, format);
  return path;
}

void OutlineFontsForm_Paint(object sender, PaintEventArgs e) {
  Graphics g = e.Graphics;
  string s = "Outline";
```

FIGURE 5.7: Using a GraphicsPath Object to Simulate an Outline-Only Font

```
RectangleF rect = this.ClientRectangle;
Font font = this.Font;
StringFormat format = StringFormat.GenericTypographic;
float dpi = g.DpiY;
using( GraphicsPath path =
        GetStringPath(s, dpi, rect, font, format) ) {
  g.DrawPath(Pens.Black, path);
}

}
```

Notice that even though I have ClearType on and the TextRendering-Hint set to SystemDefault, the outline path was not drawn smoothly. As soon as the string was used to create a path, it stopped being text and became a shape, which is drawn smoothly or not based on the Smoothing-Mode property. Also, you'll notice that I showed an example of a really big font (72-point). The string-as-path trick doesn't work very well at lower resolutions because of the translation of font family characters into a series of lines and curves.

Even more interesting uses of paths are available when you apply transforms, which you'll read about in Chapter 6: Advanced Drawing.

Where Are We?

We've finished up the basics of drawing that we started in Chapter 4. In Chapter 6, we talk about advanced drawing topics, such as coordinate systems, regions, and transformations.

■ 6 ■
Advanced Drawing

C HAPTERS 4 AND 5 COVER the basics of drawing, including colors, pens, brushes, shapes, paths, images, fonts, and string drawing. This chapter takes a look at advanced topics such as page units, world transforms, regions, and optimization techniques. And as if that weren't enough, Chapter 7 wraps up the tour of the System.Drawing namespace with a look at printing.

Page Units

So far, we've been concentrating on drawing to the screen. By default, if you're drawing in the Paint event handler, you're drawing in units of pixels. Even if you create a graphics object from a form using Form.Create-Graphics, you'll be drawing in units of pixels. This is handy because the units of the user interface elements, such as the client rectangle and the position and sizes of the controls, are all in pixels.

Pixels translate into real-world coordinates based on system settings for Normal or Small versus Large or Custom fonts, the resolution at which the display adapter is running, and the size of the monitor. Taking all that into account, only some of which is available programmatically, it would be remarkably difficult to display physically correct sizes on a monitor—for example, the ruler you see at the top of a word processing program. Luckily, because you can usually adjust all this using various systemwide and application-specific settings, people generally size things so that they are comfortable, and the real-world sizes are not so important. That is, they're not important until you need to output to a specific physical size.

For example, it's not important that the ruler at the top of the document I'm typing this sentence into is currently showing an inch as $1\frac{9}{16}$ inches.[1] What is important is the proportion of the dimensions of each line to the units shown as "inches" as compared to the width of each line as I type. The principle of WYSIWYG (What You See Is What You Get) dictates that I should be able to print something very similar to what I'm seeing on the screen. When my word processing program shows a line wrapping at a certain word when I get close to the 6.5-inch area inside my margins (standard 8.5-inch wide paper with a 1-inch margin on each side), I want that same wrap to happen at the same word when I print the document. To make that happen, we need to be able to write a program that can wrap text at units other than pixels, as shown in Figure 6.1.

Figure 6.1 shows a ruler marked off in half-inch increments and text wrapped to a right margin of 6.5 inches. We can accomplish this by using the following function to manually convert coordinates and sizes to inches:

```
float InchesToPixels(float inches) {
  using( Graphics g = this.CreateGraphics() ) {
    return inches * g.DpiX;
  }
}
```

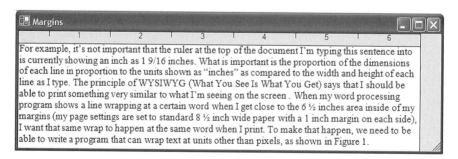

FIGURE 6.1: Manually Drawing in Inches

---

1. I measured it with a ruler from the physical world.

This function is used to calculate the width of the ruler, the half-inch tick marks, and the width of the text box. For example, the code that draws the outline of the ruler looks like this:

```
using( Font rulerFont = new Font("MS Sans Serif", 8.25f) ) {
  int pixelsPerInch = 72;

  // Inches
  float rulerFontHeight = rulerFont.SizeInPoints/pixelsPerInch;

  // Specify units in inches
  RectangleF rulerRect =
    new RectangleF(
    0, 0,
    6.5f, rulerFontHeight * 1.5f);

  // Draw in pixels
  g.DrawRectangle(
    Pens.Black,
    InchesToPixels(rulerRect.X), InchesToPixels(rulerRect.Y),
    InchesToPixels(rulerRect.Width), InchesToPixels(rulerRect.Height));
  ...
}
```

The conversion from inches to pixels is necessary because the units of the Graphics object passed to the Paint event are pixels, which represent the *device units* for the display adapter. All units eventually need to be translated to device units for rendering, but this doesn't mean that you need to specify drawing in device units. Instead, the Graphics object is drawing using *page units*, which default to pixels in the Paint event but don't need to stay that way. The PageUnit and PageScale properties of the Graphics object allow you to specify different units in which to draw:

```
// Set page units and scale
g.PageUnit = GraphicsUnit.Inch;
g.PageScale = 1; // 1 unit is 1 inch

using( Font rulerFont = new Font("MS Sans Serif", 8.25f) )
using( Pen blackPen = new Pen(Color.Black, 0) ) {
  // Inches
  float rulerFontHeight = rulerFont.GetHeight(g);

  // Specify units in inches
  RectangleF rulerRect =
    new RectangleF(
```

continues

```
      0, 0,
      6.5f, rulerFontHeight * 1.5f);

  // Draw in inches
  g.DrawRectangle(
    blackPen,
    rulerRect.X, rulerRect.Y,
    rulerRect.Width, rulerRect.Height);
  . . .
}
```

Before the code does any drawing, the first thing it does is to set the page unit for the graphics object to GraphicsUnit.Inch[2] and the page scale to 1, which will turn every one unit, whether it's specified for a position or a size, into 1 inch. Notice that we're using floating point numbers to enable fractional inches; the floating point numbers will be converted to device units by the Graphics object. The PageUnit property can be any value from the GraphicsUnit enumeration, so units can be in points or millimeters as well as pixels or inches. The PageScale can be a floating point number, so if we had wanted to specify a scale of 0.1 when specifying a PageUnit of Inch, then 1 unit would equal 0.1 inch, and 10 units would equal 1 inch.

Note the use of a new black pen, in spite of the presence of the Pens.Black pen that was used in the earlier sample. All the default pens default to 1 unit in width. When the unit was pixels, that was fine, but when the unit is inches, a 1-unit pen became 1 inch wide. Pens are specified in units that are interpreted when the pen is used. To avoid having a very wide pen, the code specifies 0 for the width of the pen, and that causes the pen to be 1 device unit wide no matter what the page unit is currently set to.

Also note that the Font object is not affected by the page units. Instead, recall from Chapter 5: Drawing Text that Fonts are specified using a GraphicsUnit argument passed to the constructor, and they default to GraphicsUnit.Point. Finally, notice that the code uses the GetHeight method of the Font class, passing the Graphics object. Unlike the Height property, the GetHeight method is scaled appropriately to the current units of the Graphics object.

---

2. Recall the GraphicsUnit enumeration from Chapter 4: Drawing Basics.

Converting Pixels to Page Units

If a method doesn't take a Graphics object as an argument, then it won't be affected by the page units. For example, the ClientRectangle of the form or control being drawn is always specified in pixels, making some consideration necessary when units other than pixels are being used. To convert back and forth between device and page units, the Graphics object provides the TransformPoints method:

```
using( Graphics g = this.CreateGraphics() ) {
  // Set page unit to inches
  g.PageUnit = GraphicsUnit.Inch;
  g.PageScale = 1;
  PointF[] bottomRight =
    new PointF[] {
      new PointF(this.ClientSize.Width, this.ClientSize.Height)
    };

  // Convert client size to inches from pixels
  g.TransformPoints(
    CoordinateSpace.Page, CoordinateSpace.Device, bottomRight);
  ...
}
```

The TransformPoints method can convert between any types of coordinates from the CoordinateSpace enumeration (from the System. Drawing.Drawing2D namespace). This code converts to page units (set to inches in this example) from device units (also known as pixels). The CoordinateSpace enumeration has the following values:

```
enum CoordinateSpace {
  Device,
  Page,
  World,
}
```

The value we haven't yet discussed is CoordinateSpace.World, which is a whole other world of coordinates (if you'll excuse the pun).

Transforms

Page units are useful for specifying things conveniently and letting the Graphics object sort it out, but there are all kinds of effects that can't be achieved with such a simple transform. A *transform* is a mathematical function by which units are specified and then transformed into other units. So far, we've talked about transforming from page units to device units, but a more general-purpose transformation facility is provided via the Transform property of the Graphics object, which is an instance of the Matrix class from the System.Drawing.Drawing2D namespace:

```
sealed class Matrix : MarshalByRefObject, IDisposable {
  // Constructors
  public Matrix(...); // various overloads

  // Properties
  public float[] Elements { get; }
  public bool IsIdentity { get; }
  public bool IsInvertible { get; }
  public float OffsetX { get; }
  public float OffsetY { get; }

  // Methods
  public void Invert();
  public void Multiply(...);
  public void Reset();
  public void Rotate(...);
  public void RotateAt(...);
  public void Scale(...);
  public void Shear(...);
  public void TransformPoints(...);
  public void TransformVectors(...);
  public void Translate(...);
  public void VectorTransformPoints(Point[] pts);
}
```

The Matrix class provides an implementation of a 3×3 mathematical *matrix*, which is a rectangular array of numbers. The specifics of what make up a matrix in math are beyond the scope of this book, but the Matrix class provides all kinds of interesting methods that let you use a matrix without doing any of the math.[3]

---

3. Of course, as with all technology, understanding the underlying principles is always helpful. Martin Heller, my series editor, recommends *Introduction to Computer Graphics*, by James D. Foley, Andries Van Dam, and Steven K. Feiner (Addison-Wesley, 1993), for the details of matrix math as related to graphics programming.

The graphics transformation matrix is used to transform *world coordinates*, which is what units involved with graphics operations are really specified in. Graphical units are passed as world coordinates, transformed by the transformation matrix into page units, and finally transformed again from page units to display units. As you've seen, the default page units for the screen are pixels, and that's why no page unit conversion happens without our changing the page unit or the scale or both. Similarly, by default, the transformation matrix is the *identity matrix*, which means that it doesn't actually do any conversions.

Scaling

Using an instance of a Matrix object instead of page units, we could perform the simple scaling we did in the preceding example:

```
// Set units to inches using a transform
Matrix matrix = new Matrix();
matrix.Scale(g.DpiX, g.DpiY);
g.Transform = matrix;

using( Font rulerFont = new Font("MS Sans Serif", 8.25f / g.DpiY) )
using( Pen blackPen = new Pen(Color.Black, 0) ) {
  float rulerFontHeight = rulerFont.GetHeight(g); // Inches
  // Specify units in inches
  RectangleF rulerRect =
    new RectangleF(
    0, 0,
    6.5f, rulerFontHeight * 1.5f);
  // Draw in inches
  g.DrawRectangle(
    blackPen,
    rulerRect.X, rulerRect.Y,
    rulerRect.Width, rulerRect.Height);
  ...
}
```

This code creates a new instance of the Matrix class, which defaults to the identity matrix. Instead of directly manipulating the underlying 3×3 matrix numbers, the code uses the Scale method to put the numbers in the right place to scale from inches to pixels using the dpi settings for the current Graphics object. This transformation is exactly the same result that we got by setting the page unit to inches and the page scale to 1, except for one detail: the font. Although the page unit and scale do not affect the size of fonts, the current transform affects everything, including fonts. This is why the point size being passed to the Font's constructor in the sample code is first scaled back by the current dpi setting, causing it to come out right after the transformation has occurred. I'd show you the result of using the transform instead of page units, but because it looks just like Figure 6.1, it'd be pretty boring.

Scaling Fonts

The fact that the world transform works with fonts as well as everything else makes scaling fonts an interesting use of the world transform all by itself. Usually, fonts are specified by height only, but using a transforms allows a font's height and width to be adjusted independently of each other, as shown in Figure 6.2.

Notice that scaling can even be used in the negative direction, as shown on the far right of Figure 6.2, although you'll want to make sure you specify the rectangle appropriately:

```
Matrix matrix = new Matrix();
matrix.Scale(-1, -1);
g.Transform = matrix;
g.DrawString("Scale(-1, -1)", this.Font, Brushes.Black,
  new RectangleF(-x - width, -y - height, width, height), format);
```

Because scaling by –1 in both dimensions causes all coordinates to be multiplied by –1, to get a rectangle at the appropriate place in the window requires negative coordinates. Notice that the width and height are still positive, however, because a rectangle needs positive dimensions to have positive area.

FIGURE 6.2: Scaling Font Height Independently of Font Width

Rotation

Scaling by a negative amount can look very much like rotation, but only in a limited way. Luckily, matrices support rotation directly, as in this code sample, which draws a line rotated along a number of degrees (as shown in Figure 6.3):

```
for( int i = 0; i <= 90; i += 10 ) {
  Matrix matrix = new Matrix();
  matrix.Rotate(i);
  g.Transform = matrix;
  g.DrawLine(Pens.Black, 0, 0, 250, 0);
  g.DrawString(
    i.ToString(), this.Font, Brushes.Black, textRect, format);
}
```

Notice that rotation takes place starting to the right horizontally and proceeding clockwise. Both shapes and text are rotated, as would anything else drawn into the rotated graphics object.

Rotate works well if you're rotating around graphical elements with origins at (0, 0), but if you're drawing multiple lines originating at a different origin, the results may prove unintuitive (although mathematically sound), as shown in Figure 6.4.

To rotate more intuitively around a point other than (0, 0), use the RotateAt method (as shown in Figure 6.5):

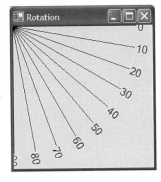

FIGURE 6.3: Line from (0, 0) to (250, 0) Rotated by Degrees 0–90

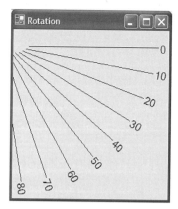

FIGURE 6.4: Line from (25, 25) to (275, 25) Rotated by Degrees 0–90

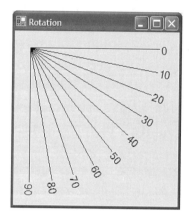

FIGURE 6.5: Line from (25, 25) to (275, 25) Rotated by Degrees 0–90 at (25, 25)

```
for( int i = 0; i <= 90; i += 10 ) {
  Matrix matrix = new Matrix();
  matrix.RotateAt(i, new PointF(25, 25));
  g.Transform = matrix;
  g.DrawLine(Pens.Black, 25, 25, 275, 25);
  g.DrawString(
    i.ToString(), this.Font, Brushes.Black, textRect, format);
}
```

Translation

Instead of moving our shapes relative to the origin, as we did when drawing the lines, it's often handy to move the origin itself by translating the matrix (as demonstrated in Figure 6.6).

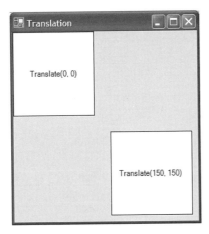

FIGURE 6.6: Rectangle(0, 0, 125, 125) Drawn at Two Origins

Translation is very handy when you've got a figure to draw that can take on several positions around the display area. You can always draw starting from the origin and let the translation decide where the figure actually ends up:

```
void DrawLabeledRect(Graphics g, string label) {
  // Always draw at (0, 0) and let the client
  // set the position using a transform
  RectangleF rect = new RectangleF(0, 0, 125, 125);
  StringFormat format = new StringFormat();
  format.Alignment = StringAlignment.Center;
  format.LineAlignment = StringAlignment.Center;
  g.DrawRectangle(Pens.Black, rect.X, rect.Y, rect.Width, rect.Height);
  g.DrawString(label, this.Font, Brushes.Black, rect, format);
}

void TranslationForm_Paint(object sender, PaintEventArgs e) {
  Graphics g = e.Graphics;

  // Origin at (0, 0)
  DrawLabeledRect(g, "Translate(0, 0)");

  // Move origin to (150, 150)
  Matrix matrix = new Matrix();
  matrix.Translate(150, 150);
  g.Transform = matrix;
  DrawLabeledRect(g, "Translate(150, 150)");
}
```

In fact, this technique can be used for any of the matrix transformation effects covered so far, in addition to the one yet to be covered: shearing.

Shearing

Shearing is like drawing on a rectangle and then pulling along an edge while holding the opposite edge down. Shearing can happen in both directions independently. A shear of zero represents no shear, and the "pull" is increased as the shear increases. The shear is the proportion of the opposite dimension from one corner to another. For example, the rectangle (0, 0, 200, 50) sheared 0.5 along the x dimension will have its top-left edge at (0, 0) but its bottom-left edge at (25, 50). Because the shear dimension is x, the top edge follows the coordinates of the rectangle, but the bottom edge is offset by the height of the rectangle multiplied by the shear value:

$$bottomLeftX = height * xShear = 50 * 0.5 = 25$$

Here's the code that results in the middle sheared rectangle and text in Figure 6.7:

```
RectangleF rect = new RectangleF(0, 0, 200, 50);
matrix = new Matrix();
matrix.Translate(200, 0);
matrix.Shear(.5f, 0f); // Shear in x dimension only
g.Transform = matrix;
g.DrawString("Shear(.5, 0)", this.Font, Brushes.Black, rect, format);
g.DrawRectangle(Pens.Black, rect.X, rect.Y, rect.Width, rect.Height);
```

Combining Transforms

In addition to a demonstration of shearing, the preceding code snippet offers another interesting thing to notice: the use of two operations—a translation and a shear—on the matrix. Multiple operations on a matrix are cumulative. This is useful because the translation allows you to draw the

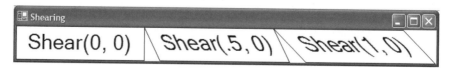

FIGURE 6.7: Drawing a Constant-Size Rectangle at Various Shearing Values

sheared rectangle in the middle at a translated (0, 0) without stepping on the rectangle at the right (and the rectangle at the right is further translated out of the way of the rectangle in the middle).

It's a common desire to combine effects in a matrix, but be careful, because order matters. In this case, because translation works on coordinates and shear works on sizes, the two operations can come in any order. However, because scaling works on coordinates as well as sizes, the order in which scaling and translation are performed matters very much:

```
Matrix matrix = new Matrix();
matrix.Translate(10, 20); // Move origin to (10, 20)
matrix.Scale(2, 3); // Scale x/width and y/width by 2 and 3

Matrix matrix = new Matrix();
matrix.Scale(2, 3); // Scale x/width and y/width by 2 and 3
matrix.Translate(10, 20); // Move origin to (20, 60)
```

If you find that you'd like to reuse a Matrix object but don't want to undo all the operations you've done so far, you can use the Reset method to set it back to the identity matrix. Similarly, you can check whether it's already the identity matrix:

```
Matrix matrix = new Matrix(); // Starts as identity
matrix.Rotate(...); // Touched by inhuman hands
if( !matrix.IsIdentity ) matrix.Reset(); // Back to identity
```

Transformation Helpers

If you've been following along with this section on transformations, you may have been tempted to reach into the Graphics object's Transform property and call Matrix methods directly:

```
Matrix matrix = new Matrix();
matrix.Shear(.5f, .5f);
g.Transform = matrix; // works

g.Transform.Shear(.5f, .5f); // compiles, but doesn't work
```

Although the Transform property will return its Matrix object, it's returning a copy, so performing operations on the copy will have no effect on the transformation matrix of the graphics object. However, instead of creating Matrix objects and setting the Transform property all the time, you can use several helper methods of the Graphics class that affect the transformation matrix directly:

```
// Transformation methods of the Graphics class
sealed class Graphics : MarshalByRefObject, IDisposable {
  ...
  public void ResetTransform();
  public void RotateTransform(...);
  public void ScaleTransform(...);
  public void TranslateTransform(...);
}
```

These methods are handy for simplifying transformation code (although you'll notice that there's no ShearTransform method):

```
// No new Matrix object required
g.TranslateTransform(200, 0);
g.DrawString("(0, 0)", this.Font, Brushes.Black, 0, 0);
```

Path Transformations

As you've seen in previous chapters, GraphicsPath objects are very similar to Graphics objects, and the similarity extends to transformations. A GraphicsPath object can be transformed just as a Graphics object can, and that's handy when you'd like some parts of a drawing, as specified in paths, to be transformed but not others.

Because a path is a collection of figures to be drawn as a group, a transformation isn't a property to be set and changed; instead, it is an operation that is applied. To transform a GraphicsPath, you use the Transform method:

```
GraphicsPath CreateLabeledRectPath(string label) {
  GraphicsPath path = new GraphicsPath();
  ... // Add rectangle and string
  return path;
}

void PathTranslationForm_Paint(object sender, PaintEventArgs e) {
  Graphics g = e.Graphics;
  using( GraphicsPath path = CreateLabeledRectPath("My Path") ) {

    // Draw at (0, 0)
    g.DrawPath(Pens.Black, path);
```

```
   // Translate all points in path by (150, 150)
   Matrix matrix = new Matrix();
   matrix.Translate(150, 150);
   path.Transform(matrix);
   g.DrawPath(Pens.Black, path);
 }
}
```

In addition, GraphicsPath provides transformations that do flattening, widening, and warping via the Flatten, Widen, and Warp methods, respectively (as shown in Figure 6.8).

Each of these methods takes a Matrix object in case you'd like to, for example, translate and widen at the same time. Passing the identity matrix allows each of the specific operations to happen without an additional transformation. The Flatten method takes a flatness value; the larger the value, the fewer the number of points used along a curve, and therefore the more "flat." Figure 6.8 shows an ellipse flattened by 10:

```
// Pass the identity matrix as the first argument to
// stop any transformation except for the flattening
path.Flatten(new Matrix(), 10);
g.DrawPath(Pens.Black, path);
```

The Widen method takes a Pen whose width is used to widen the lines and curves along the path. Figure 6.8 shows an ellipse widened by a pen of width 10:

```
using( Pen widenPen = new Pen(Color.Empty /* ignored */, 10) ) {
  path.Widen(widenPen);
  g.DrawPath(Pens.Black, path);
}
```

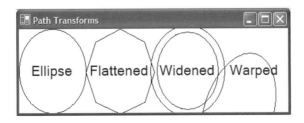

FIGURE 6.8: Path Flattening, Widening, and Warping

One of the overloads of the Widen method takes a flatness value, in case you'd like to widen and flatten simultaneously, in addition to the matrix that it also takes for translation.

The Warp method acts very like the skewing of an image discussed in Chapter 4: Drawing Basics. Warp takes, at a minimum, a set of points that define a parallelogram that describes the target, and a rectangle that describes a chunk of the source. It uses these arguments to skew the source chunk to the destination parallelogram. Figure 6.8 shows the top half of an ellipse skewed left:

```
PointF[] destPoints = new PointF[3];
destPoints[0] = new PointF(width/2, 0);
destPoints[1] = new PointF(width, height);
destPoints[2] = new PointF(0, height/2);
RectangleF srcRect = new RectangleF(0, 0, width, height/2);
path.Warp(destPoints, srcRect);
g.DrawPath(Pens.Black, path);
```

Regions

Whereas paths define a set of figures, with both a frame and an area, a *region* defines only an area. A region can be used for filling or, most importantly, clipping. A region is modeled in .NET with the Region class from the System.Drawing namespace:

```
sealed class Region : MarshalByRefObject, IDisposable {
  // Constructors
  public Region(...);

  // Methods
  public void Complement(...);
  public void Exclude(...);
  public static Region FromHrgn(IntPtr hrgn);
  public RectangleF GetBounds(Graphics g);
  public IntPtr GetHrgn(Graphics g);
  public RegionData GetRegionData();
  public RectangleF[] GetRegionScans(Matrix matrix);
  public void Intersect(...);
  public bool IsEmpty(Graphics g);
  public bool IsInfinite(Graphics g);
  public bool IsVisible(...);
  public void MakeEmpty();
  public void MakeInfinite();
```

```
  public void Transform(...);
  public void Union(...);
  public void Xor(...);
}
```

Constructing and Filling a Region

Because the underlying Win32 implementation also has a construct that represents a region (managed using the Win32 HRGN data type), the Region class can be translated back and forth for interoperability reasons. In addition to constructing a region from an HRGN, you can construct regions from Rectangle objects or, more generally, from GraphicsPath objects:

```
using( GraphicsPath path = new GraphicsPath() ) {
  path.AddEllipse(rect);
  path.Flatten(new Matrix(), 13f);
  path.AddString("Flattened Ellipse", ...);
  using( Region region = new Region(path) ) {
    g.FillRegion(Brushes.Red, region);
  }
}
```

You might be curious about what might drive you to fill a region, especially given that paths can be drawn or filled but regions can only be filled. The answer is that you probably won't be using regions to draw. You'll probably be using regions to decide what not to draw.

Clipping to a Region

Every Graphics object has a region to which all drawing is *clipped*; any drawing outside the clip region is ignored. By default, the clip region is an *infinite* region, and this means that it has no bounds and nothing inside the region being drawn will be thrown out. Windows itself will clip outside the region that isn't part of the invalid region that triggered the Paint event, but that's a separate region from the region exposed by the Graphics object. You can set the clip region on the Graphics object by setting the Clip property (as shown in Figure 6.9):

```
using( GraphicsPath path = new GraphicsPath() ) {
  path.AddEllipse(this.ClientRectangle);
  using( Region region = new Region(path) ) {
```

continues

FIGURE 6.9: Rectangle Clipped to an Ellipse Region

```
// Frame clipping region (for illustration only)
g.DrawPath(Pens.Red, path);

// Don't draw outside the ellipse region
g.Clip = region;

// Draw a rectangle
Rectangle rect = this.ClientRectangle;
rect.Offset(10, 10);
rect.Width -= 20;
rect.Height -= 20;
g.FillRectangle(Brushes.Black, rect);
g.DrawString("Rectangle clipped to Ellipse", ...);
  }
}
```

If you'd rather call a method than set a property when setting the clip region, you can use the SetClip method. It has overloads that take rectangles and paths and create the underlying clip region itself from those. If you'd like to go back to no clipping, you can use the ResetClip method. There are also several clip-related methods on the Region class that deal with intersecting and combining clip regions. All these operate on the underlying methods of the Region class itself, which supports various combination techniques.

Region Combination Operations

Regions support several combination operations for creating more complicated regions from several combined simpler regions. These operations are complement, exclude, intersect, union, and xor, as shown in Figure 6.10.

Each region combination method takes a path, a region, or a rectangle and combines it with the existing one. By default, a Region with no

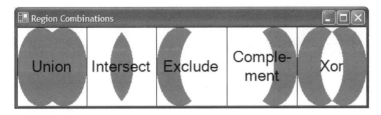

FIGURE 6.10: Region Combination Operations

constructor argument is infinite, but you can make it empty by calling MakeEmpty. Creating a Region with a constructor argument is like creating it as empty and then using the Union method to add a new shape to the region. The following are equivalent:

```
// Intersect the easy way
using( Region region = new Region(path1) ) {
  region.Intersect(path2);
  g.FillRegion(Brushes.Red, region);
}

// Intersect the hard way
using( Region region = new Region() ) {
  // Defaults to region.IsInfinite(g) == true
  if( !region.IsEmpty(g) ) region.MakeEmpty();
  region.Union(path1); // Add a path
  region.Intersect(path2); // Intersect with another path
  g.FillRegion(Brushes.Red, region);
}
```

Taken together, these combining operations provide a complete set of ways to combine regions for filling and clipping.

Optimized Drawing

If you're drawing using page units, transformations, and regions, it's likely that you're heavy into drawing. If that's the case, you'll be interested in ways to optimize your drawings for responsiveness and smooth operation. First and foremost, you'll want to avoid drawing anything that doesn't need drawing. You can do that in one of two ways: redraw only what needs to be redrawn, or don't draw unnecessarily in the first place.

First, invalidate only the portion of your drawing surface that needs to be refreshed. In other words, when drawing the internal state of your form or control, don't invalidate the whole thing if only a small part of the state has changed:

```
float[] lotsOfNumbers;

Region GetRegionWhereNumberIsShown(int number) {...}

public float OneNumber {
  set {
    lotsOfNumbers[1] = value;

    // Don't do this:
    this.Invalidate();

    // Do this:
    this.Invalidate(GetRegionWhereNumberIsShown(1));
  }
}
```

The Invalidate function takes an optional rectangle or region as the first argument, so you'll want to invalidate only the portion that needs redrawing, not the entire client area. Now, when the Paint event is triggered, all drawing outside the invalid rectangle will be ignored:

```
void NumbersForm_Paint(object sender, PaintEventArgs e) {
  for( int i = 0; i != lotsOfNumbers.Length; ++i ) {
    DrawNumber(g, i); // Will draw only in invalid region
  }
}
```

Also, there's an optional second argument that says whether to invalidate children. If the state of your children doesn't need updating, don't invalidate.

What's even better than having drawing operations ignored for efficiency? Not drawing at all. Sometimes the client area will be too small to show all of the state.[4] When that happens, there's no need to draw something that lies entirely outside the visible clip region. To determine whether that's the case, you can use the IsVisible method of the Graphics object,

---

4. This often involves scrolling, which is covered in Chapter 8: Controls.

which checks to see whether a point or any part of a rectangle is visible in the current clipped region:

```
Rectangle GetNumberRectangle(int i) {...}

void DrawNumber(Graphics g, int i) {
  // Avoid something that takes a long time to draw
  if( !g.IsVisible(GetNumberRectangle(i)) ) return;

  // Draw something that takes a long time...
}
```

Be careful when doing the calculations that produce the region to invalidate or checking to see whether a hunk of data is in the invalid region; it may take more cycles to do the checking than it does to simply do the drawing. As always when performance is what you're after, your best bet is to profile various real-world scenarios.

Double Buffering

Another way to make your graphics-intensive programs come out sweet and nice is to eliminate flicker. *Flicker* is caused by Windows showing things as they're drawn—whether you're drawing shapes back to front or Windows is erasing the invalid region before you even get a chance to handle the Paint event.[5] To eliminate the problem of displaying the drawing while it's happening, you can use a technique known as double buffering.

Double buffering is the act of creating a second buffer for the graphics operations to take place in and then, when they're all finished, blowing all the bits onto the screen at once. You can enable double buffering in a form or a control by setting the DoubleBuffer style from the ControlStyles enumeration to true:

```
public Form1() {
  // Required for Windows Form Designer support
  InitializeComponent();

  // Constructor code after InitializeComponent call
  this.SetStyle(ControlStyles.DoubleBuffer, true);
}
```

---

5. You can handle background painting manually by overriding the OnPaintBackground method.

Double buffering by itself solves only half the problem, however, because Windows does your painting in three phases. First, it erases the invalid region by painting it with a Windows-level background brush. Second, it sends the PaintBackground event for your form or control to paint the background, something that your base class generally handles for you using the BackColor and BackgroundImage properties. You can handle it yourself, though:

```
// There is no PaintBackground event, only this virtual method
protected override void OnPaintBackground(PaintEventArgs e) {
  // Make sure to paint the entire client area or call the
  // base class, or else you'll have stuff from below showing through
  //base.OnPaintBackground(e);
  e.Graphics.FillRectangle(Brushes.Black, this.ClientRectangle);
}
```

The third phase of painting is the Paint event handler. Double buffering, by default, collapses the drawing of the PaintBackground and Paint events into a single operation, but the initial erase phase will still show up as flicker. To eliminate the erase phase, you must also set the AllPainting-InWmPaint control style:

```
public Form1() {
  // Required for Windows Form Designer support
  InitializeComponent();

  // Constructor code after InitializeComponent call
  this.SetStyle(ControlStyles.DoubleBuffer, true);
  this.SetStyle(ControlStyles.AllPaintingInWmPaint, true);

  // Needed for controls that are double-buffered
  this.SetStyle(ControlStyles.UserPaint, true);
}
```

Notice the use of the UserPaint style. This is needed for controls that are double-buffered (and doesn't hurt anything for forms that are double-buffered).

Although double buffering (without the initial erasing of the background) can make all the difference in the user experience, double buffering requires enough memory to capture the entire visible region at the current color quality. At 32 bits per pixel, a 200×200 region requires 156K in additional memory per drawing operation for that region. In memory-constrained systems, this extra memory usage could degrade instead of improve the user experience.

Other Drawing Options

There are a few other drawing-related ControlStyles you may be interested in:

```
// Drawing-related control styles
enum ControlStyles {
  AllPaintingInWmPaint, // Collapse drawing phases into Paint event
  DoubleBuffer, // Don't show drawing until Paint event returns
  UserPaint, // Control that paints itself specially
  Opaque, // OnPaintBackground skipped, Paint draws all client area
  ResizeRedraw, // Invalidate entire client area on resize
  SupportsTransparentBackColor, // Simulated transparent controls
  ...
}
```

For example, it's common for controls that need double buffering to want to automatically redraw when they're resized. For this, you use the ResizeRedraw style:

```
public Form1() {
  // Required for Windows Form Designer support
  InitializeComponent();

  // Double buffering
  this.SetStyle(ControlStyles.DoubleBuffer, true);
  this.SetStyle(ControlStyles.AllPaintingInWmPaint, true);
  this.SetStyle(ControlStyles.UserPaint, true);

  // Redraw when resized
  this.SetStyle(ControlStyles.ResizeRedraw, true);
}
```

The ControlStyles settings apply at the point where WinForms starts wrapping the functionality of Windows itself, which is the Control base class (Forms ultimately derive from Control). Several of the ControlStyles settings have nothing to do with drawing but rather govern how the Control class interacts with the underlying operating system. For more information, see the reference documentation for the ControlStyles enumeration.

Where Are We?

If Chapters 4, 5, and 6 haven't convinced you of .NET's very rich support for drawing, then Chapter 7, on drawing to the printer, should do the trick.

7

Printing

U SUALLY, DRAWING TO THE SCREEN is pretty easy because screen settings are generally constant during the run of the application. Drawing to a printer, on the other hand, is more complicated because users may
change the printer or the printer settings many times, even for a single document. Also, paper costs money and can't be sent through the printer twice
(unless you don't care what's on the back), so before users print their documents they want to see what they will look like. The actual drawing is
largely the same for a printer as it is for the screen, but the printer settings
are the interesting part, and the settings are covered in this chapter.

Print Documents

The basic unit of printing in WinForms is the print document. A *print document* describes the characteristics of what's to be printed, such as the title of
the document, and provides the events at various parts of the printing process, such as when it's time to print a page. .NET models the print document using the PrintDocument component from the System.Drawing.
Printing namespace (and available on the VS.NET Toolbox):

```
class PrintDocument : Component, IComponent, IDisposable {
  // Constructors
  public PrintDocument();
```

continues

```
    // Properties
    public PageSettings DefaultPageSettings { get; set; }
    public string DocumentName { get; set; }
    public PrintController PrintController { get; set; }
    public PrinterSettings PrinterSettings { get; set; }

    // Events
    public event PrintEventHandler BeginPrint;
    public event PrintEventHandler EndPrint;
    public event PrintPageEventHandler PrintPage;
    public event QueryPageSettingsEventHandler QueryPageSettings;

    // Methods
    public void Print();
}
```

The basic usage of a PrintDocument object is to create an instance, subscribe to at least the PrintPage event, call the Print method, and handle the PrintPage event:

```
PrintDocument printDocument1;

void InitializeComponent() {
  this.printDocument1 = new PrintDocument();
  ...
  this.printDocument1.PrintPage +=
    new PrintPageEventHandler(this.printDocument1_PrintPage);
  ...
}

void printButton_Click(object sender, System.EventArgs e) {
  printDocument1.DocumentName = fileName;
  printDocument1.Print();
}

void printDocument1_PrintPage(object sender, PrintPageEventArgs e) {
  // Draw to the printer
  Graphics g = e.Graphics;
  using( Font font = new Font("Lucida Console", 72) ) {
    g.DrawString("Hello,\nPrinter", font, ...);
  }
}
```

The PrintPage event is triggered by a call to the PrintDocument object's Print method. The PrintPage event is responsible for actually rendering the state of the document to the printer surface using the Graphics object. The

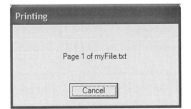

actual drawing is just like drawing on any other Graphics object, as discussed in Chapters 4, 5, and 6.

Notice that this sample sets the DocumentName property of the document. This string shows up in the queue for the printer so that the user can manage the document being printed.

Print Controllers

The name of the print document also shows up in the dialog that the print document displays during printing. The Printing dialog lets the user cancel the print job as it's being spooled to the printer, as shown in Figure 7.1.

The Printing dialog is provided by a print controller. The *print controller*, modeled as the PrintController abstract base class and exposed via the PrintController property of the PrintDocument object, actually manages the underlying printing process and fires the events as printing progresses. The core print controller is StandardPrintController, which provides the Graphics object that wraps the printer device, causing the drawing commands to make it to the printer itself. However, the default print controller is an instance of the PrintControllerWithStatusDialog class, which is the one that shows the Printing dialog. The PrintControllerWithStatusDialog class doesn't do anything except show the dialog; it relies on StandardPrintController to communicate with the printer. In fact, creating an instance of the PrintControllerWithStatusDialog class requires an instance of the StandardPrintController class as a constructor argument. So, by

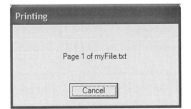

FIGURE 7.1: The Printing Dialog shown by the PrintControllerWithStatusDialog

default, the print control provided by the print document acts as if you'd written this code:

```
void printButton_Click(object sender, EventArgs e) {
  PrintController standard = new StandardPrintController();
  // Can change the title from "Printing" to something else
  PrintController status =
    new PrintControllerWithStatusDialog(standard, "Printing");
  printDocument1.PrintController = status;
  printDocument1.Print();
}
```

If you'd prefer to print without showing a dialog—for example, when you're printing in the background—you can use StandardPrintController directly:

```
void printButton_Click(object sender, EventArgs e) {
  // Suppress the Printing dialog
  PrintController standard = new StandardPrintController();
  printDocument1.PrintController = standard;
  printDocument1.Print();
}
```

Print Preview

Another print controller that .NET provides is PreviewPrintController, which is used for previewing a document before it's printed. Figure 7.2 shows a preview print controller being used to prepare a document for preview.

PreviewPrintController is primarily used by PrintPreviewControl, which shows document previews one page at a time. PrintPreviewControl is available on the Toolbox and uses the drawing commands performed in

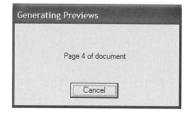

FIGURE 7.2: The PreviewPrintController in use by the PrintPreviewControl

PrintDocument's PrintPage event handler to display the client area for a standard print preview-style dialog, as shown in Figure 7.3.

The client area in Figure 7.3 consists of a PrintPreviewControl set to fill the client area (using DockStyle.Fill). Notice that it draws what looks like a piece of paper in miniature, showing the drawing performed by the Print-Page event handler. The PrintPreviewControl class has all kinds of interesting properties and methods for implementing a print preview-style dialog:

```
class PrintPreviewControl : Control,  IComponent, IDisposable, ... {
  // Constructors
  public PrintPreviewControl();

  // Properties
  public bool AutoZoom { get; set; }
  public int Columns { get; set; }
  public PrintDocument Document { get; set; }
  public int Rows { get; set; }
  public int StartPage { get; set; }
  public bool UseAntiAlias { get; set; }
  public double Zoom { get; set; }

  // Methods
  public void InvalidatePreview();
  public virtual void ResetBackColor();
  public virtual void ResetForeColor();
}
```

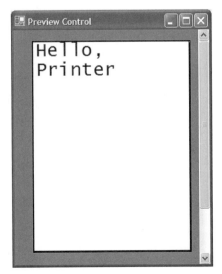

FIGURE 7.3: The PrintPreviewControl Hosted in a Custom Form

The only requirement is that the Document property be set to an instance of a PrintDocument so that the preview control can get the contents of each page to be displayed. Displaying multiple pages at once is a matter of setting the Rows and Columns properties. Figure 7.4 shows a PrintPreviewControl with Rows set to 1 and Columns set to 2.

Displaying the next page (or the next set of pages) is a matter of setting the StartPage property, which dictates the page shown in the upper left of the control. In addition, PrintPreviewControl interprets Page Up and Page Down to move between pages.

The Zoom property is a multiplier: A Zoom of 1.0 is 100%, a Zoom of 0.5 is 50%, and a Zoom of 2.0 is 200%. The AutoZoom property is handy when PrintPreviewControl can resize. When AutoZoom is true (the default), PrintPreviewControl sets the Zoom property to scale the page (or pages) to a size as large as possible inside the control.

Finally, the UseAntiAlias property applies antialiasing to the preview image (this defaults to false to let the printer's higher resolution print smoothly without the need to antialias).

Although it's useful to be able to implement a custom print preview-style dialog with zooming, page count, and multipage support, often a "standard" print preview dialog is all that's required. In those cases, the PrintPreviewDialog component from the Toolbox is your friend. Figure 7.5 shows the PrintPreviewDialog component in action.

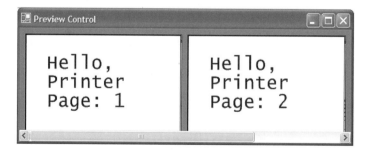

FIGURE 7.4: Previewing Multiple Pages at Once in PrintPreviewControl

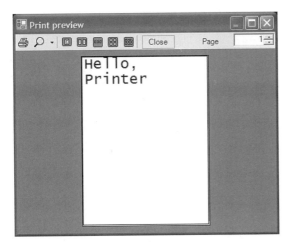

FIGURE 7.5: The PrintPreviewDialog Component

The PrintPreviewDialog component uses PrintPreviewControl and your PrintDocument instance to provide a full-featured, preview-style dialog:

```
PrintPreviewDialog printPreviewDialog1;

void InitializeComponent() {
  ...
  this.printPreviewDialog1 = new PrintPreviewDialog();
  ...
}

void previewButton_Click(object sender, EventArgs e) {
  printPreviewDialog1.Document = printDocument1;
  printPreviewDialog1.ShowDialog();
}
```

Basic Print Events

All print controller implementations rely on the print document's print events to gather the drawing commands into the graphics object, either to spool to the printer or to show on the screen:

```
void printDocument1_PrintPage(object sender, PrintPageEventArgs e) {
  // Draw to the e.Graphics object
```

continues

```
    Graphics g = e.Graphics;
    using( Font font = new Font("Lucida Console", 72) ) {
        g.DrawString("Hello,\nPrinter", font, ...);
    }
}
```

Notice that this sample PrintPage event handler creates a font only for printing. For a single page, this code is fine, because it creates the font and then reclaims the font resources when the printing is complete. However, if we're printing more than one page, it's wasteful to create the font anew on each page. On the other hand, creating a font for printing and then caching it in a field seems wasteful if the font is never used again after the print job. What we'd really like is to be notified when a print job is started and ended so that we can have tight control over print-related resources. For this, we use the print document's BeginPrint and EndPrint events:

```
Font font = null;

void printDocument1_BeginPrint(object sender, PrintEventArgs e) {
    // Create font for printing
    font = new Font("Lucida Console", 72);
}

void printDocument1_EndPrint(object sender, PrintEventArgs e) {
    // Reclaim font
    font.Dispose();
    font = null;
}
```

Notice that the BeginPrint and EndPrint events come with an instance of the PrintEventArgs class. The PrintEventArgs class derives from the CancelEventArgs class and provides no extra members. As you might guess, the Cancel property of the PrintEventArgs class (inherited from the CancelEventArgs base class) is used primarily by a print controller that shows a UI, such as PrintControllerWithStatusDialog, to cancel a print job.

Unlike BeginPrint and EndPrint, the PrintPage event comes with an instance of the PrintPageEventArgs class:

```
class PrintPageEventArgs : EventArgs {
    public bool Cancel { get; set; }
    public Graphics Graphics { get; }
    public bool HasMorePages { get; set; }
```

```
  public Rectangle MarginBounds { get; }
  public Rectangle PageBounds { get; }
  public PageSettings PageSettings { get; }
}
```

As you've seen, the Cancel property is used to cancel a print job, and the Graphics property is used for drawing. HasMorePages defaults to false. If there are more pages to print, you set HasMorePages to true during the PrintPage handler for all pages except the last page of a multipage document:

```
int totalPages = 13;
int page = 1;

void printDocument1_PrintPage(object sender, PrintPageEventArgs e) {
  Graphics g = e.Graphics;
  g.DrawString("Hello,\nPrinter\nPage: " + page, ...);
  ++page;
  e.HasMorePages = (page < totalPages);
}
```

This example has 13 pages, of which as many as 6 can be shown in the print preview dialog at once (as shown in Figure 7.6).

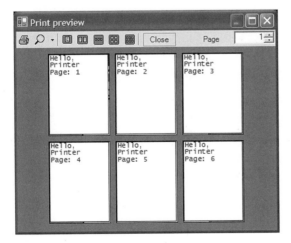

FIGURE 7.6: Printing Multiple Pages

Margins

The PageBounds rectangle property of the PrintPageEventArgs class represents the entire rectangle of the page, all the way to the edge. The MarginBounds rectangle represents the area inside the margins. Figure 7.7 shows the difference.

Both PageBounds and MarginBounds are always scaled to units of 100 dpi, so a standard 8.5 × 11 inch piece of paper will always have a PageBounds rectangle {0, 0, 750, 1000}. With the default margin of 1 inch all the way around, the MarginBounds will be at {100, 100, 650, 900}. To match the bounds, by default the GraphicsUnit for the Graphics object will be 100 dpi, too, and will be scaled to whatever is appropriate for the printer resolution. For example, my laser printer is 600 × 600 dpi.

The margin is useful not only because users often want some white space around their pages when they print, but also because many printers can't print to the edge of the page, so anything printed all the way to the edge is bound to be cut off to some degree. To avoid this, the Graphics object you get when you're printing starts at the top-left corner of the printable area of the page. That's useful for printing outside the margins, such as for headers or footers.

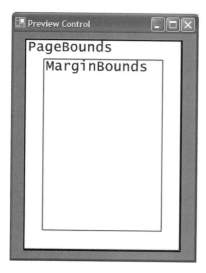

FIGURE 7.7: PageBounds Versus MarginBounds

However, because printers normally can't print to the edge of the page, the PageBounds rectangle will be too large. To get the actual size of the bounding rectangle, you can use the Graphics object's VisibleClipBounds rectangle:

```
// Get a page bounds with an accurate size
RectangleF pageBounds = e.Graphics.VisibleClipBounds;

// Draw a header
g.DrawString("header", font, Brushes.Black, pageBounds);
```

Unfortunately, for some reason VisibleClipBounds contains nonsense values when the page is previewed, so in that case, the PageBounds rectangle should be used. Also, if the Graphics object is using a nondefault Page-Unit (as discussed in Chapter 6: Advanced Drawing), VisibleClipBounds will be in different units than PageBounds (which is always in units of 100 dpi). To handle these variables, it's useful to have a helper method to return the "real" page bounds in a consistent unit of measure:

```
// Get real page bounds based on printable area of the page
static
  Rectangle GetRealPageBounds(PrintPageEventArgs e, bool preview) {
  // Return in units of 1/100th of an inch
  if( preview ) return e.PageBounds;

  // Translate to units of 1/100th of an inch
  RectangleF vpb = e.Graphics.VisibleClipBounds;
  PointF[]
    bottomRight = { new PointF(vpb.Size.Width, vpb.Size.Height) };
  e.Graphics.TransformPoints(
    CoordinateSpace.Device, CoordinateSpace.Page, bottomRight);
  float dpiX = e.Graphics.DpiX;
  float dpiY = e.Graphics.DpiY;
  return new Rectangle(
    0,
    0,
    (int)(bottomRight[0].X * 100 /  dpiX),
    (int)(bottomRight[0].Y * 100 / dpiY));
}
```

GetRealPageBounds returns the PageBounds rectangle if in preview mode[1] and always scales the returned Rectangle in the same units. This

---

1. Whether the application is printing in preview mode must be managed by the application itself. There is nothing to indicate printing versus print preview in the printing classes.

helper allows you to write your printing code to stay within the real bounds of the page:

```
// Get the real page bounds
Rectangle pageBounds = GetRealPageBounds(e, this.preview);

// Draw a header in the upper left
g.DrawString("header", font, Brushes.Black, pageBounds);

// Draw a footer in the lower right
StringFormat farFormat = new StringFormat();
farFormat.Alignment = StringAlignment.Far;
farFormat.LineAlignment = StringAlignment.Far;
g.DrawString("footer", font, Brushes.Black, pageBounds, farFormat);
```

For the bulk of the printed content, however, you should be printing inside the MarginBounds rectangle:

```
void printDocument1_PrintPage(object sender, PrintPageEventArgs e) {
  Graphics g = e.Graphics;
  g.DrawString(..., e.MarginBounds);
}
```

Unfortunately, because MarginBounds is offset from PageBounds and because PageBounds is offset to stay inside the printable region of the page, MarginBounds is often lined up at offsets that don't match the user-specified margins along the edge of the page.

For example, on my Hewlett-Packard LaserJet 2100, the left edge of the PageBounds rectangle is actually $\frac{1}{4}$ inch in from the left edge of the page, and the top edge is $\frac{1}{8}$ inch down from the top. This affects MarginBounds, lining up the 1-inch margin I expect at $1\frac{1}{4}$ inches from the left edge of the page. This poses a problem because neither PageBounds nor VisibleClip-Bounds nor any other information provided by WinForms actually tells you how much the PageBounds is offset from the edge of the paper.

To get the physical offsets, you must turn to interoperability with Win32 and the GetDeviceCaps function. Using that, you can get the printer's physical X and Y offset from the top left and adjust the margins appropriately. However, the X and Y offset is in printer coordinates, which may not be the same units as MarginBounds, so you must convert those units as well. The following helper methods do all that work:

```
[System.Runtime.InteropServices.DllImport("gdi32.dll")]
static extern int GetDeviceCaps(IntPtr hdc, DeviceCapsIndex index);

enum DeviceCapsIndex {
  PhysicalOffsetX = 112,
  PhysicalOffsetY = 113,
}

// Adjust MarginBounds rectangle when printing based
// on the physical characteristics of the printer
static
  Rectangle GetRealMarginBounds(PrintPageEventArgs e, bool preview) {
  if( preview ) return e.MarginBounds;

  int cx = 0;
  int cy = 0;
  IntPtr hdc = e.Graphics.GetHdc();

  try {
    // Both of these come back as device units and are not
    // scaled to 1/100th of an inch
    cx = GetDeviceCaps(hdc, DeviceCapsIndex.PhysicalOffsetX);
    cy = GetDeviceCaps(hdc, DeviceCapsIndex.PhysicalOffsetY);
  }
  finally {
    e.Graphics.ReleaseHdc(hdc);
  }

  // Create the real margin bounds by scaling the offset
  // by the printer resolution and then rescaling it
  // back to 1/100th of an inch
  Rectangle marginBounds = e.MarginBounds;
  int dpiX = (int)e.Graphics.DpiX;
  int dpiY = (int)e.Graphics.DpiY;
  marginBounds.Offset(-cx * 100 / dpiX , -cy * 100 / dpiY);
  return marginBounds;
}
```

The GetRealMarginBounds method takes preview mode into account and, when you use a real printer, adjusts MarginBounds using the physical offsets, always returning a rectangle in the same units. With this in place, you can safely print inside the margins based on the edges of the paper, as you'd expect:

```
void printDocument1_PrintPage(object sender, PrintPageEventArgs e) {
  ...
```

continues

```
    g.DrawString(..., GetRealMarginBounds(e, this.preview));
}
```

As an alternative to using these helper functions, the .NET 1.1 Framework provides a property on PrintDocument called OriginAtMargins. This property defaults to false, but setting it to true sets the offset of the Page-Bounds rectangle to be at the margin offset from the physical edge of the page, letting you print at the appropriate margins using the PageBounds rectangle. However, this property doesn't have any effect in preview mode, doesn't adjust the PageBounds size, and keeps the MarginBounds as offset from the now further offset PageBounds. For these reasons, I don't find it particularly useful when compared with the GetRealPageBounds and GetRealMarginBounds helper methods.

Page Settings

You may have noticed that both the MarginBounds and the PageSettings properties of the PrintPageEventArgs class are read-only. Changing Page-Settings on-the-fly (including the margins) requires handling the print document's QueryPageSettings event:

```
void printDocument1_QueryPageSettings(
  object sender, QueryPageSettingsEventArgs e) {
  // Set margins to 0.5" all the way around
  // (measured in 100ths of an inch)
  e.PageSettings.Margins = new Margins(50, 50, 50, 50);
}
```

QueryPageSettingsEventArgs provides only a Cancel property and a PageSettings property. The latter is an instance of the PageSettings class:

```
class PageSettings : ICloneable {
  // Constructors
  public PageSettings();
  public PageSettings(PrinterSettings printerSettings);

  // Properties
  public Rectangle Bounds { get; }
  public bool Color { get; set; }
  public bool Landscape { get; set; }
  public Margins Margins { get; set; }
  public PaperSize PaperSize { get; set; }
```

```
  public PaperSource PaperSource { get; set; }
  public PrinterResolution PrinterResolution { get; set; }
  public PrinterSettings PrinterSettings { get; set; }
}
```

In addition to setting the margins, the PageSettings object can be set to indicate whether color is allowed, the size and source of the paper, the printer resolution, and other printer-specific settings. You could adjust these properties programmatically during the printing process, but it's friendlier to let the user do it before the printing begins. For that, you use the PageSetupDialog component shown in Figure 7.8.

Before the page setup dialog can be shown, the Document property must be set:

```
PageSetupDialog pageSetupDialog1;

void InitializeComponent() {
  ...
  this.pageSetupDialog1 = new PageSetupDialog();
  ...
}
```

continues

FIGURE 7.8: PageSetupDialog Component with Default Page Settings

```
void pageSetupButton_Click(object sender, EventArgs e) {
  // Let the user select page settings
  pageSetupDialog1.Document = printDocument1;
  pageSetupDialog1.ShowDialog();
}
```

When the user presses OK, the PageSettings properties are adjusted for that instance of the PrintDocument and are used at the next printing. The PageSetupDialog itself provides some useful options:

```
class PageSetupDialog : CommonDialog, IComponent, IDisposable {
  // Constructors
  public PageSetupDialog();

  // Properties
  public bool AllowMargins { get; set; }
  public bool AllowOrientation { get; set; }
  public bool AllowPaper { get; set; }
  public bool AllowPrinter { get; set; }
  public PrintDocument Document { get; set; }
  public Margins MinMargins { get; set; }
  public PageSettings PageSettings { get; set; }
  public PrinterSettings PrinterSettings { get; set; }
  public bool ShowHelp { get; set; }
  public bool ShowNetwork { get; set; }

  // Events
  public event EventHandler HelpRequest;

  // Methods
  public virtual void Reset();
}
```

The AllowXxx properties dictate whether the dialog allows the user to change things, such as the margins or the orientation (all these properties default to true). The MinMargins property sets the minimum margins that the user can't go below. The ShowHelp property indicates whether the help button should be shown. By default it isn't shown, because there's no built-in help to show (other than the pop-up help). If you set ShowHelp to true, make sure to subscribe to the HelpRequest event so that when the user presses the help button, you can provide help. Finally, the Show-Network property determines whether the user can navigate the network to find a printer after pressing the Printer button (assuming AllowPrinter is set to true).

Printer Settings

So far, all the printing in this chapter has been done to the default printer, as defined by Windows itself. The user can change the printer for a document via the Printer button on the PageSetupDialog. It's more common, however, to allow the user to choose the printer after choosing the Print item from the File menu. For this you use the PrintDialog component, as shown in Figure 7.9.

Using the PrintDialog component looks like this:

```
PrintDialog printDialog1;

void InitializeComponent() {
  ...
  this.printDialog1 = new PrintDialog();
  ...
  // Can set the PrintDialog's Document property
  // in the Property Browser
  this.printDialog1.Document = this.printDocument1;
  ...
}

void printButton_Click(object sender, System.EventArgs e) {
  // Let the user choose the printer
  if( printDialog1.ShowDialog() == DialogResult.OK ) {
    printDocument1.Print();
  }
}
```

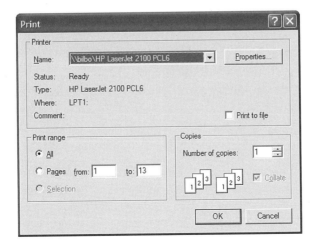

FIGURE 7.9: The PrintDialog Component

Like PageSetupDialog, the PrintDialog component allows you to set a number of options before it is shown:

```
sealed class PrintDialog : CommonDialog, IComponent, IDisposable {
  // Constructors
  public PrintDialog();

  // Properties
  public bool AllowPrintToFile { get; set; }
  public bool AllowSelection { get; set; }
  public bool AllowSomePages { get; set; }
  public PrintDocument Document { get; set; }
  public PrinterSettings PrinterSettings { get; set; }
  public bool PrintToFile { get; set; }
  public bool ShowHelp { get; set; }
  public bool ShowNetwork { get; set; }

  // Events
  public event EventHandler HelpRequest;

  // Methods
  public virtual void Reset();
}
```

You must set the Document property before showing a PrintDialog object. The other PrintDialog properties are similar in function to the Page-SetupDialog properties. A couple of properties are special, however, because they determine what to print. Let's take a look.

Print Range

The AllowSelection property of the PrintDialog lets the user print only the current selection,[2] and AllowSomePages allows the user to decide on a subset of pages to be printed. Both settings require you to print specially, based on the PrintRange property of the PrinterSettings class, which is of type PrintRange:

---

2. What, if anything, the "current selection" means is application-specific. However, Betsy Hardinger, the copy editor for this book, made an impassioned plea during her editing of this book that when the print dialog is invoked while there is a current selection, the print dialog default to printing only the selection and not all 75 pages of the document (which Betsy often finds herself printing when she doesn't want to). Thank you.

```
enum PrintRange {
  AllPages, // Print all pages (default)
  Selection, // Print only the current selection
  SomePages, // Print pages from FromPage to ToPage
}
```

Before you can set a print range that's different from AllPages, you must set AllowSelection or AllowSomePages (or both) to true (they both default to false). AllowSomePages also requires that the PrinterSettings FromPage and ToPage be set greater than the default of zero:

```
int totalPages = 13;
int page;
int maxPage;

void printButton_Click(object sender, System.EventArgs e) {
  printDocument1.PrinterSettings.FromPage = 1;
  printDocument1.PrinterSettings.ToPage = totalPages;
  printDocument1.PrinterSettings.MinimumPage = 1;
  printDocument1.PrinterSettings.MaximumPage = totalPages;
  printDialog1.AllowSomePages = true;
  if( printDialog1.ShowDialog() == DialogResult.OK ) {
    printDocument1.Print();
  }
}
```

Although it's not required, it's a good idea when setting AllowSome-Pages to true to also set MinimumPage and MaximumPage so that users can't accidentally ask for a page out of the allowed range. If AllowSelection or AllowSomePages is set to true, the PrintPage event will have to check the PrintRange and FromPage/ToPage properties to see what to print:

```
int totalPages = 13;
int page;
int maxPage;

void printButton_Click(object sender, System.EventArgs e) {
  ...
  if( printDialog1.ShowDialog() == DialogResult.OK ) {
    if( printDialog1.PrinterSettings.PrintRange ==
        PrintRange.SomePages ) {
      // Set first page to print to FromPage
      page = printDocument1.PrinterSettings.FromPage;
```

continues

```
      // Set last page to print to ToPage
      maxPage = printDocument1.PrinterSettings.ToPage;
    }
    else {
      // Print all pages
      page = 1;
      maxPage = totalPages;
    }

    // Print from first page to last page
    printDocument1.Print();
  }
}

void printDocument1_PrintPage(object sender, PrintPageEventArgs e) {
  Graphics g = e.Graphics;
  // print current page...

  // Check whether there are more pages to print
  ++page;
  e.HasMorePages = (page <= maxPage);
}
```

In addition to the PrintRange, FromPage, and ToPage properties, the PrinterSettings class has many more settings for use in determining exactly how the user would like to print:

```
class PrinterSettings : ICloneable {
  // Constructors
  public PrinterSettings();

  // Properties
  public bool CanDuplex { get; }
  public bool Collate { get; set; }
  public short Copies { get; set; }
  public PageSettings DefaultPageSettings { get; }
  public Duplex Duplex { get; set; }
  public int FromPage { get; set; }
  public static StringCollection InstalledPrinters { get; }
  public bool IsDefaultPrinter { get; }
  public bool IsPlotter { get; }
  public bool IsValid { get; }
  public int LandscapeAngle { get; }
  public int MaximumCopies { get; }
  public int MaximumPage { get; set; }
  public int MinimumPage { get; set; }
  public PaperSizeCollection PaperSizes { get; }
  public PaperSourceCollection PaperSources { get; }
```

```
  public string PrinterName { get; set; }
  public PrinterResolutionCollection PrinterResolutions { get; }
  public PrintRange PrintRange { get; set; }
  public bool PrintToFile { get; set; }
  public bool SupportsColor { get; }
  public int ToPage { get; set; }

  // Methods
  public Graphics CreateMeasurementGraphics();
}
```

One thing of particular interest is the CreateMeasurementGraphics method, which returns a Graphics object based on the printer and its settings. You can use this Graphics object for making measurement calculations and for enumerating the font families (using the FontFamily. GetFamilies method), all without having to actually start a print operation.

Targeting the Printer

I'd like to remind you again that because the drawing happens on a Graphics object, all the drawing techniques from Chapters 4, 5, and 6 work just as well with printers as they do with screens. However, unlike the screen, where page units default to Pixel, the page units for the printer default to Display. Furthermore, whereas Display means Pixel on the screen, for the printer, Display maps the printer resolution to a logical 100 dpi. Because printers often have different resolutions both vertically and horizontally and are almost never 100 dpi anyway, this may seem unintuitive. However, because the default system font setting is 96 dpi on the screen, mapping the printer to a logical 100 dpi means that the default mappings for both screen and printer yield a quick and dirty near-WYSIWYG, without your having to change a thing. If you want something even closer, you're free to use page units such as inches or millimeters, as discussed in Chapter 6: Advanced Drawing.

If you do change the units, remember to convert PageBounds and MarginBounds to the new units as well. You can use the Graphics method TransformPoints:

```
static RectangleF TranslateBounds(Graphics g, Rectangle bounds) {
  // Translate from units of 1/100th of an inch to page units
  float dpiX = g.DpiX;
  float dpiY = g.DpiY;
```

continues

```
PointF[] pts = new PointF[2];
pts[0] =
  new PointF(bounds.X * dpiX / 100, bounds.Y * dpiY / 100);
pts[1] =
  new PointF(bounds.Width * dpiX / 100, bounds.Height * dpiX / 100);
g.TransformPoints(
  CoordinateSpace.Page, CoordinateSpace.Device, pts);
return new RectangleF(
  pts[0].X,
  pts[0].Y,
  pts[1].X,
  pts[1].Y);
}
```

The TranslateBounds helper method uses the current Graphics object to translate a PageBounds or MarginBounds rectangle from units of 100 dpi to whatever the page unit is set to. This helper is meant to be used from the PrintPage handler:

```
void printDocument1_PrintPage(object sender, PrintPageEventArgs e) {
  Graphics g = e.Graphics;
  g.PageUnit = GraphicsUnit.Inch;

  using( Pen thinPen = new Pen(Color.Black, 0) ) {
    RectangleF pageBounds = GetRealPageBounds(e, preview);
    pageBounds = TranslateBounds(g, Rectangle.Truncate(pageBounds));
    g.DrawRectangle(
      thinPen,
      pageBounds.X,
      pageBounds.Y,
      pageBounds.Width,
      pageBounds.Height);
    . . .
  }
  . . .
}
```

Notice that PageUnit is set on the Graphics object right away so that any drawing that takes place in the PrintPage handler will be in those units.

Finally, notice that the PrintPage handler sets the PageUnit during each page being printed. Each time the PrintPage handler is called, it gets a fresh Graphics object, so don't forget to reset its options every time.

Where Are We?

The nucleus around which the entire .NET printing architecture revolves is the print document. It's the one that initiates the printing process, fires the print events (through the use of a print controller), holds the page and printer settings, and gathers the drawing commands for rendering to the printer or to the preview control. You implement the actual drawing using the Graphics object, as discussed in Chapters 4, 5, and 6, and this drawing is governed by the settings held by the print document.

■8■
Controls

T HE BASIC UNIT OF THE USER INTERFACE in WinForms is the control. Everything that interacts directly with the user in a region defined by a container is a control. This includes controls that do everything themselves, as well as standard controls such as the TextBox, user controls (controls that contain other controls), and even the Form class itself.

This chapter covers the broad categories of the standard controls provided by WinForms. It explains how to build custom and user controls and how to provide support for drag and drop, the most popular kind of inter-control communication. If you'd like a survey of the standard controls, refer to Appendix D: Standard WinForms Components and Controls.

Standard Controls

A *control* is a class that derives from the System.Windows.Forms.Control base (either directly or indirectly) and is responsible for drawing a chunk of the *container*, which is either a form or another control. WinForms comes with several standard controls available by default on the Toolbox in VS.NET. These controls can be broken into the following ad hoc categories:

- **Action controls.** Controls such as Button and Toolbar exist to allow the user to click on them to cause something to happen.

- **Value controls.** Controls such as Label and PictureBox show the user a value, such as text or a picture, but don't allow the user to change the value. Other value controls, such as TextBox or DateTimePicker, allow the user to change the value being displayed.

- **List controls.** Controls such as ListBox and ComboBox show the user a list of data. Other list controls, such as DataGrid, allow the user to change the data directly.

- **Container controls.** GroupBox, Panel, and TabControl exist to contain and arrange other controls.

Although Appendix D: Standard WinForms Components and Controls lists and shows each of the standard controls, it's useful to consider each category for the features that the controls share in common.

Action Controls

The action controls are Button, ToolBar, MainMenu, and ContextMenu.[1] These controls exist to provide something for the user to click on to trigger an action in the application. Each of the available actions is labeled and, in the case of ToolBar, can have an optional image. The major event the action controls is the Click event:

```
void button1_Click(object sender, EventArgs e) {
  MessageBox.Show("Ouch!");
}
```

Except for Button, the rest of the action controls are actually containers of multiple subobjects that the user interacts with. For example, a Main-Menu object contains one or more MenuItem objects, one for each menu item that can fire a Click event:

```
void exitMenuItem_Click(object sender, EventArgs e) {
  this.Close();
}
```

---

1. Technically, MenuBar and the ContextMenu classes aren't controls because they don't derive from the Control base class, but they fit so nicely into this category that I didn't have the heart to remove them. The details of these two components can be found in Chapter 2: Forms.

The ToolBar control also contains a collection of objects, of type ToolBar-Button. However, when the user clicks, the event is sent for ToolBar itself, so the event handler is responsible for using the Button property of the ToolBarButtonClickEventArgs to figure out which button was pressed:

```
void toolBar1_ButtonClick(
  object sender, ToolBarButtonClickEventArgs e) {

  if( e.Button == fileExitToolBarButton ) {
    this.Close();
  }
  else if( e.Button == helpAboutToolBarButton ) {
    MessageBox.Show("The standard controls are cool");
  }
}
```

Because menu items and toolbar buttons often result in the same action, such as showing the About box, it's good practice to centralize the code and call it from both event handlers:

```
void FileExit() {...}
void HelpAbout() {...}

void fileExitMenuItem_Click(object sender, EventArgs e) {
  FileExit();
}

void helpAboutMenuItem_Click(object sender, EventArgs e) {
  HelpAbout();
}

void toolBar1_ButtonClick(
  object sender, ToolBarButtonClickEventArgs e) {
  if( e.Button == fileExitToolBarButton ) {
    FileExit();
  }
  else if( e.Button == helpAboutToolBarButton ) {
    HelpAbout();
  }
}
```

If you centralize the handling of an action, you don't have to worry about which controls trigger it; no matter how many do, all of them will get the same behavior.

While we're on the topic of ToolBar control, you may be curious as to how images are assigned to each button. Assigning an image to a toolbar button involves creating and indexing into an ImageList, which is a component that holds a list of images for use by controls that display images. Image lists are discussed later in this chapter.

Value Controls

The value controls make up the set of controls that show and optionally allow editing of a single value. They can be broken down further by the data type of the value:

- **String values:** Label, LinkLabel, TextBox, RichTextBox, StatusBar
- **Numeric values:** NumericUpDown, HScrollBar, VScrollBar, Progress-Bar, TrackBar
- **Boolean values:** CheckBox, Radio Button
- **Date values:** DateTimePicker, MonthCalendar
- **Graphical values:** PictureBox, PrintPreviewControl

The string value controls expose a property called Text that contains the value of the control in a string format. The Label control merely displays the text. The LinkLabel control displays the text as if it were an HTML link, firing an event when the link is clicked. The StatusBar control displays the text in the same way a Label does (but, by default, docked to the bottom of the container), but it also allows for multiple chunks of text separated into panels.

In addition to displaying text, the TextBox control allows the user to edit the text in single or multiline mode (depending on the value of Multiline property). The RichTextBox control allows for editing like TextBox but also supports RTF (Rich Text Format) data, which includes font and color information as well as graphics. When the Text value of either of these controls changes, the TextChanged event is fired.

All the numeric value controls expose a numeric Value property, whose value can range from the Minimum to the Maximum property. The difference is only a matter of which UI you'd like to show to the user. When the Value properties change, the ValueChanged property is fired.

The Boolean value controls—CheckBox and RadioButton—expose a Checked property that reflects whether or not they're checked. Both Boolean value controls can also be set to a third, "indeterminate" state, which is one of the three possible values exposed from the CheckState property. When the CheckState is changed, the CheckedChanged and CheckStateChanged events are fired.

The date value controls allow the user to pick one or more instances of the DateTime type. MonthCalendar allows the choice of beginning and ending dates as exposed by the SelectionRange property (signaled by the SelectionRangeChanged event). DateTimePicker allows the user to enter a single date and time as exposed by the Value property (signaled by the ValueChanged event).

The graphical value controls show images, although neither allows the images to be changed. The PictureBox control shows any image as set by the Image property. PrintPreviewControl shows, one page at a time, a preview of print data generated from a PrintDocument object (as described in Chapter 7: Printing).

List Controls

If one value at a time is good, then several values at a time must be better. The list controls—ComboBox, CheckedListBox, ListBox, DomainUpDown, ListView, DataGrid, and TreeView—can show more than one value at a time.

Most of the list controls—ComboBox, CheckedListBox, ListBox, and DomainUpDown—show a list of objects exposed by the Items collection. To add a new item you use this collection:

```
void Form1_Load(object sender, EventArgs e) {
  listBox1.Items.Add("an item");
}
```

This sample adds a string object to the list of items, but you can add any object:

```
void Form1_Load(object sender, EventArgs e) {
  DateTime bday = DateTime.Parse("1995-08-30 6:02pm");
  listBox1.Items.Add(bday);
}
```

To come up with a string to display, the list controls that take objects as items call the ToString method. To show your own custom items in a list control, you simply implement the ToString method:

```
class Person {
  string name;
  int age;

  public Person(string name, int age) {
    this.name = name;
    this.age = age;
  }

  public string Name {
    get { return name; }
    set { name = value; }
  }

  public int Age {
    get { return age; }
    set { age = value; }
  }

  public override string ToString() {
    return string.Format("{0} is {1} years old", Name, Age);
  }
}

void Form1_Load(object sender, EventArgs e) {
  Person[] boys = { new Person("Tom", 7), new Person("John", 8) };
  foreach( Person boy in boys ) {
    listBox1.Items.Add(boy);
  }
}
```

Figure 8.1 shows the instances of the custom type shown in a ListBox control.

Because the ListView control can show items with multiple columns and states, its Items collection is populated with instances of the List-ViewItem class. Each item has a Text property, which represents the text of the first column, and then a collection of subitems that represent the rest of the columns:

FIGURE 8.1: Custom Type Shown in a ListBox Control

```
void Form1_Load(object sender, EventArgs e) {
  Person[] boys = { new Person("Tom", 7), new Person("John", 8) };
  foreach( Person boy in boys ) {
    // NOTE: Assumes Columns collection already has 2 columns
    ListViewItem item = new ListViewItem();
    item.Text = boy.Name;
    item.SubItems.Add(boy.Age.ToString());
    listView1.Items.Add(item);
  }
}
```

Figure 8.2 shows the multicolumn ListView filled via this code.

The TreeView control shows a hierarchy of items that are instances of the TreeNode type. Each TreeNode object contains the text, some optional images, and a Nodes collection containing subnodes. Which node you add to determines where the newly added node will show up in the hierarchy:

```
void Form1_Load(object sender, EventArgs e) {
  TreeNode parentNode = new TreeNode();
  parentNode.Text = "Chris";

  // Add a node to the root of the tree
  treeView1.Nodes.Add(parentNode);

  TreeNode childNode = new TreeNode();
  childNode.Text = "John";

  // Add a node under an existing node
  parentNode.Nodes.Add(childNode);
}
```

Figure 8.3 shows the result of filling a TreeView control using this sample code.

Name	Age	
Tom	7	
John	8	

FIGURE 8.2: Multicolumn ListView

```
⊟ Chris
    ⋮⋯ John
```

FIGURE 8.3: A Parent Node and a Child Node in a TreeView Control

The DataGrid control gets its data from a collection set by using the DataSource property:

```
void Form1_Load(object sender, EventArgs e) {
  Person[] boys = { new Person("Tom", 7), new Person("John", 8) };
  dataGrid1.DataSource = boys;
}
```

The DataGrid shows each public property of the objects in the collection as a column, as shown in Figure 8.4.

A DataGrid can also show hierarchical data and do all kinds of other fancy things. You'll find many more details about the DataGrid control in Chapter 13: Data Binding and Data Grids.

List Item Selection

Each of the list controls exposes a property to report the current selection (or a list of selections, if the list control supports multiple selections) and fires an event when the selection changes. For example, the following code handles the SelectedIndexChanged event of the ListBox control and uses the SelectedIndex property to pull out the currently selected object:

```
void listBox1_SelectedIndexChanged(object sender, EventArgs e) {
  // Get the selected object
  object selection = listBox1.Items[listBox1.SelectedIndex];
  MessageBox.Show(selection.ToString());

  // The object is still the same type as when we added it
  Person boy = (Person)selection;
  MessageBox.Show(boy.ToString());
}
```

Notice that the SelectedIndex property is an offset into the Items collection that pulls out the currently selected item. The item comes back as the

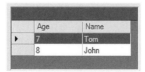

FIGURE 8.4: A DataGrid Showing a Collection of Custom Types

"object" type, but a simple cast allows us to treat it as an instance of exactly the same type as when it was added. This is useful when a custom type shows data using ToString but has another characteristic, such as a unique identifier, that is needed programmatically. In fact, for the list controls that don't take objects, such as TreeView and ListView, each of the items supports a Tag property for stashing away unique ID information:

```
void Form1_Load(object sender, EventArgs e) {
  TreeNode parentNode = new TreeNode();
  parentNode.Text = "Chris";
  parentNode.Tag = "000-00-0000"; // Put in extra info
  treeView1.Nodes.Add(parentNode);
}

void treeView1_AfterSelect(object sender, TreeViewEventArgs e) {
  TreeNode selection = treeView1.SelectedNode;
  object tag = selection.Tag; // Pull out extra info
  MessageBox.Show(tag.ToString());
}
```

List controls support either custom types or the Tag property but not both. The idea is that because the lists contain instances of custom types, any extra information can simply be kept as needed. Unfortunately, the lack of a Tag property makes it more difficult to associate ID information with simple types, such as strings. However, a simple wrapper will allow you to add a tag to a list item of any type:

```
class TaggedItem {
  public object Item;
  public object Tag;

  public TaggedItem(object item, object tag) {
    this.Item = item;
    this.Tag = tag;
  }

  public override string ToString() {
    return Item.ToString();
  }
}

void Form1_Load(object sender, EventArgs e) {
  // Add two tagged strings
  comboBox1.Items.Add(new TaggedItem("Tom", "000-00-0000"));
```

continues

```
  comboBox1.Items.Add(new TaggedItem("John",  "000-00-0000"));
}

void comboBox1_SelectedIndexChanged(object sender, EventArgs e) {
  TaggedItem selection =
    (TaggedItem)comboBox1.Items[comboBox1.SelectedIndex];
  object tag = selection.Tag;
  MessageBox.Show(tag.ToString());
}
```

The TaggedItem wrapper keeps track of an item and a tag. The ToString method lets the item decide how it should be displayed, and the Item and Tag properties expose the parts of the TaggedItem object for use in processing the current selection.

Container Controls

Whereas the list controls hold multiple objects, the job of the container controls (GroupBox, Panel, and TabControl) is to hold multiple controls. The Splitter control is not itself a container, but it can be used with container controls docked to a container's edge for sizing. All the anchoring, docking, splitting, and grouping principles covered in Chapter 2: Forms also apply to container controls. Figure 8.5 shows examples of container controls in action.

Figure 8.5 shows a GroupBox on the left, docked to the left edge of the containing form, and a TabControl with two TabPage controls on the right, split with a Splitter control in the middle.

The GroupBox sets the caption of the group using its Text property. The Panel has no label. The TabControl is really a container of TabPage controls. It's the TabPage controls that contain other controls, and the Text property shows up as the label of the tab.

FIGURE 8.5: Container Controls in Action

The only other interesting member of a container control is the Controls collection, which holds the list of contained controls. For example, the list box in Figure 8.5 is contained by the Controls collection of the group box:

```
void InitializeComponent() {
    ...
    // groupBox1
    this.groupBox1.Controls.AddRange(
        new System.Windows.Forms.Control[] {
            this.listBox1});
    ...
    // Form1
    this.Controls.AddRange(
        new System.Windows.Forms.Control[] {
            this.tabControl1,
            this.splitter1,
            this.groupBox1});
    ...
}
```

Notice in the form's InitializeComponent that the group box's Controls collection is used to contain the list box and that the form's Controls collection is used to contain the tab control, the splitter, and the group box. It's a child control's container that determines how a control is arranged. For example, when the list box's Dock property is set to Fill, the docking is relative to its container (the group box) and not to the form that actually creates the control. When a control is added to a container's Controls collection, the container control becomes the child control's parent. A child control can discover its container by using its Parent property.

ImageLists

In addition to showing text data, several of the controls—including TabPage, ToolBarButton, ListView, and TreeView—can show optional images. These controls get their images from an instance of the ImageList component. The ImageList component provides Designer support for adding images at design time and then exposes them by index number to controls that use them.

Each image-capable control exposes one or more properties of type ImageList. This property is named "ImageList" if the control supports a single set of images. But if the control supports more than one list of images, the property name contains a phrase that includes the term "ImageList." For example, the TabControl exposes the ImageList property for use by all the contained TabPage controls, whereas the ListView control exposes the LargeImageList, SmallImageList, and StateImageList properties for the three kinds of images it can display.

Regardless of the number of ImageList properties a control supports, when an item requires a certain image from the ImageList, the item exposes an index property to offset into the ImageList component's list of images. The following is an example of adding an image to each of the items in a TreeView control:

```
void InitializeComponent() {
  ...
  this.treeView1 = new TreeView();
  this.imageList1 = new ImageList(this.components);
  ...
  // ImageList associated with the TreeView
  this.treeView1.ImageList = this.imageList1;
  ...
  // Images read from Form's resources
  this.imageList1.ImageStream = ...;
  ...
}

void Form1_Load(object sender, EventArgs e) {
  TreeNode parentNode = new TreeNode();
  parentNode.Text = "Chris";
  parentNode.ImageIndex = 0; // Dad image
  parentNode.SelectedImageIndex = 0;
  treeView1.Nodes.Add(parentNode);

  TreeNode childNode = new TreeNode();
  childNode.Text = "John";
  childNode.ImageIndex = 1; // Son image
  childNode.SelectedImageIndex = 1;
  parentNode.Nodes.Add(childNode);
}
```

Using the Designer to associate images with the ImageList component causes the images themselves to be stored in form-specific resources.[2] InitializeComponent pulls them in at run time by setting the image list's

---

2. Resources are covered in detail in Chapter 10: Resources.

ImageStream property; InitializeComponent also associates the image list with the tree view by setting the tree view's ImageList property. Each node in a tree view supports two image indexes: the default image and the selected image. Each of these properties indexes into the image list associated with the tree view. Figure 8.6 shows the result.

When you collect related images in an ImageList component, setting images in a control is as simple as associating the appropriate image list (or image lists) with the control and then setting each image index as appropriate. The control itself handles the work of drawing the image.

Owner-Draw Controls

Image lists allow you to augment the display of certain controls with an image. If you'd like to take over the drawing of a control, owner-draw controls support this very thing. An *owner-draw control* provides events that allow a control's owner (or the control itself) to take over the drawing chores from the control in the underlying operating system.

Controls that allow owner draw—such as menus, some of the list controls, the tab page control, and status bar panel control—expose a property that turns owner drawing on and then fires events to let the container know that it should do the drawing. For example, the ListBox control exposes the DrawMode property, which can be one of the following values from the DrawMode enumeration:

```
enum DrawMode {
  Normal, // Control draws its own items (default)
  OwnerDrawFixed, // Fixed-size custom drawing of each item
  OwnerDrawVariable, // Variable-size custom drawing of each item
}
```

Figure 8.7 shows an owner-draw ListBox control that changes the style to Italics when it's drawing the selected item.

FIGURE 8.6: A TreeView Using an ImageList

FIGURE 8.7: Owner-Drawn List Box

To handle the drawing for a ListBox, you first set the DrawMode property to something other than Normal (the default), and then you handle the ListBox control's DrawItem event:

```
void InitializeComponent() {
  ...
  this.listBox1.DrawMode = DrawMode.OwnerDrawFixed;
  ...
}


void listBox1_DrawItem(object sender, DrawItemEventArgs e) {
  // Draw the background
  e.DrawBackground();

  // Get the default font
  Font drawFont = e.Font;
  bool ourFont = false;

  // Draw in italics if selected
  if( (e.State & DrawItemState.Selected) == DrawItemState.Selected ) {
    ourFont = true;
    drawFont = new Font(drawFont, FontStyle.Italic);
  }

  using( Brush brush = new SolidBrush(e.ForeColor) ) {
    // Draw the list box item
    e.Graphics.DrawString(listBox1.Items[e.Index].ToString(),
      drawFont,
      new SolidBrush(e.ForeColor),
      e.Bounds);

    if( ourFont ) drawFont.Dispose();
  }

  // Draw the focus rectangle
  e.DrawFocusRectangle();
}
```

The DrawItem method comes with the DrawItemEventArgs object:

```
class DrawItemEventArgs : EventArgs {
  // Properties
  public Color BackColor { get; }
  public Rectangle Bounds { get; }
  public Font Font { get; }
  public Color ForeColor { get; }
  public Graphics Graphics { get; }
  public int Index { get; }
  public DrawItemState State { get; }

  // Methods
  public virtual void DrawBackground();
  public virtual void DrawFocusRectangle();
}
```

The DrawItem event is called whenever the item is drawn or when the item's state changes. The DrawItemEventArgs object provides all the information you'll need to draw the item in question, including the index of the item being drawn, the bounds of the rectangle to draw in, the preferred font, the preferred color of the foreground and background, and the Graphics object to do the drawing on. DrawItemEventArgs also provides the selection state so that you can draw selected items differently (as our example does). DrawItemEventArgs also gives you a couple of helper methods for drawing the background and the focus rectangle if necessary. You'll usually use the latter to bracket your own custom drawing.

When you set DrawMode to OwnerDrawFixed, each item's size is set for you. If you'd like to influence the size, too, you can set DrawMode to OwnerDrawVariable, and, in addition to doing the drawing in the DrawItem handler, you can specify the height in the MeasureItem handler:

```
void InitializeComponent() {
  ...
  this.listBox2.DrawMode = OwnerDrawVariable;
  ...
}

void listBox2_MeasureItem(object sender, MeasureItemEventArgs e) {
  // Make every even item twice as high
  if( e.Index % 2 == 0 ) e.ItemHeight *= 2;
}
```

The MeasureItem event provides an instance of the MeasureItemEventArgs class, which gives you useful properties for getting and setting each item's height:

```
class MeasureItemEventArgs : EventArgs {
  // Properties
  public Graphics Graphics { get; }
  public int Index { get; }
  public int ItemHeight { get; set; }
  public int ItemWidth { get; set; }
}
```

Figure 8.8 shows the effects of doubling the heights of the even items (as well as continuing to show the selection in italics).

Unlike the DrawItem event, the MeasureItem event is called only once for every item in the control, so things such as selection state can't be a factor when you decide how big to make the space for the item.

ControlPaint

Often, owner drawing is used to draw a control that looks just like an existing Windows control but has one minor addition, such as an image added to a menu item. In those cases, you'd like to avoid spending any time duplicating the way every version of Windows draws its controls, and you can use the ControlPaint helper class for that purpose. The ControlPaint class has static members for drawing common controls, lines, grids, and types of text:

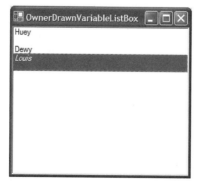

FIGURE 8.8: An Owner-Drawn List Box Using Variable Height

```
sealed class ControlPaint {
  // Properties
  public static Color ContrastControlDark { get; }

  // Methods
  public static IntPtr CreateHBitmap16Bit(...);
  public static IntPtr CreateHBitmapColorMask(...);
  public static IntPtr CreateHBitmapTransparencyMask(...);
  public static Color Dark(...);
  public static Color DarkDark(...);
  public static void DrawBorder(...);
  public static void DrawBorder3D(...);
  public static void DrawButton(...);
  public static void DrawCaptionButton(...);
  public static void DrawCheckBox(...);
  public static void DrawComboButton(...);
  public static void DrawContainerGrabHandle(...);
  public static void DrawFocusRectangle(...);
  public static void DrawGrabHandle(...);
  public static void DrawGrid(...);
  public static void DrawImageDisabled(...);
  public static void DrawLockedFrame(...);
  public static void DrawMenuGlyph(...);
  public static void DrawMixedCheckBox(...);
  public static void DrawRadioButton(...);
  public static void DrawReversibleFrame(...);
  public static void DrawReversibleLine(...);
  public static void DrawScrollButton(...);
  public static void DrawSelectionFrame(...);
  public static void DrawSizeGrip(...);
  public static void DrawStringDisabled(...);
  public static void FillReversibleRectangle(...);
  public static Color Light(...;
  public static Color LightLight(...);
}
```

For example, you can use ControlPaint to draw disabled text in an owner-draw status bar panel:

```
void statusBar1_DrawItem(object sender, StatusBarDrawItemEventArgs e) {
  // Panels don't draw with their BackColor,
  // so it's not set to something reasonable, and
  // therefore e.DrawBackground() isn't helpful.
  // Instead, use the BackColor of the StatusBar, which is the sender
  StatusBar statusBar = (StatusBar)sender;
  using( Brush brush = new SolidBrush(statusBar.BackColor) ) {
    e.Graphics.FillRectangle(SystemBrushes.Control, e.Bounds);
  }
```

continues

```
// Draw text as disabled
StringFormat format = new StringFormat();
format.LineAlignment = StringAlignment.Center;
format.Alignment = StringAlignment.Center;
ControlPaint.DrawStringDisabled(
  e.Graphics, "Hi!", this.Font, this.ForeColor, e.Bounds, format);
}
```

What makes the ControlPaint class handy is that it takes into account the conventions between versions of the operating system about the latest way to draw whatever it is you're trying to draw. So, instead of manually trying to duplicate how Windows draws disabled text this time, we can let ControlPaint do it for us, as shown in Figure 8.9.

As nifty as ControlPaint is, as of .NET 1.1 it doesn't take theming into account. If you are using a themed operating system (such as Windows XP or Windows 2003 Server), the artifacts drawn by ControlPaint will not be themed. But even though ControlPaint doesn't support themed drawing, WinForms has some support for it in the standard controls, as discussed in Chapter 2: Forms.

Custom Controls

Owner-draw controls allow a great deal of control over how a control draws itself, but to take full command of how a control acts you must build a *custom control*. There are three main kinds of custom controls:

- Controls that derive directly from the Control base class, allowing you to handle your control's input and output completely
- Controls that derive from ScrollableControl, which are like controls that derive from Control but also provide built-in support for scrolling

FIGURE 8.9: An Owner-Drawn Status Bar Panel Using ControlPaint

- Controls that derive from an existing control to extend their behavior

The kind of control you choose depends on the kind of functionality you need. If you need something that's fundamentally new, you'll derive from Control or ScrollingControl, depending on whether you need scrolling. Deriving from one of the existing controls is useful if an existing control almost does what you want. The following sections discuss how to build all three kinds of custom controls.

Deriving Directly from the Control Class

In VS.NET, if you right-click on your project in Solution Explorer and choose Add | Add New Item | Custom Control, you'll get the following skeleton:

```
using System;
using System.Collections;
using System.ComponentModel;
using System.Drawing;
using System.Data;
using System.Windows.Forms;

namespace MyCustomControls {
  /// <summary>
  /// Summary description for CustomControl1.
  /// </summary>
  public class CustomControl1 : System.Windows.Forms.Control {
    public CustomControl1() {
    }

    protected override void OnPaint(PaintEventArgs pe) {
      // TODO: Add custom paint code here

      // Calling the base class OnPaint
      base.OnPaint(pe);
    }
  }
}
```

This skeleton derives from the Control base class and provides a handler for the Paint event. It even provides a helpful comment letting you know where to add your custom code to render your custom control's state.

Testing Custom Controls

After you've worked with your custom control for a while, you'll want it to show up on the Toolbox so that you can use it in various places. To do this, right-click on the Toolbox and choose Add/Remove Items.[3] When you do that, you will get the Customize Toolbox dialog showing the .NET components that VS.NET knows about, as shown in Figure 8.10. To choose a .NET assembly, click on the .NET Framework Component tab and press the Browse button.

Choose the assembly that your control lives in and press OK. If you are writing a Windows Forms application and writing your custom control in the same assembly, select the application's .EXE file as the assembly. Even controls from applications are available for reuse, although DLLs are the preferred vehicle for distributing reusable controls.

After you've chosen the assembly to add, the custom controls will be added to the Toolbox, as shown in Figure 8.11.

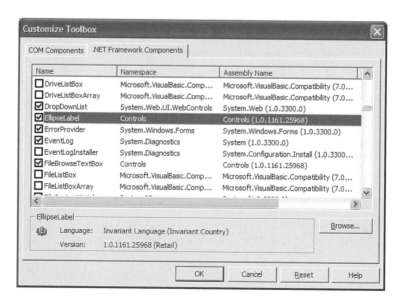

FIGURE 8.10: Customizing the Toolbox

---

3. In VS.NET 2002, "Add/Remove Items" is called "Customize Toolbox."

FIGURE 8.11: Custom Controls Added to the Toolbox in VS.NET

Although it's possible to customize any of the tabs on the Toolbox, it's handy to have custom tabs for custom controls so that they don't get lost among the standard controls and components. Figure 8.11 shows custom controls organized on the My Custom Controls tab.

When your control is available on the Toolbox, you can drop it onto a Form and use the Property Browser to set all public properties and handle all public events. Because your custom controls inherit from the Control base, all this comes essentially for free. For the details of how to customize your control's interaction with the Designer and the Property Browser, see Chapter 9: Design-Time Integration.

Control Rendering

Looking back at the skeleton code generated by the Designer for a custom control, remember that it handles the Paint event by deriving from the Control base class and overriding the OnPaint method. Because we're deriving from the Control class, we have two options when deciding how to handle a method. The first option is to add a delegate and handle the event. This is the only option available when you're handling a control's event from a container. The second option is to override the virtual method that the base class provides that actually fires the methods. By convention, these methods are named On<EventName> and take an object of the EventArgs (or EventArgs-derived) class. When you override an event method, remember to call to the base class's implementation of the method so that all the event subscribers will be notified.

For example, here's how to implement OnPaint for a custom label–like control:

```
public class EllipseLabel : Control {
  public EllipseLabel() {
    // Required for Designer support
    InitializeComponent();
  }

  protected override void OnPaint(PaintEventArgs pe) {
    // Custom paint code
    Graphics g = pe.Graphics;
    using( Brush foreBrush = new SolidBrush(this.ForeColor) )
    using( Brush backBrush = new SolidBrush(this.BackColor) ) {
      g.FillEllipse(foreBrush, this.ClientRectangle);

      StringFormat fmt = new StringFormat();
      fmt.Alignment = StringAlignment.Center;
      fmt.LineAlignment = StringAlignment.Center;
      g.DrawString(
        this.Text, this.Font, backBrush, this.ClientRectangle, fmt);
    }

    // Calling the base class OnPaint
    base.OnPaint(pe);
  }
}
```

In this code, notice how much functionality is available from the base class without the need to add any new properties, methods, or events. In fact, the sheer amount of functionality in the base Control class is too large to list here.

Many of the properties have corresponding <PropertyName>Changed events to track when they change. For example, the state of our custom label–like control depends on the state of the BackColor, ForeColor, Text, Font, and ClientRectangle properties; so when any of these properties changes, we must apply the principles of drawing and invalidation from Chapter 4: Drawing Basics to keep the control visually up-to-date:

```
public EllipseLabel() {
  // Required for Designer support
  InitializeComponent();
```

```
  // Automatically redraw when resized
  // (See Chapter 6: Advanced Drawing for ControlStyles details)
  this.SetStyle(ControlStyles.ResizeRedraw, true);
}

void InitializeComponent() {
  this.TextChanged += new EventHandler(this.EllipseLabel_TextChanged);
}

void EllipseLabel_TextChanged(object sender, EventArgs e) {
  this.Invalidate();
}
```

In this case, we track when the Text property has changed by using the Designer[4] to set up an event handler for the TextChanged event (saving us from typing in the event handler skeleton or remembering to call the base class). When the text changes, we invalidate our control's client area. However, we don't need to track any of the BackColorChanged, FontChanged, or ForeColorChanged events because the base class knows to invalidate the client area of the control in those cases for us. Those properties are special, as explained next.

Ambient Properties

The reason that the base class knows to treat some properties specially is that they are ambient properties. An *ambient property* is one that, if it's not set in the control, will be "inherited" from the container. Of all the standard properties provided by the Control base class, only four are ambient: Back-Color, ForeColor, Font, and Cursor. For example, imagine an instance of the EllipseLabel control and a button hosted on a form container, as in Figure 8.12.

FIGURE 8.12: The EllipseLabel Custom Control Hosted on a Form

---

4. Be careful when using the Designer with custom controls. It adds an InitializeComponent method if there isn't already one in the class, but it doesn't add a call from your control's constructor to InitializeComponent, so you must do that manually.

All the settings for the Form, the EllipseLabel control, and the Button control are the defaults with respect to the Font property; this means that on my Windows XP machine running at normal-sized fonts, the two controls show with MS Sans Serif 8.25-point font. Because the EllipseLabel control takes its own Font property into account when drawing, changing its Font property to Impact 10-point in the Property Browser yields this code:

```
void InitializeComponent() {
  ...
  this.ellipseLabel1.Font = new Font("Impact", 10F, ...);
  ...
}
```

The result looks like Figure 8.13.

This works great if you're creating a funhouse application in which different controls have different fonts, but more commonly, all the controls in a container will share the same font. Although it's certainly possible to use the Designer to set the fonts for each of the controls individually, it's even easier to leave the font alone on the controls and set the font on the form:

```
void InitializeComponent() {
  ...
  this.Font = new Font("Impact", 10F, ...);
  ...
}
```

Because the Font property is ambient, setting the font on the container also sets the fonts on the contained controls, as shown in Figure 8.14.

When you set the Font property on the container and leave the Font property at the default value[5] for the controls, the control "inherits" the Font property from the container. Similarly, a contained control can "override" an ambient property if you set it to something other than the default:

FIGURE 8.13: Setting the Font Property on the EllipseLabel Control

FIGURE 8.14: Setting the Font Property on the Hosting Form

```
void InitializeComponent() {
   ...
   this.ellipseLabel1.Font = new Font("Times New Roman", 10F, ...);
   ...
   this.Font = new Font("Impact", 10F, ...);
   ...
}
```

Notice that the form's font is set after the EllipseLabel control's font. It doesn't matter in which order the ambient properties are set. If a control has its own value for an ambient property, that value will be used instead of the container's value. The result of the contained EllipseLabel control overriding the ambient Font property is shown in Figure 8.15.

Also, if you need to reset the ambient properties to a default value, you can do this by using the Control class's Reset<PropertyName> methods:

```
ellipseLabel1.ResetFont();
```

Ambient properties exist to allow containers to specify a look and feel that all the contained controls share without any special effort. However, in the event that a particular control needs to override the property inherited from its container, that can happen without incident.

FIGURE 8.15: A Contained Control Overriding the Value of the Ambient Font Property

---

5. You can return a property to its "default" value in the Property Browser by right-clicking on the property name and choosing Reset.

Custom Functionality

In addition to the standard properties that a control gets from the Control base class, the state that a control must render will come from new public methods and properties that are exposed as they would be exposed from any .NET class:

```
// Used to prepend to Text property at output
string prefix = "";

public void ResetPrefix() {
  this.Prefix = ""; // Uses Prefix setter
}

public string Prefix {
  get { return this.prefix; }
  set {
    this.prefix = value;
    this.Invalidate();
  }
}

protected override void OnPaint(PaintEventArgs pe) {
  ...
  g.DrawString(this.prefix + this.Text, ...);
  ...
}
```

In this case, we've got some extra control state modeled with a string field named "prefix." The prefix is shown just before the Text property when the control paints itself. The prefix field itself is private, but you can affect it by calling the public ResetPrefix method or getting or setting the public Prefix property. Notice that whenever the prefix field changes, the control invalidates itself so that it can maintain a visual state that's consistent with its internal state.

Because the Prefix property is public, it shows up directly in the Property Browser when an instance of the Ellipse Control is chosen on a design surface, as shown in Figure 8.16.

FIGURE 8.16: A Custom Property in the Property Browser

Custom Events

The Property Browser will show any public property without your doing anything special to make it work. Similarly, any public events[6] will show up there, too. For example, if you want to fire an event when the Prefix property changes, you can expose a public property:

```
// Let clients know of changes in the Prefix property
public event EventHandler PrefixChanged;

public string Prefix {
  get { return this.prefix; }
  set {
    this.prefix = value;

    // Fire PrefixChanged event
    if( this.PrefixChanged != null ) {
      PrefixChanged(this, EventArgs.Empty);
    }

    this.Invalidate();
  }
}
```

---

6. For an introduction to delegates and events, see Appendix B: Delegates and Events.

Notice that this code exposes a custom event called PrefixChanged of type EventHandler, which is the default delegate type for events that don't need special data. When the prefix field is changed, the code looks for event subscribers and lets them know that the prefix has changed, passing the sender (the control itself) and an empty EventArgs object, because we don't have any additional data to send.

When your control has a public event, it will show up as just another event in the Property Browser, as shown in Figure 8.17.

Just like handling any other event, handling a custom event yields a code skeleton for the developer to fill in with functionality—again, without your doing anything except exposing the event as public.

If, when defining your event, you find that you'd like to pass other information, you can create a custom delegate:

```
public class PrefixEventArgs : EventArgs {
  public string Prefix;
  public PrefixEventArgs(string prefix) { Prefix = prefix; }
}

public delegate
  void PrefixedChangedEventHandler(object sender, PrefixEventArgs e);
public event PrefixedChangedEventHandler PrefixChanged;

public string Prefix {
  get { return this.prefix; }
  set {
    this.prefix = value;

    // Fire PrefixChanged event
    if( this.PrefixChanged != null ) {
      PrefixChanged(this, new PrefixEventArgs(value));
    }
```

FIGURE 8.17: A Custom Event Shown in the Property Browser

```
    this.Invalidate();
  }
}
```

Notice that the custom delegate we created uses the same pattern of no return value, an object sender argument, and an EventArgs-derived type as the last argument. This is the pattern that .NET follows, and it's a good one for you to emulate with your own custom events. In our case, we're deriving from EventArgs to pass along a PrefixEventArgs class, which derives from EventArgs and sends the new prefix to the event handlers. But you can define new EventArgs-derived classes as appropriate for your own custom controls.

Control Input

In addition to providing output and exposing custom methods, properties, and events, custom controls often handle input, whether it's mouse input, keyboard input, or both.

Mouse Input

For example, if we wanted to let users click on EllipseControl and, as they drag, adjust the color of the ellipse, we could do so by handling the Mouse-Down, MouseMove, and MouseUp events:

```
// Track whether mouse button is down
bool mouseDown = false;

void SetMouseForeColor(MouseEventArgs e) {
  int red = (e.X * 255/(this.ClientRectangle.Width - e.X))%256;
  if( red < 0 ) red = -red;
  int green = 0;
  int blue = (e.Y * 255/(this.ClientRectangle.Height - e.Y))%256;
  if( blue < 0 ) blue = -blue;
  this.ForeColor = Color.FromArgb(red, green, blue);
}

void EllipseLabel_MouseDown(object sender, MouseEventArgs e) {
  mouseDown = true;
  SetMouseForeColor(e);
}
```

continues

```
void EllipseLabel_MouseMove(object sender, MouseEventArgs e) {
  if( mouseDown ) SetMouseForeColor(e);
}

void EllipseLabel_MouseUp(object sender, MouseEventArgs e) {
  SetMouseForeColor(e);
  mouseDown = false;
}
```

The MouseDown event is fired when the mouse is clicked inside the client area of the control. The control continues to get MouseMove events until the MouseUp event is fired, even if the mouse moves out of the region of the control's client area. The code sample watches the mouse movements when the button is down and calculates a new ForeColor using the X and Y coordinates of the mouse as provided by the MouseEventArgs argument to the events:

```
class MouseEventArgs : EventArgs {
  public MouseButtons Button { get; } // Which buttons are pressed
  public int Clicks { get; } // How many clicks since the last event
  public int Delta { get; } // How many mouse wheel ticks
  public int X { get; } // Current X position relative to the screen
  public int Y { get; } // Current Y position relative to the screen
}
```

MouseEventArgs is meant to provide you with the information you need in order to handle mouse events. For example, to eliminate the need to track the mouse button state manually, we could use the Button property to check for a click of the left mouse button:

```
void EllipseLabel_MouseDown(object sender, MouseEventArgs e) {
  SetMouseForeColor(e);
}

void EllipseLabel_MouseMove(object sender, MouseEventArgs e) {
  if( (e.Button & MouseButtons.Left) == MouseButtons.Left ) {
    SetMouseForeColor(e);
  }
}

void EllipseLabel_MouseUp(object sender, MouseEventArgs e) {
  SetMouseForeColor(e);
}
```

Additional mouse-related input events are MouseEnter, MouseHover, and MouseLeave, which can tell you that the mouse is over the control, that it's hovered for "a while" (useful for showing tooltips), and that it has left the control's client area.

If you'd like to know the state of the mouse buttons or the mouse position outside a mouse event, you can access this information from the static MouseButtons and MousePosition properties of the Control class. In addition to MouseDown, MouseMove, and MouseUp, there are five other mouse-related events. MouseEnter, MouseHover, and MouseLeave allow you to track when a mouse enters, loiters in, and leaves the control's client area. Click and DoubleClick provide an indication that the user has clicked or double-clicked the mouse in the control's client area.

Keyboard Input

In addition to providing mouse input, forms (and controls) can capture keyboard input via the KeyDown, KeyUp, and KeyPress events. For example, to make the keys i, j, k, and l move our elliptical label around on the container, the EllipseLabel control could handle the KeyPress event:

```
void EllipseLabel_KeyPress(object sender, KeyPressEventArgs e) {
  Point location = new Point(this.Left, this.Top);

  switch( e.KeyChar ) {
    case 'i':
      --location.Y;
      break;

    case 'j':
      --location.X;
      break;

    case 'k':
      ++location.Y;
      break;

    case 'l':
      ++location.X;
      break;
  }

  this.Location = location;
}
```

The KeyPress event takes a KeyPressEventArgs argument:

```
class KeyPressEventArgs : EventArgs {
  public bool Handled { get; set; } // Whether this key is handled
  public char KeyChar { get; } // Character value of the key pressed
}
```

The KeyPressEventArgs object has two properties. The Handled property defaults to false but can be set to true to indicate that no other handlers should handle the event. The KeyChar property is the character value of the key after the modifier has been applied. For example, if the user presses the I key, the KeyChar will be i, but if the user presses Shift and the I key, the KeyChar property will be I. On the other hand, if the user presses Ctrl+I or Alt+I, we won't get a KeyPress event at all, because those are special sequences that aren't sent via the KeyPress event. To handle these kinds of sequences along with other special characters such as F-keys or arrows, you need the KeyDown event:

```
void TransparentForm_KeyDown(object sender, KeyEventArgs e) {
  Point location = new Point(this.Left, this.Top);

  switch( e.KeyCode ) {
    case Keys.I:
    case Keys.Up:
      --location.Y;
      break;

    case Keys.J:
    case Keys.Left:
      --location.X;
      break;

    case Keys.K:
    case Keys.Down:
      ++location.Y;
      break;

    case Keys.L:
    case Keys.Right:
      ++location.X;
      break;
  }
```

```
    this.Location = location;
}
```

Notice that the KeyDown event takes a KeyEventArgs argument (as does the KeyUp event), which is shown here:

```
class KeyEventArgs : EventArgs {
  public bool Alt { virtual get; } // Whether Alt is pressed
  public bool Control { get; } // Whether Ctrl is pressed
  public bool Handled { get; set; } // Whether this key is handled
  public Keys KeyCode { get; } // The key being pressed, w/o modifiers
  public Keys KeyData { get; } // The key and the modifiers
  public int KeyValue { get; } // KeyData as an integer
  public Keys Modifiers { get; } // Only the modifiers
  public bool Shift { virtual get; } // Whether Shift is pressed
}
```

Although it looks as if the KeyEventArgs object contains a lot of data, it really contains only one thing: a private field exposed via the KeyData property. KeyData is a bit field of the combination of the keys being pressed (from the Keys enumeration) and the modifiers being pressed (also from the Keys enumeration). For example, if the I key is pressed by itself, KeyData will be Keys.I, whereas if Ctrl+Shift+F2 is pressed, KeyData will be a bitwise combination of Keys.F2, Keys.Shift, and Keys.Control.

The rest of the properties in the KeyEventArgs object are handy views of the KeyData property, as shown in Table 8.1. Also shown is the KeyChar that would be generated in a corresponding KeyPress event.

Even though we're handling the KeyDown event specifically to get special characters, some special characters, such as arrows, aren't sent to the control by default. To enable them, the custom control overrides the IsInputKey method from the base class:

```
protected override bool IsInputKey(Keys keyData) {
  // Make sure we get arrow keys
  switch( keyData ) {
    case Keys.Up:
    case Keys.Left:
    case Keys.Down:
    case Keys.Right:
      return true;
  }
```

continues

TABLE 8.1: KeyEventArgs and KeyPressEventArgs Examples

Keys Pressed	KeyData	KeyCode	Modifiers	Alt	Ctrl	Shift	KeyValue	KeyChar
I	Keys.I	Keys.I	Keys.None	false	false	false	73	i
Shift+I	Keys.Shift + Keys.I	Keys.I	Keys.Shift	false	false	true	73	I
Ctrl+Shift+I	Keys.Ctrl + Keys.Shift + Keys.I	Keys.I	Keys.Ctrl + Keys.Shift	false	true	true	73	n/a
Ctrl	Keys.ControlKey + Keys.Ctrl	Keys.ControlKey	Keys.Control	false	true	false	17	n/a

```
  // The rest can be determined by the base class
  return base.IsInputKey(keyData);
}
```

The return from IsInputKey indicates whether or not the key data should be sent in events to the control. In this example, IsInputKey returns true for all the arrow keys and lets the base class decide what to do about the other keys.

If you'd like to know the state of a modifier key outside a key event, you can access the state in the static ModifierKeys property of the Control class. For example, the following checks to see whether the Ctrl key is the only modifier to be pressed during a mouse click event:

```
void EllipseLabel_Click(object sender, EventArgs e) {
  if( Control.ModifierKeys == Keys.Control ) {
    MessageBox.Show("Ctrl+Click detected");
  }
}
```

Windows Message Handling

The paint event, the mouse and keyboard events, and most of the other events handled by a custom control come from the underlying Windows operating system. At the Win32 level, the events start out life as Windows messages. A *Windows message* is most often generated by Windows because of some kind of hardware event, such as the user pressing a key, moving the mouse, or bringing a window from the background to the foreground. The window that needs to react to the message gets the message queued in its *message queue*. That's where WinForms steps in.

The Control base class is roughly equivalent to the concept of a window in the operating system. It's the job of WinForms to take each message off the Windows message queue and route it to the Control responsible for handling the message. The base Control class turns this message into an event, which Control then fires by calling the appropriate method in the base class. For example, the WM_PAINT Windows message eventually turns into a call on the OnPaint method, which in turn fires the Paint event to all interested listeners.

However, not all Windows messages are turned into events by WinForms. For those cases, you can drop down to a lower level and handle the messages as they come into the Control class. You do this by overriding the WndProc method:

```
protected override void WndProc(ref Message m) {
  // Process and/or update message
  ...

  // Let base class handle it if you don't
  base.WndProc(ref m);
}
```

As a somewhat esoteric example of handling Windows messages directly, the following is a rewrite of the code from Chapter 2: Forms to move the nonrectangular form around the screen:

```
protected override void WndProc(ref Message m) {
  // Let the base class have first crack
  base.WndProc(ref m);
  int WM_NCHITTEST = 0x84; // winuser.h
  if( m.Msg != WM_NCHITTEST ) return;

  // If the user clicked on the client area,
  // ask the OS to treat it as a click on the caption
  int HTCLIENT = 1;
  int HTCAPTION = 2;
  if( m.Result.ToInt32() == HTCLIENT )
    m.Result = (IntPtr)HTCAPTION;
}
```

This code handles the WM_NCHITTEST message, which is one of the few that WinForms doesn't expose as an event. In this case, the code calls to the Windows-provided handler for this message to see whether the user is moving the mouse over the client area of the form. If that's the case, the code pretends that the entire client area is the caption so that when the user clicks and drags on it, Windows will take care of moving the form for us.

There aren't a whole lot of reasons to override the WndProc method and handle the Windows message directly, but it's nice to know that the option is there in case you need it.

Scrolling Controls

Although directly inheriting from Control gives you a bunch of functionality, you may find the need to create a control that scrolls. You could use a custom control to handle the logic involved in creating the scrollbar(s) and handling repainting correctly as the user scrolls across the drawing surface. Luckily, though, the .NET Framework provides a class that handles most of these chores for you.

To create a scrolling control, you derive from ScrollableControl instead of Control:

```
class ScrollingEllipseLabel : ScrollableControl {...}
```

When you implement a scrolling control, the ClientRectangle represents the size of the control's visible surface, but there could be more of the control that isn't currently visible because it's been scrolled out of range. To get to the entire area of the control, use the DisplayRectangle property instead. DisplayRectangle is a property of the ScrollableControl class that represents the virtual drawing area. Figure 8.18 shows the difference between the ClientRectangle and the DisplayRectangle.

An OnPaint method for handling scrolling should look something like this:

```
protected override void OnPaint(PaintEventArgs pe) {
  Graphics g = pe.Graphics;
  using( Brush foreBrush = new SolidBrush(this.ForeColor) )
  using( Brush backBrush = new SolidBrush(this.BackColor) ) {
    g.FillEllipse(foreBrush, this.DisplayRectangle);

    StringFormat format = new StringFormat();
    format.Alignment = StringAlignment.Center;
    format.LineAlignment = StringAlignment.Center;
```

continues

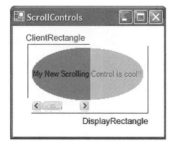

FIGURE 8.18: DisplayRectangle Versus ClientRectangle (See Plate 20)

```
    g.DrawString(
      this.Text, this.Font, backBrush, this.DisplayRectangle, format);
  }

  base.OnPaint(pe);
}
```

The only difference between this OnPaint method and the custom control is that we are painting to the DisplayRectangle instead of the ClientRectangle.

Setting the Scroll Dimension

Unlike the ClientRectangle, which is determined by the container of the control, the DisplayRectangle is determined by the control itself. The scrollable control gets to decide the minimum when you set the AutoScrollMinSize property from the ScrollableControl base class. For example, the following code uses the control's font settings to calculate the size needed for the scrollable label based on the size of the Text property:

```
void ScrollingEllipseLabel_TextChanged(object sender, EventArgs e) {
  this.Invalidate();

  // Text changed -- calculate new DisplayRectangle
  SetScrollMinSize();
}

void ScrollingEllipseLabel_FontChanged(object sender, EventArgs e) {
  // Font changed -- calculate new DisplayRectangle
  SetScrollMinSize();
}

void SetScrollMinSize() {
  // Create a Graphics Object to measure with
  using( Graphics g = this.CreateGraphics() ) {
    // Determine the size of the text
    SizeF sizeF = g.MeasureString(this.Text, this.Font);
    Size size =
      new Size(
      (int)Math.Ceiling(sizeF.Width),
      (int)Math.Ceiling(sizeF.Height));

    // Set the minimum size to the text size
    this.AutoScrollMinSize = size;
  }
}
```

The SetScrollMinSize helper measures the size that the text will be in the particular font and then creates a Size structure. The AutoScrollMinSize property of the Size structure is used to tell the control when to show the scrollbars. If the DisplayRectangle is larger in either dimension than the ClientRectangle, scrollbars will appear.

The ScrollableControl base class has a few other interesting properties. The AutoScroll property (set to true by the Designer by default) enables the DisplayRectangle to be a different size than the ClientRectangle. Otherwise, the DisplayRectangle is always the same size as the ClientRectangle.

The AutoScrollPosition property lets you programmatically change the position within the scrollable area of the control. The AutoScrollMargin property is used to set a margin around scrollable controls that are also container controls. The DockPadding property is similar but is used for child controls that dock. Container controls could be controls such as GroupBox or Panel, or they could be custom controls, such as user controls, covered later in this chapter.

Checking MSDN Library, ScrollableControl control does not have either HScroll or VScroll events. Except for the scrolling capability, scrollable controls are just like controls that derive from the Control base class.

Extending Existing Controls

If you'd like a control that's similar to an existing control but not exactly the same, you don't want to start by deriving from Control or ScrollableControl and building everything from scratch. Instead, you should derive from the existing control, whether it's one of the standard controls provided by WinForms or one of your own controls.

For example, let's assume that you want to create a FileTextBox control that's just like the TextBox control except that it indicates to the user whether or not the currently entered file exists. Figures 8.19 and 8.20 show the FileTextBox control in use.

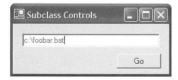

FIGURE 8.19: FileTextBox with a File That *Does Not* Exist (See Plate 21)

FIGURE 8.20: FileTextBox with a File Name That *Does* Exist (See Plate 22)

By putting this functionality into a reusable control, you can drop it on any form without making the form itself provide this functionality. By deriving the FileTextBox from the TextBox base control class, you can get most of the behavior you need without any effort, letting you focus on the interesting new functionality:

```
class FileTextBox : TextBox {
  protected override void OnTextChanged(EventArgs e) {
    // If the file does not exist, color the text red
    if( !File.Exists(this.Text) ) {
      this.ForeColor = Color.Red;
    }
    else { // Make it black
      this.ForeColor = Color.Black;
    }

    // Call the base class
    base.OnTextChanged(e);
  }
}
```

Notice that implementing FileTextBox is merely a matter of deriving from the TextBox base class (which provides all the editing capabilities that the user will expect) and overriding the OnTextChanged method. (I also could have handled the TextChanged event.) When the text changes, we use the Exists method of the System.IO.File class to check whether the currently entered file exists in the file system and to set the foreground color of the control accordingly. Often, you can easily create new controls that have application-specific functionality using as little code as this because the bulk of the code is provided by the base control class.

User Controls

Deriving from an existing control is one way to reuse it, but the most popular form of reuse for a control is simple containment, as you're accustomed to doing when building custom forms using existing controls. A *user control* is a way to contain a set of other controls for reuse as a set, producing a kind of "subform." For example, imagine that we wanted a control that composed our FileTextBox control with a "..." button for browsing. In use, it would look like the one shown in Figure 8.21.

It's hard to tell from the picture, but as far as the form in Figure 8.21 is concerned, it's containing only a single control (named FileBrowseText-Box). The control is a user control because it derives from the UserControl base class and contains two other controls: a FileTextBox control and a Button control.

To create a custom user control, you right-click on your project in Solution Explorer, choose Add | Add User Control, and press OK.[7] When you do, you'll get the design surface for your user control to arrange with controls, as shown in Figure 8.22.

Building a user control that brings the FileTextBox together with a browse button is a matter of dropping each onto the form and arranging to taste. Also, to enable browsing, you'll probably want to use an instance of the OpenFileDialog component, capturing all that functionality into a single user control for reuse, as shown in Figure 8.23.

FIGURE 8.21: A Sample User Control in Action

---

7. If you'd like to start a new project to hold user controls, you can do so with the Windows Controls Library project template in the New Project dialog.

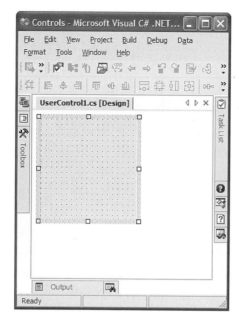

FIGURE 8.22: A New User Control

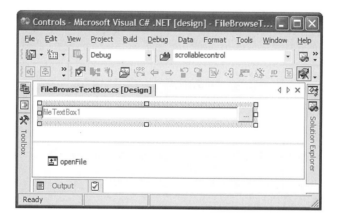

FIGURE 8.23: The FileBrowseTextBox User Control in the Designer

All the control arranging that you're already accustomed to—such as anchoring and docking—works the same way in a user control as in a custom form. You also use the same techniques for setting properties or handling events. After arranging the existing controls and components on the user control design surface, you simply write a tiny chunk of code to handle the click on the browse button to make it all work:

```
void browseButton_Click(object sender, EventArgs e) {
  if( this.openFileDialog1.ShowDialog() == DialogResult.OK ) {
    fileTextBox1.Text = this.openFile.FileName;
  }
}
```

User controls allow you to build reusable controls using the same tools you use when building forms, but with the added advantage of being able to drop a user control onto anything that can contain controls, including container controls, forms, and even other user controls.

Drag and Drop

No matter what kind of controls you're using or building, often you'd like to enable the user to drag data from one to another. This communication protocol, known as *drag and drop*, has long been standardized and is fully supported in WinForms for both targets and sources.

The Drop Target

Adding drag and drop to your application involves two elements: the drop target and the drop source. First, you must have a control that supports having things dragged and dropped onto it. This kind of control is known as the *drop target*. You designate your target by setting the AllowDrop property of the control to true.

Next, you make the target control subscribe to one or more of the drag-and-drop events:

- **DragEnter** is fired when the mouse enters the area of a control containing drag-and-drop data. It is used by the target to indicate whether it can accept the data.
- **DragOver** is called as the user hovers the mouse over the target.
- **DragLeave** is called when the mouse leaves the area of a control containing the drag-and-drop data.
- **DragDrop** is called when the user drops the data onto the target.

All target controls must implement the DragEnter event, or else they won't be able to accept any dropped data. The DragEnter event comes along with an instance of the DragEventArgs class, which gives the target information about the data:

```
class DragEventArgs : EventArgs {
  // Properties
  public DragDropEffects AllowedEffect { get; }
  public IDataObject Data { get; }
  public DragDropEffects Effect { get; set; }
  public int KeyState { get; }
  public int X { get; }
  public int Y { get; }
}
```

A target control's DragEnter event handler checks the Data property to see whether it can be accepted when dropped. The object returned from the Data property implements IDataObject to make that determination possible:

```
interface IDataObject {
  // Methods
  public virtual
    object GetData(string format, bool autoConvert);
  public virtual object GetData(string format);
  public virtual object GetData(Type format);

  public virtual void
    SetData(string format, bool autoConvert, object data);
  public virtual void SetData(string format, object data);
  public virtual void SetData(Type format, object data);
  public virtual void SetData(object data);

  public virtual
    bool GetDataPresent(string format, bool autoConvert);
  public virtual bool GetDataPresent(string format);
  public virtual bool GetDataPresent(Type format);

  public virtual string[] GetFormats(bool autoConvert);
  public virtual string[] GetFormats();
}
```

The IDataObject interface is actually defined from .NET's Component Object Model (COM) cousin, where drag and drop was born. WinForms continues to work with the COM-based protocol so that managed and unmanaged applications can participate in drag-and-drop operations between each other.

Furthermore, the COM-based protocol itself is based on the Windows convention for the way the Clipboard works. All data passed around using drag and drop is represented in Clipboard formats. Some Clipboard formats are customized for your own application, and others are well known to allow Clipboard and drag-and-drop operations between applications. The format strings used to specify the well-known formats are predefined as static fields of the DataFormats class:

```
class DataFormats {
  // Fields
  public static readonly string Bitmap;
  public static readonly string CommaSeparatedValue;
  public static readonly string Dib;
  public static readonly string Dif;
  public static readonly string EnhancedMetafile;
  public static readonly string FileDrop;
  public static readonly string Html;
  public static readonly string Locale;
  public static readonly string MetafilePict;
  public static readonly string OemText;
  public static readonly string Palette;
  public static readonly string PenData;
  public static readonly string Riff;
  public static readonly string Rtf;
  public static readonly string Serializable;
  public static readonly string StringFormat;
  public static readonly string SymbolicLink;
  public static readonly string Text;
  public static readonly string Tiff;
  public static readonly string UnicodeText;
  public static readonly string WaveAudio;

  // Methods
  public static DataFormats.Format GetFormat(string format);
  public static DataFormats.Format GetFormat(int id);
}
```

In addition to support for well-known data formats, .NET provides a conversion from some .NET types, such as String, to a corresponding format string, such as DataFormats.Text. Using a format string and the Get-DataPresent method of the IDataObject, the target can determine whether the type of data being dragged is acceptable for a drop:

```
void textBox3_DragEnter(object sender, DragEventArgs e) {
  // Could check against DataFormats.Text as well
  if( e.Data.GetDataPresent(typeof(string)) ) {
    e.Effect = DragDropEffects.Copy;
  }
  else {
    e.Effect = DragDropEffects.None;
  }
}
```

GetDataPresent checks the format of the data to see whether it matches the Clipboard format (or a .NET type converted to a Clipboard format). To find out whether the data is in a convertible format, you can call the GetFormats() function, which returns an array of formats. Calling any of the IDataObject methods with the autoConvert parameter set to false will disable anything except a direct match of data types.

If the data is acceptable, the DragEnter event handler must set the Effect property of the DragEffectArgs object to one or more flags indicating what the control is willing to do with the data if it's dropped, as determined by the flags in the DragDropEffects enumeration:

```
enum DragDropEffects {
  Copy, // Take a copy of the data
  Move, // Take ownership of the data
  Link, // Link to the data
  Scroll, // Scrolling is happening in the target
  All, // All of the above
  None, // Reject the data
}
```

If a drop is allowed and it happens while the mouse is over the target, the target control will receive the DragDrop event:

```
void textBox3_DragDrop(object sender, DragEventArgs e) {
  textBox3.Text = (string)e.Data.GetData(typeof(string));
}
```

When you implement the DragDrop handler, the Effect property of the DragEventArgs will be the effect that the source and target agreed on, should multiple effects be allowed. Retrieving the data is a matter of calling GetData—using either a DataFormat format string or a .NET Type object—and casting the result.

Drop Targets and COM

When you enable a control as a target, you open yourself up to the possibility that the user will receive the cryptic message shown in Figure 8.24.

Because drag and drop is a feature provided using COM, COM must be initialized on the UI thread for drag and drop to work. Although .NET is smart enough to lazily initialize COM on the running thread as needed, for reasons of efficiency it picks the UI-hostile Multi-Threaded Apartment (MTA) for the thread to join unless told to do otherwise. Unfortunately, for drag and drop, the UI thread must join the Single-Threaded Apartment (STA). To ensure that that's the case, always double-check that the Main function on all your WinForms applications is marked with STAThreadAttribute:

```
[STAThread]
static void Main() {
  Application.Run(new Form1());
}
```

(Note that STAThread is a C# shortcut for STAThreadAttribute.)

By default, any VS.NET-generated code will contain this attribute on the Main function (even Console applications), but just in case it somehow goes missing, this is the first thing to check when you see the message box from Figure 8.24.

The Drop Source

With the target implemented, what's left is initiating a drag-and-drop operation from the *drop source* using the DoDragDrop method of the

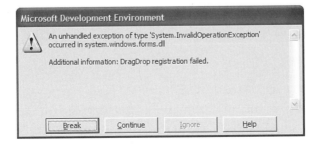

FIGURE 8.24: Cryptic Drag-and-Drop Error Message

Control class. DoDragDrop is almost always placed in the handler for a MouseDown event:

```
void button3_MouseDown(object sender, MouseEventArgs e) {
  // Start a drag-and-drop operation
  DoDragDrop(button3.Text, DragDropEffects.Copy);
}
```

The DoDragDrop method's first parameter is the data, which can be any object. The second parameter is a combination of the drag-and-drop effects that the source supports. For example, Figure 8.25 shows the button initiating the drag and drop.

As the drag-and-drop operation progresses, the DoDragDrop method tracks the mouse as it moves over controls, looking to see whether they are potential drop targets (as set with the AllowDrop property) and firing the DragEnter event to see whether potential targets can accept the data. Depending on whether the target can accept the data, DoDragDrop sets the cursor based on the current effect indicated by the target to communicate to users what would happen if they were to drop at any point. Notice in Figure 8.25 that the button itself is not a drop target, so the cursor indicates that a drop on the button would have no effect.

On the other hand, when the data is dragged over a text box that is enabled to accept string data, the DragEnter event is fired, and the control indicates the effect that it will support. This causes the cursor to be updated appropriately, as shown in Figure 8.26.

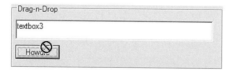

FIGURE 8.25: A Drag-and-Drop Operation Showing the None Effect

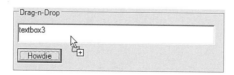

FIGURE 8.26: Drop Target Indicating the Copy Effect

When the user releases the mouse button, dropping the data, the Drag-Drop event is fired on the target, and the target accepts the data, as shown in Figure 8.27.

When the drag and drop is completed, the DoDragDrop method returns with the effect that was performed. If the effect was a Move, the source knows to remove its copy of the data.

Supporting Multiple Effects

If you want to support more than one effect, such as Copy and Move, you can check the KeyState property of the DragEventArgs structure. KeyState is a set of flags that determines which keys are being pressed. By Windows convention, the lack of modifier keys indicates a Move, the Ctrl modifier indicates a Copy, and the Ctrl+Shift modifier indicates a Link (which your application may or may not support).

Unfortunately, the KeyState property is an integer, and WinForms provides no data type for checking the flags. So you'll need your own, such as this KeyState enumeration:[8]

```
// KeyState Values (not available in WinForms)
[FlagsAttribute] enum KeyState {
  LeftMouse = 1,
  RightMouse = 2,
  ShiftKey = 4,
  CtrlKey = 8,
  MiddleMouse = 16,
  AltKey = 32,
}
```

Because users may change the keys they're pressing at any time to get the effect they're looking for, you will want to notify the drag operation of

FIGURE 8.27: Completed Drag-and-Drop Copy Operation

---

8. The FlagsAttribute makes instances of the KeyState enumeration show up in a friendlier manner when debugging, such as "LeftMouse, CtrlKey" instead of "9."

which operation they are trying to do while the mouse is hovering. To do this you check the DragEnter and DragOver events:

```
void textBox3_DragEnter(object sender, DragEventArgs e) {
  SetDropEffect(e);
}

void textBox3_DragOver(object sender, DragEventArgs e) {
  SetDropEffect(e);
}

void SetDropEffect(DragEventArgs  e) {
  KeyState keyState = (KeyState)e.KeyState;

  // If the data is a string, we can handle it
  if( e.Data.GetDataPresent(typeof(string)) ) {
    // If only Ctrl is pressed, copy it
    if( (keyState & KeyState.CtrlKey) == KeyState.CtrlKey ) {
      e.Effect = DragDropEffects.Copy;
    }
    else { // Else, move it
      e.Effect = DragDropEffects.Move;
    }
  }
  // We don't like the data, so do not allow anything
  else {
    e.Effect = DragDropEffects.None;
  }
}
```

The SetDropEffect method makes sure that the data is a string because that is all we are expecting. If it finds a string, it tests to see whether the Ctrl key is pressed. If so, it specifies that the operation is a copy; otherwise, it specifies that it will do a move. Figure 8.28 shows what the drag operation now looks like over the text box without the Ctrl key pressed, indicating a move effect.

FIGURE 8.28: Dragging *without* Ctrl, Causing a Move

Figure 8.29 shows the same operation with the Ctrl key pressed, indicating a copy effect.

In our sample, when the user drops the data with no modifiers, indicating a move, the text is removed from the button when it drops the text to the text box, as shown in Figure 8.30.

To handle multiple effects in the drop source, you must specify which effects are allowed and check the resulting effect after the DoDragDrop method returns:

```
void button3_MouseDown(object sender, MouseEventArgs e) {
  DragDropEffects effect =
    DoDragDrop(
      button3.Text,
      DragDropEffects.Copy | DragDropEffects.Move);

  // If the effect was move, remove the text of the button
  // If the effect was a copy, we don't have anything to do
  if( effect == DragDropEffects.Move ) {
    button3.Text = "";
  }
}
```

Drag and drop is a great way to allow your mouse-oriented users to directly manipulate the data that your application presents without an undue development burden on you.

FIGURE 8.29: Dragging *with* Ctrl, Causing a Copy

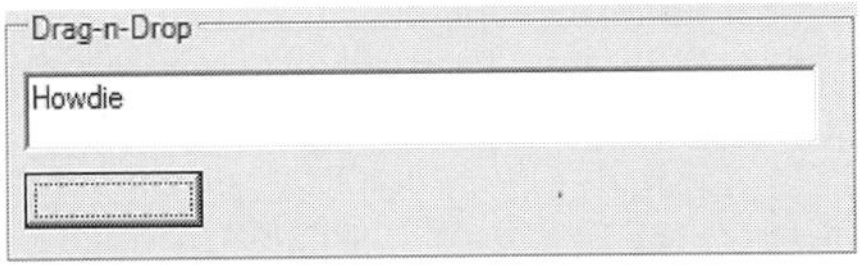

FIGURE 8.30: After a Drag-and-Drop Move Operation

Where Are We?

Controls are a way to repackage hunks of user interaction and behavior for the user. Controls can also provide a great many niceties to make them more approachable for the developer. That's what Chapter 9 is all about, for non-GUI components as well as GUI controls.

■9■
Design-Time Integration

A COMPONENT IS A NONVISUAL CLASS designed specifically to integrate with a design-time environment such as Visual Studio .NET. WinForms provides several standard components, and .NET lets you build your own, gaining a great deal of design-time integration with very little work.

On the other hand, with a bit more effort, you can integrate nonvisual components and controls very tightly into the design-time environment, providing a rich development experience for the programmer using your custom components and controls.

Components

Recall from Chapter 8: Controls that controls gain integration into VS.NET merely by deriving from the Control base class in the System.Windows.Forms namespace. That's not the whole story. What makes a control special is that it's one kind of *component*: a .NET class that integrates with a design-time environment such as VS.NET. A component can show up on the Toolbox along with controls and can be dropped onto any design surface. Dropping a component onto a design surface makes it available to set the property or handle the events in the Designer, just as a control is. Figure 9.1 shows the difference between a hosted control and a hosted component.

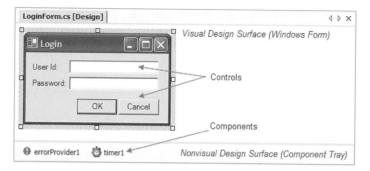

FIGURE 9.1: Locations of Components and Controls Hosted on a Form

Standard Components

It's so useful to be able to create instances of nonvisual components and use the Designer to code against them that WinForms comes with several components out of the box:

- **Standard dialogs.** The ColorDialog, FolderBrowserDialog, FontDialog, OpenFileDialog, PageSetupDialog, PrintDialog, PrintPreviewDialog, and SaveFileDialog classes make up the bulk of the standard components that WinForms provides. The printing-related components are covered in detail in Chapter 7: Printing.

- **Menus.** The MainMenu and ContextMenu components provide a form's menu bar and a control's context menu. They're both covered in detail in Chapter 2: Forms.

- **User information.** The ErrorProvider, HelpProvider, and ToolTip components provide the user with varying degrees of help in using a form and are covered in Chapter 2: Forms.

- **Notify icon.** The NotifyIcon component puts an icon on the shell's TaskBar, giving the user a way to interact with an application without the screen real estate requirements of a window. For an example, see Appendix D: Standard WinForms Components and Controls.

- **Image List.** The ImageList component keeps track of a developer-provided list of images for use with controls that need images when drawing. Chapter 8: Controls shows how to use them.

- **Timer.** The Timer component fires an event at a set interval measured in milliseconds.

Using Standard Components

What makes components useful is that they can be manipulated in the design-time environment. For example, imagine that you'd like a user to be able to set an alarm in an application and to notify the user when the alarm goes off. You can implement that using a Timer component. Dropping a Timer component onto a Form allows you to set the Enabled and Interval properties as well as handle the Tick event in the Designer, which generates code such as the following into InitializeComponent:

```
void InitializeComponent() {
  this.components = new Container();
  this.timer1 = new Timer(this.components);
  ...
  // timer1
  this.timer1.Enabled = true;
  this.timer1.Tick += new EventHandler(this.timer1_Tick);
  ...
}
```

As you have probably come to expect by now, the Designer-generated code looks very much like what you'd write yourself. What's interesting about this sample InitializeComponent implementation is that when a new component is created, it's put on a list with the other components on the form. This is similar to the Controls collection that is used by a form to keep track of the controls on the form.

After the Designer has generated most of the Timer-related code for us, we can implement the rest of the alarm functionality for our form:

```
DateTime alarm = DateTime.MaxValue; // No alarm

void setAlarmButton_Click(object sender, EventArgs e) {
  alarm = dateTimePicker1.Value;
}

// Handle the Timer's Tick event
void timer1_Tick(object sender, System.EventArgs e) {
  statusBar1.Text = DateTime.Now.TimeOfDay.ToString();
```

continues

```
// Check to see whether we're within 1 second of the alarm
double seconds = (DateTime.Now - alarm).TotalSeconds;
if( (seconds >= 0) && (seconds <= 1) ) {
  alarm = DateTime.MaxValue; // Show alarm only once
  MessageBox.Show("Wake Up!");
}
}
```

In this sample, when the timer goes off every 100 milliseconds (the default value), we check to see whether we're within 1 second of the alarm. If we are, we shut off the alarm and notify the user, as shown in Figure 9.2.

If this kind of single-fire alarm is useful in more than one spot in your application, you might choose to encapsulate this functionality in a custom component for reuse.

Custom Components

A component is any class that implements the IComponent interface from the System.ComponentModel namespace:

```
interface IComponent : IDisposable {
  ISite Site { get; set; }
  event EventHandler Disposed;
}

interface IDisposable {
  void Dispose();
}
```

A class that implements the IComponent interface can be added to the Toolbox[1] in VS.NET and dropped onto a design surface. When you drop a

FIGURE 9.2: The Timer Component Firing Every 100 Milliseconds

component onto a form, it shows itself in a tray below the form. Unlike controls, components don't draw themselves in a region on their container. In fact, you could think of components as nonvisual controls, because, just like controls, components can be managed in the design-time environment. However, it's more accurate to think of controls as visual components because controls implement IComponent, which is where they get their design-time integration.

A Sample Component

As an example, to package the alarm functionality we built earlier around the Timer component, let's build an AlarmComponent class. To create a new component class, right-click on the project and choose Add | Add Component, enter the name of your component class, and press OK. You'll be greeted with a blank design surface, as shown in Figure 9.3.

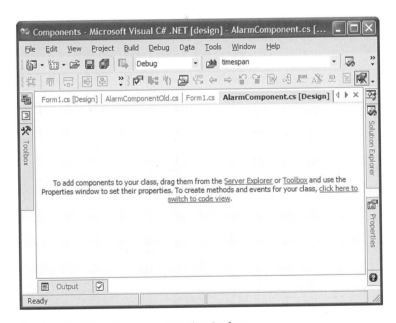

FIGURE 9.3: A New Component Design Surface

---

1. The same procedure for adding a custom control to the Toolbox in Chapter 8: Controls can be used to add a custom component to the Toolbox.

The design surface for a component is meant to host other components for use in implementing your new component. For example, we can drop our Timer component from the Toolbox onto the alarm component design surface. In this way, we can create and configure a timer component just as if we were hosting the timer on a form. Figure 9.4 shows the alarm component with a timer component configured for our needs.

Switching to the code view[2] for the component displays the following skeleton generated by the component project item template and filled in by the Designer for the timer:

```
using System;
using System.ComponentModel;
using System.Collections;
using System.Diagnostics;

namespace Components {
  /// <summary>
  /// Summary description for AlarmComponent.
  /// </summary>
```

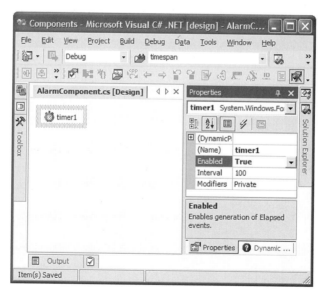

FIGURE 9.4: A Component Design Surface Hosting a Timer Component

---

2. You can switch to code view from designer view by choosing View | Code or pressing F7. Similarly, you can switch back by choosing View | Designer or by pressing Shift+F7.

```
public class AlarmComponent : System.ComponentModel.Component {
  private Timer timer1;
  private System.ComponentModel.IContainer components;

  public AlarmComponent(System.ComponentModel.IContainer container) {
    /// <summary>
    /// Required for Windows.Forms Class Composition Designer support
    /// </summary>
    container.Add(this);
    InitializeComponent();

    //
    // TODO: Add any constructor code after InitializeComponent call
    //
  }

  public AlarmComponent() {
    /// <summary>
    /// Required for Windows.Forms Class Composition Designer support
    /// </summary>
    InitializeComponent();

    //
    // TODO: Add any constructor code after InitializeComponent call
    //
  }

#region Component Designer generated code
  /// <summary>
  /// Required method for Designer support - do not modify
  /// the contents of this method with the code editor.
  /// </summary>
  private void InitializeComponent() {
    this.components = new System.ComponentModel.Container();
    this.timer1 = new System.Windows.Forms.Timer(this.components);
    //
    // timer1
    //
    this.timer1.Enabled = true;
  }
#endregion
  }
}
```

Notice that the custom component derives from the Component base class from the System.ComponentModel namespace. This class provides an implementation of IComponent for us.

After the timer is in place in the alarm component, it's a simple matter to move the alarm functionality from the form to the component by handling the timer's Tick event:

```
public class AlarmComponent : Component {
  ...
  DateTime alarm = DateTime.MaxValue; // No alarm
  public DateTime Alarm {
    get { return this.alarm; }
    set { this.alarm = value; }
  }

  // Handle the Timer's Tick event
  public event EventHandler AlarmSounded;

  void timer1_Tick(object sender, System.EventArgs e) {
    // Check to see whether we're within 1 second of the alarm
    double seconds = (DateTime.Now - this.alarm).TotalSeconds;
    if( (seconds >= 0) && (seconds <= 1) ) {
      this.alarm = DateTime.MaxValue; // Show alarm only once
      if( this.AlarmSounded != null ) {
        AlarmSounded(this, EventArgs.Empty);
      }
    }
  }
}
```

This implementation is just like what the form was doing before, except that the alarm date and time are set via the public Alarm property; when the alarm sounds, an event is fired. Now we can simplify the form code to contain merely an instance of the AlarmComponent, setting the Alarm property and handling the AlarmSounded event:

```
public class AlarmForm : Form {
  AlarmComponent alarmComponent1;
  ...
  void InitializeComponent() {
    ...
    this.alarmComponent1 = new AlarmComponent(this.components);
    ...
    this.alarmComponent1.AlarmSounded +=
      new EventHandler(this.alarmComponent1_AlarmSounded);
    ...
  }
}
```

```
void setAlarmButton_Click(object sender, EventArgs e) {
  alarmComponent1.Alarm = dateTimePicker1.Value;
}

void alarmComponent1_AlarmSounded(object sender, EventArgs e) {
  MessageBox.Show("Wake Up!");
}
```

In this code, the form uses an instance of AlarmComponent, setting the Alarm property based on user input and handling the AlarmSounded event when it's fired. The code does all this without any knowledge of the actual implementation, which is encapsulated inside the AlarmComponent itself.

Component Resource Management

Although components and controls are similar as far as their design-time interaction is concerned, they are not identical. The most obvious difference lies in the way they are drawn on the design surface. A less obvious difference is that the Designer does not generate the same hosting code for components that it does for controls. Specifically, a component gets extra code so that it can add itself to the container's list of components. When the container shuts down, it uses this list of components to notify all the components that they can release any resources that they're holding.

Controls don't need this extra code because they already get the Closed event, which is an equivalent notification for most purposes. To let the Designer know that it would like to be notified when its container goes away, a component can implement a public constructor that takes a single argument of type IContainer:

```
public AlarmComponent(IContainer container) {
  // Add object to container's list so that
  // we get notified when the container goes away
  container.Add(this);
  InitializeComponent();
}
```

Notice that the constructor uses the passed container interface to add itself as a container component. In the presence of this constructor, the Designer generates code that uses this constructor, passing it a container for the component to add itself to. Recall that the code to create the Alarm-Component uses this special constructor:

```
public class AlarmForm : Form {
  IContainer components;
  AlarmComponent alarmComponent1;
  ...
  void InitializeComponent() {
    this.components = new Container();
    ...
    this.alarmComponent1 = new AlarmComponent(this.components);
    ...
  }
}
```

By default, most of the VS.NET-generated classes that contain components will notify each component in the container as part of the Dispose method implementation:

```
public class AlarmForm : Form {
  ...
  IContainer components;
  ...
  // Overridden from the base class Component.Dispose method
  protected override void Dispose( bool disposing ) {
    if( disposing ) {
      if (components != null) {
        // Call each component's Dispose method
        components.Dispose();
      }
    }
    base.Dispose( disposing );
  }
}
```

As you may recall from Chapter 4: Drawing Basics, the client is responsible for calling the Dispose method from the IDisposable interface. The IContainer interface derives from IDisposable, and the Container implementation of Dispose walks the list of components, calling IDisposable. Dispose on each one. A component that has added itself to the container can override the Component base class's Dispose method to catch the notification that it is being disposed of:

```
public class AlarmComponent : Component {
  Timer timer1;
  IContainer components;
  ...
  void InitializeComponent() {
    this.components = new Container();
    this.timer1 = new Timer(this.components);
    ...
  }

  protected override void Dispose(bool disposing) {
    if( disposing ) {
      // Release managed resources
      ...

      // Let contained components know to release their resources
      if( components != null ) {
        components.Dispose();
      }
    }

    // Release unmanaged resources
    ...
  }
}
```

Notice that, unlike the method that the client container is calling, the alarm component's Dispose method takes an argument. The Component base class routes the implementation of IDisposable.Dispose() to call its own Dispose(bool) method, with the Boolean argument disposing set to true. This is done to provide optimized, centralized resource management.

A disposing argument of true means that Dispose was called by a client that remembered to properly dispose of the component. In the case of our alarm component, the only resources we have to reclaim are those of the timer component we're using to provide our implementation, so we ask our own container to dispose of the components it's holding on our behalf. Because the Designer-generated code added the timer to our container, that's all we need to do.

A disposing argument of false means that the client forgot to properly dispose of the object and that the .NET Garbage Collector (GC) is calling our object's finalizer. A *finalizer* is a method that the GC calls when it's about to reclaim the memory associated with the object. Because the GC calls the finalizer at some indeterminate time—potentially long after the component is no longer needed (perhaps hours or days later)—the finalizer is a bad place to reclaim resources, but it's better than not reclaiming them at all.

The Component base class's finalizer implementation calls the Dispose method, passing a disposing argument of false, which indicates that the component shouldn't touch any of the managed objects it may contain. The other managed objects should remain untouched because the GC may have already disposed of them, and their state is undefined.

Any component that contains other objects that implement IDisposable, or handles to unmanaged resources, should implement the Dispose(bool) method to properly release those objects' resources when the component itself is being released by its container.

Design-Time Integration Basics

Because a component is a class that's made to be integrated into a design-time host, it has a life separate from the run-time mode that we normally think of for objects. It's not enough for a component to do a good job when interacting with a user at run time as per developer instructions; a component also needs to do a good job when interacting with the developer at design time.

Hosts, Containers, and Sites

In Visual Studio .NET, the Windows Forms Designer is responsible for providing design-time services during Windows Forms development. At a high level, these services include a form's UI and code views. The responsibility of managing integration between design-time objects and the designer is handled by the designer's internal implementation of IDesignerHost (from the System.ComponentModel.Design namespace). The designer host stores IComponent references to all design-time objects on the current form and also stores the form itself (which is also a component). This collection of components is available from the IDesignerHost interface through the Container property of type IContainer (from the System.ComponentModel namespace):

```
interface IContainer : IDisposable {
  ComponentCollection Components { get; }
  void Add(IComponent component);
  void Add(IComponent component, string name);
  void Remove(IComponent component);
}
```

This implementation of IContainer allows the designer host to establish a relationship that helps it manage each of the components placed on the form. Contained components can access the designer host and each other through their container at design time. Figure 9.5 illustrates this two-way relationship.

In Figure 9.5 you can see that the fundamental relationship between the designer host and its components is established with an implementation of the ISite interface (from the System.ComponentModel namespace):

```
interface ISite : IServiceProvider {
  IComponent Component { get; }
  IContainer Container { get; }
  bool DesignMode { get; }
  string Name { get; set; }
}
```

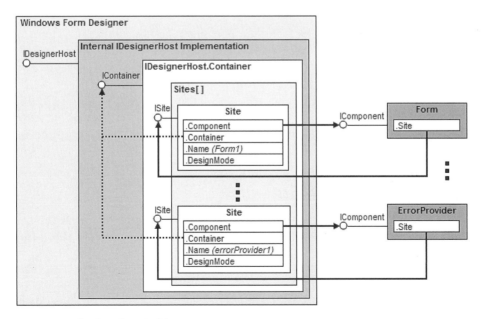

FIGURE 9.5: Design-Time Architecture

Internally, a container stores an array of sites. When each component is added to the container, the designer host creates a new site, connecting the component to its design-time container and vice versa by passing the ISite interface in the IComponent.Site property implementation:

```
interface IComponent : IDisposable {
  ISite Site { get; set; }
  event EventHandler Disposed;
}
```

The Component base class implements IComponent and caches the site's interface in a property. It also provides a helper property to go directly to the component's container without having to go first through the site:

```
class Component : MarshalByRefObject, IComponent, IDisposable {
  public IContainer Container { get; }
  public virtual ISite Site { get; set; }
  protected bool DesignMode { get; }
  protected EventHandlerList Events { get; }
}
```

The Component base class gives a component direct access to both the container and the site. A component can also access the Visual Studio .NET designer host itself by requesting the IDesignerHost interface from the container:

```
IDesignerHost designerHost = this.Container as IDesignerHost;
```

In Visual Studio .NET, the designer has its own implementation of the IDesignerHost interface, but, to fit into other designer hosts, it's best for a component to rely only on the interface and not on any specific implementation.

Debugging Design-Time Functionality

To demonstrate the .NET Framework's various design-time features and services, I've built a sample.[3] Because components and controls share the

---

3. While I use the term "I" to maintain consistency with the rest of the prose, it was actually Michael Weinhardt who built this sample as well as doing the initial research and even the initial draft of much of the material in this chapter. Thanks, Michael!

same design-time features and because I like things that look snazzy, I built a digital/analog clock control with the following public members:

```
public class ClockControl : Control {
  public ClockControl();
  public DateTime Alarm { get; set; }
  public bool IsItTimeForABreak { get; set; }
  public event AlarmHandler AlarmSounded;
  ...
}
```

Figure 9.6 shows the control in action.

When you build design-time features into your components,[4] you'll need to test them and, more than likely, debug them. To test run-time functionality, you simply set a breakpoint in your component's code and run a test application, relying on Visual Studio .NET to break at the right moment.

What makes testing design-time debugging different is that you need a design-time host to debug against; an ordinary application won't do. Because the hands-down hosting favorite is Visual Studio .NET itself, this means that you'll use one instance of Visual Studio .NET to debug another instance of Visual Studio .NET with a running instance of the component loaded. This may sound confusing, but it's remarkably easy to set up:

FIGURE 9.6: Snazzy Clock Control

---

4. Remember that nonvisual components as well as controls are components for the purposes of design-time integration.

1. Open the component solution to debug in one instance of Visual Studio .NET.

2. Set a second instance of Visual Studio .NET as your debug application by going to Project | Properties | Configuration Properties | Debugging and setting the following properties:

    a. Set Debug Mode to Program.

    b. Set Start Application to <your devenv.exe path>\devenv.exe.

    c. Set Command Line Arguments to <your test solution path>\yourTestSolution.sln.

3. Choose Set As StartUp Project on your component project.

4. Set a breakpoint in the component.

5. Use Debug | Start (F5) to begin debugging.

At this point, a second instance of Visual Studio.NET starts up with another solution, allowing you to break and debug at will, as illustrated in Figure 9.7.

The key to making this setup work is to have one solution loaded in one instance of VS.NET that starts another instance of VS.NET with a completely different solution to test your component in design mode.

The DesignMode Property

To change the behavior of your component at design time, often you need to know that you're running in a Designer. For example, the clock control uses a timer component to track the time via its Tick event handler:

```
public class ClockControl : Control {
  ...
  Timer timer = new Timer();
  ...
  public ClockControl() {
    ...
    // Initialize timer
    timer.Interval = 1000;
    timer.Tick += new System.EventHandler(this.timer_Tick);
    timer.Enabled = true;
  }
  ...
```

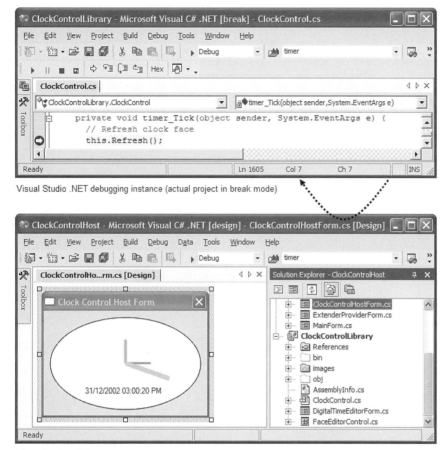

Visual Studio .NET debugging instance (actual project in break mode)

Visual Studio .NET with running control instance (simulated project in design mode)

FIGURE 9.7: Design-Time Control Debugging

```
void timer_Tick(object sender, EventArgs e) {
  // Refresh clock face
  this.Invalidate();
  ...
  }
}
```

Inspection reveals that the control is overly zealous in keeping time both at design time and at run time. Such code should really be executed at run time only. In this situation, a component or control can check the

DesignMode property, which is true only when it is executing at design time. The timer_Tick event handler can use DesignMode to ensure that it is executed only at run time, returning immediately from the event handler otherwise:

```
void timer_Tick(object sender, EventArgs e) {
  // Don't execute event if running in design time
  if( this.DesignMode ) return;
  this.Invalidate();
  ...
}
```

Note that the DesignMode property should not be checked from within the constructor or from any code that the constructor calls. A constructor is called before a control is sited, and it's the site that determines whether or not a control is in design mode. DesignMode will always be false in the constructor.

Attributes

Design-time functionality is available to controls in one of two ways: programmatically and declaratively. Checking the DesignMode property is an example of the programmatic approach. One side effect of using a programmatic approach is that your implementation takes on some of the design-time responsibility, resulting in a blend of design-time and run-time code within the component implementation.

The declarative approach, on the other hand, relies on attributes to request design-time functionality implemented somewhere else, such as the designer host. For example, consider the default Toolbox icon for a component, as shown in Figure 9.8.

If the image is important to your control, you'll want to change the icon to something more appropriate. The first step is to add a 16×16, 16-color icon or bitmap to your project and set its Build Action to Embedded

FIGURE 9.8: Default Toolbox Icon

Resource (embedded resources are discussed in Chapter 10: Resources). Then add the ToolboxBitmapAttribute to associate the icon with your component:

```
[ToolboxBitmapAttribute(
  typeof(ClockControlLibrary.ClockControl),
  "images.ClockControl.ico")]
public class ClockControl : Control {...}
```

The parameters to this attribute specify the use of an icon resource located in the "images" project subfolder.

You'll find that the Toolbox image doesn't change if you add or change ToolboxBitmapAttribute after the control has been added to the Toolbox. However, if your implementation is a component, its icon is updated in the component tray. One can only assume that the Toolbox is not under the direct management of the Windows Form Designer, whereas the component tray is. To refresh the Toolbox, remove your component and then add it again to the Toolbox. The result will be something like Figure 9.9.

You can achieve the same result without using ToolboxBitmap-Attribute: Simply place a 16×16, 16-color bitmap in the same project folder as the component, and give it the same name as the component class. This is a special shortcut for the ToolboxBitmapAttribute only; don't expect to find similar shortcuts for other design-time attributes.

Property Browser Integration

No matter what the icon is, after a component is dragged from the Toolbox onto a form, it can be configured through the designer-managed Property Browser. The Designer uses reflection to discover which properties the design-time control instance exposes. For each property, the Designer calls the associated get accessor for its current value and renders both the

FIGURE 9.9: New and Improved Toolbox Icon

property name and the value onto the Property Browser. Figure 9.10 shows how the Property Browser looks for the basic clock control.

The System.ComponentModel namespace provides a comprehensive set of attributes, shown in Table 9.1, to help you modify your component's behavior and appearance in the Property Browser.

By default, public read and read/write properties—such as the Alarm property highlighted in Figure 9.10—are displayed in the Property Browser under the "Misc" category. If a property is intended for run time only, you can prevent it from appearing in the Property Browser by adorning the property with BrowsableAttribute:

```
[BrowsableAttribute(false)]
public bool IsItTimeForABreak {
  get { ... }
  set { ... }
}
```

With IsItTimeForABreak out of the design-time picture, only the custom Alarm property remains. However, it's currently listed under the Property Browser's Misc category and lacks a description. You can improve the situation by applying both CategoryAttribute and DescriptionAttribute:

```
[
  CategoryAttribute("Behavior"),
  DescriptionAttribute("Alarm for late risers")
]
public DateTime Alarm {
  get { ... }
  set { ... }
}
```

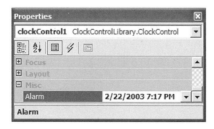

FIGURE 9.10: Visual Studio.NET with a Clock Control Chosen

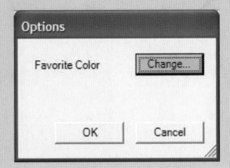

PLATE 1 (FIGURE 1.15): A Dialog Box

PLATE 2 (FIGURE 1.16): ErrorProvider Providing an Error

PLATE 3 (FIGURE 1.17): Custom Drawing

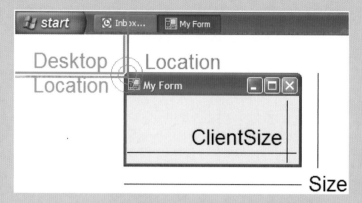

PLATE 4 (FIGURE 2.3): The DesktopLocation, Location, ClientSize, and Size Properties

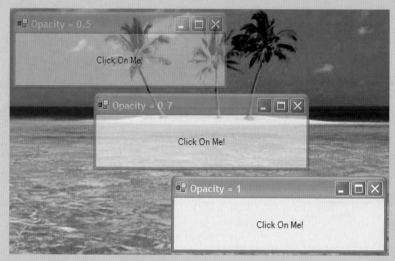

PLATE 5 (FIGURE 2.4): Opacity

PLATE 6 (FIGURE 4.3): A Sample Form Used as a Dialog

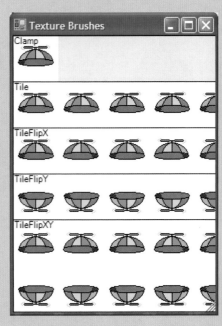

PLATE 7 (FIGURE 4.4): Various Texture-Brush WrapMode Values

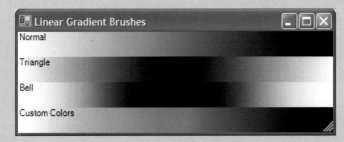

PLATE 8 (FIGURE 4.6): Normal, Triangle, and Bell Linear Gradient Brushes

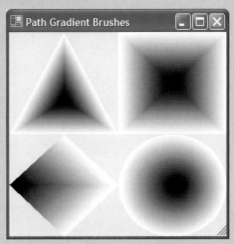

PLATE 9 (FIGURE 4.7): Four Sample Uses of the PathGradientBrush Class

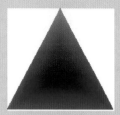

PLATE 10 (FIGURE 4.8):
A PathGradientBrush
with One Red
Surrounding Point
and Two Blue Ones

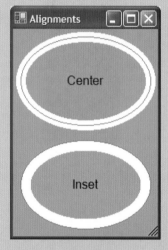

PLATE 11 (FIGURE 4.12): Pen
Alignment Options

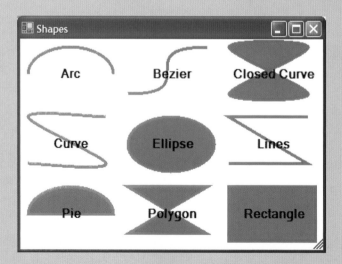

PLATE 12 (FIGURE 4.15): The Basic Shapes

PLATE 13 (FIGURE 4.19):
A Rounded Rectangle
Composed of Arc
Figures in a
GraphicsPath Object

PLATE 14 (FIGURE 4.20):
Starting a New Figure
in a Path Without
Closing the Current
Figure

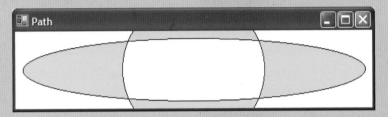

PLATE 15 (FIGURE 4.22): Overlapping Figures and the Alternate FillMode

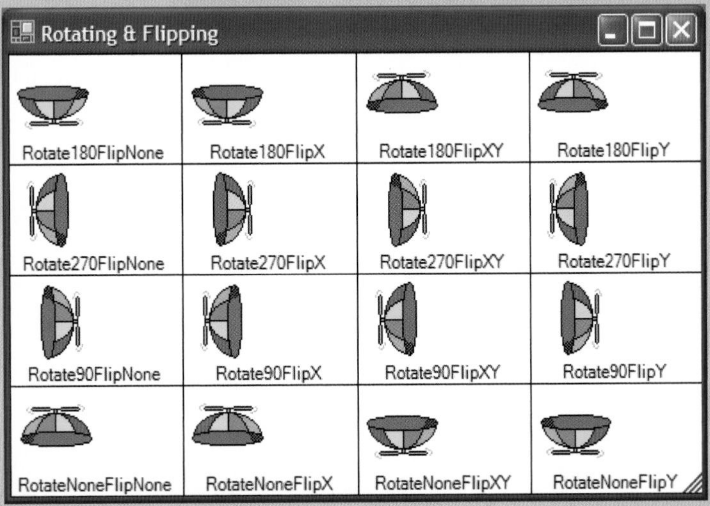

PLATE 16 (FIGURE 4.26): The Rotating and Flipping Types from the
RotateFlipType Enumeration

PLATE 17 (FIGURE 4.27): An Example of Mapping Color.Lime to Color.White

PLATE 18 (FIGURE 4.28): Using Color.Transparent in a Color Map

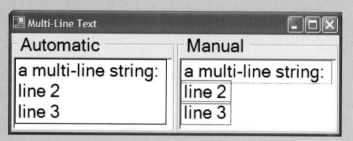

PLATE 19 (FIGURE 5.1): Automatic Word-Wrap Performed by Draw-String Compared with Manual Word-Wrap Using Font.GetHeight

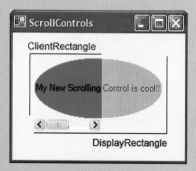

PLATE 20 (FIGURE 8.18): DisplayRectangle Versus ClientRectangle

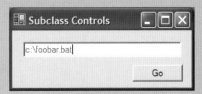

PLATE 21 (FIGURE 8.19): FileTextBox with a File That Does Not Exist

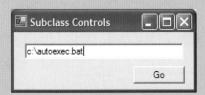

PLATE 22 (FIGURE 8.20): FileTextBox with a File That Does Exist

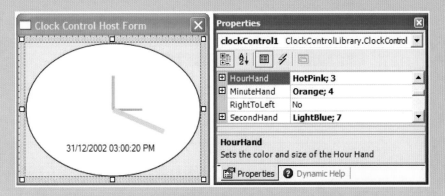

PLATE 23 (FIGURE 9.23): HandConverter in Action

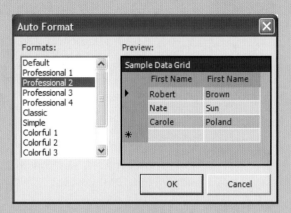

PLATE 24 (FIGURE 13.33): The Data Grid Auto Format
Dialog

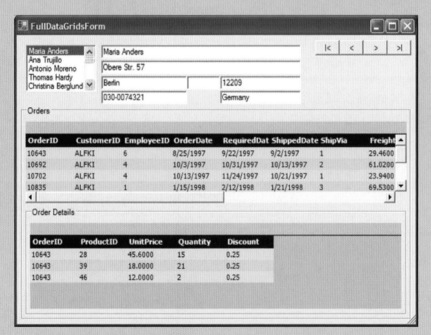

PLATE 25 (FIGURE 13.34): An Example of What WinForms Provides for Data
Programmers

PLATE 26 (FIGURE D.7):
A Sample Usage of the
NotifyIcon Component

Table 9.1: Design-Time Property Browser Attributes

Attribute	Description
AmbientValueAttribute	Specifies the value for this property that causes it to acquire its value from another source, usually its container (see the section titled Ambient Properties in Chapter 8: Controls).
BrowsableAttribute	Determines whether the property is visible in the Property Browser.
CategoryAttribute	Tells the Property Browser which group to include this property in.
DescriptionAttribute	Provides text for the Property Browser to display in its description bar.
DesignOnlyAttribute	Specifies that the design-time value of this property is serialized to the form's resource file. This attribute is typically used on properties that do not exist at run time.
MergablePropertyAttribute	Allows this property to be combined with properties from other objects when more than one are selected and edited.
ParenthesizePropertyNameAttribute	Specifies whether this property should be surrounded by parentheses in the Property Browser.
ReadOnlyAttribute	Specifies that this property cannot be edited in the Property Browser.

After adding these attributes and rebuilding, you will notice that the Alarm property has relocated to the desired category in the Property Browser, and the description appears on the description bar when you select the property (both shown in Figure 9.11). You can actually use CategoryAttribute to create new categories, but you should do so only if the existing categories don't suitably describe a property's purpose. Otherwise, you'll confuse users looking for your properties in the logical category.

FIGURE 9.11: Alarm Property with CategoryAttribute and DescriptionAttribute Applied

In Figure 9.11, some property values are shown in boldface and others are not. Boldface values are those that differ from the property's default value, which is specified by DefaultValueAttribute:

```
[
  CategoryAttribute("Appearance"),
  DescriptionAttribute("Whether digital time is shown"),
  DefaultValueAttribute(true)
]
public bool ShowDigitalTime {
  get { ... }
  set { ... }
}
```

Using DefaultValueAttribute also allows you to reset a property to its default value using the Property Browser, which is available from the property's context menu, as shown in Figure 9.12.

This option is disabled if the current property is already the default value. Default values represent the most common value for a property.

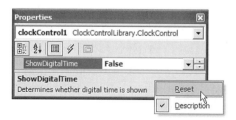

FIGURE 9.12: Resetting a Property to Its Default Value

Some properties, such as Alarm or Text, simply don't have a default that's possible to define, whereas others, such as Enabled and ControlBox, do.

Just like properties, a class can have defaults. You can specify a default event by adorning a class with DefaultEventAttribute:

```
[DefaultEventAttribute("AlarmSounded")]
class ClockControl : Control { ... }
```

Double-clicking the component causes the Designer to automatically hook up the default event; it does this by serializing code to register with the specified event in InitializeComponent and providing a handler for it:

```
class ClockControlHostForm : Form {
  ...
  void InitializeComponent() {
    ...
    this.clockControl1.AlarmSounded +=
      new AlarmHandler(this.clockControl1_AlarmSounded);
    ...
  }
  ...
  void clockControl1_AlarmSounded(
    object sender,
    ClockControlLibrary.AlarmType type) {
  }
  ...
}
```

You can also adorn your component with DefaultPropertyAttribute:

```
[DefaultPropertyAttribute("ShowDigitalTime")]
public class ClockControl : Windows.Forms.Control { ... }
```

This attribute causes the Designer to highlight the default property when the component's property is first edited, as shown in Figure 9.13.

Default properties aren't terribly useful, but setting the correct default event properly can save a developer's time when using your component.

Code Serialization

Whereas DefaultEventAttribute and DefaultPropertyAttribute affect the behavior only of the Property Browser, DefaultValueAttribute serves a dual purpose: It also plays a role in helping the Designer determine which

FIGURE 9.13: Default Property Highlighted in the Property Browser

code is serialized to InitializeComponent. Properties that don't have a default value are automatically included in InitializeComponent. Those that have a default value are included only if the property's value differs from the default. To avoid unnecessarily changing a property, your initial property values should match the value set by DefaultValueAttribute.

DesignerSerializationVisibilityAttribute is another attribute that affects the code serialization process. The DesignerSerializationVisibilityAttribute constructor takes a value from the DesignerSerializationVisibility enumeration:

```
enum DesignerSerializationVisibility {
  Visible, // initialize this property if nondefault value
  Hidden, // don't initialize this property
  Content // initialize sets of properties on a subobject
}
```

The default, Visible, causes a property's value to be set in Initialize-Component if the value of the property is not the same as the value of the default. If you'd prefer that no code be generated to initialize a property, use Hidden:

```
[
  DefaultValueAttribute(true),
  DesignerSerializationVisibilityAttribute(
    DesignerSerializationVisibility.Hidden)
]
public bool ShowDigitalTime {
  get { ... }
  set { ... }
}
```

You can use Hidden in conjunction with BrowsableAttribute set to false for run-time-only properties. Although BrowsableAttribute determines whether a property is visible in the Property Browser, its value may still be serialized unless you prevent that by using Hidden.

By default, properties that maintain a collection of custom types cannot be serialized to code. Such a property is implemented by the clock control in the form of a "messages to self" feature, which captures a set of messages and displays them at the appropriate date and time. To enable serialization of a collection, you can apply DesignerSerializationVisibility. Content to instruct the Designer to walk into the property and serialize its internal structure:

```
[
  CategoryAttribute("Behavior"),
  DescriptionAttribute ("Stuff to remember for later"),
  DesignerSerializationVisibilityAttribute
      (DesignerSerializationVisibility.Content)
]
public MessageToSelfCollection MessagesToSelf {
  get { ... }
  set { ... }
}
```

The generated InitializeComponent code for a single message looks like this:

```
void InitializeComponent() {
  ...
  this.clockControl1.MessagesToSelf.AddRange(
  new ClockControlLibrary.MessageToSelf[] {
    new ClockControlLibrary.MessageToSelf(
      new System.DateTime(2003, 2, 22, 21, 55, 0, 0), "Wake up")});
  ...
}
```

This code also needs a "translator" class to help the Designer serialize the code to construct a MessageToSelf type. This is covered in detail in the section titled "Type Converters" later in this chapter.

Host Form Integration

While we're talking about affecting code serialization, there's another trick that's needed for accessing a component's hosting form. For example, consider a clock control and a clock component, both of which offer the ability to place the current time in the hosting form's caption. Each needs to acquire a reference to the host form to set the time in the form's Text property. The control comes with native support for this requirement:

```
Form hostingForm = this.Parent as Form;
```

Unfortunately, components do not provide a similar mechanism to access their host form. At design time, the component can find the form in the designer host's Container collection. However, this technique will not work at run time because the Container is not available at run time. To get its container at run time, a component must take advantage of the way the Designer serializes code to the InitializeComponent method. You can write code that takes advantage of this infrastructure to seed itself with a reference to the host form at design time and run time. The first step is to grab the host form at design time using a property of type Form:

```
Form hostingForm = null;

[BrowsableAttribute(false)]
public Form HostingForm {
  // Used to populate InitializeComponent at design time
  get {
    if( (hostingForm == null) && this.DesignMode ) {
    // Access designer host and obtain reference to root component
      IDesignerHost designer =
        this.GetService(typeof(IDesignerHost)) as IDesignerHost;
      if( designer != null ) {
        hostingForm = designer.RootComponent as Form;
      }
    }
    return hostingForm;
  }

  set {...}
}
```

The HostingForm property is used to populate the code in Initialize-Component at design time, when the designer host is available. Stored in the designer host's RootComponent property, the root component represents the primary purpose of the Designer. For example, a Form component is the root component of the Windows Forms Designer. DesignerHost.RootComponent is a helper function that allows you to access the root component without enumerating the Container collection. Only one component is considered the root component by the designer host. Because the HostingForm property should go about its business transparently, you should decorate it with BrowsableAttribute set to false, thereby ensuring that the property is not editable from the Property Browser.

Because HostForm is a public property, the Designer retrieves Hosting-Form's value at design time to generate the following code, which is needed to initialize the component:

```
void InitializeComponent() {
  ...
  this.myComponent1.HostingForm = this;
  ...
}
```

At run time, when InitializeComponent runs, it will return the hosting form to the component via the HostingForm property setter:

```
Form hostingForm = null;

[BrowsableAttribute(false)]
public Form HostingForm {
  get { ... }

  // Set by InitializeComponent at run time
  set {
    if( !this.DesignMode ) {
      // Don't change hosting form at run time
      if( (hostingForm != null) && (hostingForm != value) ) {
        throw new
          InvalidOperationException
            ("Can't set HostingForm at run time.");
      }
    }
    else hostingForm = value;
  }
}
```

In this case, we're using our knowledge of how the Designer works to trick it into handing our component a value at run-time that we pick at design-time.

Batch Initialization

As you may have noticed, the code that eventually gets serialized to InitializeComponent is laid out as an alphanumerically ordered sequence of property sets, grouped by object. Order isn't important until your component exposes range-dependent properties, such as Min/Max or Start/Stop pairs. For example, the clock control also has two dependent properties: PrimaryAlarm and BackupAlarm (the Alarm property was split into two for extra sleepy people).

Internally, the clock control instance initializes the two properties 10 minutes apart, starting from the current date and time:

```
DateTime primaryAlarm = DateTime.Now;
DateTime backupAlarm = DateTime.Now.AddMinutes(10);
```

Both properties should check to ensure that the values are valid:

```
public DateTime PrimaryAlarm {
  get { return primaryAlarm; }
  set {
    if( value >= backupAlarm )
      throw new ArgumentOutOfRangeException
          ("Primary alarm must be before Backup alarm");
    primaryAlarm = value;
  }
}

public DateTime BackupAlarm {
  get { return backupAlarm; }
  set {
    if( value < primaryAlarm )
      throw new ArgumentOutOfRangeException
          ("Backup alarm must be after Primary alarm");
    backupAlarm = value;
  }
}
```

With this dependence checking in place, at design time the Property Browser will show an exception in an error dialog if an invalid property is entered, as shown in Figure 9.14.

This error dialog is great at design time, because it lets the developer know the relationship between the two properties. However, there's a problem when the properties are serialized into InitializeComponent alphabetically:

```
void InitializeComponent() {
  ...
  // clockControl1
  this.clockControl1.BackupAlarm =
      new System.DateTime(2003, 11, 24, 13, 42, 47, 46);
  ...
  this.clockControl1.PrimaryAlarm =
      new System.DateTime(2003, 11, 24, 13, 57, 47, 46);
  ...
}
```

Notice that even if the developer sets the two alarms properly, as soon as BackupAlarm is set and is checked against the default value of Primary-Alarm, a run-time exception will result.

To avoid this, a component must be notified when its properties are being set from InitializeComponent in "batch mode" so that they can be validated all at once at the end. Implementing the ISupportInitialize interface (from the System.ComponentModel namespace) provides this capability, with two notification methods to be called before and after initialization:

```
public interface ISupportInitialize {
  public void BeginInit();
```

continues

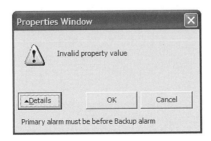

FIGURE 9.14: Invalid Value Entered into the Property Browser

```
  public void EndInit();
}
```

When a component implements this interface, calls to BeginInit and
EndInit are serialized to InitializeComponent:

```
void InitializeComponent() {
  ...
  ((System.ComponentModel.ISupportInitialize)
      (this.clockControl1)).BeginInit();
  ...
  // clockControl1
  this.clockControl1.BackupAlarm =
      new System.DateTime(2003, 11, 24, 13, 42, 47, 46);
  ...
  this.clockControl1.PrimaryAlarm =
      new System.DateTime(2003, 11, 24, 13, 57, 47, 46);
  ...
  ((System.ComponentModel.ISupportInitialize)
      (this.clockControl1)).EndInit();
  ...
}
```

The call to BeginInit signals the entry into initialization batch mode, a
signal that is useful for turning off value checking:

```
public class ClockControl : Control, ISupportInitialize {
  ...
  bool initializing = false;
  ...
  void BeginInit() { initializing = true; }
  ...
  public DateTime PrimaryAlarm {
    get { ... }
    set {
      if( !initializing ) { /* check value */ }
      primaryAlarm = value;
    }
  }

  public DateTime BackupAlarm {
    get { ... }
    set {
      if( !initializing ) { /* check value */ }
      backupAlarm = value;
    }
  }
}
```

Placing the appropriate logic into EndInit performs batch validation:

```
public class ClockControl : Control, ISupportInitialize {
  void EndInit() {
    if( primaryAlarm >= backupAlarm )
      throw new ArgumentOutOfRangeException
          ("Primary alarm must be before Backup alarm");
  }
  ...
}
```

EndInit also turns out to be a better place to avoid the timer's Tick event, which currently fires once every second during design time. Although the code inside the Tick event handler doesn't run at design time (because it's protected by a check of the DesignMode property), it would be better not to even start the timer at all until run time. However, because DesignMode can't be checked in the constructor, a good place to check it is in the EndInit call, which is called after all properties have been initialized at run time or at design time:

```
public class ClockControl : Control, ISupportInitialize {
  ...
  void EndInit() {
    ...
    if( !this.DesignMode ) {
      // Initialize timer
      timer.Interval = 1000;
      timer.Tick += new System.EventHandler(this.timer_Tick);
      timer.Enabled = true;
    }
  }
}
```

The Designer and the Property Browser provide all kinds of design-time help to augment the experience of developing a component, including establishing how a property is categorized and described to the developer and how it's serialized for the InitializeComponent method.

Extender Property Providers

So far the discussion has focused on the properties implemented by a control for itself. TimeZoneModifier, an example of such a property, allows the clock control to be configured to display the time in any time zone. One way to use this feature is to display the time in each time zone where your organization has offices. If each office were visually represented with a picture box, you could drag one clock control for each time zone onto the form, manually adjusting the TimeZoneModifier property on each clock control. The result might look like Figure 9.15.

This works quite nicely but could lead to real estate problems, particularly if you have one clock control for each of the 24 time zones globally and, consequently, 24 implementations of the same logic on the form. If you are concerned about resources, this also means 24 system timers. Figure 9.16 shows what this might look like.

Another approach is to have a single clock control and update its TimeZoneModifier property with the relevant time zone from the Click event of each picture box. This is a cumbersome approach because it requires developers to write the code associating a time zone offset with each control, a

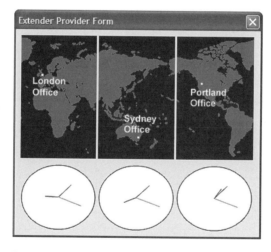

FIGURE 9.15: Form with Multiple Time Zones

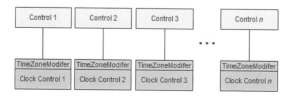

FIGURE 9.16: One Provider Control for Each Client Control

situation controls are meant to help avoid. Figure 9.17 illustrates this approach.

A nicer way to handle this situation is to provide access to a single implementation of the clock control without forcing the developer to write additional property update code. .NET offers extender property support to do just this, allowing components to extend property implementations to other components.

Logically, an *extender property* is a property provided by an extender component, like the clock control, on other components in the same container, like picture boxes. Extender properties are useful whenever a component needs data from a set of other components in the same host. For example, WinForms itself provides several extender components, including ErrorProvider, HelpProvider, and ToolTip. In the case of the ToolTip component, it makes a lot more sense to set the ToolTip property on each control on a form than it does to try to set tooltip information for each control using an editor provided by the ToolTip component itself.

In our case, by implementing TimeZoneModifier as an extender property, we allow each picture box control on the form to get its own value, as shown in Figure 9.18.

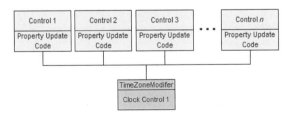

FIGURE 9.17: One Provider Control for All Client Controls, Accessed with Code

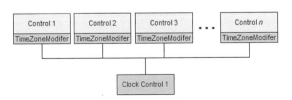

FIGURE 9.18: One Provider Control for All Client Controls, Accessed with a Property Set

Exposing an extender property from your control requires that you first use ProvidePropertyAttribute to declare the property to be extended:

```
[ProvidePropertyAttribute("TimeZoneModifier", typeof(PictureBox))]
public class ClockControl : Control { ... }
```

The first parameter to the attribute is the name of the property to be extended. The second parameter is the "receiver" type, which specifies the type of object to extend, such as PictureBox. Only components of the type specified by the receiver can be extended. If you want to implement a more sophisticated algorithm, such as supporting picture boxes and panels, you must implement the IExtenderProvider CanExtend method:

```
class ClockControl : ..., IExtenderProvider {
  bool IExtenderProvider.CanExtend(object extendee) {
    // Don't extend self
    if( extendee == this ) return false;

    // Extend suitable controls
    return( (extendee is PictureBox) ||
            (extendee is Panel) );
  }
  ...
}
```

As you saw in Figure 9.18, the provider supports one or more extendee controls. Consequently, the provider control must be able to store and distinguish one extendee's property value from that of another. It does this in the Get<PropertyName> and Set<PropertyName> methods, in which PropertyName is the name you provided in ProvidePropertyAttribute. Then GetTimeZoneModifier simply returns the property value when requested by the Property Browser:

```
public class ClockControl : Control, IExtenderProvider {
  // Mapping of components to numeric timezone offsets
  HashTable timeZoneModifiers = new HashTable();

  public int GetTimeZoneModifier(Control extendee) {
    // Return component's timezone offset
    return int.Parse(timeZoneModifiers[extendee]);
  }
  ...
}
```

SetTimeZoneModifier has a little more work to do. Not only does it put the property value into a new hash table for the extendee when provided, but it also removes the hash table entry when the property is cleared. Also, with the sample TimeZoneModifier property, you need to hook into each extendee control's Click event, unless the control isn't using the extender property. SetTimeZoneModifier is shown here:

```
class ClockControl : ..., IExtenderProvider {
  HashTable timeZoneModifiers = new HashTable();
  ...
  public void SetTimeZoneModifier(Control extendee, object value) {
    // If property isn't provided
    if( value == null ) {
      // Remove it
      timeZoneModifiers.Remove(extendee);
      if( !this.DesignMode ) {
        extendee.Click -= new EventHandler(extendee_Click);
      }
    }
    else {
      // Add the offset as an integer
      timeZoneModifiers[extendee] = int.Parse(value);
      if( !this.DesignMode ) {
        extendee.Click += new EventHandler(extendee_Click);
      }
    }
  }
}
```

As with other properties, you can affect the appearance of an extender property in the Property Browser by adorning the Get<PropertyName> method with attributes:

```
class ClockControl : ..., IExtenderProvider {
  [
    Category("Behavior"),
    Description("Sets the timezone difference from the current time"),
    DefaultValue("")
  ]
  public int GetTimeZoneModifier(Control extendee) { ... }
  ...
}
```

These attributes are applied to the extendee's Property Browser view.

With all this in place, you can compile your extender component to see the results. Extended properties will appear in the extendee component's properties with the following naming format:

```
<ExtendedPropertyName> on <ExtenderProviderName>
```

Figure 9.19 shows the TimeZoneModifier extender property behaving like any other property on a PictureBox control.

If a property is set and is not the default value, it is serialized to InitializeComponent(), as a SetTimeZoneModifier method call, and grouped with the extendee component:

```
void InitializeComponent() {
  ...
  this.clockControl1.SetTimeZoneModifier(this.pictureBox1, -11);
  ...
}
```

Extender properties allow a component to add to the properties of other components in the same host. In this way, the developer can keep the data with the intuitive component, which is not necessarily the component that provides the service.

Type Converters

When you select a component on a design surface, the entries in the Property Browser are rendered from the design-time control instance. When you edit properties in the Property Browser, the component's design-time instance is updated with the new property values. This synchronicity isn't

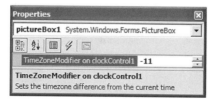

FIGURE 9.19: Extended Property in Action

as straightforward as it seems, however, because the Property Browser displays properties only as text, even though the source properties can be of any type. As values shuttle between the Property Browser and the design-time instance, they must be converted back and forth between the string type and the type of the property.

Enter the *type converter*, the translator droid of .NET, whose main goal in life is to convert between types. For string-to-type conversion, a type converter is used for each property displayed in the Property Browser, as shown in Figure 9.20.

.NET offers the TypeConverter class (from the System.Component-Model namespace) as the base implementation type converter. .NET also gives you several derivations—including StringConverter, Int32Converter, and DateTimeConverter—that support conversion between common .NET types. If you know the type that needs conversion at compile time, you can create an appropriate converter directly:

```
// Type is known at compile time
TypeConverter converter = new Int32Converter();
```

Or, if you don't know the type that needs conversion until run time, let the TypeDescriptor class (from the System.ComponentModel namespace) make the choice for you:

```
// Don't know the type before run time
object myData = 0;
TypeConverter converter = TypeDescriptor.GetConverter(myData.GetType());
```

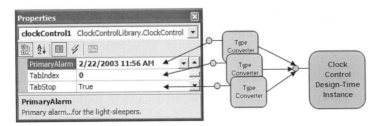

FIGURE 9.20: The Property Browser and Design-Time Conversion

The TypeDescriptor class provides information about a particular type or object, including methods, properties, events, and attributes. Type-Descriptor.GetConverter evaluates a type to determine a suitable Type-Converter based on the following:

1. Checking whether a type is adorned with an attribute that specifies a particular type converter.
2. Comparing the type against the set of built-in type converters.
3. Returning the TypeConverter base if no other type converters are found.

Because the Property Browser is designed to display the properties of any component, it can't know specific property types in advance. Consequently, it relies on TypeDescriptor.GetConverter to dynamically select the most appropriate type converter for each property.

After a type converter is chosen, the Property Browser and the design-time instance can perform the required conversions, using the same fundamental steps as those shown in the following code:

```
// Create the appropriate type converter
object myData = 0;
TypeConverter converter = TypeDescriptor.GetConverter(myData.GetType());

// Can converter convert int to string?
if( converter.CanConvertTo(typeof(string)) ) {
  // Convert it
  object intToString = converter.ConvertTo(42, typeof(string));
}

// Can converter convert string to int?
if( converter.CanConvertFrom(typeof(string)) ) {
  // Convert it
  object stringToInt = converter.ConvertFrom("42");
}
```

When the Property Browser renders itself, it uses the type converter to convert each design-time instance property to a string representation using the following steps:

1. CanConvertTo: Can you convert from the design-time property type to a string?
2. ConvertTo: If so, please convert property value to string.

The string representation of the source value is then displayed at the property's entry in the Property Browser. If the property is edited and the value is changed, the Property Browser uses the next steps to convert the string back to the source property value:

1. CanConvertFrom: Can you convert back to the design-time property type?
2. ConvertFrom: If so, please convert string to property value.

Some intrinsic type converters can do more than just convert between simple types. To demonstrate, let's expose a Face property of type Clock-Face, allowing developers to decide how the clock is displayed, including options for Analog, Digital, or Both:

```
public enum ClockFace {
  Analog = 0,
  Digital = 1,
  Both = 2
}

class ClockControl : Control {
  ClockFace face = ClockFace.Both;
  public ClockFace Face {
    get { … }
    set { … }
  }
  ...
}
```

TypeDescriptor.GetConverter returns an EnumConverter, which contains the smarts to examine the source enumeration and convert it to a drop-down list of descriptive string values, as shown in Figure 9.21.

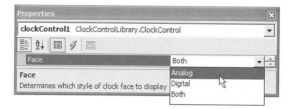

FIGURE 9.21: Enumeration Type Displayed in the Property Browser via Enum-Converter

Custom Type Converters

Although the built-in type converters are useful, they aren't enough if your component or control exposes properties based on custom types, such as the clock control's HourHand, MinuteHand, and SecondHand properties, shown here:

```
public class Hand {
  public Hand(Color color, int width) {
    this.color = color;
    this.width = width;
  }
  public Color Color {
    get { return color; }
    set { color = value; }
  }
  public int Width {
    get { return width; }
    set { width = value; }
  }
  Color  color = Color.Black;
  int    width = 1;
}

public class ClockControl : Control {
  public Hand HourHand { ... }
  public Hand MinuteHand { ... }
  public Hand SecondHand { ... }
}
```

The idea is to give developers the option to pretty up the clock's hands with color and width values. Without a custom type converter,[5] the unfortunate result is shown in Figure 9.22.

---

5. Be careful when you use custom types for properties. If the value of the property is null, you won't be able to edit it in the Property Browser at all.

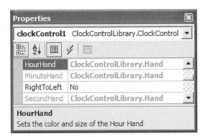

FIGURE 9.22: Complex Properties in the Property Browser

Just as the Property Browser can't know which types it will be displaying, .NET can't know which custom types you'll be developing. Consequently, there aren't any type of converters capable of handling them. However, you can hook into the type converter infrastructure to provide your own. Building a custom type converter starts by deriving from the TypeConverter base class:

```
public class HandConverter : TypeConverter { ... }
```

To support conversion, HandConverter must override CanConvertFrom, ConvertTo, and ConvertFrom:

```
public class HandConverter : TypeConverter {
  public override bool
    CanConvertFrom(
      ITypeDescriptorContext context, Type sourceType) {...}

  public override object
    ConvertFrom(
      ITypeDescriptorContext context,
      CultureInfo info,
      object value) {...}

  public override object
    ConvertTo(
      ITypeDescriptorContext context,
      CultureInfo culture,
      object value,
      Type destinationType) {...}
}
```

CanConvertFrom lets clients know what it can convert from. In this case, HandConverter reports that it can convert from a string type to a Hand type:

```
public override bool CanConvertFrom(
  ITypeDescriptorContext context, Type sourceType) {

  // We can convert from a string to a Hand type
  if( sourceType == typeof(string) ) { return true; }
  return base.CanConvertFrom(context, sourceType);
}
```

Whether the string type is in the correct format is left up to Convert-From, which actually performs the conversion. HandConverter expects a multivalued string. It splits this string into its atomic values and then uses it to instantiate a Hand object:

```
public override object ConvertFrom(
  ITypeDescriptorContext context, CultureInfo info, object value) {

    // If converting from a string
    if( value is string ) {
      // Build a Hand type
      try {
        // Get Hand properties
        string propertyList = (string)value;
        string[] properties = propertyList.Split(';');
        return new Hand(Color.FromName(properties[0].Trim()),
                    int.Parse(properties[1]));
      }
      catch {}
      throw new ArgumentException("The arguments were not valid.");
    }
    return base.ConvertFrom(context, info, value);
  }
  ...
}
```

ConvertTo converts from a Hand type back to a string:

```
public override object ConvertTo(
  ITypeDescriptorContext context,
  CultureInfo culture,
  object value,
  Type destinationType) {
```

```
  // If source value is a Hand type
  if( value is Hand ) {
    // Convert to string
    if( (destinationType == typeof(string)) ) {
      Hand hand = (Hand)value;
      string color = (hand.Color.IsNamedColor ?
                       hand.Color.Name :
                       hand.Color.R + ", " +
                         hand.Color.G + ", " +
                         hand.Color.B);
      return string.Format("{0}; {1}", color, hand.Width.ToString());
    }
  }
  return base.ConvertTo(context, culture, value, destinationType);
}
```

You may have noticed that HandConverter doesn't implement a Can-ConvertTo override. The base implementation of TypeConverter.Can-ConvertTo returns a Boolean value of true when queried for its ability to convert to a string type. Because this is the right behavior for HandConverter (and for most other custom type converters), there's no need to override it.

When the Property Browser looks for a custom type converter, it looks at each property for a TypeConverterAttribute:

```
public class ClockControl : Control {
  ...
  [ TypeConverterAttribute (typeof(HandConverter)) ]
  public Hand HourHand { ... }

  [TypeConverterAttribute (typeof(HandConverter)) ]
  public Hand MinuteHand { ... }

  [TypeConverterAttribute (typeof(HandConverter)) ]
  public Hand SecondHand { ... }
  ...
}
```

However, this is somewhat cumbersome, so it's simpler to decorate the type itself with TypeConverterAttribute:

```
[ TypeConverterAttribute(typeof(HandConverter)) ]
public class Hand { ... }
```

continues

```
public class ClockControl : Control {
  ...
  public Hand HourHand { ... }
  public Hand MinuteHand { ... }
  public Hand SecondHand { ... }
  ...
}
```

Figure 9.23 shows the effect of the custom HandConverter type converter.

Expandable Object Converter

Although using the UI shown in Figure 9.23 is better than not being able to edit the property at all, there are still ways it can be improved. For instance, put yourself in a developer's shoes. Although it might be obvious what the first part of the property is, it's disappointing not to be able to pick the color from one of those pretty drop-down color pickers. And what is the second part of the property meant to be? Length, width, degrees, something else?

As an example of what you'd like to see, the Font type supports browsing and editing of its subproperties, as shown in Figure 9.24.

This ability to expand a property of a custom type makes it a lot easier to understand what the property represents and what sort of values you need to provide. To allow subproperty editing, you simply change the base type from TypeConverter to ExpandableObjectConverter (from the System.ComponentModel namespace):

```
public class HandConverter : ExpandableObjectConverter { ... }
```

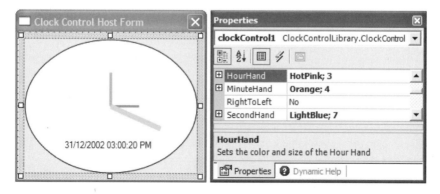

FIGURE 9.23: HandConverter in Action (See Plate 23)

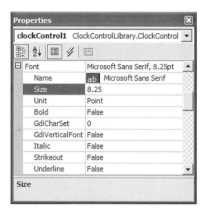

FIGURE 9.24: Expanded Property Value

This change gives you multivalue and nested property editing support, as shown in Figure 9.25.

Although you don't have to write any code to make this property expandable, you must write a little code to fix an irksome problem: a delay in property updating. In expanded mode, a change to the root property value is automatically reflected in the nested property value list. This occurs because the root property entry refers to the design-time property instance, whereas its nested property values refer to the design-time instance's properties directly, as illustrated in Figure 9.26.

When the root property is edited, the Property Browser calls Hand-Converter.ConvertFrom to convert the Property Browser's string entry to a new SecondHand instance, and that results in a refresh of the Property Browser. However, changing the nested values only changes the current instance's property values, rather than creating a new instance, and that doesn't result in an immediate refresh of the root property.

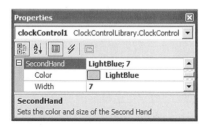

FIGURE 9.25: HandConverter Derived from ExpandableObjectConverter

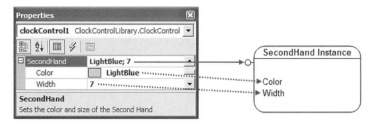

FIGURE 9.26: Relationship between Root and Nested Properties and Design-Time Property Instance

TypeConverters offer a mechanism you can use to force the creation of a new instance whenever instance property values change, something you achieve by overriding GetCreateInstanceSupported and CreateInstance. The GetCreateInstanceSupported method returns a Boolean indicating whether this support is available and, if it is, calls CreateInstance to implement it:

```
public class HandConverter : ExpandableObjectConverter {
  public override bool
  GetCreateInstanceSupported(
    ITypeDescriptorContext context) {

    // Always force a new instance
    return true;
  }

  public override object
  CreateInstance(
    ITypeDescriptorContext context, IDictionary propertyValues) {

    // Use the dictionary to create a new instance
    return new Hand(
      (Color)propertyValues["Color"],
      (int)propertyValues["Width"]);
  }
  ...
}
```

If GetCreateInstanceSupported returns true, then CreateInstance will be used to create a new instance whenever any of the subproperties of an expandable object are changed. The propertyValues argument to Create-Instance provides a set of name/value pairs for the current values of the object's subproperties, and you can use them to construct a new instance.

Custom Type Code Serialization with TypeConverters

Although the Hand type now plays nicely with the Property Browser, it doesn't yet play nicely with code serialization. In fact, at this point it's not being serialized to InitializeComponent at all. To enable serialization of properties exposing complex types, you must expose a public Should-Serialize<PropertyName> method that returns a Boolean:

```
public class ClockControl : Control {
  public Hand SecondHand { ... }
  bool ShouldSerializeSecondHand() {
    // Only serialize nondefault values
    return(
      (secondHand.Color != Color.Red) || (secondHand.Width != 1) );
  }
  ...
}
```

Internally, the Designer looks for a method named ShouldSerialize <PropertyName> to ask whether the property should be serialized. From the Designer's point of view, it doesn't matter whether your ShouldSerial-ize<PropertyName> is public or private, but choosing private removes it from client visibility.

To programmatically implement the Property Browser reset functional-ity, you use the Reset<PropertyName> method:

```
public Hand SecondHand { ... }

void ResetSecondHand() {
  SecondHand = new Hand(Color.Red, 1);
}
```

Implementing ShouldSerialize lets the design-time environment know whether the property should be serialized, but you also need to write custom code to help assist in the generation of appropriate Initialize-Component code. Specifically, the Designer needs an *instance descriptor*, which provides the information needed to create an instance of a particular type. The code serializer gets an InstanceDescriptor object for a Hand by asking the Hand type converter:

```
public class HandConverter : ExpandableObjectConverter {
  public override bool
```

continues

```
    CanConvertTo(
      ITypeDescriptorContext context, Type destinationType) {

      // We can be converted to an InstanceDescriptor
      if( destinationType == typeof(InstanceDescriptor) ) return true;
      return base.CanConvertTo(context, destinationType);
    }

  public override object
    ConvertTo(
      ITypeDescriptorContext context, CultureInfo culture,
      object value, Type destinationType) {

    if( value is Hand ) {
      // Convert to InstanceDescriptor
      if( destinationType == typeof(InstanceDescriptor) ) {
        Hand      hand = (Hand)value;
        object[] properties = new object[2];
        Type[]    types = new Type[2];

        // Color
        types[0] = typeof(Color);
        properties[0] = hand.Color;

        // Width
        types[1] = typeof(int);
        properties[1] = hand.Width;

        // Build constructor
        ConstructorInfo ci = typeof(Hand).GetConstructor(types);
        return new InstanceDescriptor(ci, properties);
      }
      ...
    }
    return base.ConvertTo(context, culture, value, destinationType);
  }
  ...
}
```

To be useful, an instance descriptor requires two pieces of information. First, it needs to know what the constructor looks like. Second, it needs to know which property values should be used if the object is instantiated. The former is described by the ConstructorInfo type, and the latter is simply an array of values, which should be in constructor parameter order. After the control is rebuilt and assuming that ShouldSerialize<Property-Name> permits, all Hand type properties will be serialized using the information provided by the HandConverter-provided InstanceDescriptor:

```
public class ClockControlHostForm : Form {
  ...
  void InitializeComponent() {
    ...
    this.clockControl1.HourHand =
      new ClockControlLibrary.Hand(System.Drawing.Color.Black, 2);
    ...
  }
}
```

Type converters provide all kinds of help for the Property Browser and the Designer to display, convert, and serialize properties of custom types for components that use such properties.

UI Type Editors

ExpandableObjectConverters help break down a complex multivalue property into a nested list of its atomic values. Although this technique simplifies editing of a complicated property, it may not be suitable for other properties that exhibit the following behavior:

- Hard to construct, interpret, or validate, such as a regular expression
- One of a list of values so large it would be difficult to remember all of them
- A visual property, such as a ForeColor, that is not easily represented as a string

Actually, the ForeColor property satisfies all three points. First, it would be hard to find the color you wanted by typing comma-separated integers like 33, 86, 24 or guessing a named color, like PapayaWhip. Second, there are a lot of colors to choose from. Finally, colors are just plain visual.

In addition to supporting in-place editing in the Property Browser, properties such as ForeColor help the developer by providing an alternative UI-based property-editing mechanism. You access this tool, shown in Figure 9.27, from a drop-down arrow in the Property Browser.

The result is a prettier, more intuitive way to select a property value. This style of visual editing is supported by the *UI type editor*, a design-time feature that you can leverage to similar effect. There are two types of "editor"

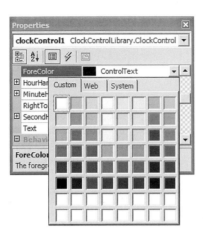

FIGURE 9.27: Color Property Drop-Down UI Editor

you can choose from: modal or drop-down. Drop-down editors support single-click property selection from a drop-down UI attached to the Property Browser. This UI might be a nice way to enhance the clock control's Face property, allowing developers to visualize the clock face style as they make their selection, shown in Figure 9.28.

You begin implementing a custom UI editor by deriving from the UITypeEditor class (from the System.Drawing.Design namespace):

```
public class FaceEditor : UITypeEditor { ... }
```

The next step requires you to override the GetEditStyle and EditValue methods from the UITypeEditor base class:

```
public class FaceEditor : UITypeEditor {
  public override UITypeEditorEditStyle GetEditStyle(
```

FIGURE 9.28: Custom View Drop-Down UI Editor

```
    ITypeDescriptorContext context)
  {...}

  public override object EditValue(
    ITypeDescriptorContext context,
    IServiceProvider provider,
    object value)
  {...}
}
```

As with type converters, the appropriate UI type editor, provided by the GetEditor method of the TypeDescription class, is stored with each property. When the Property Browser updates itself to reflect a control selection in the Designer, it queries GetEditStyle to determine whether it should show a drop-down button, an open dialog button, or nothing in the property value box when the property is selected. This behavior is determined by a value from the UITypeEditorEditStyle enumeration:

```
enum UITypeEditorEditStyle {
  DropDown, // Display drop-down UI
  Modal, // Display modal dialog UI
  None, // Don't display a UI
}
```

Not overriding GetEditStyle is the same as returning UITypeEditorEditStyle.None, which is the default edit style. To show the drop-down UI editor, the clock control returns UITypeEditorEditStyle.DropDown:

```
public class FaceEditor : UITypeEditor {
  public override UITypeEditorEditStyle GetEditStyle(
    ITypeDescriptorContext context) {

    if( context != null ) return UITypeEditorEditStyle.DropDown;
    return base.GetEditStyle(context);
  }
  ...
}
```

ITypeDescriptorContext is passed to GetEditStyle to provide contextual information regarding the execution of this method, including the following:

- The container and, subsequently, the designer host and its components

- The component design-time instance being shown in the Property Browser
- A PropertyDescriptor type describing the property, including the TypeConverter and UITypeEditor assigned to the component
- A PropertyDescriptorGridEntry type, which is a composite of the PropertyDescriptor and the property's associated grid entry in the Property Browser

Whereas GetEditStyle is used to initialize the way the property behaves, EditValue actually implements the defined behavior. Whether the UI editor is drop-down or modal, you follow the same basic steps to edit the value:

1. Access the Property Browser's UI display service, IWindowsForms-EditorService.
2. Create an instance of the editor UI implementation, which is a control that the Property Browser will display.
3. Pass the current property value to the UI editor control.
4. Ask the Property Browser to display the UI editor control.
5. Choose the value and close the UI editor control.
6. Return the new property value from the editor.

Drop-Down UI Type Editors

Here's how the clock control implements these steps to show a drop-down editor for the Face property:

```
public class FaceEditor : UITypeEditor {
  ...
  public override object EditValue(
    ITypeDescriptorContext context,
    IServiceProvider provider,
    object value) {

    if( (context != null) && (provider != null) ) {
      // Access the Property Browser's UI display service
      IWindowsFormsEditorService editorService =
        (IWindowsFormsEditorService)
          provider.GetService(typeof(IWindowsFormsEditorService));
```

```
    if( editorService!= null ) {
      // Create an instance of the UI editor control
      FaceEditorControl dropDownEditor =
        new FaceEditorControl(editorService);

      // Pass the UI editor control the current property value
      dropDownEditor.Face = (ClockFace)value;

      // Display the UI editor control
      editorService.DropDownControl(dropDownEditor);

      // Return the new property value from the UI editor control
      return dropDownEditor.Face;
    }
  }
  return base.EditValue(context, provider, value);
}
}
```

When it comes to displaying the UI editor control, you must play nicely in the design-time environment, particularly regarding UI positioning in relation to the Property Browser. Specifically, drop-down UI editors must appear flush against the bottom of the property entry and must be sized to the width of the property entry.

To facilitate this, the Property Browser exposes a service, an implementation of the IWindowsFormsEditorService interface, to manage the loading and unloading of UI editor controls as well as their positioning inside the development environment. The FaceEditor type references this service and calls its DropDownControl method to display the FaceEditorControl, relative to Property's Browser edit box. When displayed, FaceEditorControl has the responsibility of capturing the user selection and returning control to EditValue with the new value. This requires a call to IWindowsFormsEditorService.CloseDropDown from FaceEditorControl, something you do by passing to FaceEditorControl a reference to the IWindowsFormsEditorService interface:

```
public class FaceEditorControl : UserControl {
  ClockFace face = ClockFace.Both;
  IWindowsFormsEditorService editorService = null;
  ...
  public FaceEditorControl(IWindowsFormsEditorService editorService) {
    ...
```

continues

```
    this.editorService = editorService;
  }

  public ClockFace Face {
    get { ... }
    set { ... }
  }

  void picBoth_Click(object sender, System.EventArgs e) {
    face = ClockFace.Both;

    // Close the UI editor control upon value selection
    editorService.CloseDropDown();
  }

  void picAnalog_Click(object sender, System.EventArgs e) {
    face = ClockFace.Analog;

    // Close the UI editor control upon value selection
    editorService.CloseDropDown();
  }

  void picDigital_Click(object sender, System.EventArgs e) {
    face = ClockFace.Digital;

    // Close the UI editor control upon value selection
    editorService.CloseDropDown();
  }
  ...
}
```

The final step is to associate FaceEditor with the Face property by adorning the property with EditorAttribute:

```
[
  CategoryAttribute("Appearance"),
  DescriptionAttribute("Which style of clock face to display"),
  DefaultValueAttribute(ClockFace.Both),
  EditorAttribute(typeof(FaceEditor), typeof(UITypeEditor))
]
public ClockFace Face { ... }
```

Now FaceEditor is in place for the Face property. When a developer edits that property in Propery Browser, it will show a drop-down arrow and the FaceEditorControl as the UI for the developer to use to choose a value of the ClockFace enumeration.

Modal UI Type Editors

Although drop-down editors are suitable for single-click selection, there are times when unrestricted editing is required. In such situations, you would use a modal UITypeEditor implemented as a modal form. For example, the clock control has a digital time format sufficiently complex to edit with a separate dialog outside the Property Browser:

```
public class ClockControl : Control {
  ...
  string digitalTimeFormat = "dd/MM/yyyy hh:mm:ss tt";
  ...
  [
    CategoryAttribute("Appearance"),
    DescriptionAttribute("The digital time format, ..."),
    DefaultValueAttribute("dd/MM/yyyy hh:mm:ss tt"),
  ]
  public string DigitalTimeFormat {
    get { return digitalTimeFormat; }
    set {
      digitalTimeFormat = value;
      this.Invalidate();
    }
  }
}
```

Date and Time format strings are composed of a complex array of format specifiers that are not easy to remember and certainly aren't intuitive in a property browser, as shown in Figure 9.29.

Modal UITypeEditors are an ideal way to provide a more intuitive way to construct hard-to-format property values. By providing a custom form, you give developers whatever editing experience is the most conducive for

FIGURE 9.29: The DigitalTimeFormat Property

that property type. Figure 9.30 illustrates how the Digital Time Format Editor dialog makes it easier to edit the clock control's DigitTimeFormat property.

A modal UITypeEditor actually requires slightly different code from that of its drop-down counterpart. You follow the same logical steps as with a drop-down editor, with three minor implementation differences:

- Returning UITypeEditorEditStyle.Modal from UITypeEditor.GetEdit-Style
- Calling IWindowsFormsEditorService.ShowDialog from EditValue to open the UI editor dialog
- Not requiring an editor service reference to be passed to the dialog, because a Windows Form can close itself

The clock control's modal UI type editor is shown here:

```
public class DigitalTimeFormatEditor : UITypeEditor {
  public override UITypeEditorEditStyle GetEditStyle(
    ITypeDescriptorContext context) {
    if( context != null ) {
      return UITypeEditorEditStyle.Modal;
    }
    return base.GetEditStyle(context);
  }

  public override object EditValue(
    ITypeDescriptorContext context,
    IServiceProvider provider,
    object value) {
```

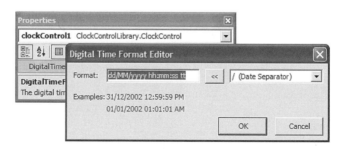

FIGURE 9.30: Custom DigitalTimeFormat Modal UI Editor

```
    if( (context != null) && (provider != null) ) {
      // Access the Property Browser's UI display service
      IWindowsFormsEditorService editorService =
        (IWindowsFormsEditorService)
          provider.GetService(typeof(IWindowsFormsEditorService));

      if( editorService != null ) {
        // Create an instance of the UI editor form
        DigitalTimeFormatEditorForm modalEditor =
          new DigitalTimeFormatEditorForm();

        // Pass the UI editor dialog the current property value
        modalEditor.DigitalTimeFormat = (string)value;

        // Display the UI editor dialog
        if( editorService.ShowDialog(modalEditor) == DialogResult.OK ) {
          // Return the new property value from the UI editor form
          return modalEditor.DigitalTimeFormat;
        }
      }
    }
    return base.EditValue(context, provider, value);
  }
}
```

At this point, normal dialog activities (as covered in Chapter 3: Dialogs) apply for the UI editor's modal form:

```
public class DigitalTimeFormatEditorForm : Form {
  ...
  string digitalTimeFormat = "dd/MM/yyyy hh:mm:ss tt";

  public string DigitalTimeFormat {
    get { return digitalTimeFormat; }
    set { digitalTimeFormat = value; }
  }
  ...
  void btnOK_Click(object sender, System.EventArgs e) {
    DialogResult = DialogResult.OK;
    digitalTimeFormat = txtFormat.Text;
  }
  ...
}
```

Again, to associate the new UI type editor with the property requires applying the EditorAttribute:

```
[
  CategoryAttribute("Appearance"),
  DescriptionAttribute("The digital time format, ..."),
  DefaultValueAttribute("dd/MM/yyyy hh:mm:ss tt"),
  EditorAttribute(typeof(DigitalTimeFormatEditor), typeof(UITypeEditor))
]
public string DigitalTimeFormat { ... }
```

After EditorAttribute is applied, the modal UITypeEditor is accessed via an ellipsis-style button displayed in the Property Browser, as shown in Figure 9.31.

UI type editors allow you to provide a customized editing environment for the developer on a per-property basis, whether it's a drop-down UI to select from a list of possible values or a modal dialog to provide an entire editing environment outside the Property Browser.

Custom Designers

So far, you have seen how properties are exposed to the developer at design time, and you've seen some of the key infrastructure provided by .NET to improve the property-editing experience, culminating in UIType-Editor. Although the focus has been on properties, they aren't the only aspect of a control that operates differently in design-time mode compared with run-time mode. In some situations, a control's UI might render differently between these modes.

For example, the Splitter control displays a dashed border when its BorderStyle is set to BorderStyle.None. This design makes it easier for developers to find this control on the form's design surface in the absence of a visible border, as illustrated in Figure 9.32.

FIGURE 9.31: Accessing a Modal UITypeEditor

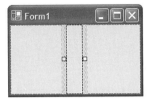

FIGURE 9.32: Splitter Dashed Border When BorderStyle Is None

Because BorderStyle.None means "don't render a border at run time," the dashed border is drawn only at design time for the developer's benefit. Of course, if BorderStyle is set to BorderStyle.FixedSingle or BorderStyle.Fixed3D, the dashed border is not necessary, as illustrated by Figure 9.33.

What's interesting about the splitter control is that the dashed border is not actually rendered from the control implementation. Instead, this work is conducted on behalf of them by a *custom designer*, another .NET design-time feature that follows the tradition, honored by type converters and UI type editors, of separating design-time logic from the control.

Custom designers are not the same as designer hosts or the Windows Forms Designer, although a strong relationship exists between designers and designer hosts. As every component is sited, the designer host creates at least one matching designer for it. As with type converters and UI type editors, the TypeDescriptor class does the work of creating a designer in the CreateDesigner method. Adorning a type with DesignerAttribute ties it to the specified designer. For components and controls that don't possess their own custom designers, .NET provides ComponentDesigner and

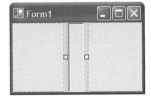

FIGURE 9.33: Splitter with BorderStyle.Fixed3D

ControlDesigner, respectively, both of which are base implementations of IDesigner:

```
public interface IDesigner : IDisposable {
  public void DoDefaultAction();
  public void Initialize(IComponent component);
  public IComponent Component { get; }
  public DesignerVerbCollection Verbs { get; }
}
```

For example, the clock face is round at design time when the clock control either is Analog or is Analog and Digital. This makes it difficult to determine where the edges and corners of the control are, particularly when the clock is being positioned against other controls. The dashed border technique used by the splitter would certainly help, looking something like Figure 9.34.

Because the clock is a custom control, its custom designer will derive from the ControlDesigner base class (from the System.Windows.Forms. Design namespace):

```
public class ClockControlDesigner : ControlDesigner { ... }
```

To paint the dashed border, ClockControlDesigner overrides the Initialize and OnPaintAdornments methods:

```
public class ClockControlDesigner : ControlDesigner {
  ...
```

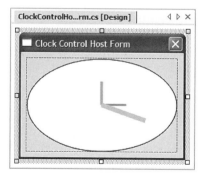

FIGURE 9.34: Border Displayed from ClockControlDesigner

```
    public override void Initialize(IComponent component) { ... }
    protected override void OnPaintAdornments(PaintEventArgs e) { ... }
    ...
}
```

Initialize is overridden to deploy initialization logic that's executed as the control is being sited. It's also a good location to cache a reference to the control being designed:

```
public class ClockControlDesigner : ControlDesigner {
  ClockControl clockControl = null;
  public override void Initialize(IComponent component) {
    base.Initialize(component);

    // Get clock control shortcut reference
    clockControl = (ClockControl)component;
  }
  ...
}
```

You could manually register with Control.OnPaint to add your design-time UI, but you'll find that overriding OnPaintAdornments is a better option because it is called only after the control's design-time or run-time UI is painted, letting you put the icing on the cake:

```
public class ClockControlDesigner : ControlDesigner {
  ...
  protected override void OnPaintAdornments(PaintEventArgs e) {
    // Let the base class have a crack
    base.OnPaintAdornments(e);

    // Don't show border if it does not have an Analog face
    if( clockControl.Face == ClockFace.Digital ) return;

    // Draw border
    Graphics g = e.Graphics;
    using( Pen pen = new Pen(Color.Gray, 1) ) {
      pen.DashStyle = DashStyle.Dash;
      g.DrawRectangle(
        pen, 0, 0, clockControl.Width - 1, clockControl.Height - 1);
    }
  }
  ...
}
```

Adding DesignerAttribute to the ClockControl class completes the association:

```
[ DesignerAttribute(typeof(ClockControlDesigner)) ]
public class ClockControl : Control { ... }
```

Design-Time-Only Properties

The clock control is now working as shown in Figure 9.34. One way to improve on this is to make it an option to show the border, because it's a feature that not all developers will like. Adding a design-time-only Show-Border property will do the trick, because this is not a feature that should be accessible at run time. Implementing a design-time-only property on the control itself is not ideal because the control operates in both design-time and run-time modes. Designers are exactly the right location for design-time properties.

To add a design-time-only property, start by adding the basic property implementation to the custom designer:

```
public class ClockControlDesigner : ControlDesigner {
  ...
  bool showBorder = true;
  ...
  protected override void OnPaintAdornments(PaintEventArgs e) {
    ...
    // Don't show border if hidden or
    // does not have an Analog face
    if( (!showBorder) ||
        (clockControl.Face == ClockFace.Digital) ) return;
    ...
  }

  // Provide implementation of ShowBorder to provide
  // storage for created ShowBorder property
  bool ShowBorder {
    get { return showBorder; }
    set {
      showBorder = value;
      clockControl.Refresh();
    }
  }
}
```

This isn't enough on its own, however, because the Property Browser won't examine a custom designer for properties when the associated component is selected. The Property Browser gets its list of properties from TypeDescriptor's GetProperties method (which, in turn, gets the list of properties using .NET reflection). To augment the properties returned by the TypeDescriptor class, a custom designer can override the PreFilter-Properties method:

```
public class ClockControlDesigner : ControlDesigner {
  . . .
  protected override void PreFilterProperties(
    IDictionary properties) {

    // Let the base have a chance
    base.PreFilterProperties(properties);

    // Create design-time-only property entry and add it to
    // the Property Browser's Design category
    properties["ShowBorder"] = TypeDescriptor.CreateProperty(
      typeof(ClockControlDesigner),
      "ShowBorder",
      typeof(bool),
      CategoryAttribute.Design,
      DesignOnlyAttribute.Yes);
  }
  . . .
}
```

The properties argument to PreFilterProperties allows you to populate new properties by creating PropertyDescriptor objects using the Type-Descriptor's CreateProperty method, passing the appropriate arguments to describe the new property. One of the parameters to TypeDescriptor. CreateProperty is DesignOnlyAttribute.Yes, which specifies design-time-only usage. It also physically causes the value of ShowBorder to be persisted to the form's resource file rather than to InitializeComponent, as shown in Figure 9.35.

If you need to alter or remove existing properties, you can override PostFilterProperties and act on the list of properties after TypeDescriptor has filled it using reflection. Pre/Post filter pairs can also be overridden for methods and events if necessary. Figure 9.36 shows the result of adding the ShowBorder design-time property.

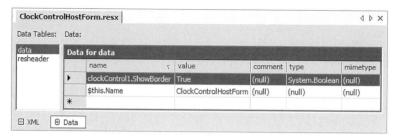

FIGURE 9.35: ShowBorder Property Value Serialized to the Host Form's Resource File

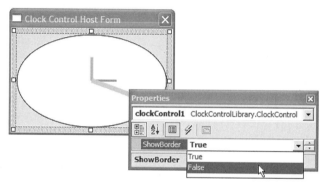

FIGURE 9.36: ShowBorder Option in the Property Browser

Design-Time Context Menu Verbs

To take the design-time-only property even further, it's possible to add items to a component's design-time context menu. These items are called *verbs*, and ShowBorder would make a fine addition to our clock control's verb menu.

Adding to the verb menu requires that we further augment the custom designer class:

```
public class ClockControlDesigner : ControlDesigner {
  ...
  public override DesignerVerbCollection Verbs {
    get {
      // Return new list of context menu items
      DesignerVerbCollection verbs = new DesignerVerbCollection();
      showBorderVerb =
        new DesignerVerb(
```

```
            GetVerbText(),
            new EventHandler(ShowBorderClicked));
        verbs.Add(showBorderVerb);
        return verbs;
    }
  }
  ...
}
```

The Verbs override is queried by the Designer shell for a list of Designer-Verbs to insert into the component's context menu. Each DesignerVerb in the DesignerVerbCollection takes a string name value plus the event handler that responds to verb selection. In our case, this is ShowBorderClicked:

```
public class ClockControlDesigner : ControlDesigner {
  ...
  void ShowBorderClicked(object sender, EventArgs e) {
    // Toggle property value
    ShowBorder = !ShowBorder;
  }
  ...
}
```

This handler simply toggles the ShowBorder property. However, because the verb menu for each component is cached, it takes extra code to show the current state of the ShowBorder property in the verb menu:

```
public class ClockControlDesigner : ControlDesigner {
  ...
  bool ShowBorder {
    get { return showBorder; }

    set {
      // Change property value
      PropertyDescriptor property =
        TypeDescriptor.GetProperties(typeof(ClockControl))["ShowBorder"];
      this.RaiseComponentChanging(property);
      showBorder = value;
      this.RaiseComponentChanged(property, !showBorder, showBorder);

      // Toggle Show/Hide Border verb entry in context menu
      IMenuCommandService  menuService =
        (IMenuCommandService)this.GetService
            (typeof(IMenuCommandService));
      if( menuService != null ) {
```

continues

```
    // Re-create Show/Hide Border verb
    if( menuService.Verbs.IndexOf(showBorderVerb) >= 0 ) {
      menuService.Verbs.Remove(showBorderVerb);
      showBorderVerb =
        new DesignerVerb(
          GetVerbText(),
          new EventHandler(ShowBorderClicked));
      menuService.Verbs.Add(showBorderVerb);
    }
  }

    // Update clock UI
    clockControl.Invalidate ();
    }
  }
  . . .
}
```

ShowBorder now performs two distinct operations. First, the property value is updated between calls to RaiseComponentChanging and Raise-ComponentChanged, helper functions that wrap calls to the designer host's IComponentChangeService. The second part of ShowBorder re-creates the Show/Hide Border verb to reflect the new property value. This manual intervention is required because the Verbs property is called only when a component is selected on the form. In our case, "Show/Hide Border" could be toggled any number of times after the control has been selected.

Fortunately, after the Verbs property has delivered its DesignerVerbCollection payload to the Designer, it's possible to update it via the designer host's IMenuCommandService. Unfortunately, because the Text property is read-only, you can't implement a simple property change. Instead, the verb must be re-created and re-associated with ShowBorderClicked every time the ShowBorder property is updated.

On top of adding Show/Hide Border to the context menu, .NET throws in a clickable link for each verb, located on the Property Browser above the property description bar. Figure 9.37 illustrates all three options, including the original editable property.

Custom designers allow you to augment an application developer's design-time experience even further than simply adding the effects to the Property Browser. Developers can change how a control renders itself, controlling the properties, methods, and events that are available at design time and augmenting a component's verbs.

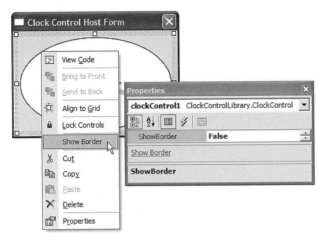

FIGURE 9.37: ShowBorder Option in the Property Browser and the Context Menu

Where Are We?

Although components (and, by association, controls) gain all kinds of integration into a .NET design-time environment with very little work, .NET also provides a rich infrastructure to augment the design-time experience for your custom components.

■ 10 ■
Resources

A RESOURCE IS A NAMED PIECE OF DATA that is bound into an assembly[1] at build time. Resources are an enormously useful way to bundle arbitrary data into your applications and components for use at run time for tasks as diverse as setting the background image on a form and setting the label of a button. And because applications and components can find themselves being used in countries other than those in which they were written, the .NET resource architecture supports no-compile deployment of localized resources.

Resource Basics

Imagine setting the background image of a form in your application by loading a bitmap from a file:

```
public Form1() {
  ...
  // Load a file from the file system
  this.BackgroundImage =
    new Bitmap(@"C:\WINDOWS\Web\Wallpaper\Azul.jpg");
}
```

---

1. Recall from Chapter 1: Hello, Windows Forms, that an assembly is a .NET executable or library (DLL).

The problem with this code is that not all installations of Windows will have Azul.jpg, and even those that do have it may not have it in the same place. Even if you shipped this picture with your application, a space-conscious user may decide to remove it, causing your application to fault. The only safe way to make sure that the picture, or any file, stays with code is to embed it and load it as a *resource*, a named piece of data embedded in the assembly itself.

Manifest Resources

Resources are added to an assembly at compile time. To embed a file into an assembly using VS.NET requires that you add the file to your VS.NET project.[2] To add a file to a project, right-click on your project in Solution Explorer, choose Add Existing Item, and choose the file you'd like to add. If it's not already there, it will be copied into your project's directory, but it is not yet embedded as a resource. To embed the file as a resource, right-click on the file and choose Properties, changing Build Action from Content (the default) to Embedded Resource, as shown in Figure 10.1.

When it's marked as an Embedded Resource, a file gets embedded in the assembly's set of manifest resources. The *manifest* of an assembly is composed of a set of metadata that's part of the assembly. Part of that metadata is the name and data associated with each embedded resource.

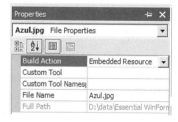

FIGURE 10.1: Setting a File's Build Action to Embedded Resource

---

2. The .NET Framework SDK command line compilers, such as csc.exe and vbc.exe, provide options for bundling files into assemblies as resources (for csc.exe and vbc.exe, the switch is /resource). In addition, the /embedresource switch for al.exe will create a new assembly from an existing assembly and a set of files to embed as resources.

Naming Manifest Resources

To check that a file has been embedded properly into your project's output assembly, you can use the .NET Framework SDK tool ildasm.exe. This tool shows all embedded resources in the Manifest view of your assembly, as shown in Figure 10.2.

As shown in ildasm with the .mresource entry, embedding a file as a resource will cause VS.NET to name the resource using the project's default namespace, an optional subfolder name, and the resource file name itself in the following format:

```
<defaultNamespace>.<folderName>.<fileName>
```

The default namespace portion of the resource name is the default namespace of the project itself, as set via Solution Explorer | <project-Name>(right-click) | Properties | Common Properties | General | Default Namespace, as shown in Figure 10.3.

If the file happens to be in a subfolder of your project, the folder name of the resource will include a version of that folder name, replacing the back slashes with dots. For example, Figure 10.4 shows the Azul.jpg file in the foo\bar project subfolder, and Figure 10.5 shows the resulting name of the resource in ildasm.

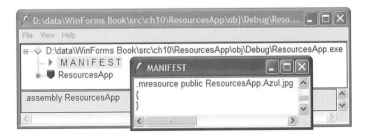

FIGURE 10.2: ildasm Showing an Embedded Manifest Resource

FIGURE 10.3: A VS.NET Project's Default Namespace

FIGURE 10.4: The Azul.jpg Resource File in the foo\bar Project Subfolder

FIGURE 10.5: How VS.NET Composes the Name of a Resource in a Project Subfolder

Loading Manifest Resources

To discover the resources embedded in an assembly, you can enumerate the list of manifest resources, as ildasm is doing, by using the GetManifestResourceNames method of the System.Reflection.Assembly[3] class:

```
using System.Reflection;
...
// Get this type's assembly
Assembly assem = this.GetType().Assembly;

// Enumerate the assembly's manifest resources
foreach( string resourceName in assem.GetManifestResourceNames() ) {
  MessageBox.Show(resourceName);
}
```

When you know the name of a manifest resource, either by enumerating it or by hard-coding the one you want, you can load it as a raw

---

3. A type's assembly can be retrieved from the associated Type object's Assembly property. Similarly, the Assembly class itself provides several methods for retrieving assemblies of interest: GetAssembly, GetCallingAssembly, GetEntryAssembly, and GetExecutingAssembly.

stream of bytes via the Assembly class's GetManifestResourceStream method:

```
using System.IO;

namespace ResourcesApp {
  public Form1() {
    ...

    // Get this type's assembly
    Assembly assem = this.GetType().Assembly;

    // Get the stream that holds the resource
    // from the "ResourcesApp.Azul.jpg" resource
    // NOTE1: Make sure not to close this stream,
    //        or the Bitmap object will lose access to it
    // NOTE2: Also be very careful to match the case
    //        on the resource name itself
    Stream stream =
      assem.GetManifestResourceStream("ResourcesApp.Azul.jpg");

    // Load the bitmap from the stream
    this.BackgroundImage = new Bitmap(stream);
  }
}
```

Notice that the resource name passed to GetManifestResourceStream is the full, case-sensitive name of the resource, including the namespace and the file name. If the resource is embedded from a subfolder of the project, remember to include the "dottified" version of the folder name as well:

```
Stream stream =
  assem.GetManifestResourceStream("ResourcesApp.foo.bar.Azul.jpg");
```

Manifest Resource Namespaces

If you pass a System.Type object to the GetManifestResourceStream method, it will use the type's namespace as the namespace prefix portion of the embedded resource. This is especially useful because, by default, a newly generated class in VS.NET is contained in the project's default namespace, allowing for an easy match between a type's namespace and the project's default namespace:

```
namespace ResourcesApp {
  public class Form1 : Form {
    ...
    // Load the stream for resource "ResourcesApp.Azul.jpg"
    Stream stream =
      assem.GetManifestResourceStream(this.GetType(), "Azul.jpg");
    ...
  }
}
```

This namespace-specification shortcut also works for some types that can directly load files that are embedded as resources. For example, the Bitmap class can load an image from a resource, eliminating the need to get the manifest stream manually:

```
namespace ResourcesApp {
  public class Form1 : Form {
    ...
    public Form1() {
      ...
      // Get this form's assembly
      Assembly assem = this.GetType().Assembly;

      // Load image from "ResourcesApp.Azul.jpg"
      this.BackgroundImage = new Bitmap(this.GetType(), "Azul.jpg");
    }
  }
}
```

To help you keep track of where all the parts of a manifest resource come from and how they're specified, Figure 10.6 shows a summary.

Although manifest resources are useful, their degree of integration with VS.NET and the type system is limited. However, manifest resources serve as the needed foundation for typed resources, which address both of these issues.

Typed Resources

Despite the file's extension, manifest resources are embedded with no type information. For example, if the name of the Azul.jpg file were Azul.quux, that would make no difference to the Bitmap class, which is looking at the data itself for the type—for example, JPEG, PNG, GIF, and so on. It's up to you to properly map the type of each resource to the type of the object needed to load it.

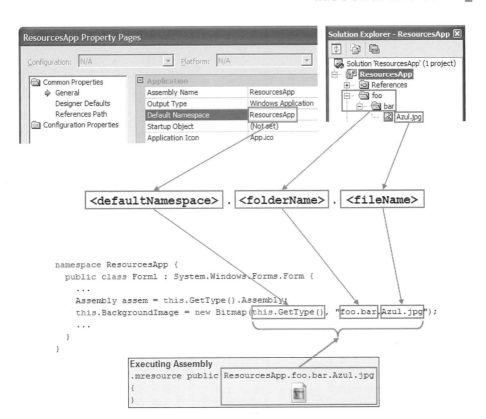

FIGURE 10.6: A Summary of Manifest Resource Naming and Name Resolution

However, you can tag your resources with a type if you're willing to take an extra step. .NET supports an extended set of metadata for a resource that includes Multipurpose Internet Mail Extensions (MIME) type information in two formats: one text and one binary. Both formats have readers so that you can pull out the properly typed resources at run time.

Text-Based Typed Resources

The text-based format is a .NET-specific XML format called ResX (.resx files). In spite of its text basis, this format is not meant to be read by humans (as few XML formats are). However, VS.NET provides a rudimentary editor for .resx files. To add a new .resx file to your VS.NET project, choose Add New Item from the Project menu and pick the Assembly Resource File template, as shown in Figure 10.7.

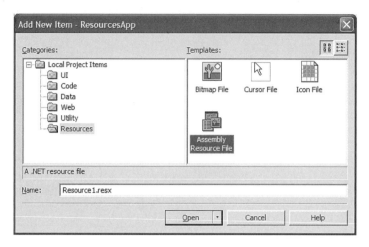

FIGURE 10.7: Adding a .resx File to a Project

As of this writing, even an empty .resx file is 42 lines of XML, most of which is the schema information. The schema allows for any number of entries in the .resx file, each of which has a name, value, comment, type, and MIME type. Figure 10.8 shows a .resx file with two entries: a string named MyString and an image named MyImage.

The corresponding XML data for the entries is shown here:

```
<?xml version="1.0" encoding="utf-8" ?>
<root>
  ...
  <data name="MyString">
    <value>a string value</value>
    <comment>a comment</comment>
  </data>
```

Resource1.resx					
Data Tables: Data:					
data resheader	**Data for data**				
	name	value	comment	type	mimetype
▶	MyString	a string value	a comment	(null)	(null)
	MyImage		(null)	System.Drawing.Bitmap,	application/x-microsoft.net.object.bytearray.base64
*					
⊡ XML ⊟ Data					

FIGURE 10.8: A Simple .resx File in the Data View of the Designer

```
  <data name="MyImage"
    type="System.Drawing.Bitmap, ..."
    mimetype="application/x-microsoft.net.object.bytearray.base64">
    <value>
      ... base64-encoded image data ...
    </value>
  </data>
</root>
```

Of the two entries, only the string entry can actually be edited in the Data view of the .resx editor. The image entry was added by hand in the XML view (the Base64-encoded data being particularly challenging). For this reason, the direct use of .resx files in VS.NET is useful only for string resources (although indirect usage makes .resx files very useful for any kind of data, as you'll see later in this chapter).

After you've got a .resx file, you can load it and enumerate it using the ResXResourceReader class from the System.Resources namespace:

```
using System.Collections;
using System.Resources;
...
using( ResXResourceReader reader =
  new ResXResourceReader(@"c:\Resource1.resx") ) {
  foreach( DictionaryEntry entry in reader ) {
    string s = string.Format("{0} ({1})= '{2}'",
      entry.Key, entry.Value.GetType(), entry.Value);
    MessageBox.Show(s);
  }
}
```

The ResXResourceReader class parses the XML file and exposes a set of named, typed values, but it provides no random access to them. Pulling out a specific entry requires first finding it:

```
public Form1() {
  ...

  using( ResXResourceReader reader =
    new ResXResourceReader(@"Resource1.resx") ) {
    foreach( DictionaryEntry entry in reader ) {
      if( entry.Key.ToString() == "MyString" ) {
        // Set form caption from string resource
        this.Text = (string)entry.Value;
      }
    }
  }
}
```

The benefit of the .resx file is that type information is embedded along with the data itself, requiring a simple cast to get to a typed version of the data.

Binary Typed Resources

To add a .resx file to your project as an embedded resource, you use the Add New Item dialog. Building the project causes the .resx data to be embedded as *nested resources*, which are resources grouped into a named container. When a .resx file is embedded as a resource in a VS.NET project, it becomes the container for the nested resources it holds. As part of that process, the .resx file is compiled from the text format to the .resources binary format. Assuming a project's default namespace of ResourcesApp and a .resx file named Resources1.resx, the container of nested resources is named ResourcesApp.Resources1.resources, as shown in ildasm in Figure 10.9.

The .resources extension comes from the resgen.exe tool, which VS.NET uses on the .resx file before embedding it as a resource. You can compile a .resx file into a .resources file yourself by using the following command line (which produces Resource1.resources in this case):

```
C:\> resgen.exe Resource1.resx
```

After you've compiled a .resx file into a .resources file in the file system, you can load it and enumerate it using ResourceReader from the System.Resources namespace. Other than the name of the class and the input format, usage of the ResourceReader class is identical to that of ResXResourceReader, including the lack of random access for named entries:

```
using( ResourceReader reader =
```

FIGURE 10.9: An Embedded .resources File

```
new ResourceReader(@"c:\Resource1.resources") ) {
foreach( DictionaryEntry entry in reader ) {
  string s = string.Format("{0} ({1})= '{2}'",
    entry.Key, entry.Value.GetType(), entry.Value);
  MessageBox.Show(s);
}
}
```

You can read a .resources file from the file system, but because VS.NET compiles a .resx file and embeds the resulting .resources file for you, it's easier to access a .resources file directly from its manifest resource stream:

```
// Load embedded .resources file
using( Stream stream =
        assem.GetManifestResourceStream(
          this.GetType(), "Resource1.resources") ) {
  // Find resource in .resources file
  using( ResourceReader reader = new ResourceReader(stream) ) {
    foreach( DictionaryEntry entry in reader ) {
      if( entry.Key.ToString() == "MyString" ) {
        // Set form caption from string resource
        this.Text = entry.Value.ToString();
      }
    }
  }
}
```

This two-step process—loading the .resx file or the .resources nested resource and then enumerating all values looking for the one you want—is an inconvenience, so .NET provides the ResourceManager class, which provides random access to resources.

Resource Manager

The ResourceManager class, also from the System.Resources namespace, is initialized with an embedded .resources file:

```
public Form1() {
  ...

  // Get this type's assembly
  Assembly assem = this.GetType().Assembly;

  // Load the .resources file into the ResourceManager
  // Assumes a file named "Resource1.resx" as part of the project
  ResourceManager resman =
```

continues

```
new ResourceManager("ResourcesApp.Resource1", assem);
   ...
}
```

Notice the use of the project's default namespace appended to the Resource1.resources file. You name your .resources files in exactly the same way that you name any other kind of resource, except that the .resources extension is assumed and cannot be included in the name.

As a further convenience, if you name a .resx file with the name of a type, such as MyCustomType.resx, the name of the .resources file and the assembly can be determined from the type:

```
namespace ResourcesApp {
  class MyCustomType {
    public MyCustomType() {
      // Load "ResourcesApp.MyCustomType.resources"
      // from the MyCustomType class's assembly
      ResourceManager resman = new ResourceManager(this.GetType());
      ...
    }
  }
}
```

Using a type's namespace and name to name a .resx file is a useful way to keep per-type resources. This is how WinForms Designer associates resources with custom forms and other types with design surfaces, as you'll see soon.

Accessing Resources from a Resource Manager

After you've created a resource manager, you can pull out nested resources by name using the GetObject method, casting to the appropriate type. But if you're using the .resx file for string resources, you'll want to use the Get-String method instead. This method performs the cast to the System.String type for you:

```
namespace ResourcesApp {
  class MyCustomType {
    public MyCustomType() {
      // Load "ResourcesApp.MyCustomType.resources"
      ResourceManager resman = new ResourceManager(this.GetType());

      // Access the MyString string from the ResourceManager
```

```
    // (both of these techniques are equivalent for strings)
    string s1 = (string)resman.GetObject("MyString");
    string s2 = resman.GetString("MyString");
  }
 }
}
```

The resource manager acts as a logical wrapper around a resource reader, exposing the nested resources by name, as shown in Figure 10.10.

Again, because the naming scheme for embedded resources is somewhat obscured, Figure 10.11 shows a summary of how VS.NET settings influence the names used with the ResourceManager.

Using a resource manager directly, especially one associated with a specific type, is a useful thing to do, but somewhat labor-intensive. WinForms Designer often makes such manual coding unnecessary.

Designer Resources

Although the resource manager code is lots friendlier to write than resource reader code, the lack of a decent editor for .resx files makes it difficult to use them for anything but string resources. Not only do you have to write the code manually to bring the data in at run time, but also you don't get to see what your resources will look like at design time. That's a problem for resources such as a form's background image.

In addition to all its other duties, WinForms Designer provides support for associating resource data with objects hosted on your custom forms and

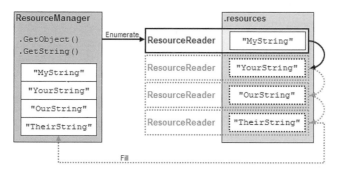

FIGURE 10.10: Logical View of the Way ResourceManager Uses ResourceReader

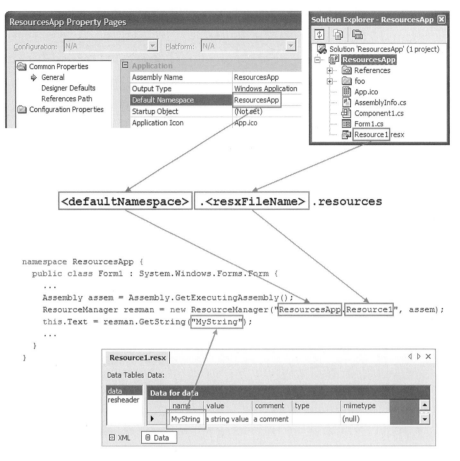

FIGURE 10.11: Resource Naming and ResourceManager

other component types.[4] If you open the VS.NET Solution Explorer and press the Show All Files button, you'll see that each component type, whether it's a form, a control, or a simple component, has a corresponding .resx file. This keeps resources associated with properties of the component, as set in the Property Browser. For example, if you set the Background-Image property of a form, not only will the form show the background image in the Designer, but also the form's .resx file will contain an entry for that image. Similarly, if you set the Image property of a PictureBox control

---

4. What makes a component type is discussed in detail in Chapter 9: Design-Time Integration.

on the same form, the .resx file will have grown to include that resource as well. Figure 10.12 shows both of these entries.

Each component's .resx file is compiled and embedded as a .resources file, just as if you'd added your own .resx file to your project, thereby making the resources available to the component at run time. In addition to the entries in the component's .resx file, the Designer adds the code to InitializeComponent to load a resource manager for the component. The Designer-added code populates the component's properties using the objects pulled from the resources:

```
namespace ResourcesApp {
  public class Form1 : Form {
    ...
    void InitializeComponent() {
      ResourceManager resources = new ResourceManager(typeof(Form1));
      ...
      this.pictureBox1.Image =
        (System.Drawing.Bitmap)resources.GetObject("pictureBox1.Image");
      ...
      this.BackgroundImage =
        (System.Drawing.Bitmap)resources.GetObject(
          "$this.BackgroundImage");

      ...
    }
  }
}
```

Notice that the ResourceManager object is constructed using the type of the component, which is used to construct the .resources resource name for the component. Notice also the naming convention used by the Designer to

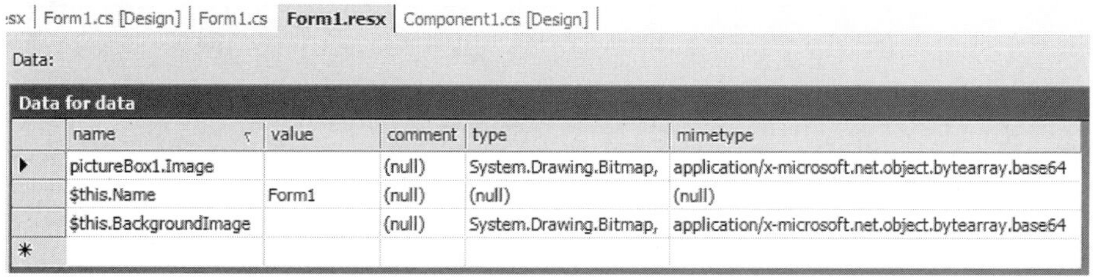

	name	value	comment	type	mimetype
▶	pictureBox1.Image		(null)	System.Drawing.Bitmap,	application/x-microsoft.net.object.bytearray.base64
	$this.Name	Form1	(null)	(null)	(null)
	$this.BackgroundImage		(null)	System.Drawing.Bitmap,	application/x-microsoft.net.object.bytearray.base64
✱					

FIGURE 10.12: A Component's .resx File

name resources. For properties on fields of the component, the format of the name is as follows:

```
<fieldName>.<propertyName>
```

For properties on the component itself, the format of the name looks like this:

```
$this.<propertyName>
```

If you'd like to add custom string properties for use in an existing Designer-managed .resx file, you can, but make sure to stay away from the format of the Designer-generated names:

```
$mine.<resourceName>
```

By using a leading dollar sign or another character that's illegal for use as a field name, and by avoiding the "$this" prefix (and the ">>" prefix, which is used by localized resources), you're likely to stay out of the way of the current Designer implementation while still allowing yourself per-component typed resources. However, because the implementation of the Designer could change, adding your own .resx file to the project is the surest way of maintaining custom resources outside the influence of the Designer.

Designer Resource Issues

As of this writing there are two main problems with resources as supported in VS.NET. The first is that when you set a property from a file, the data from the file is copied directly into the .resx file, so changes to the original file are not automatically replicated in the resource. This is exacerbated by the fact that after data from a file has been added to a .resx file, there is no way in VS.NET to edit it. Instead, to get updated data into a .resx file, you must use VS.NET to remove the entry from VS.NET, after which you must add it again manually.

The second problem is that, except for a single icon, C# projects don't support the addition of unmanaged resources. All files marked as Embedded Resource or pulled into a .resx file are managed resources. This makes them unavailable for use by unmanaged components, such as those used in the COM-based DirectX API. To support some interoperability scenarios, you'll need to use the /win32resource compiler command line switch, which can't be used from within VS.NET builds, or you must use a third-party tool that will add unmanaged resources after a build.[5] Microsoft provides no tools, as of this writing, that provide this functionality.

Resource Localization

In addition to simplified access to typed resources, the ResourceManager class provides one other important feature: the ability to *localize* resources for your components without recompiling them. The act of *localization* (l10n[6]) is a process of providing culture-specific information to display to a user in that culture. For example, a form has been localized when it shows "OK" in English but "Le OK" in French (or whatever the French actually say when they mean OK). The act of *internationalization* (i18n), on the other hand, is taking advantage of localized information. This could mean using localized resources in the UI or using code that formats currency or dates according to the current locale, as shown in Figure 10.13.

Culture Information

I generated the currencies and dates in Figure 10.13 by enumerating all the cultures that .NET knows about (centralized in the System.Globalization namespace) and using the information about each culture to provide formatting information:

```
using System.Globalization;
. . .
```

continues

---

5. This chapter's source code includes a tool from Peter Chiu called ntcopyres.exe that adds unmanaged resources to a managed assembly. It was obtained from http://www.code-guru.com/cpp_mfc/rsrc-simple.html.

6. The l10n abbreviation came from the need to spell out "localization" so often that the middle 10 letters were replaced with the number 10. Similarly, "internationalization" is abbreviated i18n. In this same spirit, I plan to switch from "abbreviation" to "a10n" any day now.

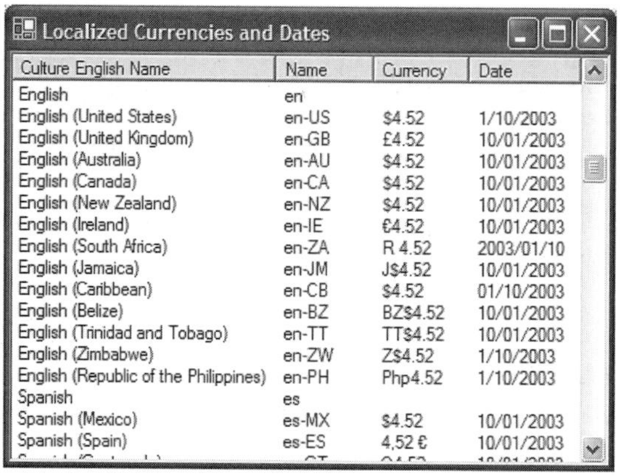

FIGURE 10.13: Localized Currencies and Dates

```
void Form1_Load(object sender, EventArgs e) {
  double amount = 4.52;
  DateTime date = DateTime.Now;

  foreach( CultureInfo info in
    CultureInfo.GetCultures(CultureTypes.AllCultures) ) {
    ListViewItem item = listView1.Items.Add(info.EnglishName);
    item.SubItems.Add(info.Name);
    if( !info.IsNeutralCulture ) {
      item.SubItems.Add(amount.ToString("C", info.NumberFormat));
      item.SubItems.Add(date.ToString("d", info.DateTimeFormat));
    }
  }
}
```

This code enumerates all known cultures, pulling out the name, the number formatting information, and the date formatting information; the latter two are passed to the ToString function to govern formatting. The intrinsic ToString implementations format strings by using the culture stored in the CurrentCulture property of the current thread (available via System.Threading.Thread.CurrentThread). The CurrentCulture property on the System.Windows.Forms.Application class is just a wrapper around the CurrentCulture property of the current thread, so either can be used to test your programs in alternative cultures:

```
static void Main() {
  double amount = 4.52;
```

```
// Show currency using default culture
MessageBox.Show(amount.ToString("C"),
   Application.CurrentCulture.EnglishName);

// Change current culture (one way)
Application.CurrentCulture = new CultureInfo("fr-CA");

// Change current culture (another way)
System.Threading.Thread.CurrentThread.CurrentCulture =
   new CultureInfo("fr-CA");

// Show currency in current culture (Canadian French)
MessageBox.Show(amount.ToString("C"),
   Application.CurrentCulture.EnglishName);
}
```

By default, the current culture is whatever users have set in their machines. Changing it requires an instance of the CultureInfo object, which is most easily constructed with a culture name. A *culture name* is composed of unique identifiers of a language and a country and is formatted this way:

```
<twoLetterLanguageId>-<twoLetterCountryId>
```

For example, U.S. English is "en-US," and Australian English is "en-AU."

Resource Probing

The ResourceManager class was written with internationalization and localization in mind. Each new ResourceManager uses the CurrentUI-Culture property[7] of the current thread to determine which culture's resources to load. When it's created, the resource manager *probes* the file system for an assembly that contains the appropriate culture-specific resources. Based on the namespace of the type it's loaded with, the resource manager looks in 16 places for an assembly, either DLL or EXE. First it looks for country- and language-specific resources, and then it falls back on country-neutral, language-specific resources. Assuming a

---

7. The CurrentUICulture property is not to be confused with the CurrentCulture property, which is used for a different purpose.

namespace of LocalizedApp, Table 10.1 shows the relative paths that the resource manager probes looking for localized resources.

The assemblies that the resource manager is looking for are known as *satellite assemblies* in that they're separate assemblies that can be found near the location of the *main assembly,* which is the assembly containing the code for the localized form(s).

TABLE 10.1: Resource Manager Probing for Localized Resources

Relative Probed Assembly Name
Country- and Language-Specific Probing
1. en-US/***LocalizedApp***.resources.DLL
2. en-US/***LocalizedApp***.resources/***LocalizedApp***.resources.DLL
3. bin/en-US/***LocalizedApp***.resources.DLL
4. bin/en-US/***LocalizedApp***.resources/***LocalizedApp***.resources.DLL
5. en-US/***LocalizedApp***.resources.EXE
6. en-US/***LocalizedApp***.resources/***LocalizedApp***.resources.EXE
7. bin/en-US/***LocalizedApp***.resources.EXE
8. bin/en-US/***LocalizedApp***.resources/***LocalizedApp***.resources.EXE
Country-Neutral and Language-Specific Probing
9. en/***LocalizedApp***.resources.DLL
10. en/***LocalizedApp***.resources/***LocalizedApp***.resources.DLL
11. bin/en/***LocalizedApp***.resources.DLL
12. bin/en/***LocalizedApp***.resources/***LocalizedApp***.resources.DLL
13. en/***LocalizedApp***.resources.EXE
14. en/***LocalizedApp***.resources/***LocalizedApp***.resources.EXE
15. bin/en/***LocalizedApp***.resources.EXE
16. bin/en/***LocalizedApp***.resources/LocalizedApp.resources.EXE

The resources embedded in the main assembly get loaded only if no culture-specific resources are found. By default, these resources are *culture-neutral* in that they aren't specialized for any culture. To mark resources embedded with code as *culture-specific*, you can apply the Neutral-ResourcesLanguageAttribute attribute (from the System.Resources namespace) to the assembly as a whole.[8] The following is an example of marking an assembly's resources as country- and language-specific:

```
using System.Resources;

// Mark all resources in this assembly as U.S. English.
// No probing will be done in the en-US culture.
[assembly: NeutralResourcesLanguageAttribute("en-US")]
```

The following is an example of marking an assembly's resources as country-neutral and language-specific:

```
using System.Resources;

// Mark all resources in this assembly as country-neutral English.
// Probing will be done for country-specific resources but
// will stop when country-neutral resources are needed.
[assembly: NeutralResourcesLanguageAttribute("en")]
```

The reason to mark an assembly's resources as culture-specific is to avoid the resource probing process for satellite assemblies when the main assembly code also contains the culture-specific resources.

Resource Localization

Whereas culture-specific resource assemblies are loaded at the namespace level, resources themselves are localized at the form level. A form is localized if the Localizable property is set in the Property Browser to true (the default is false). When the Localizable property is false, a new form has no entries in the .resx file. However, when the Localizable property is set to true, the .resx file expands to hold 26 entries, each corresponding to a property to be read from a localized resource during execution of the Initialize-Component method:

---

8. The wizard-generated AssemblyInfo source file is a handy place to put assembly-level attributes.

```
void InitializeComponent() {
  ResourceManager resources = new ResourceManager(typeof(Form1));

  // Form1
  this.AccessibleDescription =
    ((string)(resources.GetObject("$this.AccessibleDescription")));
  this.AccessibleName =
    ((string)(resources.GetObject("$this.AccessibleName")));
  this.Anchor =
    ((AnchorStyles)(resources.GetObject("$this.Anchor")));
  this.AutoScaleBaseSize =
    ((Size)(resources.GetObject("$this.AutoScaleBaseSize")));
  this.AutoScroll =
    ((bool)(resources.GetObject("$this.AutoScroll")));
  this.AutoScrollMargin =
    ((Size)(resources.GetObject("$this.AutoScrollMargin")));
  this.AutoScrollMinSize =
    ((Size)(resources.GetObject("$this.AutoScrollMinSize")));
  this.BackgroundImage =
    ((Image)(resources.GetObject("$this.BackgroundImage")));
  this.ClientSize =
    ((Size)(resources.GetObject("$this.ClientSize")));
  this.Dock =
    ((DockStyle)(resources.GetObject("$this.Dock")));
  this.Enabled =
    ((bool)(resources.GetObject("$this.Enabled")));
  this.Font =
    ((Font)(resources.GetObject("$this.Font")));
  this.Icon =
    ((Icon)(resources.GetObject("$this.Icon")));
  this.ImeMode =
    ((ImeMode)(resources.GetObject("$this.ImeMode")));
  this.Location =
    ((Point)(resources.GetObject("$this.Location")));
  this.MaximumSize =
    ((Size)(resources.GetObject("$this.MaximumSize")));
  this.MinimumSize =
    ((Size)(resources.GetObject("$this.MinimumSize")));
  this.Name = "Form1";
  this.RightToLeft =
    ((RightToLeft)(resources.GetObject("$this.RightToLeft")));
  this.StartPosition =
    ((FormStartPosition)(resources.GetObject("$this.StartPosition")));
  this.Text =
    resources.GetString("$this.Text");
  this.Visible =
    ((bool)(resources.GetObject("$this.Visible")));
}
#endregion
```

For a localized form, the InitializeComponent method checks satellite resources for any property that could be culture-specific. When a form has

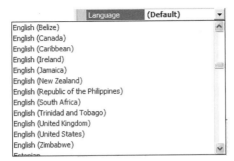

FIGURE 10.14: Choosing a Culture in the Property Browser

been set to localizable, you can choose a culture from the Language property in the Property Browser, as shown in Figure 10.14.

For each culture you choose, a corresponding .resx file containing culture-specific data will be associated with the form. Figure 10.15 shows a form in the Property Browser after the developer has chosen to support several languages—some country-specific and others country-neutral.

When the project is built, all of the form's culture-specific resources are bundled together into a satellite assembly, one per culture, and placed into the appropriately named folder. The folders and satellite assemblies are named so that the resource manager, looking for the culture-specific resources, can find the ones it's looking for:

```
LocalizedApp.exe
en\LocalizedApp.resources.dll
en-CA\LocalizedApp.resources.dll
en-US\LocalizedApp.resources.dll
fr\LocalizedApp.resources.dll
fr-CA\LocalizedApp.resources.dll
```

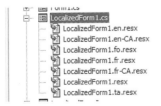

FIGURE 10.15: One Form with Localization Information for Several Cultures

Notice that the main application is at the top level, containing the culture-neutral resources, and the culture-specific resource assemblies are in subfolders named after the culture. Notice also that VS.NET has chosen the names of the subfolders and satellite assemblies that the resource manager will look for first (as shown in Table 10.1), saving probing time.

The presence of a new satellite assembly in the file system in a place that the resource manager can find it is all that's required to localize an assembly's form for a new culture. When a localized form is loaded, the resource manager will find the new satellite assembly and will load the resources from it as appropriate, without the need to recompile the main assembly itself. This provides *no-compile deployment* for localized resources.

Resource Localization for Nondevelopers

VS.NET is a handy tool for resource localization, but it's not something you want to force nondevelopers to use. Luckily, after you set the Localizable property to true for each localizable form and rebuild your component, your user can localize a set of forms in an assembly without further use of VS.NET.

To allow nondevelopers to localize resources, the .NET Framework SDK ships with a tool called Windows Resource Localization Editor (winres.exe). To use it, you open a culture-neutral .resx file for a localizable form—that is, a form with the Language property set to (Default).[9] After you've loaded the .resx file, you're presented with a miniature version of the VS.NET forms Designer, which you can use to set culture-specific resource information as shown in Figure 10.16.

Before you make any changes, I recommend choosing File | Save As to choose a culture. The culture will be used to format a culture-specific name for the .resx file. For example, LocalizedForm1.resx will be saved as LocalizedForm1.en-US.resx for the U.S. English culture, just as VS.NET does it. After you save the culture-specific .resx file, make the culture-specific changes and save again.

Next, you create the set of culture-specific .resx files for an assembly, one per form, to use in creating a satellite assembly. To do that, you start by

---

9. WinRes and VS.NET can share culture-neutral .resx files but not culture-specific .resx files, so it's best to pick only one resource localization tool and stick with it.

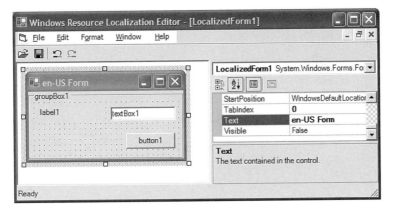

FIGURE 10.16: Localizing a Form Using winres.exe

bundling them into a set of .resources files. You can do that using the res-gen.exe tool shown earlier. To execute resgen.exe on more than one .resx file at a time, use the /compile switch:

```
C:/> resgen.exe /compile Form1.en-US.resx Form2.en-US.resx ...
```

Running resgen.exe in this manner will produce multiple .resources files, one per .resx file. After you've got the .resources files for all the local-ized forms for a particular culture, you can bundle them into a single resource assembly by using the assembly linker command line tool, al.exe:

```
C:/> al.exe /out:en-US\App.resources.dll /culture:en-US /embed-
resource:Form1.en-US.resources,App.Form1.en-US.resources /embed-
resource:Form2.en-US.resources,App.Form2.en-US.resources ...
```

The assembly linker is a tool with all kinds of uses in .NET. In this case, we're using it to bundle a number of .resources files into a single satellite assembly. The /out argument determines the name of the produced assem-bly. Make sure to pick one of the file names that the Resource Manager will probe for (as shown in Table 10.1).

The /culture argument determines the culture of the resource assembly and must match the culture name for the resources you're building. The /embedresource arguments provide the .resources files along with the *alternative names* to match the names that the resource manager will look for. By default, al.exe bundles each resource into a named container based on the file name. However, to match what the resource manager is looking for, you must use the alternative name syntax to prepend the resource namespace.

Again, ildasm is a useful tool to make sure that you have things right when it comes to building satellite resources. Figure 10.17 shows the result of running ildasm on the App.resources.dll produced by the earlier call to al.exe.

Figure 10.17 shows two localized forms, one for each of the .resources files passed to the al.exe file. In addition, notice that the locale has been set to en-US in the .assembly block. This locale setting is reserved for resource-only satellite assemblies and is used by the resource manager to confirm that the loaded resources match the folder and assembly name used to find the satellite assembly.

Resource Resolution

When there are multiple resources that match the current culture, the resource manager must choose among them. For example, if an application is running under the en-US culture, a resource with the same name can be present in an en-US satellite assembly, in an en satellite assembly, and in the main assembly itself. When multiple assemblies can contain a resource, the resource manager looks first in the most specific assembly, that is, the culture-specific assembly. If that's not present, the language-specific assembly is checked, and finally the culture-neutral resources.

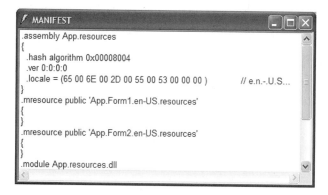

FIGURE 10.17: ildasm Showing a Culture-Specific Resource Satellite Assembly

For example, imagine a form that has three resource-specific Text properties: one for a Label control, one for a Button control, and one for the Form itself. Imagine further that there are two satellite assemblies—one for en-US and one for en—along with the neutral resources bundled into the form's assembly itself. Figure 10.18 shows how the resource manager resolves the resources while running in the en-US culture.

Remember that the resource manager always looks for the most specific resource it can find. So even though there are three instances of the button's Text property, the most culture-specific resource in the en-US assembly "overrides" the other two. Similarly, the language-specific resource for the label is pulled from the en assembly only because it's not present in the en-US assembly. Finally, the culture-neutral resource is pulled from the main assembly for the form's Text property when it's not found in the satellite assemblies. This resolution algorithm enables resources that are shared between all cultures to be set in the culture-neutral resources, leaving the culture-specific resources for overriding only the things that are culture-specific.

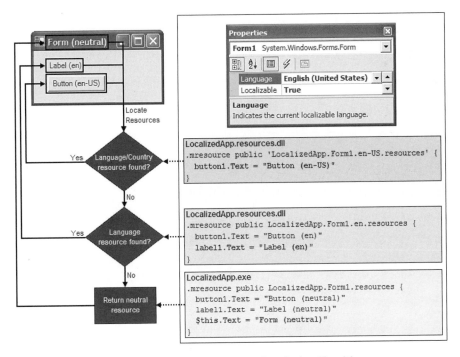

FIGURE 10.18: The Resource Manager's Resource Resolution Algorithm

However, resolving resources in less culture-specific assemblies works only when a resource is missing from the more culture-specific assembly. VS.NET is smart about putting only properties that have changed into a more culture-specific assembly, but that is not the case with WinRes. Because of the way it works, WinRes duplicates all the culture-neutral resource information to the culture-specific resource files. This means that when using WinRes, all the resources will need to be localized to a more specific culture, even if they aren't changed from a less specific culture.

Testing Resource Resolution

To test that resource resolution is working the way you think it should, you can manually set the CurrentUICulture property of the current thread:

```
static void Main() {
  // Test localized resources under fr-CA culture
  System.Threading.Thread.CurrentThread.CurrentUICulture =
    new CultureInfo("fr-CA");
  Application.Run(new MainForm());
}
```

Although the CurrentUICulture property defaults to the current culture setting of Windows itself, it can be changed. Whatever the value is when a resource manager is created will be the culture that the resource manager uses to resolve resources.

Input Language

Closely related to a thread's current culture is the *input language* to which the keyboard is currently mapped, which determines which keys map to which characters. As a further means of testing your application in alternative cultures, the WinForms Application object supports switchable input languages. The list of installed layouts is available from the Input-Language class's InstalledInputLanguages property:

```
foreach( InputLanguage l in InputLanguage.InstalledInputLanguages ) {
  MessageBox.Show(l.LayoutName);
}
```

You can change the current input language by setting one of the installed input languages to the InputLanguage class's property (which is also wrapped by the Application.CurrentInputLanguage property):

```
InputLanguage lang = ...; // Select an input language
Application.CurrentInputLanguage = lang; // one way
InputLanguage.CurrentInputLanguage = lang; // another way
```

The default system input language is available via the DefaultInput-Language property of the InputLanguage class, should you need to reinstate it.

Where Are We?

Resources are a great way to bundle arbitrary data, both untyped (in manifest resources) and typed (in .resources resources). VS.NET provides extensive support for embedding both kinds of resources, even providing them on a per-component basis. And for forms that need to be localized, VS.NET handles that, too, although WinRes is a better choice when nondevelopers are doing the localization.

■ 11 ■
Applications and Settings

A PPLICATIONS HAVE SPECIAL SIGNIFICANCE and support in Win-
Forms. For example, you can manage and tailor your application's
lifetime, even applications such as single-instance applications and multi-
SDI applications. Applications also have an environment that can be tailored by the user and kept between sessions in any of several mechanisms
for storing settings, including environment variables, command line arguments, .config files, the Registry, special folders, and isolated storage.

Applications

An *application* is anything with an EXE extension that can be started from
the shell. However, applications are also provided for directly in WinForms
by the Application class from the System.Windows.Forms namespace:

```
sealed class Application {
  // Properties
  public static bool AllowQuit { get; }
  public static string CommonAppDataPath { get; }
  public static RegistryKey CommonAppDataRegistry { get; }
  public static string CompanyName { get; }
  public static CultureInfo CurrentCulture { get; set; }
  public static InputLanguage CurrentInputLanguage { get; set; }
  public static string ExecutablePath { get; }
  public static string LocalUserAppDataPath { get; }
  public static bool MessageLoop { get; }
  public static string ProductName { get; }
```

continues

■
■ 387

```
    public static string ProductVersion { get; }
    public static string SafeTopLevelCaptionFormat { get; set; }
    public static string StartupPath { get; }
    public static string UserAppDataPath { get; }
    public static RegistryKey UserAppDataRegistry { get; }

    // Events
    public static event EventHandler ApplicationExit;
    public static event EventHandler Idle;
    public static event ThreadExceptionEventHandler ThreadException;
    public static event EventHandler ThreadExit;

    // Methods
    public static void AddMessageFilter(IMessageFilter value);
    public static void DoEvents();
    public static void Exit();
    public static void ExitThread();
    public static ApartmentState OleRequired();
    public static void OnThreadException(Exception t);
    public static void RemoveMessageFilter(IMessageFilter value);
    public static void Run();
    public static void Run(ApplicationContext context);
    public static void Run(Form mainForm);
}
```

Notice that all the members of the Application class are static. Although there is per-application state in WinForms, there is no instance of an Application class. Instead, the Application class is a scoping mechanism for the various services that the class provides, including lifetime control, message handling, and settings.

Application Lifetime

A WinForms application starts when the Main method is called. However, to initialize a WinForms application fully and start it routing WinForms events, you need a call to Application.Run.

There are three ways to call the Application class's Run method. The first is to simply call Run with no arguments at all. This is useful only if other means have already been used to show an initial UI:

```
[STAThreadAttribute]
static void Main() {
  // Create and show the main form modelessly
```

```
Form form = new MainForm();
form.Show();

// Run the application
Application.Run();
}
```

When you call Run with no arguments, the application runs until explicitly told to stop, even when all its forms are closed. This puts the burden on some part of the application to call the Application class's Exit method:

```
void MainForm_Closed(object sender, EventArgs e) {
  // Close the application when the main form goes away
  // Only for use when Application.Run is called without
  // any arguments
  Application.Exit();
}
```

Typically, you call Application.Run without any arguments only when the application needs a secondary UI thread. A *UI thread* is one that calls Application.Run and can process the events that drive a Windows application. Because the vast majority of applications contain a single UI thread and because most of those have a *main form* that, when closed, causes the application to exit, another overload of the Run method is used far more often. This overload of Run takes as an argument a reference to the form designated as the main form. When Run is called this way, it shows the main form and doesn't return until the main form closes:

```
[STAThreadAttribute]
static void Main() {
  // Create the main form
  Form form = new MainForm();

  // Run the application until the main form is closed
  Application.Run(form);
}
```

In this case, there is no need for explicit code to exit the application. Instead, the Application watches for the main form to close and then exits itself.

Application Context

Internally, the Run method creates an instance of the ApplicationContext class from the System.Windows.Forms namespace. It's this class that subscribes to the main form's Closed event and exits the application as appropriate:

```
class ApplicationContext {
  // Constructors
  public ApplicationContext();
  public ApplicationContext(Form mainForm);

  // Properties
  public Form MainForm { get; set; }

  // Events
  public event EventHandler ThreadExit;

  // Methods
  public void ExitThread();
  protected virtual void OnMainFormClosed(object sender, EventArgs e);
}
```

In fact, the Run method allows you to pass an ApplicationContext yourself:

```
[STAThreadAttribute]
static void Main() {
  // Run the application with a context
  ApplicationContext ctx = new ApplicationContext(new MainForm());
  Application.Run(ctx);
}
```

This is useful if you'd like to derive from the ApplicationContext class and provide your own custom context:

```
class MyTimedContext : ApplicationContext {
  Timer timer = new Timer();

  public MyTimedContext(Form form) : base(form) {
    timer.Tick += new EventHandler(TimesUp);
    timer.Interval = 5000; // 5 minutes
    timer.Enabled = true;
  }
```

```
  void TimesUp(object sender, EventArgs e) {
    timer.Enabled = false;
    timer.Dispose();

    DialogResult res =
      MessageBox.Show(
        "OK to charge your credit card?",
        "Time's Up!",
        MessageBoxButtons.YesNo);
    if( res == DialogResult.No ) {
      // See ya...
      base.MainForm.Close();
    }
    ...
  }
}

[STAThreadAttribute]
static void Main() {
  // Run the application with a custom context
  ApplicationContext ctx = new MyTimedContext(new MainForm());
  Application.Run(ctx);
}
```

This custom context class waits for five minutes after an application has started and then asks to charge the user's credit card. If the answer is no, the main form of the application will be closed (available from the Main-Form property of the base ApplicationContext class), causing the application to exit.

Conversely, if you'd like to stop the application from exiting when the main form goes away, you can override the OnMainFormClosed method from the ApplicationContext base class:

```
class RemotingServerContext : ApplicationContext {
  public RemotingServerContext(Form form) : base(form) {
  }

  protected override void OnMainFormClosed(object sender, EventArgs e) {
    // Don't let base class exit application
    // NOTE: Remember to call Application.Exit
    //       later when the remoting service
    //       is finished servicing its clients
    if( ServicingRemotingClient() ) return;
```

continues

```
  // Let base class exit application
  base.OnMainFormClosed(sender, e);
}


protected bool ServicingRemotingClient() {...}
  }
}
```

This example assumes an application that is serving .NET Remoting[1] clients and so needs to stick around even if the user has closed the main form.

Application Events

During the lifetime of an application, several application events will be fired: idle, thread exit, application exit, and sometimes a thread exception. You can subscribe to application events at any time, but it's most common to do it in the Main function:

```
static void App_Exit(object sender, EventArgs e) {...}
static void App_Idle(object sender, EventArgs e) {...}
static void App_ThreadExit(object sender, EventArgs e) {...}

[STAThreadAttribute]
static void Main() {
  Application.Idle += new EventHandler(App_Idle);
  Application.ThreadExit += new EventHandler(App_ThreadExit);
  Application.ApplicationExit += new EventHandler(App_Exit);
  ...
}
```

The idle event happens when all events in a series of events have been dispatched to event handlers and no more events are waiting to be processed. The idle event can sometimes be used to perform concurrent processing in tiny chunks, but it's much more convenient and robust to use worker threads for those kinds of activities. This technique is covered in Chapter 14: Multithreaded User Interfaces.

---

1. .NET Remoting is a technology that allows objects to talk to each other across application and machine boundaries. Remoting is beyond the scope of this book but is covered very nicely in Ingo Rammer's book *Advanced .NET Remoting* (APress 2002).

When a UI thread is about to exit, it receives a notification via the thread exit event. When the last UI thread goes away, the application's exit event is fired.

UI Thread Exceptions

One other application-level event that can be handled is a thread exception event. This event is fired when a UI thread causes an exception to be thrown. This one is so important that WinForms provides a default handler if you don't.

The typical .NET unhandled exception on a user's machine behavior yields a dialog box as shown in Figure 11.1.

This kind of exception handling tends to make the user unhappy. This dialog is confusing, and worse, there is no way to continue the application to attempt to save the data being worked on at the moment. On the other hand, by default, a WinForms application that experiences an exception during the processing of an event shows a dialog like that in Figure 11.2.

Although this dialog may look functionally the same as the one in Figure 11.1, there is one major difference: The WinForms version has a Continue button. What's happening is that WinForms itself catches exceptions

FIGURE 11.1: Default .NET Unhandled-Exception Dialog Box

FIGURE 11.2: Default WinForms Unhandled-Exception Dialog Box

thrown by event handlers; in this way, even if that event handler caused an exception—for example, if a file couldn't be opened or there was a security violation—the user is allowed to continue running the application with the hope that saving will work, even if nothing else does. This is a safety net that makes WinForms applications more robust in the face of even unhandled exceptions than Windows applications of old. However, if a user has triggered an exception and it's caught, the application could be in an inconsistent state, so it's best to encourage your users to save their files and restart the application.

If you'd like to replace the WinForms unhandled-exception dialog with something application-specific, you can do so by handling the application's thread exception event:

```
using System.Threading;

static void
  App_ThreadException(object sender, ThreadExceptionEventArgs e) {
  string msg =
    "A problem has occurred in this application:\r\n" +
    "\t" + e.Exception.Message + "\r\n\r\n" +
    "Would you like to continue the application so that\r\n" +
    "you can save your work?";
  DialogResult res =
    MessageBox.Show(
      msg, "Unexpected Error", MessageBoxButtons.YesNo);

  ...
}


[STAThreadAttribute]
static void Main() {
  // Handle unhandled thread exceptions
  Application.ThreadException +=
    new ThreadExceptionEventHandler(App_ThreadException);

  // Run the application
  Application.Run(new MainForm());
}
```

Notice that the thread exception handler takes a ThreadExceptionEvent object, which includes the exception that was thrown. This is handy if you want to tell the user what happened, as shown in Figure 11.3.

FIGURE 11.3: Custom Unhandled-Exception Dialog

If you provide a thread exception handler, the default exception handler will not be used, so it's up to you to let the user know that something bad has happened. If the user decides not to continue with the application, calling Application.Exit will shut down the application:

```
static void App_ThreadException(
  object sender, ThreadExceptionEventArgs e) {

  string msg = ...
  DialogResult res =
    MessageBox.Show(msg, "Unexpected Error", MessageBoxButtons.YesNo);

  // Returning continues the application
  if( res == DialogResult.Yes ) return;

  // Shut 'er down, Clancy, she's a'pumpin' mud!
  Application.Exit();
}
```

Single-Instance Applications

By default, each EXE is an application and has an independent lifetime, even if multiple instances of the same application are running at the same time. However, it's common to want to limit an EXE to a single instance, whether it's a Single Document Interface (SDI) application with a single top-level window, a Multi-Document Interface (MDI) application, or an SDI application with multiple top-level windows. All these kinds of applications require that another instance detect the initial instance and then cut its own lifetime short. You can do this using an instance of the Mutex class from the System.Threading namespace:[2]

```
using System.Threading;
...
static void Main() {
  // Check for existing instance
  bool firstInstance = false;
  string safeName = Application.UserAppDataPath.Replace(@"\", "_");
  Mutex mutex = new Mutex(true, safeName, out firstInstance);
  if( !firstInstance ) return;

  Application.Run(new MainForm());
}
```

This code relies on a *named kernel object*, that is, an object that is managed by the Windows kernel. The fact that it's a mutex doesn't really matter. What matters is that we create a kernel object with a systemwide unique name and that we can tell whether an object with that same name already exists. When the first instance is executed, that kernel object won't exist, and we won't return from Main until Application.Run returns. When another instance is executed, the kernel object will already exist, so Main will exit before the application is run.

One interesting note on the name of the mutex is worth mentioning. To make sure we have a unique name for the mutex, we need something specific to the version of the application but also specific to the user. It's important to pick a string that's unique per application so that multiple applications don't prevent each other from starting. If there are multiple users, it's equally important that each user get his or her own instance, especially in the face of Windows XP, fast user switching, and terminal services.[3] Toward that end, we use the UserAppDataPath property of the Application object. It's a path in the file system where per-user settings for an application are meant to be stored, and it takes the following form:

---

2. This method of detecting single instances will stop multiple instances across desktops and sessions. For a detailed explanation of other definitions of "single instance," read Joseph Newcomer's treatment of this topic at http://www.pgh.net/~newcomer/nomultiples.htm.

3. However, this code doesn't take into account the possibility that the same user may be logged in to the same machine in two different sessions.

```
C:\Documents and Settings\csells\Application Data\SingleInstance\
SingleInstance\1.0.1121.38811
```

What makes this string useful is that it contains the application name, the version number, and the user name—all the things we need to make the mutex unique per version of an application and per user running the application. Also, because the back slashes are illegal in mutex names, those must be replaced with something else (such as underscores).

Passing Command Line Arguments

This single-instance scheme works fine until the first instance of the application needs to get the command line arguments from any subsequent instance. For example, if the first instance of an MDI application needs to open the file passed to the other instance of the MDI application, the other instance needs to be able to communicate with the initial instance. The easiest solution to this problem is to use .NET Remoting and threading:

```csharp
using System.Threading;
using System.Runtime.Remoting;
using System.Runtime.Remoting.Channels;
using System.Runtime.Remoting.Channels.Tcp;
...
// Make main form accessible from other instance event handler
static MainForm mainForm = new MainForm();

// Signature of method to call when other instance is detected
delegate void OtherInstanceCallback(string[] args);

[STAThreadAttribute]
static void Main(string[] args) {
  // Check for existing instance
  bool firstInstance = false;
  string safeName = Application.UserAppDataPath.Replace(@"\", "_");
  Mutex mutex = new Mutex(true, safeName, out firstInstance);
  if( !firstInstance ) {
    // Open remoting channel exposed from initial instance
    // NOTE: port (1313) and channel name (mainForm) must match below
    string formUrl = "tcp://localhost:1313/mainForm";
    MainForm otherMainForm =
      (MainForm)RemotingServices.Connect(typeof(MainForm), formUrl);

    // Send arguments to initial instance and exit this one
    otherMainForm.OnOtherInstance(args);
    return;
  }
```

continues

```
// Expose remoting channel to accept arguments from other instances
// NOTE: port (1313) and channel name (mainForm) must match above
ChannelServices.RegisterChannel(new TcpChannel(1313));
RemotingServices.Marshal(mainForm, "mainForm");

// Open file from command line
if( args.Length == 1 ) mainForm.OpenFile(args[0]);

// Show main form
Application.Run(mainForm);
}


public void OnOtherInstance(string[] args) {...}
```

The details of .NET Remoting are beyond the scope of this book, and threading isn't covered until Chapter 14: Multithreaded User Interfaces, but the details are less important than the concepts. Basically what's happening is that the first instance of the application opens a named communication channel (mainForm) on a well-known, unique port (1313) in case another instance of the application ever comes along. If one does, the other instance opens the same channel and retrieves the MainForm type from it so that it can call the OnOtherInstance method. For this to work, the .NET Remoting assembly, System.Runtime.Remoting, must be referenced in the project. The Remoting infrastructure then requires that the type being retrieved by the other instance from the first instance be *marshal-by-reference*. This means that it can be called from another *application domain*, which is basically the .NET equivalent of a process. Because the MainForm class, along with all UI classes in .NET, derives from the MarshalByRef base class, this condition is met.

Another .NET Remoting requirement is that the methods called on the marshal-by-ref type called from another app domain be instance and public, and that's why the OnOtherInstance method is defined as it is:

```
// Called via remoting channel from other instances
// NOTE: This is a member of the MainForm class
public void OnOtherInstance(string[] args) {
  // Transition to the UI thread
  if( mainForm.InvokeRequired ) {
    OtherInstanceCallback callback =
      new OtherInstanceCallback(OnOtherInstance);
    mainForm.Invoke(callback, new object[] { args });
    return;
  }
```

```
  // Open file from command line
  if( args.Length == 1 ) this.OpenFile(args[0]);

  // Bring window to the front
  mainForm.Activate();
}
```

When OnOtherInstance is called, it will be called on a non-UI thread. This requires a transition to the UI thread before any methods on the Main-Form are called that access the underlying window (perhaps to create an MDI child to show the file being opened or to activate the window). That's why we include the check on the InvokeRequired property and the call to BeginInvoke.[4]

Finally, OnOtherInstance does what it likes with the command line arguments and then activates the main form to bring it to the foreground. The details of this are somewhat complicated for the service that they provide, and this makes it a good candidate for encapsulation. The only real variables that can't be handled automatically are which method to call and what the main form is. This means that we can boil down the code to use the InitialInstanceActivator class provided in the sample code included with this book:

```
// Make main form accessible from other instance event handler
static MainForm mainForm = new MainForm();

[STAThreadAttribute]
static void Main(string[] args) {
  // Check for initial instance
  OtherInstanceCallback callback =
    new OtherInstanceCallback(OnOtherInstance);
  if( InitialInstanceActivator.Activate(mainForm, callback, args) ) {
    return;
  }

  // Open file from command line
  if( args.Length == 1 ) mainForm.OpenFile(args[0]);

  // Show main form
  Application.Run(mainForm);
}
```

continues

---

4. All these threading details are discussed in Chapter 14: Multithreaded User Interfaces.

```
// Called from other instances
static void OnOtherInstance(string[] args) {
  // Open file from command line
  if( args.Length == 1 ) mainForm.OpenFile(args[0]);

  // Activate the main window
  mainForm.Activate();
}
```

InitialInstanceActivator takes three things: a reference to the main form, a delegate indicating which method to call when another instance is detected, and the arguments from Main in case this is another instance. If the Activate method returns true, it means that this is another instance and the arguments have been passed to the initial instance. The application bails, safe in the knowledge that the initial instance has things well in hand.

When another instance activates the initial instance, the delegate is invoked, letting the initial instance handle the command line arguments and activate itself as appropriate.

The underlying communication and threading requirements are handled by InitialInstanceActivator using other parts of .NET that have nothing whatever to do with WinForms. This is one of the strengths of WinForms. Unlike forms packages of old, WinForms is only one part of a much larger, integrated whole. When its windowing classes don't meet your needs, you've still got all the rest of the .NET Framework Class Library to fall back on.

Multi-SDI Applications

A *multi-SDI* application is like an MDI application in that it has multiple windows for content, but, unlike an MDI application, each window in a multi-SDI app is a top-level window. The Internet Explorer and Office XP applications are popular examples of multi-SDI applications.[5] Figure 11.4 shows a multi-SDI sample.

A multi-SDI application typically has the following features:

---

5. Internet Explorer can be configured to show each top-level window in its own process, making it an SDI application, or to share all windows in a single process, making it a multi-SDI application.

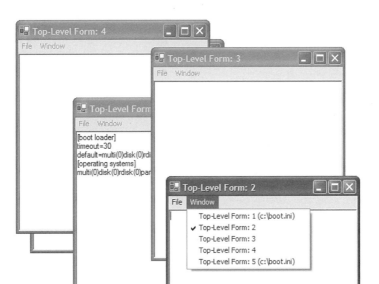

FIGURE 11.4: A Sample Multi-SDI Application

- A single instance of the application is running.
- Multiple top-level windows are running independently of each other.
- When the last window goes away, so does the application.
- A Window menu allows a user to see and select from the currently available windows.

The single-instance stuff we've already got licked with the InitialInstanceActivator class. Having multiple top-level windows running independently of each other is a matter of using the modeless Form.Show method:

```
class TopLevelForm : Form {
  ...
  void fileNewWindowMenuItem_Click(object sender, EventArgs e) {
    NewWindow(null);
  }

  static void NewWindow(string fileName) {
    // Create another top-level form
    TopLevelForm form = new TopLevelForm();
```

continues

```
    if( fileName != null ) form.OpenFile(fileName);
    form.Show();
  }
}
```

Because the default application context depends on there being only one main window, managing the lifetime of a multi-SDI application requires a custom application context. One simple way to leverage the ApplicationContext base class is to derive from it, swapping the "main" form in our multi-SDI application until there are no more top-level windows left in the application, thereby causing the application to shut down:

```
public class MultiSdiApplicationContext : ApplicationContext {

  public void AddTopLevelForm(Form form) {
    // Initial main form may add itself twice, but that's OK
    if( topLevelForms.Contains(form) ) return;

    // Add form to collection of forms and
    // watch for it to activate and close
    topLevelForms.Add(form);
    form.Activated += new EventHandler(Form_Activated);
    form.Closed += new EventHandler(Form_Closed);

    // Set initial main form to activate
    if( topLevelForms.Count == 1 ) base.MainForm = form;
  }

  void Form_Activated(object sender, EventArgs e) {
    // Whichever form activated last is the "main" form
    base.MainForm = (Form)sender;
  }

  void Form_Closed(object sender, EventArgs e) {
    // Remove form from the list
    topLevelForms.Remove(sender);

    // Set a new "main" if necessary
    if( ((Form)sender == base.MainForm) &&
      (this.topLevelForms.Count > 0) ) {
      this.MainForm = (Form)topLevelForms[0];
    }
  }

  . . .
```

```
public Form[] TopLevelForms {
  // Expose list of top-level forms for building Window menu
  get { return (Form[])topLevelForms.ToArray(typeof(Form)); }
}

ArrayList topLevelForms = new ArrayList();
}
```

The MultiSdiApplicationContext class uses the AddTopLevelForm method to keep track of a list of top-level forms as they are added. Each new form is kept in a collection and is watched for Activated and Closed events. When a top-level form is activated, it becomes the new "main" form, which is the one that the base ApplicationContext class will watch for the Closed event. When a top-level form closes, it's removed from the list. If the closed form was the main form, another form is promoted to main. When the last form goes away, the base ApplicationContext class notices and exits the application.

With this basic functionality in place, we can use the application context in Main as the argument to Application.Run:

```
// Need application context to manage top-level forms
static MultiSdiApplicationContext context =
  new MultiSdiApplicationContext();

[STAThreadAttribute]
static void Main(string[] args) {
  // Add initial form
  TopLevelForm initialForm = new TopLevelForm();
  context.AddTopLevelForm(initialForm);

  // Let initial instance show another top-level form (if necessary)
  OtherInstanceCallback callback =
    new OtherInstanceCallback(OnOtherInstance);
  if( InitialInstanceActivator.Activate(context, callback, args) ) {
    return;
  }

  // Open file from command line
  if( args.Length == 1 ) initialForm.OpenFile(args[0]);

  // Run application
  Application.Run(context);
}
```

Because we're using the application context instead of the initial form as the argument to Application.Run, it will be used to control the lifetime of the application, even as the "main" form cycles. Similarly, we're using a context to the Activate method of the InitialInstanceActivator helper class, and this means that if another instance of the application starts, the activator can ask the context for the "current" main form to use in transitioning to the UI thread, even if the initial form has been closed.

To keep the context up-to-date with the current list of top-level forms, the custom context watches for the Closed event on all forms. In addition, the custom context needs to be notified when a new top-level form has come into existence, a task that is best handled by the new form itself:

```
public TopLevelForm() {
  // Required for Windows Form Designer support
  InitializeComponent();

  // Add new top-level form to the application context
  context.AddTopLevelForm(this);
}
```

The only thing left to do is to designate and populate the Window menu with the current list of top-level forms. The forms themselves can do this by handling the pop-up event on the Window MenuItem object, using that opportunity to build the list of submenu items based on the names of all the forms (as exposed via the TopLevelForms property of the MultiSdi-ApplicationContext helper object). However, this code is pretty boiler-plate, so it's a good candidate to be handled by the custom application context in the AddWindowMenu method:

```
public class MultiMdiApplicationContext : ApplicationContext {
  ...
  public void AddWindowMenu(MenuItem menu) {
    // Add at least one dummy menu item to get pop-up event
    if( menu.MenuItems.Count == 0 ) menu.MenuItems.Add("dummy");

    // Subscribe to pop-up event
    menu.Popup += new EventHandler(WindowMenu_Popup);
  }
  ...
}
```

Each top-level form with a Window menu can add it to the context, along with itself, when it's created:

```
public TopLevelForm() {
  // Required for Windows Form Designer support
  InitializeComponent();

  // Add new top-level form to the application context
  context.AddTopLevelForm(this);

  // Add Window MenuItem to the application context
  context.AddWindowMenu(this.windowMenu);
}
```

Now, when the Window menu is shown on any top-level window, the pop-up event fires and a new menu is built on-the-fly to show the current list of top-level menus:

```
// Current Window menu items and the map to the appropriate form
Hashtable windowMenuMap = new Hashtable();

void WindowMenu_Popup(object sender, EventArgs e) {
  // Build menu from list of top-level windows
  MenuItem menu = (MenuItem)sender;
  menu.MenuItems.Clear();
  windowMenuMap.Clear();

  foreach( Form form in this.topLevelForms ) {
    MenuItem item = menu.MenuItems.Add(form.Text);
    item.Click += new EventHandler(WindowMenuItem_Click);

    // Check currently active window
    if( form == Form.ActiveForm ) item.Checked = true;

    // Associate each menu item back to the form
    windowMenuMap.Add(item, form);
  }
}
```

As each menu item is added to the Window menu, a handler is added to the Click event so that the appropriate form can be activated when it's selected. Because a MenuItem doesn't have a Tag property, we're using a Hashtable collection to map menu items to each form. The hash table is used in the Click handler to find the form that corresponds to the selected menu item:

```
void WindowMenuItem_Click(object sender, EventArgs e) {
  // Activate top-level form based on selection
  ((Form)windowMenuMap[sender]).Activate();
}
```

That's it. The extensible lifetime management of WinForms applications via a custom application context, along with a helper to find and activate application instances already running, provides all the help we need to build a multi-SDI application in only a few lines of code.

Environment

During its lifetime, an application runs in a certain environment. The environment is provided by a combination of compile-time and run-time settings supplied by .NET and Windows.

Compile-Time Settings

The Application class exposes several properties that provide the company name, product name, and product version of the currently running application:

```
void AboutBox_Load(object sender, EventArgs e) {
  this.companyNameTextBox.Text = Application.CompanyName;
  this.productNameTextBox.Text = Application.ProductName;
  this.productVersionTextBox.Text = Application.ProductVersion;
}
```

By default, these three values come from assemblywide Assembly-CompanyAttribute, AssemblyProductAttribute, and AssemblyVersion-Attribute (provided in a wizard-generated file called AssemblyInfo.cs):

```
[assembly: AssemblyCompanyAttribute("Sells Brothers, Inc.")]
[assembly: AssemblyProductAttribute("Environment Test Application")]

// Version info for an assembly consists of the following values:
//   major.minor.build.revision
```

```
// You can specify all the values, or you can default the Revision and
// Build Numbers by using the '*' as shown below:
[assembly: AssemblyVersionAttribute("1.0.*")]
```

Not only will the values you put into these attributes be available using the Application properties, but they'll also be bundled into the Win32 version information for the assembly, as shown by the Version property page in Explorer in Figure 11.5.

The rest of the version information is set via other assembly-level attributes:

```
[assembly: AssemblyTitle("Environment Test Title")]
[assembly: AssemblyDescription("Environment Test Description")]
[assembly: AssemblyCompany("Sells Brothers, Inc.")]
[assembly: AssemblyProduct("Environment Test Application")]
[assembly: AssemblyCopyright("Copyright (c) 2003, Chris Sells")]
```

continues

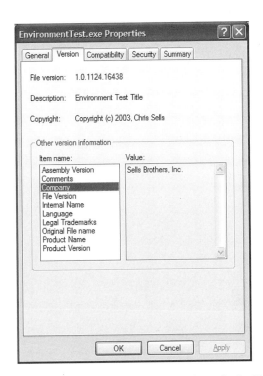

FIGURE 11.5: Assembly Properties Shown in the Shell

```
[assembly: AssemblyTrademark("Trademark nobody")]
[assembly: AssemblyVersion("1.0.*")]
```

Environment Settings

If you'd like to know where your application was started from in the file system or which folder it was run from, you can get that information from the ExecutablePath and StartupPath properties of the Application object. Table 11.1 shows examples of each.

If you want more environment settings, such as the environment variables or the command line string, you can get them from the Environment object in the System namespace:

```
sealed class Environment {
  // Properties
  public static string CommandLine { get; }
  public static string CurrentDirectory { get; set; }
  public static int ExitCode { get; set; }
  public bool HasShutdownStarted { get; }
  public static string MachineName { get; }
  public static string NewLine { get; }
  public static OperatingSystem OSVersion { get; }
  public static string StackTrace { get; }
  public static string SystemDirectory { get; }
  public static int TickCount { get; }
  public static string UserDomainName { get; }
  public static bool UserInteractive { get; }
  public static string UserName { get; }
  public static Version Version { get; }
  public static long WorkingSet { get; }

  // Methods
  public static void Exit(int exitCode);
  public static string ExpandEnvironmentVariables(string name);
```

TABLE 11.1: The Application ExecutablePath and StartupPath Properties

Application Class Static Property	Sample Property Value
ExecutablePath	D:\data\WinForms Book\src\ch11\ Settings\bin\Debug\SettingsTest.exe
StartupPath	D:\data\WinForms Book\src\ch11\ Settings\bin\Debug

```
    public static string[] GetCommandLineArgs();
    public static string GetEnvironmentVariable(string variable);
    public static IDictionary GetEnvironmentVariables();
    public static string GetFolderPath(SpecialFolder folder);
    public static string[] GetLogicalDrives();
}
```

As shown earlier, the command line arguments are also available as the array of strings argument passed to Main:

```
[STAThreadAttribute]
static void Main(string[] args) {
  bool flag = false;
  string name = "";
  int number = 0;

  // *Very* simple command line parsing
  for( int i = 0; i != args.Length; ++i ) {
    switch( args[i] ) {
      case "/flag": flag = true; break;
      case "/name": name = args[++i]; break;
      case "/number": number = int.Parse(args[++i]); break;
      default: MessageBox.Show("invalid args!"); return;
    }
  }

  MessageBox.Show(flag.ToString(), "flag");
  MessageBox.Show(name, "name");
  MessageBox.Show(number.ToString(), "number");

  ...
}
```

If you want to see more robust command line parsing support, see the Genghis class library available at http://www.genghisgroup.com.

Settings

Environment variables and command line arguments are both ways for the user to specify run-time settings to a particular application. .NET provides several more ways, including OS favorites like the Registry and special folders, as well as new ways like .config files and isolated storage.

Types of Settings

When saving settings, you should consider several different *localities* of settings:

- **Application.** These settings are shared among all users of an application on the machine. For example, the list of directories in which to search for the assemblies to show in the Add Reference dialog is a per-application setting.[6]

- **User.** These settings are specific to an application and a user. For example, Minesweeper high scores are kept per user.

- **Roaming User.** Application settings as well as user settings are specific to a machine, but roaming user settings are machine-independent. For example, if Minesweeper high scores were roaming, they'd be available to a specific user no matter what computer the user had logged in to.[7] Roaming user settings are good for things that don't depend on a machine, like a list of color preferences, but not for things that are related to current machine settings, like a window location. The use of roaming user settings presupposes that the machine is properly configured to support roaming. Otherwise, roaming user settings are equivalent to nonroaming user settings.

- **Machine.** These are application-independent settings, such as the current screen resolution or the PATH environment variable (although the PATH has a user portion).

- **Assembly.** These settings are available on a per-assembly basis so that components can have their own versioned settings.

- **Domain.** These settings are available on an *application domain* basis, which is the .NET equivalent of a process. ASP.NET hosts Web applications in their own domain and provides application domain settings.

---

6. This setting is stored at HKLM\SOFTWARE\Microsoft\.NETFramework\Assembly-Folders in the Registry.

7. Roaming user settings do depend on very specific Windows domain network settings' being enabled.

Localities and Permissions

Different storage mechanisms support different localities (as well as other characteristics, such as whether they can be written to as well as read from). In addition, different localities require different user permissions. For example, writing application settings to the Registry requires Administrator group permissions, something you cannot assume that your user has. Before shipping an application that needs to read or write settings, you should test it under the most restricted set of permissions that your users could have.

.config Files

.NET provides .config files to serve as a read-only location for text-based application settings. A *.config file* is a file placed in the same folder as the application and having the same name as the application except for a .config extension. For example, the .config file associated with foo.exe would be named foo.exe.config. .NET itself uses .config files for all kinds of things, such as resolving assemblies and assembly versions.[8]

You can add a new .config file to your VS.NET project by right-clicking on the project in Solution Explorer and choosing Add | Add New Item | Text File and naming the file "app.config" (without the quotation marks). This action will add an empty .config file to your project and, when your project is built, will copy and rename the app.config file to the output folder alongside your application. A minimal .config file looks like this:

```
<configuration>
</configuration>
```

In addition to the .NET-specific settings, .config files can be extended with custom XML sections as designated with uniquely named elements. One general-purpose custom section built into .NET is designated with the element named appSettings. For example, the following .config file

---

8. *Essential .NET, Volume 1: The Common Language Runtime* (Addison-Wesley, 2003), by Don Box, with Chris Sells, covers assembly loading and versioning in detail.

contains a custom value for pi (in case the 20 digits provided by System. Math.Pi just aren't enough):

```
<configuration>
  <appSettings>
    <add key="pi" value="3.141592653589793238462" />
  </appSettings>
</configuration>
```

Each .config section has a specific *section reader* that knows how to read values from that section. These section readers can be defined in an application's .config file or in the systemwide machine.config, as shown here for the appSettings section reader:

```
<configuration>
  <configSections>
    ...
    <section
      name="appSettings"
      type="System.Configuration.NameValueFileSectionHandler, ..." />
    ...
  </configSections>
  ...
</configuration>
```

A section reader is a class that implements IConfigurationSectionHandler and is registered with an entry in the configSections section of a .config file. For example, the NameValueFileSectionHandler class knows how to read a section in the appSettings format and return a NameValueCollection from the System.Collections.Specialized namespace. However, instead of creating an instance of NameValueFileSectionHandler yourself, it's more robust to use the ConfigurationsSettings class (from the System. Configuration namespace) to map the name of the section to a section reader for you:

```
using System.Configuration;
using System.Collections.Specialized;
...
static void Main() {
NameValueCollection settings =
(NameValueCollection)ConfigurationSettings.GetConfig("appSettings");
  ...
}
```

The ConfigurationSettings class finds the appropriate section handler. The section handler then looks in the current app configuration data for the appSettings section (parts of which can be inherited from machine.config), parses the contents, builds the NameValueCollection, and returns it.

Because different section handlers can return different data types based on the data provided in their sections, the GetConfig method returns an object that must be cast to the appropriate type. As a shortcut that doesn't require the cast, the ConfigurationSettings class provides built-in support for the appSettings section via the AppSettings property:

```
static void Main() {
  NameValueCollection settings = ConfigurationSettings.AppSettings;
  MessageBox.Show(settings["pi"]);
}
```

When you've got the settings collection, you can access the string values using the key as an indexer key. If you'd like typed data (pi is not much good as a string), you can manually parse the string using the type in question. Alternatively, you can use the AppSettingsReader class (also from the System.Configuration namespace) to provide typed access to the appSettings values:

```
static void Main() {
  // Parse the value manually
  NameValueCollection settings = ConfigurationSettings.AppSettings;
  Decimal pi1 = Decimal.Parse(settings["pi"]);

  // Let AppSettingsReader parse the value
  AppSettingsReader reader = new AppSettingsReader();
  Decimal pi2 = (Decimal)reader.GetValue("pi", typeof(Decimal));

  ...
}
```

The AppSettingsReader class's GetValue method uses .NET type conversion classes to do its work, making things a bit easier for you if your application's .config file uses different types.

Dynamic Properties

If you'd like even easier access to values from the appSettings section of the .config file, you can bind a property of a form or control to a value by using the Property Browser and dynamic properties. A *dynamic property* is a property value that's pulled from the .config file, with the extra benefit that WinForms Designer writes the reader code for you in InitializeComponent. For example, to bind the Opacity property of a form to a value in the .config file, you bring up the properties for the form and press the "…" button under the Advanced property of the DynamicProperties item, as shown in Figure 11.6.

In the Dynamic Properties dialog, check the box next to Opacity and notice the Key mapping, as shown in Figure 11.7.

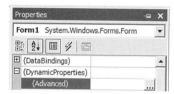

FIGURE 11.6: Dynamic Properties in the Property Browser

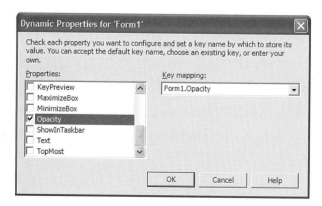

FIGURE 11.7: Dynamic Properties Dialog

The Key mapping defaults to <objectName>.<propertyName>, but you can name it whatever you like. When you press the OK button and open the project's app.config, you'll notice a new key in the appSettings section:

```
<?xml version="1.0" encoding="Windows-1252"?>
<configuration>
  <appSettings>
    <add key="Form1.Opacity" value="1" />
    <add key="pi" value="3.141592653589793238462" />
  </appSettings>
</configuration>
```

Similarly, each dynamic property has a little document icon next to it in the Property Browser, as shown in Figure 11.8.

When a property is marked as dynamic, the Designer writes the value you set in the Property Browser to the app.config file instead of to InitializeComponent. Subsequently, InitializeComponent will read the property from the .config:

```
void InitializeComponent() {
  AppSettingsReader configurationAppSettings =
    new AppSettingsReader();
  ...
  this.Opacity =
  ((System.Double)(configurationAppSettings.GetValue(
    "Form1.Opacity", typeof(System.Double)))));
  ...
}
```

Now, when your application is deployed and your power users want to change the Opacity of the form, they can crack open the .config file with any text editor and have at it. Unfortunately, if the power user removes the Opacity setting or gives it an invalid format, the application will throw an exception at run time, and the InitializeComponent method won't do anything to deal with it. If you'd like to guard against that, you need to

FIGURE 11.8: Opacity Marked as a Dynamic Property

provide a UI for your users to set their preferences that is more robust than Notepad. And if that's the case, .config files are not for you. There is no API in .NET for writing .config files, only for reading them. This makes .config files effectively read-only for applications (although read/write for humans facile in XML).[9]

The Registry

The Registry, on the other hand, has been the place to keep read/write application settings and roaming user settings from Windows 3.1 through Windows NT (it has fallen out of favor in more recent versions of Windows). The Registry gives you hierarchical, machinewide storage of arbitrary name/value pairs split into application and roaming user localities based on the path to the value. The Registry Editor (regedit.exe) is a built-in tool for setting and updating Registry values,[10] as shown in Figure 11.9.

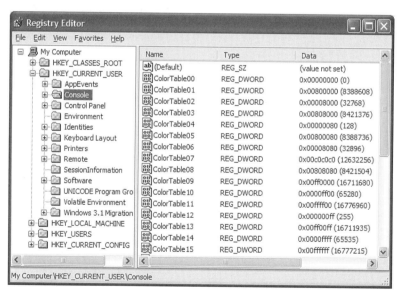

FIGURE 11.9: The Registry Editor

---

9. Some humans have also posted code on the Web to add write capabilities to .config files, although as of .NET 1.1, .config files are still officially read-only.
10. Be careful when editing Registry values. You're working on live data that's used by the entire system. One wrong move and you're reinstalling the OS, and there's no Undo!

The Registry is used a lot by Win32 applications, including the Explorer shell, so you can find yourself reading and writing Registry values whether or not you use it to store your own application's settings. For example, to use the Registry to associate a particular file extension with your application, you use the RegistryKey class from the Microsoft.Win32 namespace:

```
using Microsoft.Win32;
...
static void Main(string[] args) {
  // Create a key and set its default value
  using( RegistryKey key =
          Registry.ClassesRoot.CreateSubKey(".tlf") ) {
    // Map .tlf extension to a ProgID
    key.SetValue(null, "tlffile");
  }

  // Create another key and set its default value
  string cmdkey = @"tlffile\shell\open\command";
  using( RegistryKey key =
          Registry.ClassesRoot.CreateSubKey(cmdkey) ) {
    // Map ProgID to an Open action for the shell
    key.SetValue(null, Application.ExecutablePath + " \"%L\"");
  }
  ...
}
```

The RegistryKey class is a named "folder" in the Registry. This folder can have one or more named values, which are like the "files" (a name of null denotes the *default value* for a key). The values can be of several types, including string, unsigned integer, and arbitrary bytes. Writing to the Registry is a matter of opening or creating a subkey from one of the *hive keys* (which represent the top-level localities) and writing values. The hive keys are properties on the Registry object and translate into keys with well-known names in the Registry, as shown in Table 11.2.

Reading values from the Registry is similar to writing them:

```
static void Main(string[] args) {
  // Check whether someone has hijacked the .tlf extension
  bool mapExtension = true;

  // Open an existing key
  using( RegistryKey key =
          Registry.ClassesRoot.OpenSubKey(".tlf") ) {
```

continues

TABLE 11.2:　Registry Properties and Key Names

Registry Class Static Property	Registry Hive Key Name
Registry.ClassesRoot	HKEY_CLASSES_ROOT
Registry.CurrentConfig	HKEY_CURRENT_CONFIG
Registry.CurrentUser	HKEY_CURRENT_USER
Registry.DynData	HKEY_DYN_DATA[a]
Registry.LocalMachine	HKEY_LOCAL_MACHINE
Registry.PerformanceData	HKEY_PERFORMANCE_DATA
Registry.Users	HKEY_USERS

a. Win9x only

```
    // If the reference is null, the key doesn't exist
    if( (key != null) &&
        (key.GetValue(null).ToString().ToLower() != "tlffile" ) ) {
      string ask = "Associate .tlf with this application?";
      DialogResult res =
        MessageBox.Show(ask, "Oops!", MessageBoxButtons.YesNo);
      if( res == DialogResult.No ) mapExtension = false;
    }
  }

  if( mapExtension ) {...}
  ...
}
```

To use the Registry to store settings, Microsoft recommends putting them under the hive key using the following format:

```
<hiveKey>\Software\<companyName>\<productName>\<productVersion>
```

Here's an example:

```
HKEY_CURRENT_USER\Software\Sells Brothers, Inc.\My Settings Test\
1.0.1124.31077
```

The variable values are, coincidentally, exactly the same values provided by Application.CompanyName, Application.ProductName, and

Application.Version, so you can construct a top-level key name by using the following:

```
string appkey =
  string.Format(
    @"Software\{0}\{1}\{2}",
    Application.CompanyName,
    Application.ProductName,
    Application.ProductVersion);
using( RegistryKey key = Registry.LocalMachine.OpenSubKey(appkey) ) {
  ...
}
```

Similarly, for roaming user settings, Microsoft recommends using the same subkey but under the HKEY_CURRENT_USER hive instead of the HKEY_LOCAL_MACHINE hive. To accommodate the many people desiring to open subkeys for application and roaming user settings in the Microsoft-recommended spots, the WinForms Application object includes two properties that provide preopened registry keys at the right spot depending on whether you'd like application data or roaming user data. These properties are named CommandAppDataRegistry and UserApp-DataRegistry. For example, to save the main form's position you could use the UserAppDataRegistry key:

```
void MainForm_Closing(object sender, CancelEventArgs e) {
  // Save the form's position before it closes
  using( RegistryKey key = Application.UserAppDataRegistry ) {
    // Restore the window state to save location and
    // client size at restored state
    FormWindowState state = this.WindowState;
    this.WindowState = FormWindowState.Normal;

    key.SetValue("MainForm.Location", ToString(this.Location));
    key.SetValue("MainForm.ClientSize", ToString(this.ClientSize));
    key.SetValue("MainForm.WindowState", ToString(state));
  }
}

// Convert an object to a string
string ToString(object obj) {
  TypeConverter converter =
    TypeDescriptor.GetConverter(obj.GetType());
  return converter.ConvertToString(obj);
}
```

This example uses the Closing event to notice when the main form is about to close (but before it does) to save the window state, location, and client size. In addition to remembering to restore the window state before saving the location and the client size, this code uses the ToString helper function. This function uses a type converter, which is a helper to aid in the conversion between instances of a type and strings (for more on type converters, see Chapter 9: Design-Time Integration). Any type can have an associated type converter, and most of the simple ones do. After the application is run once, notice the settings that are saved in the Registry, as shown in Figure 11.10.

Notice that the size is shown as "292, 54" instead of "{292, 54}," as would have happened if we had used the built-in Size class's ToString method. Because Size's type converter doesn't know how to translate the surrounding braces, it's important to use the type converter's conversion to the string format instead of the type's conversion to ensure that the value can be read back during loading of the form:

```
void MainForm_Load(object sender, EventArgs e) {
  // Restore the form's position
  using( RegistryKey key = Application.UserAppDataRegistry ) {
    try {
      // Don't let the form's position be set automatically
      this.StartPosition = FormStartPosition.Manual;

      this.Location =
        (Point)FromString(
          key.GetValue("MainForm.Location"),
          typeof(Point));
```

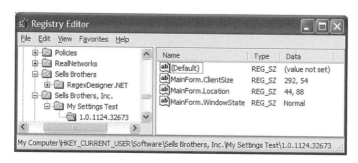

FIGURE 11.10: Using the Registry for User Settings

```
      this.ClientSize =
        (Size)FromString(
          key.GetValue("MainForm.ClientSize"),
          typeof(Size));
      this.WindowState =
        (FormWindowState)FromString(
          key.GetValue("MainForm.WindowState"),
          typeof(FormWindowState));
    }
    // Don't let missing settings scare the user
    catch {}
  }
}

// Convert a string to an object
object FromString(object obj, Type type) {
  TypeConverter converter = TypeDescriptor.GetConverter(type);
  return converter.ConvertFromString(obj.ToString());
}
```

In this case, the form's Load method uses the Registry key to load the settings that it saved during the Closing event, this time using the type converters to convert from a string to the appropriate type. Notice also that the Load method uses a try-catch block to wrap the attempts to pull values from the Registry; in this way, we avoid throwing an exception if the values aren't present. These values typically are missing when the application is first run. If you'd like, you can set defaults to avoid the exception when a value is not found:

```
this.WindowState =
  (FormWindowState)FromString(
    key.GetValue("MainForm.WindowState", "Normal"),
    typeof(FormWindowState));
```

Although the Registry can be used for application and user settings, its use has fallen out of fashion. Corruption issues with early implementations of the Registry have given it a bad reputation. There's nothing inherently wrong with it that more modern versions of Windows haven't fixed long ago. However, because the Registry doesn't support nonroaming user settings or use from partially trusted applications, you'll want to consider special folder-based settings media, discussed next.

Special Folders

Special folders are folders that Windows designates as having a special purpose. For example, the default folder where programs are installed is special and is available this way:

```
// Generally "C:\Program Files"
string programFiles =
  Environment.GetFolderPath(Environment.SpecialFolder.ProgramFiles);
```

There are three special folders for settings: one each for the application, user, and roaming user localities. Table 11.3 shows them, along with some sample paths running on Windows XP.

The special folder serves as the top-level folder in the folder under which applications can store application settings, user settings, and roaming user settings (just as Registry.LocalMachine and Registry.CurrentUser provide the top level for application and roaming user settings). Under that folder, an application is expected to construct a subfolder to avoid colliding with other applications or even versions of itself. This subfolder has the following format:

```
<specialFolder>\<companyName>\<productName>\<productVersion>
```

For example:

```
C:\Documents and Settings\csells\Local Settings\Application Data\
Sells Brothers, Inc.\My Settings Test\1.0.1124.33519
```

TABLE 11.3: Special Folders, Localities, and Examples

SpecialFolder Enum Value	Locality	Example Path
CommonApplicationData	Application	C:\Documents and Settings\ All Users\Application Data
LocalApplicationData	User	C:\Documents and Settings\ <user>\Local Settings\ Application Data
ApplicationData	Roaming user	C:\Documents and Settings\ <user>\Application Data

And just as the Application object provides shortcut access to Registry keys via properties, it also provides shortcut access to prefabricated folder names and folders via the CommonAppDataPath, LocalUserAppData-Path, and UserAppDataPath properties. For example, here's how to rewrite the Registry-based setting code using special folders:

```
using System.IO;
...
void MainForm_Closing(object sender, CancelEventArgs e) {
  // Save the form's position before it closes
  string fileName =
    Application.LocalUserAppDataPath + @"\MainForm.txt";
  using( StreamWriter writer = new StreamWriter(fileName) ) {
    // Restore the window state to save location and
    // client size at restored state
    FormWindowState state = this.WindowState;
    this.WindowState = FormWindowState.Normal;

    writer.WriteLine(ToString(this.Location));
    writer.WriteLine(ToString(this.ClientSize));
    writer.WriteLine(ToString(state));
  }
}

void MainForm_Load(object sender, EventArgs e) {
  AppSettingsReader asReader = new AppSettingsReader();
  Decimal pi = (Decimal)asReader.GetValue("pi", typeof(Decimal));
  piTextBox.Text = pi.ToString();

  // Restore the form's position
  try {
    string fileName =
      Application.LocalUserAppDataPath + @"\MainForm.txt";
    using( StreamReader reader = new StreamReader(fileName) ) {
      // Don't let the form's position be set automatically
      this.StartPosition = FormStartPosition.Manual;

      this.Location =
        (Point)FromString(
        reader.ReadLine(),
        typeof(Point));
      this.ClientSize =
        (Size)FromString(
        reader.ReadLine(),
        typeof(Size));
```

continues

```
      this.WindowState =
        (FormWindowState)FromString(
        reader.ReadLine(),
        typeof(FormWindowState));
    }
  }
  // Don't let missing settings scare the user
  catch( Exception ) {}
}
```

In this case, only two things are different from the use of the Registry. The first is the use of a file to hold the form's settings instead of a Registry key to hold the data. This means that the values must be read in the same order as they're written (unless you use a smarter serialization strategy). The second is the use of the path to the user settings data instead of roaming user settings data. With the Registry, all user data is roaming, whether you want it to be or not (unless you do something custom under the HKEY_LOCAL_MACHINE hive). User settings that are related to the capabilities of the machine itself, such as the location, size, and state of a form, are better suited to nonroaming data.

Settings and Streams

It is convenient to use type conversions with the Registry because it maintains distinct values and makes them available via the Registry Editor, but when you've got a stream, real .NET serialization[11] becomes an attractive option:

```
using System.Runtime.Serialization;
using System.Runtime.Serialization.Formatters;
using System.Runtime.Serialization.Formatters.Soap;
...
// Custom type to manage serializable form data
[SerializableAttribute]
class FormData {
  public Point Location;
  public Size ClientSize;
  public FormWindowState WindowState;
```

---

11. If you're not familiar with .NET serialization, you can read up on the basics in Appendix C: Serialization Basics.

```
  public FormData(Form form) {
    this.Location = form.Location;
    this.ClientSize = form.ClientSize;
    this.WindowState = form.WindowState;
  }
}

void MainForm_Closing(object sender, CancelEventArgs e) {
  // Save the form's position before it closes
  string fileName =
    Application.LocalUserAppDataPath + @"\MainForm.txt";
  using( Stream stream =
         new FileStream(fileName, FileMode.Create) ) {
    // Restore the window state to save location and
    // client size at restored state
    FormWindowState state = this.WindowState;
    this.WindowState = FormWindowState.Normal;

    // Serialize custom FormData object
    IFormatter formatter = new SoapFormatter();
    formatter.Serialize(stream, new FormData(this));
  }
}

void MainForm_Load(object sender, EventArgs e) {
  // Restore the form's position
  try {
    string fileName =
      Application.LocalUserAppDataPath + @"\MainForm.txt";
    using( Stream stream =
           new FileStream(fileName, FileMode.Open) ) {
      // Don't let the form's position be set automatically
      this.StartPosition = FormStartPosition.Manual;

      // Deserialize custom FormData object
      IFormatter formatter = new SoapFormatter();
      FormData data = (FormData)formatter.Deserialize(stream);

      // Set data from FormData object
      this.Location = data.Location;
      this.ClientSize = data.ClientSize;
      this.WindowState = data.WindowState;
    }
  }
  // Don't let missing settings scare the user
  catch( Exception ex ) {
    MessageBox.Show(ex.Message, ex.GetType().Name);
  }
}
```

This example serializes an instance of a custom type that represents the setting data that we'd like to keep between sessions. To *serialize* an object is to read it from or write it to a stream. A *stream* is an object that provides access to a storage medium, such as a file or a database.

To have something to serialize, we've got a custom type called Form-Data, which keeps track of the location, client size, and window state. When it's time to save the form data, the code creates an instance of the new type and then hands it to the formatter, along with the file stream opened in the special folder. Similarly, when loading, we use a formatter to deserialize the form data and use it to restore the form. This is a much easier way to go than the type converter because it takes less code. In addition, serialization provides some nice extension options as time goes on and the FormData class needs to include extra information, such as font and color preferences.

Isolated Storage

One more technology that .NET provides for reading and writing settings data is *isolated storage*. It's called "isolated" because it doesn't require the application to know where on the hard drive the settings files are stored. In fact, it's just like using the special folder shortcuts provided by the Application class except that the path to the root of the path on the file system isn't even available to the application. Instead, named chunks of data are called *streams,* and containers (and subcontainers) of streams are called *stores.* The model is such that the implementation could vary over time, although currently it's implemented on top of special folders with subfolders and files.

The special folder you get depends on the *scope* you specify when getting the store you want to work with. You specify the scope by combining one or more flags from the IsolatedStorageScope enumeration:

```
enum IsolatedStorageScope {
  Assembly, // Always required
  Domain,
  None,
  Roaming,
  User, // Always required
}
```

Isolated storage stores must be scoped by, at a minimum, assembly and user. This means that there are no user-neutral settings available from isolated storage, only user and roaming user settings (depending on whether the Roaming flag is used). In addition, you can scope settings to a .NET application domain using the Domain flag, but typically that's not useful in a WinForms application.

Table 11.4 shows the valid combinations of scope flags as related to settings localities and sample folder roots under Windows XP.

Obtaining a store to work with is a matter of specifying the scope to the GetStore method of the IsolatedStorageFile class from the System.IO. IsolatedStorage namespace:

```
IsolatedStorageScope scope =
  IsolatedStorageScope.Assembly |
  IsolatedStorageScope.User;
IsolatedStorageFile store =
  IsolatedStorageFile.GetStore(scope, null, null);
```

TABLE 11.4: Isolated Storage Scope, Locality, and Folder Roots

IsolatedStorageScope Flags	Locality	Folder Root
Assembly, User	User	C:\Documents and Settings\ <user>\Local Settings\ Application Data\ IsolatedStorage
Assembly, User, Roaming	Roaming User	C:\Documents and Settings\ <user>\Application Data\ IsolatedStorage
Assembly, User, Domain	Domain	C:\Documents and Settings\ <user>\Local Settings\ Application Data\ IsolatedStorage
Assembly, User, Domain, Roaming	Roaming User Domain	C:\Documents and Settings\ <user>\Local Settings\ Application Data\ IsolatedStorage

Because getting the user store for the assembly is so common, the IsolatedStorageFile class provides a helper with that scope already in place:

```
// Scope = User | Assembly
IsolatedStorageFile store =
  IsolatedStorageFile.GetUserStoreForAssembly();
```

After you've got the store, you can treat it like a container of streams and subcontainers by using the members of the IsolatedStorageFile class:

```
sealed class IsolatedStorageFile : IsolatedStorage, IDisposable {
  // Properties
  public object AssemblyIdentity { get; }
  public UInt64 CurrentSize { virtual get; }
  public object DomainIdentity { get; }
  public UInt64 MaximumSize { virtual get; }
  public IsolatedStorageScope Scope { get; }

  // Methods
  public void Close();
  public void CreateDirectory(string dir);
  public void DeleteDirectory(string dir);
  public void DeleteFile(string file);
  public string[] GetDirectoryNames(string searchPattern);
  public static IEnumerator GetEnumerator(IsolatedStorageScope scope);
  public string[] GetFileNames(string searchPattern);
  public static IsolatedStorageFile GetStore(...);
  public static IsolatedStorageFile GetUserStoreForAssembly();
  public static IsolatedStorageFile GetUserStoreForDomain();
  public virtual void Remove();
  public static void Remove(IsolatedStorageScope scope);
}
```

Don't be confused by the fact that the IsolatedStorageFile class is actually implemented as a directory in the file system. This is only one implementation of the IsolatedStorageStorage abstract base class. Other implementations are certainly possible (although none are currently provided by .NET).

The most common thing you'll want to do with a store is to create a stream on it using an instance of IsolatedStorageFileStream. The IsolatedStorageFileStream class is just another implementation of the virtual methods of the FileStream class to hide the details of the underlying implementation. After you've got the stream, you can write to it or read from it just as if you'd opened it yourself as a file. Here's the same code again to store the main form's location using isolated storage:

```
void MainForm_Closing(object sender, CancelEventArgs e) {
  // Save the form's position before it closes
  IsolatedStorageFile store =
    IsolatedStorageFile.GetUserStoreForAssembly();
  using( Stream stream =
          new IsolatedStorageFileStream("MainForm.txt",
          FileMode.Create,
          store) ) {
    ...
  }
}

void MainForm_Load(object sender, EventArgs e) {
  // Restore the form's position
  try {
    IsolatedStorageFile store =
      IsolatedStorageFile.GetUserStoreForAssembly();
    using( Stream stream =
            new IsolatedStorageFileStream("MainForm.txt",
            FileMode.Open,
            store) ) {
      ...
    }
  }
  // Don't let missing settings scare the user
  catch( Exception ) {}
}
```

Managing Isolated Storage and Streams

You can manage the isolated storage using the Store Admin tool (storeadm .exe) from the command line. To list the user settings, use storeadm /list, as shown in Figure 11.11.

Some records indicate storage, and others indicate streams. To remove all the user isolated storage, use storeadm /remove. Both of these commands operate by default on user settings. To act on roaming user settings, add the /roaming switch to either command. Unfortunately, the Store Admin tool does not show the contents of any storage or stream, nor does it show the mapping in the file system. So your best bet is to use the dir and find shell commands, starting at the root of the isolated storage folder you're interested in exploring.

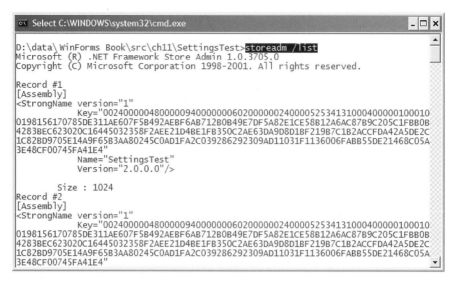

FIGURE 11.11: Using the Store Admin Tool to List Stores and Streams

Isolated Storage and Partial Trust

Although it may seem that isolated storage is only a more complicated use of special folders, there is an important benefit to using isolated storage instead of opening settings files directly: Using isolated storage lets you use partially trusted assemblies. A *partially trusted assembly* is one that runs in a security sandbox that limits its permissions—for example, a WinForms control hosted in Internet Explorer. Partially trusted assemblies are not allowed to read or write to the Registry or the file system as needed for settings, but they are allowed to read and write to isolated storage. If you need settings for a partially trusted assembly, your only option is to use isolated storage for read/write user settings and to use .config files for read-only settings. Chapter 15: Web Deployment covers partially trusted assemblies in detail.

Versioned Data Paths

You may have noticed that all the paths provided by the Application object for the Registry and the special folders are built using a version number, including the build number and revision. This means that the next version of your application will be protected from the changing format of settings data. It also means that the next version of the application cannot use the paths provided by Application to find the settings written by the preceding version.

If you're stuck on using the Registry or special folders for user settings, you can get version-independent settings in one of two ways. One way is to bypass the path helper properties on the Application object and build your own by omitting the version. For example, you could use a roaming user special folder path in the following format:

```
<specialFolder>\<companyName>\<productName>
```

Another way to get version-independent settings is to migrate the settings to the new version's path during the installation of the new version. This allows you access to the old version's settings in the new version while still letting you change the format of any settings values that have changed between versions. Of course, it also requires that you write the code to do the migration.

Each of the remaining two forms of settings management—.config files and isolated storage—has a built-in form of version independence. Settings in the appSettings portion of the .config file aren't keyed to versions at all, so those values are carried along from version to version (whether or not you want them to be). Isolated storage has two forms of versioned access to settings.

If an assembly is *unsigned*—that is, there is no key file associated with it at build time via the assemblywide AssemblyKeyFileAttribute[12]—then isolated storage is just as version-independent as .config files are (again, whether or not you want it to be). All versions of the assembly will share the same settings.

Signing an assembly requires first obtaining a key:

```
C:\>sn -k key.snk
```

---

12. Why you'd actually want to sign an assembly beyond versioning user settings data for isolated storage is beyond the scope of this book, but it is covered in gory detail in *Essential .NET* (Addison-Wesley, 2003) by Don Box, with Chris Sells.

After you have a key, you can sign an assembly by passing the name of the key as the value to the AssemblyKeyFileAttribute:

```
[assembly: AssemblyKeyFile(@"..\..\key.snk")]
```

After an assembly is signed, access to isolated storage is versioned, but only on the major part of the version number. In other words, all 1.x versions of an application will share the same settings, but 2.x versions will need their own settings. This is probably the best of both worlds. Minor versions aren't likely to change the format of existing settings and will at most gain new settings (with appropriate defaults). Major versions are likely to change fundamental things, including the format of settings data, so it makes sense to give a new major version number a clean slate when it comes to settings data. When using isolated storage, you'll still have to move user settings forward during the installation of the new version, but only if it's a major version upgrade, such as 1.1 to 2.0. No migration is needed for an upgrade from 1.1 to 1.2.

Note that this version discussion is about the paths to the data stores themselves. If you're serializing versioned types to an isolated storage stream, for example, you'll still need to deal with standard .NET versioning on those.

Choosing a Settings Mechanism

Table 11.5 summarizes the characteristics of the various mechanisms for retrieving and storing settings for WinForms applications.

Choosing which settings mechanism to use depends on what your needs are. If you have read-only application settings, the .config file is a good choice because it's simple, it has some built-in Designer support, and it works from a partially trusted environment. If you've got user settings, then isolated storage is a good choice because it supports reading and writing, partial trust, and roaming (although not roaming in combination with partial trust), and it has a nice versioning story. Special folders or the Registry is really useful only for legacy applications or read/write settings (which are pretty darn rare).

TABLE 11.5: Summary of Settings Mechanisms

Mechanism	Localities	Access	Notes
.config files	Application	Read-only	Not versioned Designer support Can be used from partially trusted assembly
Registry	Application Roaming user Machine	Read/write	Versioned when using Application paths
Special folders	Application User Roaming user	Read/write	Versioned when using Application paths
Isolated storage	User Roaming user Domain	Read/write	Not versioned when unsigned Versioned on major version number when signed Can be used from partially trusted assembly

Where Are We?

The seemingly simple application architecture in WinForms and .NET provides some useful capabilities, including tailored lifetime support for building single-instance and multi-SDI applications. It also gives you several settings storage mechanisms, depending on the environment in which you're running your application and its particular needs.

▪12▪
Data Sets and Designer Support

A LARGE MAJORITY OF EXISTING and even new Windows applications are built to access a database. If you're building that kind of application (and chances are very good that you are), you'll need to know how .NET supports access to relational data providers as well as how that support is integrated into VS.NET for ease of development of your WinForms applications.

Of course, accessing databases is a huge undertaking that can't be covered completely in anything less than an entire book (at least). This chapter introduces only the basics of ADO.NET, the part of the .NET Framework responsible for providing access to the myriad of data providers. For example, although I use this chapter to explore data sets and explain how they're used in WinForms applications, I don't cover data readers at all. The data reader can be useful, but it doesn't support WinForms data binding, a popular thing to do in WinForms (and the subject of Chapter 13: Data Binding and Data Grids).

This chapter, and the chapter that follows, give you a running start on ADO.NET, but for the complete story, including all the sordid details, you really need another book.[1]

---

1. For ADO.NET coverage, I'm partial to *Pragmatic ADO.NET* (Addison-Wesley, 2002), by Shawn Wildermuth, who was also an amazing help on the two data-centric chapters of this book. Also, for SQL beginners Shawn recommends *Instant SQL Programming* (Wrox Press, 1995), by Joe Celko.

Data Sets

The main unit of any data-centric application is the *data set*, a data-provider-neutral collection of tables with optional relationship and constraint information. Each data set contains *data tables*, each of which consists of zero or more *data rows*, which hold the actual data. In addition, each data table contains individual *data columns*, which have metadata that describes the type of data each data row can contain.

A data set can be populated by hand but is most commonly populated via a *data adapter*, which knows how to speak a data-provider-specific protocol to get and set the data. The data adapter uses a *data connection*, which is a communications pipe to the data itself, whether it lives on a file in the file system or in a database on another machine. A *data command* is used with the connection to retrieve the rows in question or to otherwise act on the data provider.

Data sets, tables, rows, and columns are data-source-neutral, but data adapters and connections are specific to a data source. The specifics serve as a bridge between the data provider and the .NET data-provider-neutral services, such as data binding (covered in Chapter 13).

The basic pieces of the .NET data architecture, known as ADO.NET, are shown in Figure 12.1.

This chapter and Chapter 13 include a lot of code samples that depend on an instance of SQL Server running with the Northwind database installed. If you don't have SQL Server running, you can install the Microsoft SQL Server Developer Edition (MSDE) that comes with the .NET Framework SDK. Follow the instructions in Start | Programs | Microsoft .NET Framework SDK | Samples and QuickStartTutorials | Install the .NET Framework Samples Database.[2]

Retrieving Data

Given this basic architecture, the following shows an example of filling a DataSet object using the classes from the System.Data namespace and the SQL Server data provider classes from the System.Data.SqlClient namespace:

---

2. If you're using SQL Server, whether it's MSDE or not, you'll want to watch out for the SQL Slammer, which is covered at http://www.microsoft.com/security/slammer.asp.

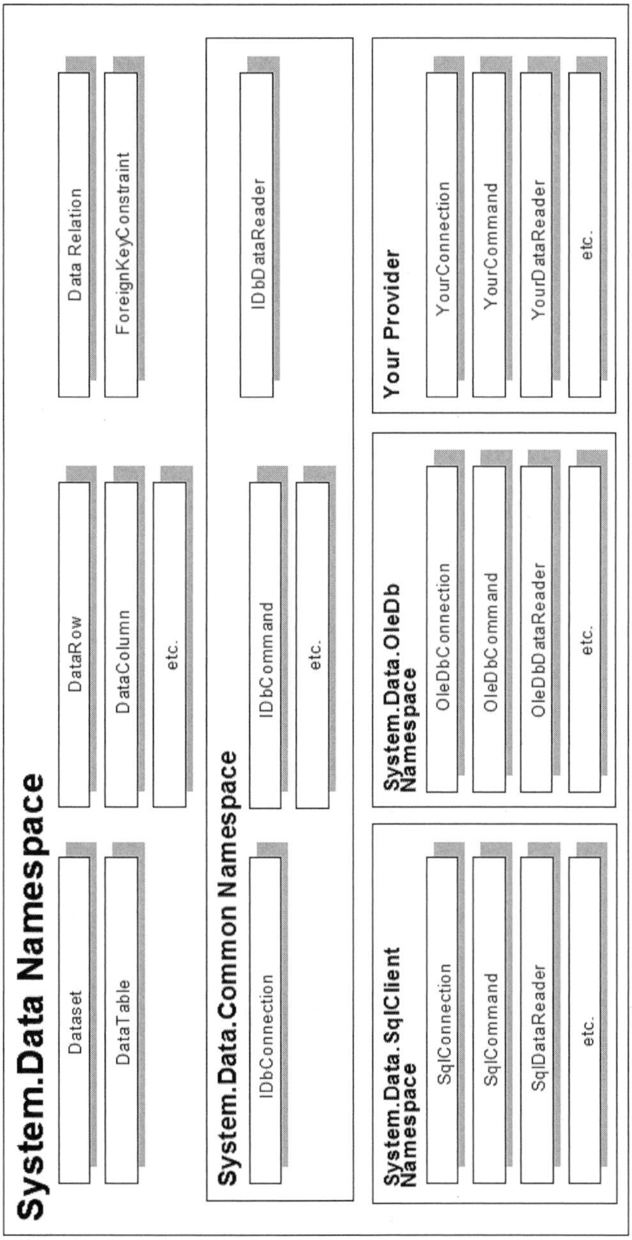

System.Data Namespace

Dataset	DataRow		Data Relation
DataTable	DataColumn		ForeignKeyConstraint
	etc.		

System.Data.Common Namespace

| IDbConnection | IDbCommand | | IDbDataReader |
| | etc. | | |

System.Data.SqlClient Namespace

| SqlConnection |
| SqlCommand |
| SqlDataReader |
| etc. |

System.Data.OleDb Namespace

| OleDbConnection |
| OleDbCommand |
| OleDbDataReader |
| etc. |

Your Provider

| YourConnection |
| YourCommand |
| YourDataReader |
| etc. |

FIGURE 12.1: .NET Data Architecture

```
using System.Data;
using System.Data.SqlClient; // Access to SQL Server
...
// A data set for use by the form
DataSet dataset = new DataSet();

void Form1_Load(object sender, EventArgs e) {
  // Configure the connection
  SqlConnection conn = new SqlConnection(@"Server=localhost;...");

  // Create the adapter from the connection
  SqlDataAdapter adapter = new SqlDataAdapter(conn.CreateCommand());
  adapter.SelectCommand.CommandText = "select * from customers";

  // Fill the data set with the Customers table
  adapter.Fill(dataset);

  // Populate list box
  PopulateListBox();
}

void PopulateListBox() {
  // Clear the list box
  listBox1.Items.Clear();

  // Enumerate cached data
  foreach( DataRow row in dataset.Tables[0].Rows ) {
    string item = row["ContactTitle"] + ", " + row["ContactName"];
    listBox1.Items.Add(item);
  }
}
```

This code creates a connection using a data-provider-specific *connection string*, which tells the connection where to go to get the data. It then creates an adapter with the appropriate *command text* to retrieve data over the connection. The adapter is used to fill the data set, which produces one table. The code then enumerates the table's rows, picking out columns by name that we happen to know that the table will contain. Then it uses the data to populate items in a list box, as shown in Figure 12.2.

Notice that although the sample code creates a connection, it never opens or closes it. Instead, the data adapter opens the connection for an operation—in this case, retrieving the data and filling the data set—and closes it when an operation is complete. The data set itself never uses the connection, nor does it know about where the data comes from. It's the

FIGURE 12.2: Showing Retrieved Data

data adapter's job to translate data in provider-specific format into the provider-neutral data set.

Because the data set has no concept of a connection to the provider, it is a cache of both data and operations on data. Data can be updated and even removed from the data set, but those operations aren't reflected to the actual provider until you tell the data adapter to do so. Before we discuss that, however, let's take a look at the rest of the common data operations: creating, updating, and deleting data.

Creating Data

Creating a new row in a table is a matter of asking the table for an empty DataRow object and filling it with column data:

```
void addRowMenuItem_Click(object sender, EventArgs e) {
  // Ask table for an empty DataRow
  DataRow row = dataset.Tables[0].NewRow();

  // Fill DataRow with column data
  row["CustomerID"] = "SELLSB";
  ...

  // Add DataRow to the table
  dataset.Tables[0].Rows.Add(row);

  // Update list box
  PopulateListBox();
}
```

Updating Data

You can update existing data by reaching into the data set, pulling out the row of interest, and updating the column data as appropriate:

```
void updateSelectedRowMenuItem_Click(object sender, EventArgs e) {
  // Get selection index from list box
  int index = listBox1.SelectedIndex;
  if( index == -1 ) return;

  // Get row from data set
  DataRow row = dataset.Tables[0].Rows[index];

  // Update the row as appropriate
  row["ContactTitle"] = "CEO";

  // Update list box
  PopulateListBox();
}
```

Deleting Data

Deleting a row from a table requires first deciding just how "deleted" you'd like it to be. If you'd like the row to be gone from the table completely, leaving no trace behind, that involves the Remove method on the DataRowCollection exposed from the DataTable:

```
void deleteSelectedRowMenuItem_Click(object sender, EventArgs e) {
  // Get selection index from list box
  int index = listBox1.SelectedIndex;
  if( index == -1 ) return;

  // Get row from data set
  DataRow row = dataset.Tables[0].Rows[index];

  // Remove the row from the data set
  dataset.Tables[0].Rows.Remove(row);

  // Update list box
  PopulateListBox();
}
```

However, this is probably more "deleted" than you'd like, especially if you plan to replicate changes made to the data set back to the originating data provider. In that case, you'll want to mark a row as deleted but not remove all traces of it from the data set. You do that using the Delete method on the DataRow itself:

```
void deleteSelectedRowMenuItem_Click(object sender, EventArgs e) {
  // Get selection index from list box
  int index = listBox1.SelectedIndex;
  if( index == -1 ) return;

  // Get row from data set
  DataRow row = dataset.Tables[0].Rows[index];

  // Mark the row as deleted
  row.Delete();

  // Update list box
  PopulateListBox();
}
```

When a DataTable contains deleted rows, you'll need to change how you access the data, because the DataTable class doesn't allow direct access to deleted rows. This is to prevent you from accidentally treating deleted rows like normal rows. Checking for a deleted row is a matter of checking a row's RowState, which is a combination of values from the DataRowState enumeration:

```
enum DataRowState {
  Added,
  Deleted,
  Detached,
  Modified,
  Unchanged,
}
```

Taking deleted rows into account looks like this:

```
void PopulateListBox() {
  // Clear the list box
  listBox1.Items.Clear();

  // Enumerate cached data
  foreach( DataRow row in dataset.Tables[0].Rows ) {
    if( (row.RowState & DataRowState.Deleted) ==
        DataRowState.Deleted ) continue;
    string item = row["ContactTitle"] + ", " + row["ContactName"];
```

continues

```
    listBox1.Items.Add(item);
  }
}
```

By default, when you access column data, you're getting the "current" data, which, for deleted columns, is missing (and attempted access to it will cause a run-time exception). All data is marked with a value from the DataRowVersion enumeration:

```
enum DataRowVersion {
  Current,
  Default,
  Original,
  Proposed,
}
```

To retrieve old or deleted column data, you can pass a value from DataRowVersion as the second argument to the row's indexer:

```
void PopulateListBox() {
  // Clear the list box
  listBox1.Items.Clear();

  // Enumerate cached data
  foreach( DataRow row in dataset.Tables[0].Rows ) {
    if( (row.RowState & DataRowState.Deleted) ==
        DataRowState.Deleted ) {
      string id =
        row["CustomerID", DataRowVersion.Original].ToString();
      listBox1.Items.Add("***deleted***: " + id);
      continue;
    }

    ...
  }
}
```

Tracking Changes

When a DataRow makes its way into a DataSet as a result of the Data-Adapter's Fill method, the RowState is set to Unchanged and, as I mentioned, using the DataRow Delete method sets the RowState to Deleted. Similarly, adding new rows and updating existing ones sets the RowState to Added and Modified, respectively. This turns the data set into not only a repository for the current state of the cached data but also a record of the changes that have been made to the data since it was initially retrieved. You can get these changes on a per-table basis by using the GetChanges method of the DataTable:

```
DataTable tableChanges =
  dataset.Tables[0].GetChanges(DataRowState.Modified);
if( tableChanges != null ) {
  foreach( DataRow changedRow in tableChanges.Rows ) {
    MessageBox.Show(changedRow["CustomerID"] + " modified");
  }
}
```

The GetChanges method takes a combination of DataRowState values and returns a table that has a copy of only those rows. The rows are copied so that there's no need to worry about accessing deleted data, an attempt that would normally throw an exception. You can use the GetChanges method to find all the modified, added, and deleted rows, together or selectively. This is a handy way to access the data that you need to replicate changes back to the data provider.

Committing Changes

The combination of the GetChanges method and the DataRowVersion enumeration allows you to build commands for replicating changes made to the data set back to the data provider. In the case of database-centric data adapters, you retrieve data using an instance of a *command*, which is responsible for selecting the data set via the SelectCommand property. In fact, recall the earlier code that set up the data adapter:

```
// Configure the connection
SqlConnection conn = new SqlConnection(@"...");

// Create the adapter from the connection
string select = "select * from customers";
SqlDataAdapter adapter = new SqlDataAdapter(select, conn);
```

This code is really just a shortcut for the following code, which creates a command to perform the select directly:

```
// Configure the connection
SqlConnection conn = new SqlConnection(@"...");
```

continues

```
// Create the adapter from the connection
string select = "select * from customers";
SqlDataAdapter adapter = new SqlDataAdapter();
adapter.SelectCommand = new SqlCommand(select, conn);
```

It's the Command object that's responsible for using the connection to retrieve the data, and it's the data adapter's job to keep track of the command it needs to retrieve the data. Similarly, the data adapter uses other commands for replicating changes back, where "changes" includes added rows, updated rows, and deleted rows. It does this using commands that are set via the InsertCommand, UpdateCommand, and DeleteCommand properties, respectively.

You can populate these commands yourself, but it's generally easier to let a command builder do that work for you. A *command builder* is an object that uses the information it gets from the select command and populates the other three commands appropriately:

```
// Create the adapter from the connection with a select command
SqlDataAdapter
  adapter = new SqlDataAdapter("select * from customers", conn);

// Let command builder build commands for insert, update, and delete
// using the information from the existing select command
new SqlCommandBuilder(adapter);
```

The command builder is so self-sufficient that you don't even need to keep it around. The mere act of creating it, passing the adapter that needs commands built, is enough. After the command builder has set up the adapter's commands appropriately, you replicate changes back to the data provider by calling the adapter's Update method:

```
void commitChangesMenuItem_Click(object sender, EventArgs e) {
  // Configure the connection
  SqlConnection conn = new SqlConnection(@"...");

  // Create the adapter from the connection with a select command
  SqlDataAdapter
    adapter = new SqlDataAdapter("select * from customers", conn);

  // Let command builder build commands for insert, update, and delete
  new SqlCommandBuilder(adapter);
```

```
  // Commit changes back to the data provider
  try {
    adapter.Update(dataset);
  }
  catch( SqlException ex ) {
    MessageBox.Show(ex.Message, "Error(s) Committing Changes");
  }

  // Update list box
  PopulateListBox();
}
```

This code uses a command builder to build the other three commands needed to update the data provider and then lets the data adapter compose the command text as necessary. If any of the updates causes an error, a run-time exception will be thrown, and that's why the code shows the call to Update wrapped in a try-catch block. Error information is kept for each row so that you can show it to the user:

```
void PopulateListBox() {
  // Clear the list box
  listBox1.Items.Clear();

  // Enumerate cached data
  foreach( DataRow row in dataset.Tables[0].Rows ) {
    if( (row.RowState & DataRowState.Deleted) !=
        DataRowState.Deleted ) continue;
    string item = row["ContactTitle"] + ", " + row["ContactName"];
    if( row.HasErrors ) item += "(***" + row.RowError + "***)";
    listBox1.Items.Add(item);
  }
}
```

The HasErrors Boolean property of each row reports whether there was an error during the last update, and the RowError string reports what that error is. If there are errors during an update, the RowState of the row will not be changed. For every row that doesn't have errors, it will be reset to DataRowState.Unchanged in preparation for the next update.

Multitable Data Sets

Data sets can hold more than one table at a time. When creating data sets that contain multiple tables, you will want to use one data adapter for each table loaded. In addition, you must be careful when filling a data set using more than one adapter. If you call the data adapter's Fill method on a data set multiple times, you'll end up appending data into a single table, so you need to be specific about what table you're trying to fill:

```
// Configure the connection
SqlConnection conn = new SqlConnection(@"...");

// Create the adapters
SqlDataAdapter customersAdapter = new SqlDataAdapter();
SqlDataAdapter ordersAdapter = new SqlDataAdapter();

// Create a data set
DataSet dataset = new DataSet();

void MultiTableForm_Load(object sender, EventArgs e) {
  // Create the Customer adapter from the connection
  customersAdapter.SelectCommand = conn.CreateCommand();
  customersAdapter.SelectCommand.CommandText =
    "select * from customers";

  // Fill the data set with the Customers table
  customersAdapter.Fill(dataset, "Customers");

  // Create the Orders adapter from the connection
  ordersAdapter.SelectCommand = conn.CreateCommand();
  ordersAdapter.SelectCommand.CommandText =
    "select * from orders";

  // Fill the data set with the Orders table
  ordersAdapter.Fill(dataset, "Orders");

  // Need one command builder for each adapter
  // in anticipation of eventually committing changes
  new SqlCommandBuilder(customersAdapter);
  new SqlCommandBuilder(ordersAdapter);

  // Populate list boxes
  PopulateListBoxes();
}
```

This code fills a data set with data from two different data adapters, one for each table. When you call the Fill method of the data adapter, you must specify which table to fill with the data from the adapter. If you fail to do this, you will get one data table (called "Table") with data from both Fill methods.

You could have used a single data adapter to fill both tables, but because the command builders use the SelectCommand to determine how to update the data provider, it is good form to have a one-to-one relationship between tables in the data set and data adapters. Notice that when the data adapters are created, one command builder is created for each of them in anticipation of committing changes for each table. With more than one table, the code to commit changes needs to be updated:

```
void commitChangesMenuItem_Click(object sender, EventArgs e) {
  // Commit customer changes back to the data provider
  try {
    customersAdapter.Update(dataset, "Customers");
  }
  catch( SqlException ex ) {
    MessageBox.Show(ex.Message,
      "Error(s) Committing Customer Changes");
  }

  // Commit order changes back to the data provider
  try {
    ordersAdapter.Update(dataset, "Orders");
  }
  catch( SqlException ex ) {
    MessageBox.Show(ex.Message,
      "Error(s) Committing Order Changes");
  }

  // Update list boxes
  PopulateListBoxes();
}
```

This code commits changes on each table by calling the Update method of the particular data adapter while specifying the table to update. Make sure not to get the adapter mixed up with the name of the table, or things won't go so well.

Constraints

If you'd like to catch problems with the data as it's added by the user instead of waiting until the data is sent back to the data provider, you can establish constraints. A *constraint* limits the kind of data that can be added to each column. The System.Data namespace comes with two constraints: the foreign key constraint and the unique value constraint, which are represented by the ForeignKeyConstraint and the UniqueConstraint classes, respectively.

For example, to make sure that no two rows have the same value in a column, you can add a unique constraint to the table's list of constraints:

```
// Add a constraint
DataTable customers = dataset.Tables["Customers"];
UniqueConstraint constraint =
  new UniqueConstraint(customers.Columns["CustomerID"]);
customers.Constraints.Add(constraint);
```

With the constraint in place, if a row is added to the table that violates the constraint, a run-time exception will be thrown immediately, without a round-trip to the data provider. Unique constraints set up a constraint between one or more columns in a single table, whereas foreign key constraints set up an existence requirement between columns in multiple tables. Foreign key constraints are set up automatically whenever a relation is established.

Relations

Data sets are not simply containers for multiple tables of data but instead are containers that have support for relational data. As with data in a database, the real power of a data set can be harnessed by relating multiple tables:

```
// Get reference to the tables
DataTable customers = dataset.Tables["Customers"];
DataTable orders = dataset.Tables["Orders"];

// Create the relation
DataRelation relation =
  new DataRelation(
    "CustomersOrders",
    customers.Columns["CustomerID"],
    orders.Columns["CustomerID"]);

// Add the relation
dataset.Relations.Add(relation);
```

This code creates a relation between the customer and order tables on each table's CustomerID column. A *relation* is a named association of columns between multiple tables. To relate columns between tables, you use an instance of a DataRelation class, passing a name and the columns from each of the two tables. Figure 12.3 shows the sample relation between the Customers and the Orders tables.

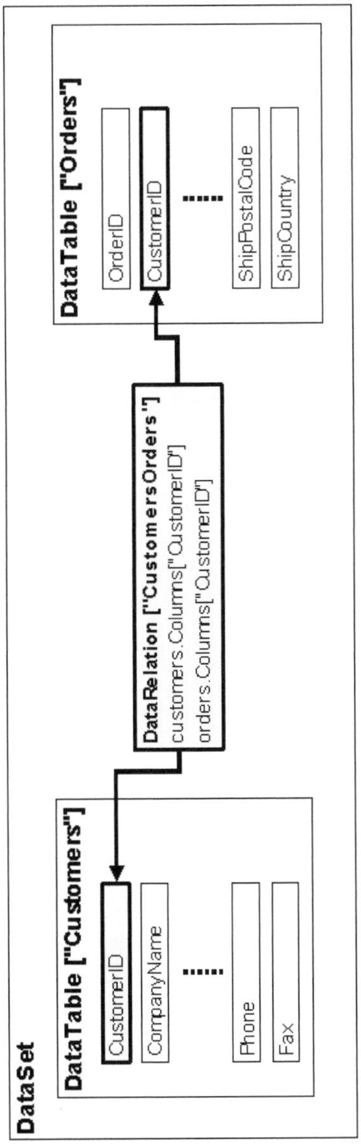

FIGURE 12.3: A Sample Relation between the Customers Table and the Orders Table

After the relation is created, it's added to the set of relations maintained on the data set, an action that also sets up the foreign key constraint. In addition, relations are used for navigation and in expressions.

Navigation

When a relation is added, the second argument to the DataRelation constructor becomes the *parent column*, and the third argument becomes the *child column*. You can navigate between the two using the DataRow methods GetParentRows and GetChildRows, respectively. This allows you to show, for example, related child rows when a parent row is selected, as shown in Figure 12.4.

In Figure 12.4, the top list box shows the customers, which form the parent in the CustomersOrders relation. When a customer is selected, the bottom list box is populated with the related rows:

```
void PopulateChildListBox() {
  // Clear the list box
  ordersListBox.Items.Clear();

  // Get the currently selected parent customer row
  int index = customersListBox.SelectedIndex;
  if( index == -1 ) return;

  // Get row from data set
  DataRow parent = dataset.Tables["Customers"].Rows[index];

  // Enumerate child rows
  foreach( DataRow row in parent.GetChildRows("CustomersOrders") ) {
    ...
  }
}
```

Similarly, from any child row, a relation can be navigated back to the parent using GetParentRows.

Expressions

Relations can also be used in expressions. An *expression* is a column of values that are calculated on-the-fly. The Expression property on the Data-Column class provides this functionality. For example, here's an expression to combine the ContactTitle and ContactName fields:

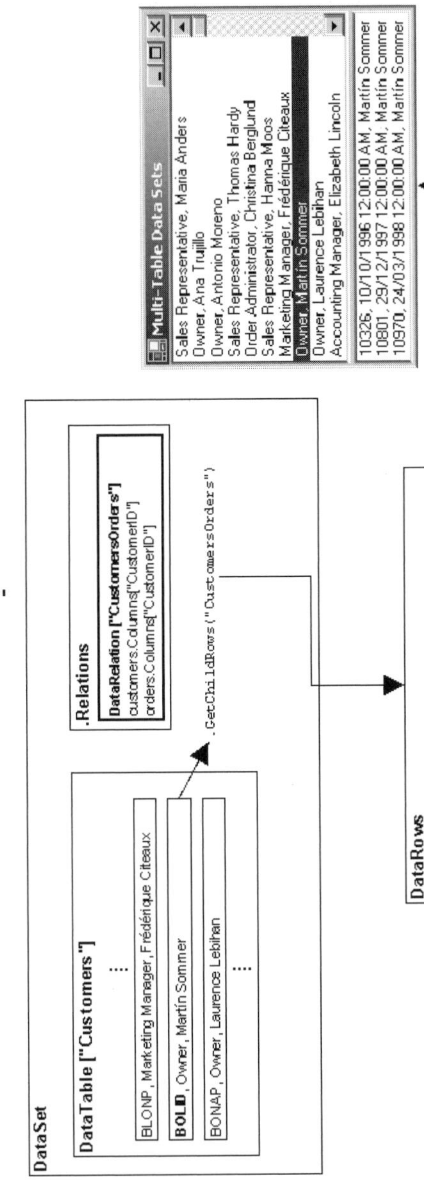

FIGURE 12.4: Showing the Results of GetChildRows Using a Relation

```
// Create the expression column
DataColumn exp = new DataColumn();
exp.ColumnName = "ContactTitleName";
exp.DataType = typeof(string);
exp.Expression = "ContactTitle + ', ' + ContactName";

// Add it to the customer table
dataset.Tables["Customers"].Columns.Add(exp);
```

This code creates a new DataColumn and specifies the name, data type, and expression. The expression syntax is fairly straightforward and is syntactically similar to SQL. You can find the complete reference to the expression syntax in the DataColumn's Expression property documentation.[3]

After you've created an expression column, you can use it like any other column:

```
void PopulateListBoxes() {
  // Clear the list box
  customersListBox.Items.Clear();

  // Enumerate cached data
  foreach( DataRow row in dataset.Tables["customers"].Rows ) {
    // Use the expression instead of composing the string
    //string item = row["ContactTitle"] + ", " + row["ContactName"];
    string item = row["ContactTitleName"].ToString();
    customersListBox.Items.Add(item);
  }

  PopulateChildListBox();
}
```

An expression can navigate a relation from child to parent or vice versa. For example, the orders table doesn't have a contact name for the parent customer, but you can use an expression to grab the data from the parent:

```
// Create the expression column
DataColumn exp2 = new DataColumn();
exp2.ColumnName = "CustomerContactName";
exp2.DataType = typeof(string);
exp2.Expression = "parent(CustomersOrders).ContactName";
```

---

3. http://msdn.microsoft.com/library/en-us/cpref/html/
   frlrfSystemDataDataColumnClassExpressionTopic.asp

```
// Add it to the customer table
dataset.Tables["Orders"].Columns.Add(exp2);
```

This code uses the parent(relationName).columnName syntax to navigate from the child orders table to the parent customers table. If there's only one relationship, then you can just use parent.columnName. Similarly, when going from a parent to a child, you use the child(relationName).columnName syntax.

Designer Support

Although ADO.NET provides a great deal of power in a small amount of code, you still may prefer not to do all the hand coding required in the earlier examples. For that reason, VS.NET provides integrated data access directly in the Windows Forms designer. In the Toolbox window there is a Data Tab, as shown in Figure 12.5.

This Toolbox contains the various kinds of data access objects you'll commonly need. These objects are instances of components, so they don't have UIs of their own. When they're added to a design surface, they cluster along the bottom just like any other component.

Connection Objects

A connection object exists to establish the connection to the data provider, and this means that you're primarily concerned with the ConnectionString property. If you're overly eager, you can type this in manually. More

FIGURE 12.5: Data Toolbox

commonly, you'll let the Property Browser provide you access to the Data Link Properties dialog, as shown in Figure 12.6.

Command Objects

As with connections, dropping a command object does not immediately add any assistance to creating a connection, but again, the Property Browser does, as shown in Figure 12.7.

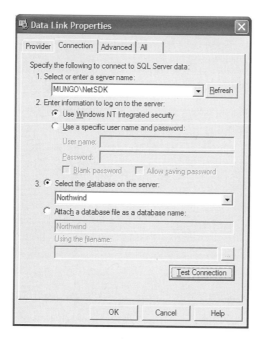

FIGURE 12.6: Data Link Properties Dialog

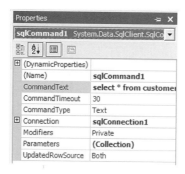

FIGURE 12.7: Command Properties

When setting the Connection property, you'll get a drop-down list of all the known connections on the form. After you select one, you can set the CommandText property using Query Builder, as shown in Figure 12.8.

When the CommandType property is set to Text, Query Builder will help you specify the type of query your command will need to generate. You can add tables, views, and functions from your database and customize the query by using the Designer as necessary. If CommandType is set to Stored Procedure or to TableDirect, you're on your own with the CommandText.

Data Adapter Objects

The data adapter continues to build on the connection objects as well as the command objects. When you drag a data adapter object onto your form, the Designer starts a Data Adapter Configuration Wizard to create a data adapter, which will include a connection object and one or more command objects. The Data Adapter Configuration Wizard can create any missing

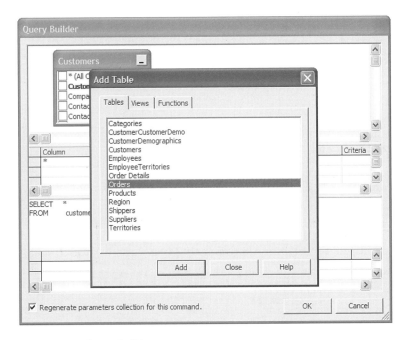

FIGURE 12.8: Query Builder

objects, saving you those steps. The wizard walks you through very specific steps:

1. You specify and create a connection.
2. You create one or more commands for the data adapter, including the select, insert, update, and delete commands.
3. You create the data adapter to tie all the objects together.

When you're finished with this wizard, the generated code creates the connection, the command objects, and the data adapter, associating objects with each other as needed.

Typed Data Sets

In addition to potential problems in creating and relating the various data objects, another source of much coding, and therefore potential for error, is in the access to columns. By default, columns are named with a string and then cast to the specific type that is expected:

```
string postalCode =
   (string)dataset.Tables["Customers"].Rows[0]["PostalCode"];
```

If you get it wrong, the best thing that can happen is an exception at run time; the worst is a silent failure that hides the error. It would be useful if we could make the compiler help figure out when there are errors so that we can find and correct them before we even run the code. That's the job of the typed data set.

Creating a Typed Data Set

To create a typed data set, you add a new data set to your project from the Add New Item menu. This adds an .xsd file to the project. In Visual Studio .NET you use an XML schema document (.xsd) to generate the classes and use DataSet Designer to configure a typed data set. Figure 12.9 shows an empty typed data set.

FIGURE 12.9: An Empty Typed Data Set

Apparently this picture is worth 18 words, and, as it states, you can drag objects from either Server Explorer or the Toolbox. Most often it will be Server Explorer, as shown in Figure 12.10.

Server Explorer allows you to navigate to various data providers. If you are using SQL Server, you can navigate directly to the servers to find databases. Otherwise, you will need to create a data connection or select an existing one. If you created new data connections in the earlier examples for adding a connection to a form, you should notice that connection shown here as well.

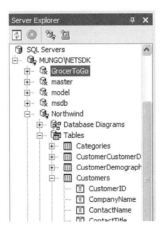

FIGURE 12.10: Server Explorer

To create a typed data set, you drag any number of tables, stored procedures, views, or functions from the database onto the Designer surface. Dragging and dropping the Customers and Orders tables form the Northwind database will show you something like Figure 12.11.

Here, dropping the tables onto the design surface created two tables: one for Customers and one for Orders. In each table, the Designer was able to ask the database for the primary key, as indicated by the key icons. In addition, notice that each column is typed, which is what puts the "typed" in "typed data set." Saving the schema generates a new type having the same name as the schema and deriving from the DataSet base class. Inside this new type are nested types that provide type-safe wrappers around each row:

```
public class CustomerSet : DataSet {
  ...
  public class CustomersRow : DataRow {
    ...
    public string CustomerID {...}
    public string CompanyName {...}
  }
}
```

With the new typed data set, the code to pull data out of a column is now shorter and more robust:

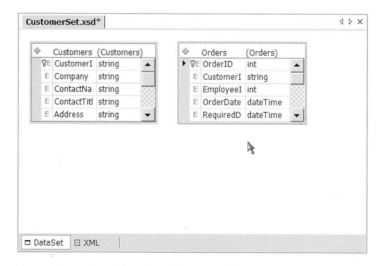

FIGURE 12.11: Typed Data Set with New Tables

```
// Create a typed data set
CustomerSet dataset = new CustomerSet();

// Fill the data set as normal
// ...

// Untyped access
// string postalCode =
//    (string)dataset.Tables["Customers"].Rows[0]["PostalCode"];

// Typed access
string postalCode = dataset.Customers[0].PostalCode;
```

Because it derives directly from the DataSet class, a CustomerSet object can be filled and manipulated exactly like a regular data set. It is a typed data set, so the new typed properties simplify the code. As an additional benefit, the tables and columns in the typed data are also available in VS.NET's IntelliSense, causing typed data sets to further decrease our typing [sic].

Using typed data sets in this way is very helpful, but what about constraints, relations, and expressions? Data Set Designer supports them, too.

Constraints in Typed Data Sets

Adding a unique constraint to a table is a matter of dropping a key onto the table from the XML Schema Toolbox, as shown in Figure 12.12.

Dropping a key produces the Edit Key dialog, as shown in Figure 12.13.

FIGURE 12.12: XML Schema Toolbox

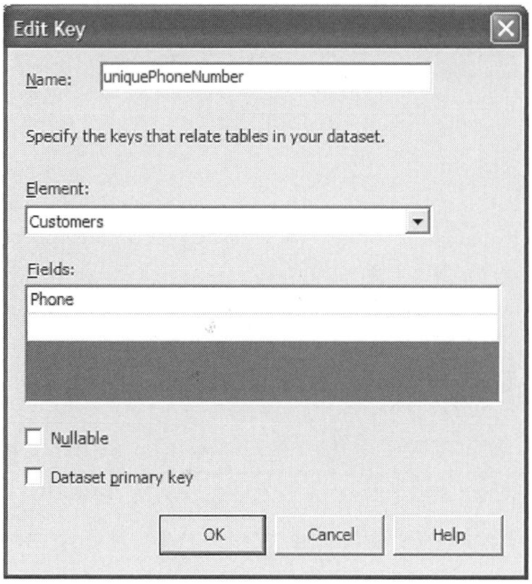

FIGURE 12.13: Edit Key Dialog

To add the unique constraint, you specify the table in the Element dropdown, and the column in the Fields. If you want to create a multicolumn unique constraint, such as requiring that the combination of first and last name be unique, you can specify more than one column under Fields. Adding a foreign key constraint requires adding a Relation from the Toolbox.

Relations in Typed Data Sets

To add a relation to a typed data set, drop a Relation onto the table that will serve as the parent of the relation. This opens the Edit Relation dialog, where you finish the job, as shown in Figure 12.14.

The Parent element will be set based on the table you dropped the Relation onto, so you'll need to set the Child element. After you do, the Name will be set to something fairly intuitive, although you can change it if you like. By default, the Key Fields (which form the relation) will be the two primary keys from the two tables, which is likely what you want to relate in the first place.

In most cases this dialog will give you all the options you need (the documentation can explain the subtleties of this dialog if you need more). A

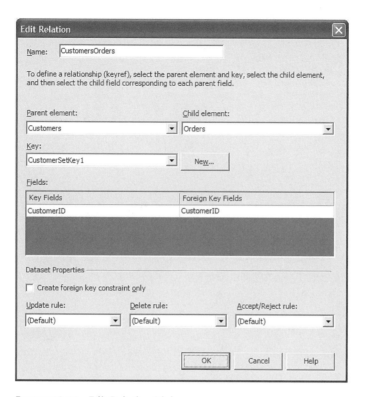

FIGURE 12.14: Edit Relation Dialog

relation will show in the Designer something like the one shown in Figure 12.15.

Not only does setting a relation in the Designer free us from writing the code to establish the relation, but it also exposes the relation as a type-safe method for navigation:

```
// Navigate the relation from the parent to the children
foreach( CustomerSet.OrdersRow row in
         dataset.Customers[0].GetOrdersRows() ) {...}
```

Expressions in Typed Data Sets

You can add expression columns to a table by typing in a new column name and type at the end of a table, as shown in Figure 12.16.

When you've got the new column, you add an Expression property in the Property Browser:

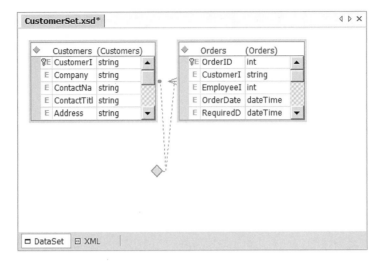

FIGURE 12.15: Typed Data Set with a New Relation

FIGURE 12.16: Adding a New Column to Be Used as an Expression Column

```
ContactTitle + ', ' + ContactName
```

Like all the other columns, the new expression column will be accessible through a strongly typed property:

```
// Get the first Contact's Title and Name
string titleName = dataset.Customers[0].ContactTitleName;
```

Adding a Typed Data Set to a Form

After you've designed the typed data set class, you can add an instance of it to a form (or any other design surface) by dropping a DataSet from the Data Toolbox onto a form. This action produces the Add Dataset dialog, as shown in Figure 12.17.

This dialog allows you to specify a typed or untyped data set. Any typed data sets that have been created in the project will show up in the drop-down list under Typed Dataset. As you'd expect, pressing OK generates the code to create an instance of the typed data set class. With the typed data set in place, and using the Data Adapter Configuration Wizard and Query Builder, we need to enter only a few lines of code to achieve the functionality of Figure 12.4:

```
void Form1_Load(object sender, EventArgs e) {
  // Connection already created
  // Adapters already created
  // Data set already created

  // Fill the data sets
  this.customersAdapter.Fill(this.customerSet1, "Customers");
  this.ordersAdapter.Fill(this.customerSet1, "Orders");
```

continues

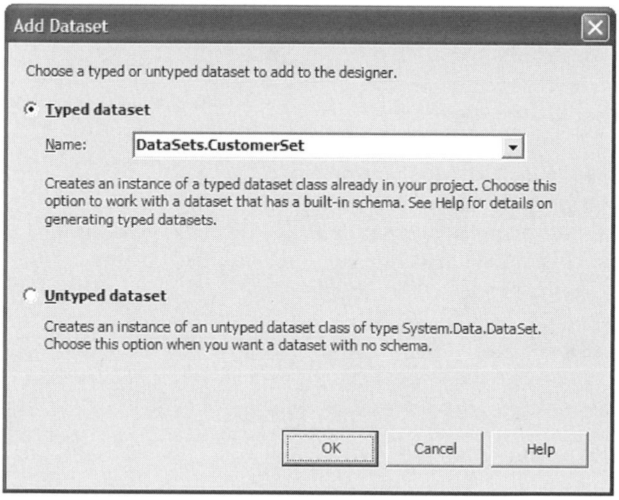

FIGURE 12.17: Adding a Typed Data Set to a Form

```csharp
    // Commands for updating already created
    // Unique constraint already added
    // Relation already established
    // Expression column already added

    // Populate list boxes
    PopulateListBoxes();
}

void PopulateListBoxes() {
  customersListBox.Items.Clear();

  // Enumerate typed customers
  foreach( CustomerSet.CustomersRow row in
           this.customerSet1.Customers.Rows ) {
    if( (row.RowState & DataRowState.Deleted) !=
        DataRowState.Deleted ) continue;

    // Use the typed expression column
    customersListBox.Items.Add(row.ContactTitleName);
  }

  PopulateChildListBox();
}

void PopulateChildListBox() {
  ordersListBox.Items.Clear();
  int index = customersListBox.SelectedIndex;
  if( index == -1 ) return;

  // Get row from data set
  CustomerSet.CustomersRow parent =
    this.customerSet1.Customers[index];

  // Enumerate typed child order rows using
  // typed relation method GetOrdersRow
  foreach( CustomerSet.OrdersRow row in parent.GetOrdersRows() ) {
    if( (row.RowState & DataRowState.Deleted) !=
        DataRowState.Deleted ) continue;

    // Use typed properties
    ordersListBox.Items.Add(row.OrderID + ", " + row.OrderDate);
  }
}

void customersListBox_SelectedIndexChanged(object sender, EventArgs e) {
  PopulateChildListBox();
}
```

Adding CRUD (create/retrieve/update/delete) functionality is also more convenient using a typed data set:

```
void addRowMenuItem_Click(object sender, EventArgs e) {
  // Add a new typed row
  CustomerSet.CustomersRow row =
    this.customerSet1.Customers.NewCustomersRow();
  row.CustomerID = "SELLSB";
  row.CompanyName = "Sells Brothers, Inc.";
  row.ContactName = "Chris Sells";
  row.ContactTitle = "Chief Cook and Bottle Washer";
  row.Address = "555 Not My Street";
  row.City = "Beaverton";
  row.Region = "OR";
  row.PostalCode = "97007";
  row.Country = "USA";
  row.Phone = "503-555-1234";
  row.Fax = "503-555-4321";
  this.customerSet1.Customers.AddCustomersRow(row);

  // Update list boxes
  PopulateListBoxes();
}

void updateSelectedRowMenuItem_Click(object sender, EventArgs e) {
  int index = customersListBox.SelectedIndex;
  if( index == -1 ) return;

  // Update a typed row
  CustomerSet.CustomersRow row = this.customerSet1.Customers[index];
  row.ContactTitle = "CEO";

  // Update list boxes
  PopulateListBoxes();
}

void deleteSelectedRowMenuItem_Click(object sender, EventArgs e) {
  int index = customersListBox.SelectedIndex;
  if( index == -1 ) return;

  // Mark a typed row as deleted
  CustomerSet.CustomersRow row = this.customerSet1.Customers[index];
  row.Delete();

  // Update list boxes
  PopulateListBoxes();
}
```

continues

```
void commitChangesMenuItem_Click(object sender, EventArgs e) {
  try {
    // Update a typed table
    this.customersAdapter.Update(dataset, "Customers");
  }
  catch( SqlException ex ) {
    MessageBox.Show(ex.Message,
      "Error(s) Committing Customer Changes");
  }

  try {
    // Update a typed table
    this.ordersAdapter.Update(dataset, "Orders");
  }
  catch( SqlException ex ) {
    MessageBox.Show(ex.Message,
      "Error(s) Committing Order Changes");
  }

  // Update list boxes
  PopulateListBoxes();
}
```

With typed data sets, the code we're responsible for typing is smaller and more robust. The DataSet Designer generates the code for coercing data, and the Forms Designer generates the code for establishing the connection, the commands, the adapters, and the data set. That leaves us to write only the fun stuff (mostly).

Where Are We?

This chapter discusses data sets and the basics of data manipulation. It explains how they're integrated into VS.NET and how to use typed data sets to produce leaner, better code. The one part that nags us through the entire chapter, however, is the need to constantly update the list boxes whenever the underlying data set changes in any way. Chapter 13 explains how to use data binding to eliminate that requirement.

13

Data Binding and Data Grids

T HE DATA SUPPORT IN ADO.NET and integrated into VS.NET discussed in Chapter 12 is only half the story for WinForms programmers. WinForms provides a rich infrastructure for bidirectional data binding between arbitrary controls and arbitrary data sources. The control that takes the most advantage of this architecture is the data grid. This chapter covers data binding and data grids and wraps up with a discussion of custom data sources.

Data Binding

In Windows Forms development, there often comes a time when you need to populate a number of controls with data from a database or other data source. Recall our example from Chapter 12: Data Sets and Designer Support, which used a data set populated from a database. Whenever the data set was changed, such as when the user added a row or deleted a row, we had to repopulate the list boxes so that the display was kept in sync with the data:

```
void addRowMenuItem_Click(object sender, EventArgs e) {
  // Add a new typed row
  CustomerSet.CustomersRow row =
    this.customerSet1.Customers.NewCustomersRow();
  row.CustomerID = "SELLSB";
  ...
```

continues

```
this.customerSet1.Customers.AddCustomersRow(row);

    // Update list box
    PopulateListBox();
}
```

Writing code to do this repopulation of the control is boring:

```
void PopulateListBox() {
    // Don't show any item more than once
    customersListBox.Items.Clear();

    // Show all rows in the Customers table
    foreach( CustomerSet.CustomersRow row in
             this.customerSet1.Customers.Rows ) {
        // Except don't show the deleted rows
        if( (row.RowState & DataRowState.Deleted) !=
            DataRowState.Deleted ) {
          continue;
        }

        // On each row, show the ContactTitleName column
        customersListBox.Items.Add(row.ContactTitleName);
    }
}
```

This code implements the following intention: "Keep the list box up-to-date by showing the ContactTitleName column from the undeleted rows of the Customers table." But what we'd really like to do is to declare this intention and let some part of WinForms keep a control up-to-date as the underlying data changes. That is the service provided by WinForms *data binding*.

Bindings and Data Sources

At the heart of the data binding architecture is the idea of a binding. A *binding* is an association between a control and a *data source*, which can be any object (although it's often an instance of the DataSet class). For example, binding a data set to a list box requires a binding be established between the list box and the data set. For the list box to be populated with the appropriate data, we must also specify, as part of the binding, the data table and the column name, which is the *data member* portion of the binding. The data member specifies the name of the data to pull from the data source. Figure 13.1 shows a logical binding from a data set to a list box, using the Contact-TitleName from the Customers table as the data member.

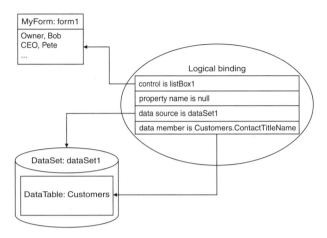

FIGURE 13.1: Complex Data Binding

Figure 13.2 shows the results of establishing this binding.

The kind of binding shown in Figures 13.1 and 13.2 is known as *complex data binding*. The binding is "complex" not because it's hard to use, but because the ListBox control must have specific support for it. Other built-in controls, such as ComboBox and DataGrid, support complex binding, but not all controls do.[1]

FIGURE 13.2: Result of Complex Data Binding

---

1. ListView is an example of a control that you'd expect to support complex binding but doesn't.

On the other hand, *simple data binding* works for all controls. Simple data binding is an association from a data source to a specific property of a control. The property can be nearly any public property that a control exposes, such as Text or BackColor. What makes this binding "simple" is that the control doesn't have to do anything to support simple binding; the data binding infrastructure itself sets the value of a control's bound property.

As an example of simple binding, Figure 13.3 shows binding the Text property of a text box to a data set, using Customers.ContactTitleName as the data member.

Because text boxes can't show lists of data, only one row from the data set can be displayed at a time, as shown in Figure 13.4.

It may not seem useful to be able to see only one row from a data set, but, as you'll see, it's possible to "scroll" through the rows of a data set, allowing a column from each row to be displayed and edited one at a time.

Both of these examples of data binding show binding against a data set, which provides a list of objects to display either all at once (in the case of

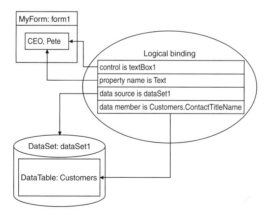

FIGURE 13.3: Simple Data Binding

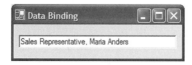

FIGURE 13.4: Simple Data Binding

complex binding) or one at a time (in the case of simple binding). A data set is an example of a *list data source*, because it provides a list of objects against which to bind. Other list data sources include arrays, collections from the System.Collections namespace, and custom collections (more on that later).

However, data binding can also happen against an *item data source*, which is an instance of any type that can queried for values to bind against. For example, Figure 13.5 shows a logical binding from a string object to the Text property of a TextBox control.

Figure 13.6 shows the results of establishing this binding.

When you're using data binding, you need to keep track of both the kind of binding you're doing (simple or complex) and the kind of data source to which you're binding (item or list). Those two factors largely determine how data binding works, as you'll see.

Simple Data Binding to Items

The binding scenario in Figure 13.5 shows the simple binding of a TextBox control to a string item data source. You implement simple binding by creating an instance of a Binding object and adding it to the list of bindings exposed by the control via the DataBindings property:

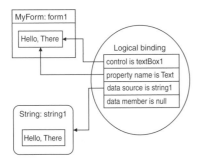

FIGURE 13.5: Simple Data Binding to an Item Data Source

FIGURE 13.6: Simple Binding to a String Object

```
void Form1_Load(object sender, EventArgs e) {
  // Data source
  string stringDataSource = "Hello, There";

  // Binding (without a data member)
  Binding binding = new Binding("Text", stringDataSource, null);

  // Bind the control to the data source
  // Control: textBox1
  // PropertyName: Text
  // DataSource: stringDataSource
  // DataMember: null
  textBox1.DataBindings.Add(binding);
}
```

You create the Binding object by passing the name of the control's property as the first argument, the data source object as the second argument, and the optional name of a data member. Then you add the new binding object to the list of the data bindings of the text box, and that's all that's needed to bind the string object's value to the Text property of the control, as shown earlier in Figure 13.6.

The Binding class, which is used to implement simple binding,[2] is from the System.Windows.Forms namespace:

```
class Binding {
  // Constructors
  public Binding(
    string propertyName, object dataSource, string dataMember);

  // Properties
  public BindingManagerBase BindingManagerBase { get; }
  public BindingMemberInfo BindingMemberInfo { get; }
  public Control Control { get; }
  public object DataSource { get; }
  public bool IsBinding { get; }
  public string PropertyName { get; }
```

---

2. Although simple and complex data binding are logically similar, only simple binding uses instances of the Binding class. The implementation details of complex binding are specific to the control and are hidden from the client of the control, as you'll see later in this chapter.

```
  // Events
  public event ConvertEventHandler Format;
  public event ConvertEventHandler Parse;
}
```

As a shortcut to creating a Binding object and adding it to a control's list of bindings, you can use the overload of the Add method (which takes the three Binding constructor arguments) and let the Add method create the Binding object for you:

```
// Data source
string stringDataSource = "Hello, There";

// Bind the control to the data source,
// letting the Add method create the Binding object
// Control: textBox1
// PropertyName: Text
// DataSource: stringDataSource
// DataMember: null
textBox1.DataBindings.Add("Text", stringDataSource, null);
```

Passing null as the data member parameter means that we can obtain the contents of the data source by calling the string object's ToString method. If you'd like to bind to a specific property of a data source, you can do so by passing the name of the property as the data member of the binding. For example, the following code binds the text box's Text property to the Length property of the string object:

```
// Bind the control to the Length property of the data source
// Control: textBox1
// PropertyName: Text
// DataSource: stringDataSource
// DataMember: Length
textBox1.DataBindings.Add("Text", stringDataSource, "Length");
```

Binding to the Length property of the string instead of binding the string itself works as shown in Figure 13.7.

FIGURE 13.7: Simple Binding to the Length Property of a String Object

Any public property of a data source can serve as a data member. Similarly, any public property of a control can serve as the property for binding. The following shows an example of binding a data source to the Font property of a text box:

```
// Data sources
string stringDataSource = "Hello, There";
Font fontDataSource = new Font("Lucida Console", 18);

// Bind the control properties to the data sources

// Control: textBox1
// PropertyName: Text
// DataSource: stringDataSource
// DataMember: null
textBox1.DataBindings.Add("Text", stringDataSource, null);

// Control: textBox1
// PropertyName: Font
// DataSource: fontDataSource
// DataMember: null
textBox1.DataBindings.Add("Font", fontDataSource, null);
```

Notice that the code provides two different bindings against the same control. A control can have any number of bindings as long as any single property has only one. The results of the combined bindings are shown in Figure 13.8.

Notice also that the data from the data source needs to be a string object for the Text property and needs to be a Font object for the Font property. By providing data sources that expose those types directly, we avoided the need for conversion. If the data being bound to isn't already in the appropriate format, a type converter is used, as discussed in Chapter 9: Design-Time Integration. Type converters are also covered in more detail later in this chapter.

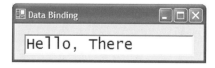

FIGURE 13.8: Binding the Text and Font Properties of a TextBox Control

Simple Data Binding to Lists

You implement simple binding to a list data source without a data member in the same way as binding to an item data source:

```
// Control: textBox1
// PropertyName: Text
// DataSource: listDataSource
// DataMember: null
string[] listDataSource = { "apple", "peach", "pumpkin" };
textBox1.DataBindings.Add("Text", listDataSource, null);
```

When you bind to a list data source, only one item is displayed at a time, as shown in Figure 13.9.

Similarly, you're allowed to bind to a particular property of the objects in the list data source by specifying a data member:

```
// Control: textBox1
// PropertyName: Text
// DataSource: listDataSource
// DataMember: Length
textBox1.DataBindings.Add("Text", listDataSource, "Length");
```

Again, this technique displays only a single item at a time, as shown in Figure 13.10.

Before we look at how to display other items from a list data set using simple binding, let's talk about binding to a data set.

FIGURE 13.9: Simple Data Binding to a List Data Source

FIGURE 13.10: Simple Data Binding to a Property of a List Data Source

Simple Binding to Data Sets

Although arrays and other kinds of list data sources are useful, the most popular list data source is the data set. You can bind to columns in a table from a data set in two ways:

```
// Fill the data set
customersAdapter.Fill(customerSet1, "Customers");
ordersAdapter.Fill(customerSet1, "Orders");

// 1. Bind to data set + table.column (good!)
textBox1.DataBindings.Add(
  "Text", customerSet1, "Customers.ContactTitleName");

// 2. Bind the table + column (BAD!)
textBox1.DataBindings.Add(
  "Text", customerSet1.Customers, "ContactTitleName");
```

Either way you do the binding, what you'll see is shown in Figure 13.11.

Although both techniques of binding to a column seem to display equivalent results, there is an "issue" in .NET 1.x that causes inconsistencies if you mix the two methods. The reason to always use technique 1 (data set + table.column) is that the Designer-generated code uses this technique when you choose a data member in the Property Browser, as shown in Figure 13.12.

The DataBindings property in the Property Browser allows you to add bindings without writing the code manually. When you choose a column from a data set hosted on your form, the generated code will use the data set + table.column technique:

```
void InitializeComponent() {
  ...
  this.textBox1.DataBindings.Add(
    new Binding(
      "Text", this.customerSet1, "Customers.ContactTitleName"));
  ...
}
```

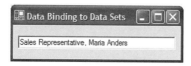

FIGURE 13.11: Simple Binding to a Data Set

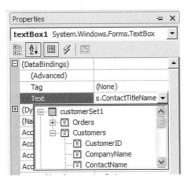

FIGURE 13.12: Adding a Data Binding in the Property Browser

You can feel free to add bindings in custom code or to use the Property Browser, whichever you find more convenient. But if you also use the data set + table.column technique, you'll avoid the inconsistencies caused by data binding support in WinForms 1.x.

So, as convenient as the Property Browser is for generating the binding code for us, it doesn't seem very useful to show only a single value from a list data source. However, when you understand binding managers (discussed next), simple binding to list data sources can be very useful.

Binding Managers

For every bound data source, the infrastructure creates a binding manager for you. *Binding managers* manage a set of bindings for a particular data source and come in two flavors: property managers and currency managers. A *property manager* is an instance of the PropertyManager class and is created for an item data source. A *currency manager* is an instance of the CurrencyManager class and is created for a list data source. Both of these managers are implementations of the abstract base class BindingManager-Base:

```
abstract class BindingManagerBase {
  // Constructors
  public BindingManagerBase();

  // Properties
  public BindingsCollection Bindings { get; }
  public int Count { virtual get; }
  public object Current { virtual get; }
```

```
public int Position { virtual get; virtual set; }

// Events
public event EventHandler CurrentChanged;
public event EventHandler PositionChanged;

// Methods
public virtual void AddNew();
public virtual void CancelCurrentEdit();
public virtual void EndCurrentEdit();
public virtual void RemoveAt(int index);
public virtual void ResumeBinding();
public virtual void SuspendBinding();
}
```

It's the job of the binding manager—whether it's a property binding manager or a currency binding manager—to keep track of all the bindings between all the controls bound to the same data source. For example, it's the binding manager's job (through the bindings) to keep all the controls up-to-date when the underlying data source changes and vice versa. To access a data source's binding manager, you can retrieve a binding for a bound property and get the binding manager from the binding's Binding-ManagerBase property:

```
void positionButton_Click(object sender, EventArgs e) {
  // Get the binding
  Binding binding = textBox1.DataBindings["Text"];

  // Get the binding manager
  BindingManagerBase manager = binding.BindingManagerBase;

  // Get current position
  int pos = manager.Position;
  MessageBox.Show(pos.ToString(), "Current Position");
}
```

Notice that after the binding manager is retrieved, the code checks the current position. This is known as the binding manager's *currency*, which is the current position in its list of items. Figure 13.13 shows how a currency manager maintains the position into a list data source.

Although only a currency manager manages an actual list, for simplicity the position is pushed into the base binding manager for both the currency manager and the property manager. This allows easy access to the

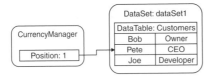

FIGURE 13.13: A Currency Manager Maintaining a Position into a List Data Source

current position for both kinds of binding managers through the Binding-ManagerBase class. For a property manager, which manages the data source of only a single object, the position will always be zero, as shown in Figure 13.14.

For a currency manager, the position can be changed, and that will update all the bindings to a new "current" object in a list data source. This arrangement allows you to build controls that let your users "scroll" through a list data source, even when you're using simple binding, as shown in Figure 13.15.

The following code shows how to implement the list data source navigation buttons using the BindingManagerBase Position property:

```
void CurrencyForm_Load(object sender, EventArgs e) {
  Binding binding = textBox1.DataBindings["Text"];
```

continues

FIGURE 13.14: A Property Manager Managers Only a Single Item

FIGURE 13.15: Managing Currency

```csharp
  // Fill the data set
  customersAdapter.Fill(customerSet1, "Customers");
}

void positionButton_Click(object sender, EventArgs e) {
  Binding binding = textBox1.DataBindings["Text"];
  BindingManagerBase manager = binding.BindingManagerBase;

  // Get current position
  int pos = manager.Position;
  MessageBox.Show(pos.ToString(), "Current Position");
}

void startButton_Click(object sender, EventArgs e) {
  // Reset the position
  Binding binding = textBox1.DataBindings["Text"];
  BindingManagerBase manager = binding.BindingManagerBase;
  manager.Position = 0;
}

void previousButton_Click(object sender, EventArgs e) {
  // Decrement the position
  Binding binding = textBox1.DataBindings["Text"];
  BindingManagerBase manager = binding.BindingManagerBase;
  --manager.Position; // No need to worry about being <0
}

void nextButton_Click(object sender, EventArgs e) {
  // Increment the position
  Binding binding = textBox1.DataBindings["Text"];
  BindingManagerBase manager = binding.BindingManagerBase;
  ++manager.Position; // No need to worry about being >Count
}

void endButton_Click(object sender, EventArgs e) {
  // Set position to end
  Binding binding = textBox1.DataBindings["Text"];
  BindingManagerBase manager = binding.BindingManagerBase;
  manager.Position = manager.Count - 1;
}
```

Taking this a step further, Figure 13.16 shows two text boxes bound to the same data source but in two different columns.

After the binding is in place for both controls, changing the position on the binding context for one will automatically affect the other. Figure 13.17 shows the currency manager and the logical bindings for the two text controls.

FIGURE 13.16: Two Controls Bound to the Same Data Source

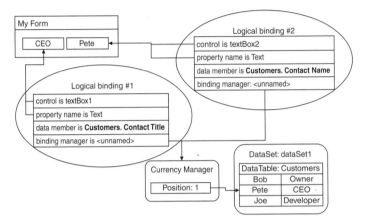

FIGURE 13.17: Two Controls Bound to the Same Data Source Sharing the Same Currency Manager

Establishing the bindings for the two text boxes works as you'd expect:

```
void InitializeComponent() {
  ...
  this.textBox1.DataBindings.Add(
    new Binding(
      "Text", this.customerSet1, "Customers.ContactTitle"));
  ...
  this.textBox2.DataBindings.Add(
    new Binding(
      "Text", this.customerSet1, "Customers.ContactName"));
  ...
}
```

A binding manager is per data source,[3] not per binding. This means that when the same data set and data table are used, the two text boxes get routed through the same currency manager to the same data source. As the currency manager's position changes, all the controls bound through the same currency manager get updated appropriately.

Because all controls bound against the same data source share access to the same binding manager, getting the binding manager from either control yields the same binding manager:

```
// Check the binding manager
BindingManagerBase manager1 =
  textBox1.DataBindings["Text"].BindingManagerBase;
BindingManagerBase manager2 =
  textBox2.DataBindings["Text"].BindingManagerBase;

// Assert that these controls are bound to the
// same data source
System.Diagnostics.Debug.Assert(manager1 == manager2);
```

In fact, the binding managers are shared at the container level, so you can go to the containing form's BindingContext collection to get the binding manager:

```
BindingManagerBase manager =
  this.BindingContext[customerSet1, "Customers"]; // 1: good!
```

Access to the binding manager from the BindingContext property is another place where there's an overload that can take a data set and a table name or only a table:

```
BindingManagerBase manager =
  this.BindingContext[customerSet1.Customers]; // 2: BAD!
```

This is another case of technique 1 versus technique 2 for specifying the data source. If you use technique 1, all the binding managers will be shared as planned, keeping everything in sync. However, *if you use technique 2, you'll get back a different binding manager, and this means that things won't be in sync when you manipulate the binding manager.* This is the issue that data binding has in .NET 1.x, and you'd be wise to avoid it by always sticking to technique 1.

---

3. Technically, a binding manager is unique per data source only within a *binding context*, which holds groups of binding managers. Every control can have its own binding context, and that allows two controls in the same container to show the same data source but different currencies. Although it's interesting, the need for multiple binding contexts is rare and not explored further in this book.

Current Data Row

The Position property is fine when it comes to navigating the rows currently shown, but it's not good for finding the current row in a data table. The problem is that as soon as items are marked as deleted in the underlying data table, they're automatically hidden from view by the binding infrastructure (just what we want to have happen). However, deleted rows are still there at exactly the same offset, and this means that the offsets will be mismatched between the underlying data table and the binding manager, which "counts" rows that haven't been deleted.

Luckily, the BindingManagerBase class provides a Current property, which always provides access to the current row in the data table regardless of the mismatch between the offsets:

```
void showButton_Click(object sender, EventArgs e) {
  // Get the binding manager
  BindingManagerBase manager =
    this.BindingContext[customerSet1, "Customers"];

  // Get the current row via the view
  DataRowView view = (DataRowView)manager.Current;
  CustomerSet.CustomersRow row =
    (CustomerSet.CustomersRow)view.Row;

  MessageBox.Show(row.ContactTitleName);
}
```

BindingManagerBase's Current property is of type Object, so it must be cast to a specific type. Normally, that type will be the type you'd expect when you set up the binding. For example, when you bind to a string, the Current property will return an object of type string. However, in the case of DataSets, the DataTable data source exposes DataRowView objects instead of DataRow objects (to tailor the view of a row when it's displayed). You'll learn more about DataRowView later in this chapter, but the trick is to get the current row from the Row property of the current DataRowView.

Changes to the Data Set

Adding data to the underlying data works in pretty much the same way it did before we started using data binding:

```
void addButton_Click(object sender, EventArgs e) {
  // Add a new row
  CustomerSet.CustomersRow row =
    this.customerSet1.Customers.NewCustomersRow();
  row.CustomerID = "SELLSB";
  ...
  this.customerSet1.Customers.AddCustomersRow(row);

  // Controls automatically updated
  // (except some controls, e.g. ListBox, need a nudge)

  // NOTE: Use C# "as" cast to ask if the binding
  //       manager is a currency manager. If the
  //       result of the "as" cast is null, then
  //       we've got a property manager, which
  //       doesn't have a Refresh method
  CurrencyManager manager =
    this.BindingContext[customerSet1, "Customers"]
    as CurrencyManager;
  if( manager != null ) manager.Refresh();
}
```

Adding a new row to the data set causes most controls to be updated, except for some complex bound controls like the ListBox. For those cases, we cast the BindingManagerBase class to a CurrencyManager to be able to call the CurrencyManager-specific Refresh method, which will bring those pesky list boxes up to speed on the new row.

As far as updates and deletes go, make sure to use the Binding-ManagerBase class's Current property instead of the Position property to get the current row. Otherwise, you could access the wrong row:

```
void updateButton_Click(object sender, EventArgs e) {
  // Update the current row
  BindingManagerBase manager =
    this.BindingContext[customerSet1, "Customers"];
  DataRowView view = (DataRowView)manager.Current;
  CustomerSet.CustomersRow row =
    (CustomerSet.CustomersRow)view.Row;
  row.ContactTitle = "CEO";

  // Controls automatically updated
}

void deleteButton_Click(object sender, EventArgs e) {
  // Mark the current row as deleted
  BindingManagerBase manager =
```

```
  this.BindingContext[customerSet1, "Customers"];
 DataRowView view = (DataRowView)manager.Current;
 CustomerSet.CustomersRow row =
   (CustomerSet.CustomersRow)view.Row;
 row.Delete();

 // Controls automatically updated
 // (no special treatment needed to avoid deleted rows!)
}
```

Notice that no code is needed to update the controls to take into account updated or deleted rows. *This is the power of data binding.* When the underlying data source is updated, we don't want to be forced to update the related controls manually. Instead, we bind them and let that happen automatically.[4]

Replacing the Data Set

Sometimes, after all the data bindings are established, it's necessary to replace a data set with a different data set. For example, if you're calling into a Web service that produces a DataSet as the return type, you might find yourself writing code like this:

```
DataSet newDataSet = myWebService.GetDataSet();
this.dataSet1 = newDataSet; // Data bindings lost
```

Unfortunately, when you replace the existing data set with a new one, all the data bindings remain with the old data set. As a shortcut, instead of manually moving all the data bindings to the new data set, you can use the Merge method of the DataSet class to bring the data from the new data set into the existing one:

```
DataSet newDataSet = myWebService.GetDataSet();
this.dataSet1.Clear();
this.dataSet1.Merge(newDataSet); // Data bindings kept
```

The trick here is that all the data bindings continue to be bound to the existing data set, but the data from the existing data set is cleared and

---

4. Not all data sources are as good about keeping the bound controls up-to-date as the DataSet-related data sources are. For the requirements of a good custom data source, see the "Custom Data Sources" section later in this chapter.

replaced with the data from the new data set. For this to work, all the schema information in the new data set, such as the names of the columns, must match the schema information that the bindings are using. Otherwise, you'll get run-time exceptions.

As an optimization when merging data sets, you'll want to temporarily turn off data binding so that you don't have to update all the bound controls after when the data set is cleared and again when the new data is merged:

```
DataSet newDataSet = myWebService.GetDataSet();
BindingManagerBase manager =
   this.BindingContext[dataSet1, "Customers"];
manager.SuspendBinding();
this.dataSet1.Clear();
this.dataSet1.Merge(newDataSet); // Data bindings kept
manager.ResumeBinding();
```

To turn off the updates that bindings cause as the data set is updated, we suspend the binding by using a call to the binding manager's Suspend-Binding method. Then, after we clear and merge the data set, to resume updates to the bound controls we resume the binding with the call to ResumeBinding. Temporarily suspending bindings isn't for use only with data sets; it's useful whenever the controls shouldn't be updated until a set of operations on the underlying data source has been performed.

Changes to the Control

Keeping the controls updated when the data source changes is half the story of data binding. The other half is keeping the underlying data source up-to-date as the data in the controls changes. By default, any change in the control's data will be replicated when the position within the currency manager is changed. For example, in Figure 13.18, even though the data in the TextBox has changed, the underlying row (as shown in the message box) has not, in spite of the change in focus that occurs when you move to the Show button.

The reason that the text box hasn't pushed the new data to the current row is that the *current edit* hasn't yet ended. When data in a control changes, that represents an "edit" of the data. Only when the current edit has ended does the data get replicated to the underlying data source. If you

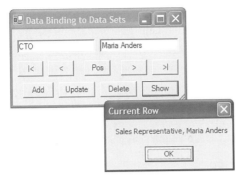

FIGURE 13.18: Losing Focus Does Not Trigger an End to the Edit

don't like waiting for the currency to change before the current edit takes effect, you can push it through yourself using the EndCurrentEdit method of the BindingManagerBase:

```
void textBox1_Leave(object sender, EventArgs e) {
  // Force the current edit to end
  BindingManagerBase manager =
    this.BindingContext[customerSet1, "Customers"];
  manager.EndCurrentEdit();
}
```

This causes the control whose data is being edited to flush it to the underlying data source immediately. If, on the other hand, you'd like to replace the dirty data with the data currently in the data source, you can use CancelCurrentEdit instead:

```
// Cancel the current edit
BindingManagerBase manager =
  this.BindingContext[customerSet1, "Customers"];
manager.CancelCurrentEdit();
```

Custom Formatting and Parsing

Sometimes the data as shown in the control is already formatted automatically the way you would like to see it. However, if you'd like to change the formatting, you can do so by handling the Format event of the Binding object:

```
void CurrencyForm_Load(object sender, EventArgs e) {
```

continues

```
  // Custom-format the ContactTitle
  // NOTE: subscribe to this before filling the data set
  Binding binding = textBox1.DataBindings["Text"];
  binding.Format += new ConvertEventHandler(textBox1_Format);

  // Fill the data set
  ...
}


void textBox1_Format(object sender, ConvertEventArgs e) {
  // Show ContactTitle as all caps
  e.Value = e.Value.ToString().ToUpper();
}
```

The Format event handler gets a ConvertEventArgs parameter:

```
class ConvertEventArgs : EventArgs {
  // Constructors
  public ConvertEventArgs(object value, Type desiredType);

  // Properties
  public Type DesiredType { get; }
  public object Value { get; set; }
}
```

The Value property of the ConvertEventArgs class is the unconverted value that will be shown if you don't change it. It's your job to convert the current Value property (which will be of the same type as the underlying data) to a value of the DesiredType (string), formatting it as you please.

If you are binding to a read-only property, this is all that is involved in getting what you need. If you expect the data to be pushed back to the data source, you should also trap the Parse event of the binding. This allows you to undo the formatting as the data is replicated from the control back to the data source:

```
void CurrencyForm_Load(object sender, EventArgs e) {
  // Custom-format and parse the ContactTitle
  // NOTE: subscribe to these before filling the data set
  Binding binding = textBox1.DataBindings["Text"];
  binding.Format += new ConvertEventHandler(textBox1_Format);
  binding.Parse += new ConvertEventHandler(textBox1_Parse);

  // Fill the data set
  ...
}
```

```
void textBox1_Parse(object sender, ConvertEventArgs e) {
  // Convert ContactTitle to mixed case
  e.Value = MixedCase(e.Value.ToString());
}
```

Parsing is the opposite of formatting. The type of Value will be string, and DesiredType will be the type needed for the underlying data source. Value will start as the data from the control, and it's your job to convert it.

Complex Data Binding

Complex binding and simple binding are more alike than not. All the considerations discussed so far about using binding managers and keeping the control and data source in sync apply equally well to complex binding as they do to simple binding.

However, unlike simple binding, a control that supports complex binding must do so in a custom fashion. It does so by exposing a custom property to specify a data source (typically called DataSource) and zero or more properties for specifying data members. For example, the list control family of controls—ListBox, CheckedListBox, and ComboBox—exposes the following properties to support complex data binding:

- **DataSource.** This takes a list data source that implements IList or IListSource.[5] This includes arrays, ArrayList data tables, and any custom type that supports one of these interfaces.
- **DisplayMember.** This is the name of the property from the data source that the list control will display (defaults to ValueMember, if that's set, or ToString otherwise).
- **ValueMember.** This is the name of the property from the data source that the list control will use as the value of the SelectedValue property (defaults to the currently selected item).
- **SelectedValue.** This is the value of the ValueMember property for the currently selected item.

---

5. The implementation of the IListSource interface is what allows a DataTable to expose multiple DataRowView objects as data sources.

- **SelectedItem.** This is the currently selected item from the list data source.

- **SelectedItems.** This is the currently selected items for a multiselect list control.

For the list controls, you must set at least the DataSource and the DisplayMember:

```
this.listBox1.DataSource = this.customerSet1;
this.listBox1.DisplayMember = "Customers.ContactTitleName";
```

This is another case of remembering to set the data source to the data set and to set the display member (and value member) to table.column. Otherwise, you can end up with mismatched binding managers. Remembering to make these settings is especially important because, unlike simple binding, complex binding using technique 2 is allowed in the Property Browser, as shown in Figure 13.19.

Instead, make sure that you pick a data set for the DataSource property and pick a table.column for the DisplayMember and ValueMember properties, as shown in Figure 13.20.

FIGURE 13.19: Don't Use the dataset.table + Column Technique to Specify the Data Source

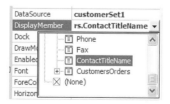

FIGURE 13.20: Use the Dataset + table.column Technique to Specify a Data Source

After you've set the data source and the display member, you'll get an automatically populated list control, just as we've been pining for since this chapter began (and as shown in Figure 13.21).

In addition to a nicely filled list box, notice that Figure 13.21 shows the data for the same row in both of the text boxes as in the currently selected list box item. As the list box selection changes, the position is updated for the shared currency manager. Using the VCR-style buttons would likewise change the position and update the list box's selection accordingly.

Also, notice that the status bar is updated with the CustomerID of the current row as the position changes. You do this using the SelectedItem property of the list control, which exposes the currently selected item:

```
void listBox1_SelectedIndexChanged(object sender, EventArgs e) {
  if( listBox1.SelectedValue == null ) return;

  // Get the currently selected row's CustomerID using current item
  DataRowView view = (DataRowView)listBox1.SelectedItem;
  CustomerSet.CustomersRow row = (CustomerSet.CustomersRow)view.Row;
  statusBar1.Text = "Selected CustomerID= " + row.CustomerID;
}
```

As a convenience, you can set the ValueMember property to designate a property as the value of the selected row. This is useful for primary keys when you want to know what was selected without knowing any of the

FIGURE 13.21: Using Data Binding to Populate a List Control

other details. Using the ValueMember property, you can directly extract the ID of the currently selected row:

```
void InitializeComponent() {
  ...
  this.listBox1.ValueMember = "Customers.CustomerID";
  ...
}

void listBox1_SelectedIndexChanged(object sender, EventArgs e) {
  if( listBox1.SelectedValue == null ) return;

  // Get the currently selected row's CustomerID
  statusBar1.Text = "Selected CustomerID= " + listBox1.SelectedValue;
}
```

Data Views

So far we've discussed how to show specific data members, such as specific columns, from a data source. However, it's also useful to filter which rows from a data table are shown as well as to sort the rows. This kind of functionality is provided by a *data view*, which allows you to transform a data table as it's being displayed in ways that the Format and Parse events can't.

Sorting

You can sort on any number of columns in either ascending or descending order. Setting the sort criteria is a matter of creating an instance of the Data-View class, setting the Sort property, and then binding to the view as the data source:

```
void CurrencyForm_Load(object sender, EventArgs e) {
  // Create a sorting view
  DataView sortView = new DataView(customerSet1.Customers);
  sortView.Sort = "ContactTitle ASC, ContactName DESC";

  // Bind to the view
  listBox1.DataSource = sortView;
  listBox1.DisplayMember = "ContactTitleName";

  // Fill the data set
  ...
}
```

Notice that the DataView object takes a DataTable argument so that it knows where to get its data. Notice also the ASC (default) and DESC designators, which indicate ascending and descending sort order, respectively. Binding to the sorted view of our customers table yields Figure 13.22.

Filtering

Similarly, filtering is a matter of creating an instance of the DataView class, setting the RowFilter property, and binding to the view:

```
void CurrencyForm_Load(object sender, EventArgs e) {
  // Create a filtering view
  DataView filterView = new DataView(customerSet1.Customers);
  filterView.RowFilter = "ContactTitle = 'Owner'";

  // Bind to the view
  listBox1.DataSource = filterView;
  listBox1.DisplayMember = "ContactTitleName";

  // Fill the data set
  ...
}
```

Binding to this view of our customers data table shows only rows where the ContactTitle column has the value of "Owner," as shown in Figure 13.23.

FIGURE 13.22: Binding to a Sort View

FIGURE 13.23: Binding to a Filtered View

The expression language used for filtering is a subset of SQL. You can find a link to the documentation in the description of the DataView class's RowFilter property.

Master-Detail Relations

While we're on the subject of filtering, one of the most popular ways to filter what's shown in one control is based on the current selection in another control. For example, when a customer is selected in the top list box of Figure 13.24, the bottom list box shows only the related orders for that customer.

Recall from Chapter 12: Data Sets and Designer Support that we implemented this functionality by repopulating the orders list box whenever the

FIGURE 13.24: Master-Detail Relations

selection in the customers list box changed. The order list box populating code uses a relation to get the child order rows from the currently selected parent customer row:

```
// Get references to the tables
DataTable customers = dataset.Tables["Customers"];
DataTable orders = dataset.Tables["Orders"];

// Create the relation
DataRelation relation =
  new DataRelation(
    "CustomersOrders",
    customers.Columns["CustomerID"],
    orders.Columns["CustomerID"]);

// Add the relation
dataset.Relations.Add(relation);
...

void PopulateChildListBox() {
  // Clear the list box
  ordersListBox.Items.Clear();

  // Get the currently selected parent custom row
  int index = customersListBox.SelectedIndex;
  if( index == -1 ) return;

  // Get row from data set
  DataRow parent = dataset.Tables["Customers"].Rows[index];

  // Enumerate child rows
  foreach( DataRow row in parent.GetChildRows("CustomersOrders") ) {
    ...
  }
}
```

Instead of our writing this code by hand, data binding allows us to bind to a relation. Then as the selection changes in the parent control, the child control is automatically populated with only the related child rows. The format for specifying the data member for a relation is the following:

```
parentTable.relationName.childColumn
```

Specifying a parent-child relationship in this manner allows us to use a binding to display master-detail data.

```
void InitializeComponent() {
  ...
  this.ordersListBox.DisplayMember =
    "Customers.CustomersOrders.OrderID";
  ...
}
```

When we use a typed data set to establish a relation, the Property Browser provides a list of possible relation bindings, as shown in Figure 13.25.

In addition, you aren't limited to a single level of master-detail binding. You can have any number of relations from parent to child to grandchild, and so on.

The combination of VS.NET design-time features, typed data sets, and data binding has reduced the amount of handwritten code in the sample shown in Figure 13.24 to the following:

```
void MasterDetailForm_Load(object sender, EventArgs e) {
  // Fill the data set
  customersAdapter.Fill(customerSet1, "Customers");
  ordersAdapter.Fill(customerSet1, "Orders");
}

void addRowMenuItem_Click(object sender, EventArgs e) {
  // Add a new typed row
  CustomerSet.CustomersRow row =
    this.customerSet1.Customers.NewCustomersRow();
  row.CustomerID = "SELLSB";
  ...
  this.customerSet1.Customers.AddCustomersRow(row);

  // Controls automatically updated
  // (except some controls, e.g. ListBox, need a nudge)
  CurrencyManager manager =
```

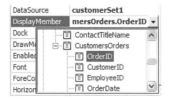

FIGURE 13.25: Composing a Data Member from a Relation in the Property Browser

```
      this.BindingContext[customerSet1, "Customers"]
      as CurrencyManager;
   if( manager != null ) manager.Refresh();
}

void updateSelectedRowMenuItem_Click(object sender, EventArgs e) {
   // Update the current row
   BindingManagerBase manager =
      this.BindingContext[customerSet1, "Customers"];
   DataRowView view = (DataRowView)manager.Current;
   CustomerSet.CustomersRow row = (CustomerSet.CustomersRow)view.Row;
   row.ContactTitle = "CEO";
}

void deleteSelectedRowMenuItem_Click(object sender, EventArgs e) {
   // Mark the current row as deleted
   BindingManagerBase manager =
      this.BindingContext[customerSet1, "Customers"];
   DataRowView view = (DataRowView)manager.Current;
   CustomerSet.CustomersRow row = (CustomerSet.CustomersRow)view.Row;
   row.Delete();
}
```

The rest, including keeping both list boxes up-to-date as the underlying data changes and synchronizing the orders list box based on the selection in the customers list box, is all written for us.

Data Grids

Although the preceding sample relies heavily on .NET and VS.NET data features to reduce our coding, the list controls can take us only so far toward data-centric application nirvana. For example, the list box supports the display only of a single column from the underlying data set and provides no built-in UI for adding, editing, or deleting rows. For those features and a boatload of others, we've got the *data grid*.

The DataGrid control supports complex binding to list data sources. However, it does it a lot more thoroughly than do the list controls discussed so far. For one thing, a data grid can show all the columns, as shown in Figure 13.26.

Binding a data source to the DataGrid control requires setting the Data-Source and DataMember properties (again, watch out for setting more than just the data set in the DataSource property):

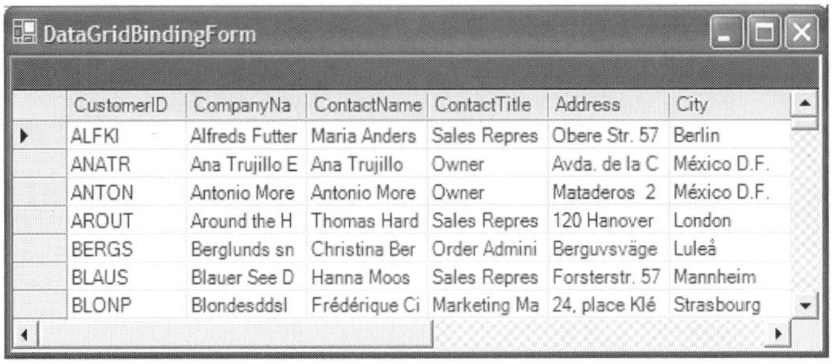

FIGURE 13.26: Binding to a DataGrid

```
void InitializeComponent() {
    ...
    this.dataGrid1.DataMember = "Customers";
    this.dataGrid1.DataSource = this.customerSet1;
    ...
}
```

The data grid supports showing not only multiple columns but also multiple tables. If you change your data set to include multiple tables and relationships between the tables, your grid will look like the one in Figure 13.27.

When you click on the small plus sign on the grid, you can see links to all the relations, as shown in Figure 13.28.

Clicking on the link brings you the related rows, shown in Figure 13.29.

You can now see and navigate through the child rows of that relationship. As a convenience, the data grid also shows a history of the parent rows that you have navigated from.

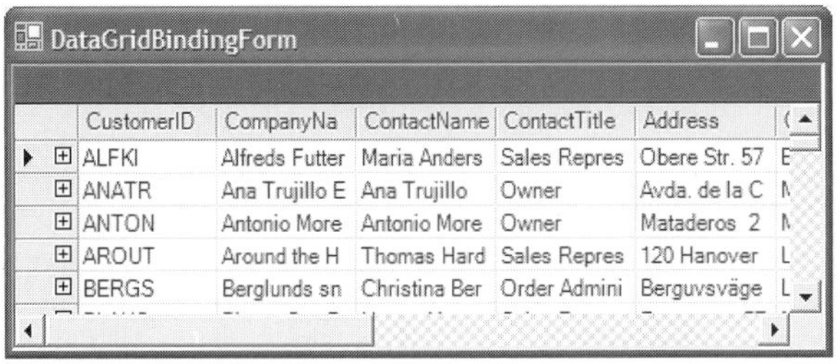

FIGURE 13.27: Showing 3-D Data in a Data Grid

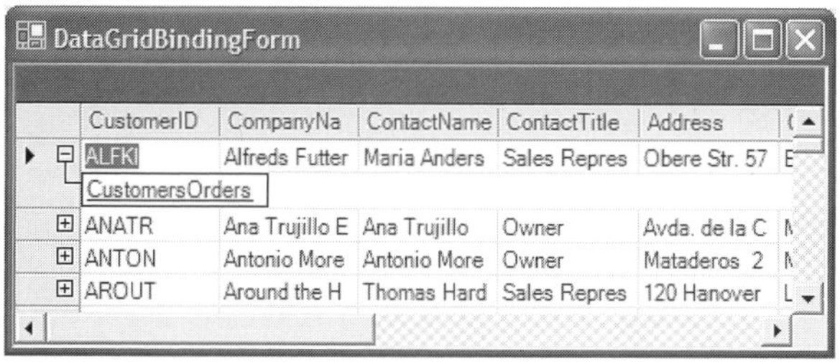

FIGURE 13.28: Showing Relations

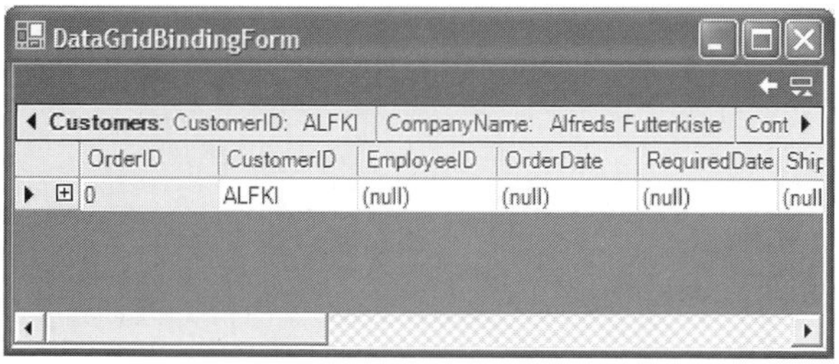

FIGURE 13.29: Drilling Through Relations

Formatting Data Grids

In spite of the ability a data grid gives you to drill down into relations, the default layout of the data grid is not very useful. For example, we don't really want to show primary key identifiers to normal humans. The way to control the look and feel of the data grid is to use data grid table styles.

Data grid table styles (or just *styles*) allow you to control which specific columns are shown, as well as column alignment, width, and header text and things like colors and fonts. Like most other things in .NET, styles are available via an object model, but the model is sufficiently complicated that I want to break with tradition and introduce you directly to DataGrid-TableStyle Collection Editor, available from the TableStyles property of the Property Browser.[6]

---

6. If you feel the need to learn the data grid styles object model at the code level, I suggest starting with the code generated by the style editor, if for no other reason than it makes a wonderful data grid table styles macro editor.

Using the style editor, you'll want to create a set of styles for each data table in the grid, as shown in Figure 13.30.

For each table style, you set the MappingName property, choosing the name of the data table to which to apply the styles.

By default, a new table style has no columns at all. To add columns, bring up DataGridColumnStyle Collection Editor using the GridColumn-Style property for each table. The column style editor is shown in Figure 13.31 with a few columns added.

Again, when you add a column, you specify the MappingName, this time choosing the column name. You'll probably also want to specify header text, or else the column will be blank. Width and alignment are other things you'll want to consider. Figure 13.32 shows an example of a data grid after some table and grid styles have been built.

If you'd like something even fancier, you can format a data grid using the various color- and font-related properties on the data grid object itself. Or, if you don't want to spend the afternoon getting those settings just right, you can click the Auto Format link in the lower-right corner of the

FIGURE 13.30: DataGridTableStyle Collection Editor

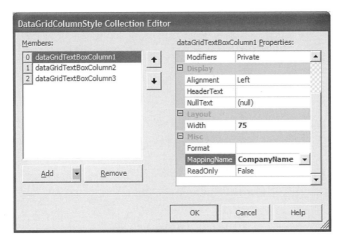

FIGURE 13.31: DataGridColumnStyle Collection Editor with Added Columns

FIGURE 13.32: A Stylish Data Grid

the Property Browser for a data grid. This opens the Auto Format dialog, where you can choose from an assortment of prefabricated formats, as shown in Figure 13.33.

Now, instead of spending the afternoon tweaking individual data grid properties, you can spend the afternoon choosing among the prepackaged sets of data grid properties. Or, if you'd like to return to the minimalist view, you can choose the Default format, which resets the data grid style properties to the defaults.

Data Exchange and Data Grids

Unlike the list controls, the data grid provides direct support for adding, updating, and deleting rows in the underlying data source. If you don't plan to replicate the data back to a data source (as discussed in Chapter 12:

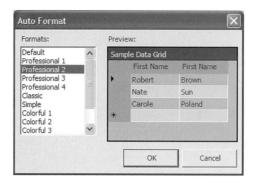

FIGURE 13.33: The Data Grid Auto Format Dialog (See Plate 24)

Data Sets and Designer Support), you may want to set the ReadOnly property of the data grid to true (it defaults to false). This will remove the capability to update the data.

Bringing It All Together

Figure 13.34 is an example of the kind of form you can produce using typed data sets, relations, expressions, the VS.NET data integration, master-detail, data binding, and data grids.

All the controls in this example bind to the same data source (customerSet1.Customers). Because they all use the same data source, the VCR navigation buttons (upper right) move the currency for all the data bound controls simultaneously. Also, this example uses two master-detail bindings to allow you to show the orders for the current customer and the order details for the current order. With data binding, the amount of code you will need to write to get this kind of core functionality working is minimal:

```
void FullDataGridsForm_Load(object sender, EventArgs e) {
  sqlDataAdapter1.Fill(customerSet1);
}

void button1_Click(object sender, EventArgs e) {
  BindingContext[customerSet1, "Customers"].Position = 0;
}

void button2_Click(object sender, EventArgs e) {
  --BindingContext[customerSet1, "Customers"].Position;
}
```

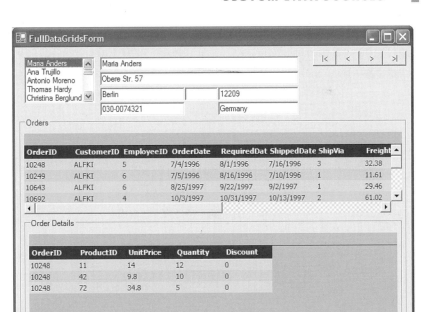

FIGURE 13.34: An Example of What WinForms Provides for Data Programmers (See Plate 25)

```
void button3_Click(object sender, EventArgs e) {
  ++BindingContext[customerSet1, "Customers"].Position;
}

void button4_Click(object sender, EventArgs e) {
  BindingContext[customerSet1, "Customers"].Position =
    BindingContext[customerSet1, "Customers"].Count - 1;
}
```

Of course, there's a whole lot more code behind Figure 13.34 than only these few lines, but the bulk of it is generated for you by VS.NET and provided by the WinForms data binding infrastructure. That, after all, is the whole point of data binding in the first place.

Custom Data Sources

Although the data set is a popular data source, it's by no means the only one. Any custom type can be a data source.

Custom Item Data Sources

The requirements of an item data source are only that it expose one or more public properties:

```
// Expose two properties for binding
class NameAndNumber {
  public string Name {
    get { return name; }
    set { name = value; }
  }

  public int Number {
    get { return number; }
    set { number = value; }
  }

  string name = "Chris";
  int number = 452;
}

NameAndNumber source = new NameAndNumber();

void CustomItemDataSourceForm_Load(object sender, EventArgs e) {
  // Bind to public properties
  textBox1.DataBindings.Add("Text", source, "Name");
  textBox2.DataBindings.Add("Text", source, "Number");
}
```

In this case, we've created a simple class that exposes two public properties and binds each of them to the Text property of two text boxes, as shown in Figure 13.35.

The binding works just as it did when we implemented binding against columns in a table. Changes in the bound control will be used to set the value of read/write properties on the object. However, by default, the binding doesn't work the other way; changes to the data source object won't automatically be reflected to the bound controls. Enabling that requires the

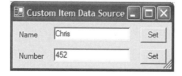

FIGURE 13.35: Binding to a Custom Item Data Source

data source to expose and fire an event of type EventHandler to which the binding can subscribe. Each property that must notify a bound control of a change must expose an event using the following naming convention:

```
public event EventHandler <propertyName>Changed;
```

When firing, the data source object passes itself as the sender of the event:

```
class NameAndNumber {

  // For bound controls
  public event EventHandler NameChanged;
  public string Name {
    get { return name; }
    set {
      name = value;
      // Notify bound control of changes
      if( NameChanged != null ) NameChanged(this, EventArgs.Empty);
    }
  }
  ...
}
```

Now, when the data source object's properties are changed, bound controls are automatically updated:

```
void setNameButton_Click(object sender, EventArgs e) {
  // Changes replicated to textBox1.Text
  source.Name = "Joe";
}
```

Type Descriptors and Data Binding

The information that the property manager uses to determine the list of properties that can be used for binding is provided by the TypeDescriptor class from the System.ComponentModel namespace. The TypeDescriptor class uses .NET Reflection[7] to gather information about an object's properties. However, before falling back on Reflection, the TypeDescriptor class first calls the GetProperties methods of the ICustomTypeDescriptor

---

7. For a discussion of .NET Reflection, see *Essential .NET* (Addison-Wesley, 2003), by Don Box, with Chris Sells.

interface to ask the object for a list of properties. The list of Property-Descriptor objects returned from this method can expose a custom set of properties or no properties at all:

```
class NameAndNumber : ICustomTypeDescriptor {
  public PropertyDescriptorCollection GetProperties(...) {
    // Expose no properties for run-time binding
    return new PropertyDescriptorCollection(null);
  }
  ...
}
```

For example, this implementation of GetProperties causes any call to the AddBinding method on our custom data source to fail at run time, because the list of properties exposed from the class is empty. Exposing a subset of properties for binding requires passing an array of objects of a custom type that derives from the PropertyDescriptor base class.[8] If you're willing to go that far, you can use the same technique to build properties at run time out of whole cloth from external data. This is how DataRowView exposes columns on tables for binding that it doesn't know about until run-time.

Type Conversion

Notice that our custom data source class uses simple types that are easy to convert to and from strings. That's important because the Text property of a control is a string.

However, you don't always want to bind simple types to string properties. For example, you may need to bind to a custom data type from a property instead of binding to a simple type. For that to work, the data must be convertible not only to a string but also back from a string to the custom data type. Otherwise, the changes that the user makes to the bound control will be lost. For example, consider beefing up the sample code to expose a custom type as the value to one of the properties being bound to:

```
class Fraction {
  public Fraction(int numerator, int denominator) {
    this.numerator = numerator;
```

---

8. Unfortunately, .NET provides no public, creatable classes that derive from Property-Descriptor, but TypeConverter.SimplePropertyDescriptor is a start.

```
    this.denominator = denominator;
  }

  public int Numerator {
    get { return this.numerator; }
    set { this.numerator = value; }
  }

  public int Denominator {
    get { return this.denominator; }
    set { this.denominator = value; }
  }

  int numerator;
  int denominator;
}

class NameAndNumber {
  ...
  // Expose a custom type from a bound property
  public event EventHandler NumberChanged;
  public Fraction Number {
    get { return number; }
    set {
      number = value;
      // Notify bound control of changes
      if( NumberChanged != null ) NumberChanged(this, EventArgs.Empty);
    }
  }

  string name = "Chris";
  Fraction number = new Fraction(452, 1);
}

NameAndNumber source = new NameAndNumber();

void CustomItemDataSourceForm_Load(object sender, EventArgs e) {
  // Bind to a custom type
  textBox2.DataBindings.Add("Text", source, "Number");
}
```

By default, this binding will show the name of the type instead of any meaningful value, as shown in Figure 13.36.

To get the string value to be set as the Text property, the binding falls back on the ToString method of the custom Fraction class, which defaults to the Object base class's implementation of returning the name of the type. Overriding the ToString method of the Fraction class solves the display problem (as shown in Figure 13.37):

FIGURE 13.36: Binding to a Custom Item Data Source without a Conversion to String

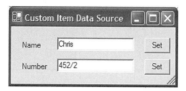

FIGURE 13.37: Binding to a Custom Item Data Source with a Conversion to String

```
class Fraction {
  ...
  public override string ToString() {
    return string.Format("{0}/{1}", numerator, denominator);
  }
}
```

However, implementing ToString fixes only half of the conversion problem. The other half is taking the value that the user enters and putting it back into the property. There is no method to override in the Fraction class that will allow that. Instead, you'll need a type converter.

As discussed in Chapter 9: Design-Time Integration, a type converter is a class that derives from the TypeConverter class in the System. ComponentModel namespace. Specifically, the virtual methods that you must override when converting between types are the CanConvertFrom and CanConvertTo methods and the ConvertFrom and ConvertTo methods. This is an example of a type converter that knows how to convert between our custom Fraction type and the string type:

```
class FractionTypeConverter : TypeConverter {
  public override bool
    CanConvertFrom(
    ITypeDescriptorContext context,
    Type sourceType) {
```

```
    return sourceType == typeof(string);
}

public override bool
  CanConvertTo(
    ITypeDescriptorContext context,
    Type destinationType) {

    return destinationType == typeof(string);
}

public override object
  ConvertFrom(
    ITypeDescriptorContext context,
    CultureInfo culture,
    object value) {

    // Very simple conversion ignores context, culture, and errors
    string from = (string)value;
    int slash = from.IndexOf("/");
    int numerator = int.Parse(from.Substring(0, slash));
    int denominator = int.Parse(from.Substring(slash + 1));
    return new Fraction(numerator, denominator);
}

public override object
  ConvertTo(
    ITypeDescriptorContext context,
    CultureInfo culture,
    object value,
    Type destinationType) {

    if( destinationType != typeof(string) ) return null;
    Fraction number = (Fraction)value;
    return string.Format(
      "{0}/{1}", number.Numerator, number.Denominator);
  }
}
```

Associating the type converter with the type is a matter of applying TypeConverterAttribute:

```
[TypeConverterAttribute(typeof(FractionTypeConverter))]
class Fraction {...}
```

Now, instead of using the ToString method to get the Fraction string to display in the bound control, the binding will use the FractionType-Converter class's CanConvertTo and ConvertTo methods.

Similarly, when new data is available, the binding will use the Can-ConvertFrom and ConvertFrom methods. Or rather, it would, if that worked. Unfortunately, as of .NET 1.1, converting control data back into data of the custom type never makes it back to the custom type converter. Instead, an untested hunk of code throws an exception that's caught and ignored, and the conversion back from the control to the custom data type silently fails. One workaround is to handle the Binding class's Parse event, as discussed earlier in this chapter, and let the client do the conversion:

```
NameAndNumber source = new NameAndNumber();

void CustomItemDataSourceForm2_Load(object sender, EventArgs e) {
  textBox1.DataBindings.Add("Text", source, "Name");

  // Bind to a property of a custom type
  // and handle the parsing
  Binding binding =
    textBox2.DataBindings.Add("Text", source, "Number");
  binding.Parse += new ConvertEventHandler(textBox2_Parse);
}

void textBox2_Parse(object sender, ConvertEventArgs e) {
  string from = (string)e.Value;
  int slash = from.IndexOf("/");
  int numerator = int.Parse(from.Substring(0, slash));
  int denominator = int.Parse(from.Substring(slash + 1));
  e.Value = new Fraction(numerator, denominator);
}
```

However, instead of building the parsing of the type into the form itself, it's much more robust to let the parsing be handled by the type's own type converter:

```
void textBox2_Parse(object sender, ConvertEventArgs e) {
  // Let the type converter do the work
  TypeConverter converter = TypeDescriptor.GetConverter(e.DesiredType);
  if( converter == null ) return;
  if( !converter.CanConvertFrom(e.Value.GetType()) ) return;
  e.Value = converter.ConvertFrom(e.Value);
}
```

Another solution that doesn't require manually handling the parsing of every property of a custom type is to derive from the Binding base class and override the OnParse method:

```
class WorkAroundBinding : Binding {
  public WorkAroundBinding(string name, object src, string member)
    : base(name, src, member) {
  }

  protected override void OnParse(ConvertEventArgs e) {
    try {
      // Let the base class have a crack
      base.OnParse(e);
    }
    catch( InvalidCastException ) {
      // Take over for base class if it fails

      // If one of the base class event handlers converted it,
      // we're finished
      if( e.Value.GetType().IsSubclassOf(e.DesiredType) ||
        (e.Value.GetType() == e.DesiredType) ||
        (e.Value is DBNull) ) {
        return;
      }

      // Ask the desired type for a type converter
      TypeConverter converter =
        TypeDescriptor.GetConverter(e.DesiredType);
      if( (converter != null) &&
          converter.CanConvertFrom(e.Value.GetType()) ) {
        e.Value = converter.ConvertFrom(e.Value);
      }
    }
  }
}
```

You use the WorkAroundBinding class instead of the standard Binding class when adding a binding to a property of a custom type:

```
void Form1_Load(object sender, EventArgs e) {
  textBox1.DataBindings.Add("Text", source, "Name");

  // Let the custom binding handle the parsing workaround
  Binding binding =
    new WorkAroundBinding("Text", source, "Number");
  textBox2.DataBindings.Add(binding);
}
```

Neither of these techniques is as nice as if custom types were fully supported, but both show the power that comes from understanding the basics of the data binding architecture.

List Data Sources

The basics of simple data binding support require only that you expose public properties. In the same way, setting the content for complex bound controls, such as the ListBox or the ComboBox, requires only a collection of your custom data source objects:

```
NameAndNumber[] source =
{ new NameAndNumber("John", 8), new NameAndNumber("Tom", 7) };

void ComplexCustomDataSourceForm_Load(object sender, EventArgs e) {
  // Bind a collection of custom data sources complexly
  listBox1.DataSource = source;
}
```

As you recall from the earlier discussion, setting only the DataSource and not the DisplayMember property shows the type of each object instead of anything useful from them, as shown in Figure 13.38.

If you'd like the object itself to decide how it's displayed, you can leave the DisplayMember property as null and let the type's implementation of ToString or its type converter determine what's shown:

```
class NameAndNumber {
  ...
  // For use by single-valued complex controls,
  // e.g. ListBox and ComboBox
  public override string ToString() {
    return this.name + ", " + this.number;
  }
}

void CustomListDataSourceForm_Load(object sender, EventArgs e) {
  // Let the object determine how it's displayed
  listBox1.DataSource = source;
}
```

FIGURE 13.38: Binding to a Custom List Data Source without a String Conversion

Binding to a collection of NameAndNumber objects with its own ToString implementation yields the kind of display shown in Figure 13.39.

The ToString method is used only in the absence of values in both the DisplayMember and the ValueMember properties. When used against custom data sources, the list controls allow the DisplayMember and ValueMember properties to be set with the names of properties to pull from the custom types in the collection:

```
NameAndNumber[] source =
{ new NameAndNumber("John", 8), new NameAndNumber("Tom", 7) };

void ComplexCustomDataSourceForm_Load(object sender, EventArgs e) {
  listBox1.DataSource = source;
  listBox1.DisplayMember = "Name";
  listBox1.ValueMember = "Number";
}

void listBox1_SelectedIndexChanged(object sender, EventArgs e) {
  // Show selected value as selected index changes
  statusBar1.Text = "selected Number= " + listBox1.SelectedValue;
}
```

The results of this binding are shown in Figure 13.40.

Binding to Custom Hierarchies

Sometimes objects are arranged in hierarchies. You can accommodate this using a property that exposes a collection class. For example, you might

FIGURE 13.39: Binding to a Custom List Data Source with a String Conversion

FIGURE 13.40: Binding Properties as Data Members

use an ArrayList, which implements the IList interface from the System.
Collections namespace:

```csharp
// Lowest-level objects:
class Fraction {
  public Fraction(int numerator, int denominator) {
    this.numerator = numerator;
    this.denominator = denominator;
  }

  public int Numerator {
    get { return this.numerator; }
    set { this.numerator = value; }
  }

  public int Denominator {
    get { return this.denominator; }
    set { this.denominator = value; }
  }

  int numerator;
  int denominator;
}

// Top-level objects:
class NameAndNumbers {
  public NameAndNumbers(string name) {
    this.name = name;
  }

  public event EventHandler NameChanged;
  public string Name {
    get { return name; }
    set {
      name = value;
      if( NameChanged != null ) NameChanged(this, EventArgs.Empty);
    }
  }

  // Expose second-level hierarchy:
  // NOTE: DataGrid doesn't bind to arrays
  public ArrayList Numbers {
    get { return this.numbers; }
  }

  // Add to second-level hierarchy
  public void AddNumber(Fraction number) {
    this.numbers.Add(number);
  }
```

```
  public override string ToString() {
    return this.name;
  }

  string name = "Chris";
  ArrayList numbers = new ArrayList(); // subobjects
}
```

When you've got a multilevel hierarchy of custom types, you can bind it against any control that supports hierarchies, such as the DataGrid control:

```
// Top-level collection:
ArrayList source = new ArrayList();

void CustomListDataSourceForm2_Load(object sender, EventArgs e) {
  // Populate the hierarchy
  NameAndNumbers nan1 = new NameAndNumbers("John");
  nan1.AddNumber(new Fraction(1, 2));
  nan1.AddNumber(new Fraction(2, 3));
  nan1.AddNumber(new Fraction(3, 4));
  source.Add(nan1);

  NameAndNumbers nan2 = new NameAndNumbers("Tom");
  nan2.AddNumber(new Fraction(4, 5));
  nan2.AddNumber(new Fraction(5, 6));
  source.Add(nan2);

  // Bind a collection of custom data sources complexly
  dataGrid1.DataSource = source;
}
```

Figure 13.41 shows the top-level collection bound to a data grid, showing a link to the second-level collection.

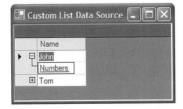

FIGURE 13.41: Showing the Top Level of an Object Hierarchy in a Data Grid

The data grid shows each public property from the object at each level, along with links to subobjects exposed as collection properties. Figure 13.42 shows the second-level collection after the link has been followed.

The data grid is pretty flexible, but each level of hierarchy needs to be a type that exposes one or more public properties. It needs property names for column names. This means that, unlike the list controls, a data grid won't use a type converter or the ToString method to show the value of the object as a whole.

A more full-featured integration with the data grid—including enabling the data grid UI to edit the data and the ability to keep the data grid up-to-date as the list data source is modified—requires an implementation of the IBindingList interface, something that is beyond the scope of this book.

Where Are We?

Data binding is the act of connecting a control to a data source. Binding lets you create an association between controls and data sources to keep a control and a data source in sync automatically. The control can be simple, like a TextBox or a ListBox, or full-featured, like the DataGrid. If the data source is an item data source, either it's an object having zero, one, or more public properties or you need a conversion to the data type to properly bind to what the control needs. A data source can also be a list data source, in which case it's a list of objects that can be shown one at a time (when simply bound) or all at once (when complexly bound). Simple binding requires no support from the control itself and allows any number of

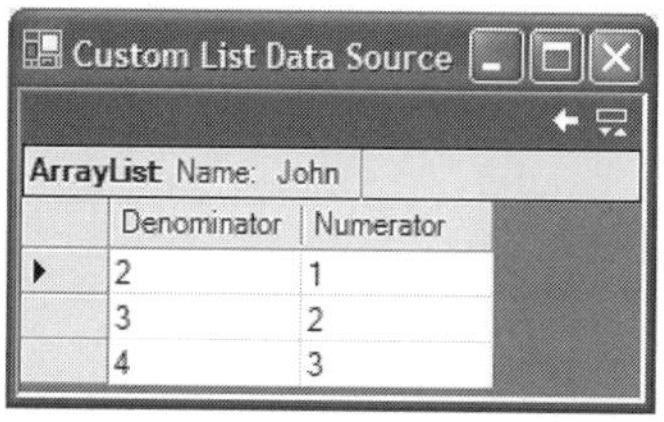

FIGURE 13.42: Showing the Second Level of an Object Hierarchy in a Data Grid

control properties to be bound to any number of data sources. Complex binding requires support from the control but allows the control greater flexibility in the way it interacts with the data source. For example, it can show multiple items from a list or show multiple columns from a table (or multiple properties from an object).

■14■
Multithreaded User Interfaces

W INFORMS APPLICATIONS OFTEN NEED to start long-running operations, such as an intensive calculation or a call to a Web service. In
those cases, it's important to run the operation so that you allow the application to continue to interact with the user without freezing, while still
allowing the user to see the progress of the operation and even to cancel it.

Before we get started, I should mention that this chapter discusses the
issues surrounding multithreaded user interfaces only. This simplifies the
discussion and covers the information you'll need most of the time when
handling long-running operations in a WinForms application. For more
details of threading specifics in .NET—including the details of the Thread
class, thread pooling, locking, synchronization, race conditions, and deadlocks—you should turn to your favorite low-level .NET book.

Long-Running Operations

Imagine that the value of pi in System.Math.PI, at only 20 digits, just isn't
accurate enough for you. In that case, you may find yourself writing an
application like the one in Figure 14.1 to calculate pi to an arbitrary number
of digits.

This program takes as input the number of digits of pi to calculate and,
when the Calc button is pressed, shows the progress as the calculation
happens.

FIGURE 14.1: Digits of Pi Application

Progress Indication

Although most applications don't need to calculate the digits of pi, many kinds of applications need to perform long-running operations, whether it's printing, making a Web service call, or calculating the interest earnings of a certain billionaire in the Pacific Northwest. Users are generally content to wait for such things as long as they can see that progress is being made. That's why even this simple application has a progress bar.

The algorithm it uses calculates pi 9 digits at a time. As each new set of digits is available, the application updates the text and the progress bar. For example, Figure 14.2 shows progress on the way to calculating 1,000 digits of pi (if 21 digits are good, then 1,000 must be better).

The following shows how the UI is updated as the digits of pi are calculated:

```
class AsyncCalcPiForm : Form {
  ...
```

FIGURE 14.2: Calculating Pi to 1,000 Digits

```
  void ShowProgress(string pi, int totalDigits, int digitsSoFar) {
    piTextBox.Text = pi;
    piProgressBar.Maximum = totalDigits;
    piProgressBar.Value = digitsSoFar;
  }

  void CalcPi(int digits) {
    StringBuilder pi = new StringBuilder("3", digits + 2);

    // Show progress
    ShowProgress(pi.ToString(), digits, 0);

    if( digits > 0 ) {
      pi.Append(".");

      for( int i = 0; i < digits; i += 9 ) {
        int nineDigits = NineDigitsOfPi.StartingAt(i+1);
        int digitCount = Math.Min(digits - i, 9);
        string ds = string.Format("{0:D9}", nineDigits);
        pi.Append(ds.Substring(0, digitCount));

        // Show progress
        ShowProgress(pi.ToString(), digits, i + digitCount);
      }
    }
  }

  void calcButton_Click (object sender, EventArgs e) {
    CalcPi((int)_digits.Value);
  }
}
```

This implementation works just fine for a small number of digits. But suppose the user switches away from the application and then returns in the middle of calculating pi to a large number of digits, as shown in Figure 14.3.

FIGURE 14.3: No Paint for You!

The problem is that the application has a single thread of execution (this kind of application is often called a *single-threaded application*), so while the thread is calculating pi, it can't also be drawing the UI. This didn't happen before the user switched the application to the background because both the text box and the progress bar force their own painting to happen immediately as their properties are set (although the progress bar seems to be better at this than the text box). However, after the user puts the application into the background and then the foreground again, the main form must paint the entire client area, and that means processing the Paint event. Because no other event can be processed until the application returns from the Click event on the Calc button, the user won't see any display of further progress until all the digits of pi are calculated.

What this application needs is a way to free the UI thread to do UI work and handle the long-running pi calculation in the background. For this, it needs another thread of execution.

Asynchronous Operations

A *thread of execution* (often called simply a *thread*) is a series of instructions and a call stack that operate independently of the other threads in the application or in any other application. In every version of Windows since Windows 95, Windows schedules each thread transparently so that a programmer can write a thread almost (but not quite) as if it were the only thing happening on the system. Starting a thread is an *asynchronous operation,* in that the current thread of execution will continue immediately, executing independently of the new thread. To start a new thread of execution in .NET is a matter of creating a Thread object from the System.Threading namespace, passing a delegate[1] as the constructor parameter, and starting the thread:

```
using System.Threading;
...
class AsyncCalcPiForm : Form {
  ...
  int digitsToCalc = 0;
```

---

1. You can read more about delegates in Appendix B: Delegates and Events.

```
void CalcPiThreadStart() {
  CalcPi(digitsToCalc);
}

void calcButton_Click(object sender, EventArgs e) {
  digitsToCalc = (int)_digits.Value;
  Thread piThread =
    new Thread(new ThreadStart(CalcPiThreadStart));
  piThread.Start();
}
}
```

This code creates a new thread and begins execution of the thread by passing a delegate wrapper around the method to call. Now, instead of waiting for CalcPi to finish before returning from the button Click event, the UI thread spawns a *worker* thread, immediately returning the UI thread to its user interaction duties. Figure 14.4 shows the two threads doing their separate jobs.

Spawning a worker thread to calculate pi leaves the UI thread free to handle events (which WinForms creates as it takes messages off the Windows message queue). When the worker thread has more digits of pi to share with the user, it directly sets the values of the text box and the progress bar controls. (Actually, letting the worker thread access controls created by the UI thread is dangerous, but we'll get to that a little later.)

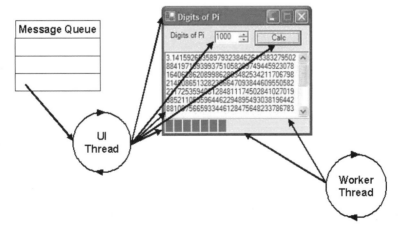

FIGURE 14.4: Naïve Multithreading

In the sample code to start a thread, notice that no arguments are passed to the worker thread's entry point, CalcPiThreadStart. This is because the delegate that is used to construct the Thread class allows no arguments to be passed. Instead, we tuck the number of digits to calculate into a field, digitsToCalc. Then we call the thread entry point, which uses digitsToCalc to call the CalcPi method in turn. Because you can't pass arguments to the thread start method, I prefer to use custom delegates for spawning threads. In addition, an asynchronous delegate will be handled on a thread from the per-process thread pool, something that scales better than does creating a new thread for each of a large number of asynchronous operations.

Here's how to declare a custom delegate suitable for calling CalcPi:

```
delegate void CalcPiDelegate(int digits);
```

After the custom delegate has been defined, the following creates an instance of the delegate to call the CalcPi method synchronously:

```
void calcButton_Click(object sender, EventArgs e) {
  CalcPiDelegate calcPi = new CalcPiDelegate(CalcPi);
  calcPi((int)digitsUpDown.Value);
}
```

Because calling CalcPi synchronously is the cause of our trouble, we need to call it asynchronously. Before we do that, however, we need to understand a bit more about how delegates work. The CalcPiDelegate declaration implicitly declares a new class derived from MultiCastDelegate with three methods: Invoke, BeginInvoke, and EndInvoke:

```
class CalcPiDelegate : MulticastDelegate {
  public void Invoke(int digits);
  public void BeginInvoke(
    int digits, AsyncCallback callback, object asyncState);
  public void EndInvoke(IAsyncResult result);
}
```

When the application created an instance of CalcPiDelegate and called it like a method, it was really calling the synchronous Invoke method, which simply turned around and called the CalcPi method on the same thread. BeginInvoke and EndInvoke, however, are the pair of methods that allow asynchronous invocation of a method on a new thread for a per-process pool of threads. To have the CalcPi method called on another thread—the aforementioned worker thread—the application uses BeginInvoke:[2]

```
void calcButton_Click(object sender, EventArgs e) {
  CalcPiDelegate calcPi = new CalcPiDelegate(CalcPi);
  calcPi.BeginInvoke((int)digitsUpDown.Value, null, null);
}
```

Notice the nulls for the last two arguments of BeginInvoke. We would need these arguments if we needed to later harvest the result from the method we're calling (which is also what EndInvoke is for). Because the CalcPi method updates the UI directly, we don't need anything but nulls for these two arguments.

At this point, we've got an application with a fully interactive UI that shows progress on a long-running operation. Unfortunately, we're not quite finished yet.

Safety and Multithreading

As it turns out, we're lucky that this application works at all. Because we start the CalcPi method on a worker thread, when CalcPi calls the ShowProgress method it's accessing the text box and progress bar controls from the worker thread, even though those controls were created on the UI thread. This violates a key requirement that's been present since Windows first got support for threads: "Thou shalt operate on a window only from its creating thread." In fact, the WinForms documentation is clear on this point: "There are four methods on a control that are safe to call from any thread: Invoke, BeginInvoke, EndInvoke, and CreateGraphics. For all other method calls, you should use one of the invoke methods to marshal the call to the control's thread." So when the CalcPi method calls the ShowProgress method, which in turn accesses two controls created by the UI thread, our application is clearly violating this rule.

Luckily, long-running operations are common in Windows applications. As a result, each UI class in WinForms—meaning every class that

---

2. If you're using VS.NET 2002, don't be alarmed that neither BeginInvoke nor EndInvoke shows up in IntelliSense from C#. They're there, I assure you, and VS.NET 2003 has been updated to show them.

ultimately derives from System.Windows.Forms.Control—has a property that you can use to find out whether it's safe to act on the control from that thread. The property is InvokeRequired, which returns true if the calling thread needs to pass control to the UI thread before calling a method on the control. A simple Assert in the ShowProgress method would have immediately shown the error in our sample application:

```
using System.Diagnostics;

void ShowProgress(string pi, int totalDigits, int digitsSoFar) {
  // Make sure we're on the UI thread
  Debug.Assert(this.InvokeRequired == false);
  ...
}
```

Because the worker thread is clearly not allowed to show progress directly, we need to pass control from the worker thread back to the UI thread. From the names of the first three methods that are safe to call from any thread—Invoke, BeginInvoke, and EndInvoke—it should be clear that you'll need another delegate to pass control appropriately. The delegate will be created on the worker thread and then executed on the UI thread so that we can have safe, single-threaded access to UI objects.

Synchronous Callbacks

Asynchronous operations, such as the call to a delegate's BeginInvoke method, return immediately, so they are *nonblocking*. This means that the thread isn't blocked waiting for the method to complete. Synchronous operations, on the other hand, are *blocking*, because they do cause the calling thread to block until the method returns.

Depending on the blocking behavior you're interested in, you can call Invoke or BeginInvoke to block or not to block, respectively, when calling into the UI thread:

```
class System.Windows.Forms.Control : ... {
  public object Invoke(Delegate method);
  public virtual object Invoke(Delegate method, object[] args);
  public IAsyncResult BeginInvoke(Delegate method);
  public virtual IAsyncResult BeginInvoke
      (Delegate method, object[] args);
```

```
public virtual object EndInvoke(IAsyncResult asyncResult);
  ...
}
```

Control.Invoke will block until the UI thread has processed the request: that is, until Control.Invoke has put a message on the UI thread's message queue and has waited for it to be processed like any other message (except that the delegate's method is called instead of an event handler). Because Invoke takes a Delegate argument, which is the base class for all delegates, it can form a call to any method, using the optional array of objects as arguments and returning an object as the return value for the called method. Using Control.Invoke looks like this:

```
void ShowProgress(string pi, int totalDigits, int digitsSoFar) {
  ...
}

delegate
  void ShowProgressDelegate(
    string pi, int totalDigits, int digitsSoFar);

void CalcPi(int digits) {
  StringBuilder pi = new StringBuilder("3", digits + 2);

  // Get ready to show progress
  ShowProgressDelegate showProgress =
    new ShowProgressDelegate(ShowProgress);

  // Show progress
  this.Invoke(showProgress,
    new object[] { pi.ToString(), digits, 0});

  if( digits > 0 ) {
    pi.Append(".");

    for( int i = 0; i < digits; i += 9 ) {
      ...
      // Show progress
      this.Invoke(showProgress,
        new object[] { pi.ToString(), digits, i + digitCount});
    }
  }
}
```

Notice the declaration of a new delegate, ShowProgressDelegate. This delegate matches the signature of the ShowProgress method we'd like to be called on the UI thread. Because ShowProgress takes three arguments, the code uses an overload to Invoke that takes an array of objects to form the arguments to the ShowProgress method.

Now the UI thread uses a delegate, calling Delegate.BeginInvoke to spawn a worker thread, and the worker thread uses Control.Invoke to pass control back to the UI thread when the progress controls need updating. Figure 14.5 shows our safe multithreading architecture.

Notice that Figure 14.5 shows only the UI thread ever touching the controls and shows that the worker thread uses the message queue to let the UI thread know when progress needs reporting.

Asynchronous Callbacks

Our use of the synchronous call to Control.Invoke works just fine, but it gives us more than we need. The worker thread doesn't get any output or return values from the UI thread when calling through the ShowProgress-Delegate. By calling Invoke, we force the worker thread to wait for the UI thread, blocking the worker thread from continuing its calculations. This is a job tailor-made for the asynchronous Control.BeginInvoke method:

```
void CalcPi(int digits) {
  StringBuilder pi = new StringBuilder("3", digits + 2);

  // Get ready to show progress
  ShowProgressDelegate showProgress =
    new ShowProgressDelegate(ShowProgress);
```

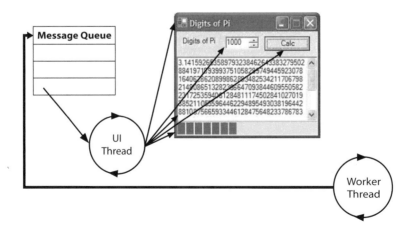

FIGURE 14.5: Safe Multithreading

```
  // Show progress
  this.BeginInvoke(showProgress,
    new object[] { pi.ToString(), digits, 0});

  if( digits > 0 ) {
    pi.Append(".");

    for( int i = 0; i < digits; i += 9 ) {
      ...
      // Show progress
      this.BeginInvoke(showProgress,
        new object[] { pi.ToString(), digits, i + digitCount});
    }
  }
}
```

Notice that the only thing different in this code is the call to Begin-Invoke instead of Invoke. All the arguments are the same, and we can ignore the return value from BeginInvoke. The BeginInvoke method returns an IAsyncResult interface, which provides access to the current status of the request and allows the worker thread to harvest any results. Because there are no results to harvest, there's no need to worry about the IAsyncResult or ever calling EndInvoke.

If you need to retrieve results from the UI thread to the worker thread, you can:

```
// Call back to the UI thread
IAsyncResult res =
  this.BeginInvoke(someDelegateWithResults, ...);

// Check for results
while( res.IsCompleted == false )
  System.Threading.Thread.Sleep(100);

// Harvest results
object methodResults = this.EndInvoke(res);

// Do something with results...
```

IAsyncResult.IsCompleted is meant to be called periodically while doing other things (such as during the Application class's Idle event, mentioned in Chapter 11: Applications and Settings). Of course, if you're doing nothing except polling for results, the Control.Invoke method is what you want.

Simplified Multithreading

The call to BeginInvoke is a bit cumbersome, especially because it happens twice in the CalcPi method. We can simplify things by updating the Show-Progress method to make the asynchronous call itself. If ShowProgress is called from the UI thread, it will update the controls, but if it's called from a worker thread, it uses BeginInvoke to call itself back on the UI thread. This lets the application go back to the earlier, simpler CalcPi implementation:

```csharp
void ShowProgress(string pi, int totalDigits, int digitsSoFar) {
  // Make sure we're on the UI thread
  if( this.InvokeRequired == false ) {
    piTextBox.Text = pi;
    piProgressBar.Maximum = totalDigits;
    piProgressBar.Value = digitsSoFar;
  }
  else {
    // Show progress asynchronously
    ShowProgressDelegate showProgress =
      new ShowProgressDelegate(ShowProgress);
    this.BeginInvoke(showProgress,
      new object[] { pi, totalDigits, digitsSoFar});
  }
}

void CalcPi(int digits) {
  StringBuilder pi = new StringBuilder("3", digits + 2);

  // Show progress
  ShowProgress(pi.ToString(), digits, 0);

  if( digits > 0 ) {
    pi.Append(".");

    for( int i = 0; i < digits; i += 9 ) {
      ...
      // Show progress
      ShowProgress(pi.ToString(), digits, i + digitCount);
    }
  }
}
```

When you build multithread UI code, it's common for the methods that interact with the controls to check that they're running on the UI thread. During development, you may need a way to track down places where you've forgotten to make the appropriate transition between threads. To make those places obvious, I recommend that in every method that might be called from a worker thread use a call that asserts that InvokeRequired is not required.

Canceling

So far, the sample application can send messages back and forth between the worker and the UI threads without a care in the world. The UI thread doesn't have to wait for the worker thread to complete or even be notified on completion, because the worker thread communicates its progress as it goes. Similarly, the worker thread doesn't have to wait for the UI thread to show progress as long as progress messages are sent at regular intervals to keep users happy.

However, one thing doesn't make users happy: not having full control of any processing that their applications are performing. Even though the UI is responsive while pi is being calculated, users would still like the option to cancel the calculation if they've decided they really need 1,000,001 digits and they mistakenly asked for only 1,000,000. Figure 14.6 shows an updated UI for CalcPi that allows cancellation.

Implementing cancel for a long-running operation is a multistep process. First, you need to provide a UI that lets the user cancel the operation. In this case, the Calc button is changed to a Cancel button after the calculation has begun. Another popular choice is to display a separate progress dialog, which typically includes current progress details, a progress bar showing percentage of work complete, and a Cancel button.

If the user decides to cancel, that is noted in a member variable. In addition, the UI is disabled for the short time between the time when the

FIGURE 14.6: Letting the User Cancel a Long-Running Operation

UI thread knows the worker thread should stop and the time the worker thread itself knows and has had a chance to stop sending progress. If you ignore this lag time, the user could start another operation before the first worker thread stops sending progress, making it the job of the UI thread to figure out whether it's getting progress from the new worker thread or the old worker thread, which is supposed to be shutting down.

You could assign each worker thread a unique ID so that the UI thread can keep such things organized (and, in the face of multiple simultaneous long-running operations, you may well need to do this), but it's often simpler to pause the UI for this brief amount of time. The sample application keeps track of its current processing state using a value from a three-value enumeration:

```
enum CalcState {
  Pending,     // No calculation running or canceling
  Calculating, // Calculation in progress
  Canceled,    // Calculation canceled in UI but not worker
}

CalcState state = CalcState.Pending;
```

Now, depending on what state the application is in, it treats the Calc button differently:

```
void calcButton_Click(object sender, EventArgs e)  {
  // Calc button does double duty as Cancel button
  switch( state ) {
    // Start a new calculation
    case CalcState.Pending:
      // Allow canceling
      state = CalcState.Calculating;
      calcButton.Text = "Cancel";

      // Async delegate method
      CalcPiDelegate calcPi = new CalcPiDelegate(CalcPi);
      calcPi.BeginInvoke((int)digitsUpDown.Value, null, null);
      break;

    // Cancel a running calculation
    case CalcState.Calculating:
      state = CalcState.Canceled;
      calcButton.Enabled = false;
      break;
```

```
    // Shouldn't be able to press Calc button while it's canceling
    case CalcState.Canceled:
      Debug.Assert(false);
      break;
  }
}
```

Notice that when the Calc/Cancel button is pressed in the Pending state, the application sets the state to Calculating, changes the label on the button, and starts the calculation asynchronously, just as it did before. If the state is Calculating when the Calc/Cancel button is pressed, the application switches the state to Canceled and disables the UI. The UI will remain disabled, preventing the start of a new calculation, for as long as it takes to communicate the canceled state to the worker thread.

After the UI thread has communicated with the worker thread that the operation has been canceled, the UI thread enables the UI again and resets the state to Pending (shown later) so that the user can start another operation. To communicate to the worker that it should cancel, the sample augments the ShowProgress method to include a new *out* parameter:

```
void ShowProgress(..., out bool cancel);

void CalcPi(int digits) {
  bool cancel = false;
  ...

  for( int i = 0; i < digits; i += 9 ) {
    ...

    // Show progress (checking for Cancel)
    ShowProgress(..., out cancel);
    if( cancel ) break;
  }
}
```

You may be tempted to make the cancel indicator a Boolean return value from ShowProgress, but I find it hard to remember whether a return value of "true" means to cancel or to continue as normal. I use the out parameter technique to make it very clear what's going on.

The only thing left to do is to update the ShowProgress method to notice whether the user has asked to cancel and to let CalcPi know accordingly. Exactly how that information is communicated depends on which technique we'd like to use.

Communication with Shared Data

Remember that the ShowProgress method is the code that actually performs the transition between the worker thread and the UI thread, so it's the one at the heart of the communication between the two threads. The obvious way to communicate the current state of the UI is to give the worker thread direct access to the state member variable:

```
void ShowProgress(..., out bool cancel) {
  if( state == CalcState.Canceled ) {
    state = CalcState.Pending;
    cancel = true;
    return;
  }
  . . .
}
```

I hope that something inside you cringed when you saw this code. If you're going to do multithreaded programming, you're going to have to watch out for any time that two threads have simultaneous access to the same data (in this case, the state member variable). Shared access to data between threads makes it very easy to get into *race conditions,* in which one thread is racing to read data that is only partially up-to-date before another thread has finished updating it. For concurrent access to shared data to work, you must monitor usage of your shared data to make sure that each thread waits patiently while the other thread works on the data.

To monitor access to shared data, .NET provides the Monitor class. You use Monitor on a shared object to act as the lock on the data, which C# wraps with the handy lock block:

```
object stateLock = new object();

void ShowProgress(..., out bool cancel) {
  lock( stateLock ) { // Monitor the lock
    if( state == CalcState.Cancel ) {
      state = CalcState.Pending;
      cancel = true;
```

```
        return;
    }
    ...
  }
}
```

The data has now been properly protected against race conditions, but the way we've done it invites another problem known as a *deadlock*. When two threads are deadlocked, each of them waits for the other to complete its work before continuing, thereby ensuring that neither will actually progress.

If all this talk of race conditions and deadlocks has caused you concern, that's good. Multithreaded programming with shared data is hard. So far we've been able to avoid these issues because we have passed copies of data around so that no two threads need to share access to any one piece of data. If you don't have shared data, there's no need for synchronization. If you find that you need access to shared data—maybe because the overhead of copying the data is too great a space or time burden—then you'll need to read up on multithreading and shared data synchronization, topics that are beyond the scope of this book.

Luckily, the vast majority of multithreading scenarios, especially as related to UI multithreading, seem to work best with the simple message-passing scheme used so far. Most of the time, you don't want the UI to have access to data being worked on in the background, such as the document being printed or the collection of objects being enumerated. For these cases, passing data to be owned by the receiving thread is just the ticket.

Communicating via Method Parameters

Because ShowProgress has already been updated with an out parameter, the sample lets it check the state variable when it's executing on the UI thread:

```
void ShowProgress(..., out bool cancel) {
  // Make sure we're on the UI thread
  if( this.InvokeRequired == false ) {
    ...
```

continues

```
    // Check for Cancel
    cancel = (state == CalcState.Canceled);

    // Check for completion
    if( cancel || (digitsSoFar == totalDigits) ) {
      state = CalcState.Pending;
      calcButton.Text = "Calc";
      calcButton.Enabled = true;
    }
  }
  // Transfer control to UI thread
  else { ... }
}
```

The UI thread is the only one to access the state member variable, so no synchronization is needed. Now it's just a matter of passing control to the UI thread in such a way as to harvest the cancel output parameter of the ShowProgressDelegate. Unfortunately, our use of Control.BeginInvoke makes this complicated, because it doesn't wait for results from the UI thread. Waiting for the ShowProgress method to complete and the cancel flag to be set requires a call to the blocking Control.Invoke, but even this is a bit tricky:

```
void ShowProgress(..., out bool cancel) {
  if( this.InvokeRequired == false ) { ... }
  // Transfer control to UI thread
  else {
    ShowProgressDelegate showProgress =
      new ShowProgressDelegate(ShowProgress);

    // Avoid boxing and losing our return value
    object inoutCancel = false;

    // Show progress synchronously (so we can check for cancel)
    Invoke(showProgress, new object[] {..., inoutCancel});
    cancel = (bool)inoutCancel;
  }
}
```

It would have been nice to simply pass a Boolean variable directly to Control.Invoke to harvest the cancel parameter, but there is a problem. The problem is that a Boolean is a value type, whereas Invoke takes an array of objects, which are reference types. A *value type* is a simple type, such as a Boolean, that is meant to be managed on the stack. A *reference type*, on the other hand, comes out of the heap. Although passing a value type where a reference type is expected is certainly legal, it causes a copy of the value type (this copying is called *boxing*).[3] So even though ShowProgress would be able to change the cancel flag, the change would occur on a temporary variable created by the run time on-the-fly in the heap, and we have no access to that variable.

To avoid losing updates to the cancel flag, ShowProgress instead manually creates and passes a reference type variable (inoutCancel), avoiding the copy. After the synchronous call to Invoke, the code casts the object variable back to a Boolean to see whether or not the operation should be canceled.

Communication via Message Passing

The simplicity of the CalcPi example, and the resulting complexity of sending around a single Boolean indicating whether to cancel, may cause you to try a solution like the following:

```
void ShowProgress(..., out bool cancel) {
  // Make sure we're on the UI thread
  if( this.InvokeRequired == false ) {...}
  // Transfer control to the UI thread
  else {
    ShowProgressDelegate
      showProgress = new ShowProgressDelegate(ShowProgress);

    // Show progress synchronously (so we can check for cancel)
    Invoke(showProgress, new object[] {...});

    // Check for Cancel the easy, but special-purpose, way
    cancel = (state == CalcState.Canceled);
  }
}
```

For our simple application, and others like it, that would work just fine. Because the worker thread reads only from the state field, it will always be valid (although a race condition could cause it to be old). However, don't be tempted to take this path. As soon as you have multiple outstanding

---

3. For the full treatment of value types, reference types, boxing, and unboxing, see *Essential .NET* (Addison-Wesley, 2003), by Don Box, with Chris Sells.

requests and you keep them in an array or any kind of data structure at all, you run the risk of attempting to access data that's been invalidated (those darn race conditions again), something you'll have to protect against using synchronization (remember deadlocks?).

It's much simpler and safer to pass around ownership of the data instead of sharing access to the same data. To avoid the complexity of boxing, I recommend that you follow the delegate idiom used by the rest of .NET:

```
class ShowProgressArgs : EventArgs {
  public string Pi;
  public int TotalDigits;
  public int DigitsSoFar;
  public bool Cancel;

  public ShowProgressArgs(string pi, int totalDigits, int digitsSoFar) {
    this.Pi = pi;
    this.TotalDigits = totalDigits;
    this.DigitsSoFar = digitsSoFar;
  }
}


delegate void ShowProgressHandler(object sender, ShowProgressArgs e);
```

This code declares the class ShowProgressArgs, which derives from the EventArgs base class, to hold event arguments. It also declares a delegate that takes a sender and an instance on the custom arguments object. With this in place, we can use the new delegate to update ShowProgress to call itself:

```
void ShowProgress(...) {
  // Make sure we're on the UI thread
  if( this.InvokeRequired == false ) {...}
  }
  // Transfer control to the UI thread
  else {
    // Create an instance of the delegate to call
    // the handler on the UI thread
    ShowProgressHandler showProgress =
      new ShowProgressHandler(AsyncCalcPiForm_ShowProgress);

    // Initialize the message parameters
    object sender = System.Threading.Thread.CurrentThread;
    ShowProgressArgs e =
      new ShowProgressArgs(pi, totalDigits, digitsSoFar);
```

```
    // Send the message, waiting for the UI thread to
    // return whether the operation should be canceled
    this.Invoke(showProgress, new object[] {sender, e});
    cancel = e.Cancel;
  }
}

// Called on the UI thread
void AsyncCalcPiForm_ShowProgress(object sender, ShowProgressArgs e) {
  // Unpack the message and forward it to the ShowProgress method
  ShowProgress(e.Pi, e.TotalDigits, e.DigitsSoFar, out e.Cancel);
}
```

ShowProgress hasn't changed its signature, so CalcPi still calls it in the same simple way. However, now the worker thread will compose an instance of the ShowProgressArgs object to pass to the UI thread via a handler that looks like any other event handler, including a sender and an EventArgs-derived object. The handler calls the ShowProgress method again, breaking out the arguments from the ShowProgressArgs object. After Control.Invoke returns in the worker thread, the worker thread pulls out the cancel flag without any concern about boxing because the ShowProgressArgs type is a reference type. However, even though it is a reference type and the worker thread passes control of it to the UI thread, there's no danger of race conditions because the worker thread waits until the UI thread is finished working with the data before accessing it again.

You can further simplify this usage by updating the CalcPi method to create an instance of the ShowProgressArgs class itself, eliminating the need for an intermediate method:

```
void ShowProgress(object sender, ShowProgressArgs e) {
  // Make sure we're on the UI thread
  if( this.InvokeRequired == false ) {
    piTextBox.Text = e.Pi;
    piProgressBar.Maximum = e.TotalDigits;
    piProgressBar.Value = e.DigitsSoFar;

    // Check for Cancel
    e.Cancel = (state == CalcState.Canceled);

    // Check for completion
    if( e.Cancel || (e.DigitsSoFar == e.TotalDigits) ) {
      state = CalcState.Pending;
      calcButton.Text = "Calc";
```

continues

```
          calcButton.Enabled = true;


        }
    }
    // Transfer control to the UI thread
    else {
        ShowProgressHandler
          showProgress =
            new ShowProgressHandler(ShowProgress);
        Invoke(showProgress, new object[] { sender, e });
    }
}

void CalcPi(int digits) {
    StringBuilder pi = new StringBuilder("3", digits + 2);
    object sender = System.Threading.Thread.CurrentThread;
    ShowProgressArgs e = new ShowProgressArgs(pi.ToString(), digits, 0);

    // Show progress (ignoring Cancel so soon)
    ShowProgress(sender, e);

    if( digits > 0 ) {
      pi.Append(".");

      for( int i = 0; i < digits; i += 9 ) {
        int nineDigits = NineDigitsOfPi.StartingAt(i+1);
        int digitCount = Math.Min(digits - i, 9);
        string ds = string.Format("{0:D9}", nineDigits);
        pi.Append(ds.Substring(0, digitCount));

        // Show progress (checking for Cancel)
        e.Pi = pi.ToString();
        e.DigitsSoFar = i + digitCount;
        ShowProgress(sender, e);
        if( e.Cancel ) break;
      }
    }
}
```

This technique represents a *message passing* model. This model is clear,
safe, general-purpose, and scalable. It's clear because it's easy to see
that the worker is creating a message, passing it to the UI, and then checking the message for information that may have been added during the UI
thread's processing of the message. It's safe because the ownership of the
message is never shared, starting with the worker thread, moving to the UI
thread, and then returning to the worker thread, with no simultaneous
access between the two threads. It's general-purpose because if the worker

or UI thread needed to communicate information in addition to a cancel flag, that information can be added to the ShowProgressArgs class. Finally, this technique is scalable because it uses a thread pool, which can handle a large number of long-running operations more efficiently than naïvely creating a new thread for each one. For long-running operations in your WinForms applications, you should first consider message passing.

Asynchronous Web Services

One specific area in which you'll want to use asynchronous WinForms applications is when calling Web services. Calling a Web service is similar to passing a message between threads, except that Web services messages travel between machines using standard protocols such as HTTP and XML.[4] Imagine a .NET Web service that calculated digits of pi using some way-cool fast pi calculation engine:

```
public class CalcPiService : System.Web.Services.WebService {
  [WebMethod]
  public string CalcPi(int digits) {
    StringBuilder pi = new StringBuilder("3", digits + 2);

    // Way-cool fast pi calculator running on a huge processor...

    return pi.ToString();
  }
}
```

Now imagine a version of the CalcPi program that used the Web service instead of our slow client-side algorithm to calculate pi on giant machines with huge processors (or even better, databases with more digits of pi cached than anyone could ever want or need). Although the underlying protocol of Web services is HTTP- and XML-based and we could form a Web service request fairly readily to ask for the digits of pi we're after, it's simpler to let VS.NET generate a class to make the Web services calls for you. You can do this in the Project menu using the Add Web Reference

---

4. For thorough coverage of the whys and wherefores of Web services, you can read *.NET Web Services: Architecture and Implementation with .NET* (Addison-Wesley, 2003), by Keith Ballinger.

item. The Add Web Reference dialog allows you to enter the URL of the WSDL (Web Service Description Language) that describes the Web service you'd like to call. For example, after installing the Web service sample that accompanies this book,[5] you can access the WSDL via the following URL:

```
http://localhost/CalcPiWebService/CalcPiService.asmx?WSDL
```

Accepting the WSDL in the Add Web Reference dialog will generate a *client-side Web services proxy class*, a helper class that turns your method calls into Web services messages. The generated proxy code for the CalcPi Web service looks like this:

```
namespace AsyncCalcPi.localhost {
  [WebServiceBindingAttribute(Name="CalcPiServiceSoap", ...)]
  public class CalcPiService : SoapHttpClientProtocol {
    public CalcPiService() {
      this.Url = "http://localhost/CalcPiWebService/CalcPiService.asmx";
    }

    [SoapDocumentMethodAttribute("http://tempuri.org/CalcPi", ...)]
    public string CalcPi(int digits) {...}

    public IAsyncResult
      BeginCalcPi(
        int digits,
        System.AsyncCallback callback,
        object asyncState) {...}

    public string EndCalcPi(IAsyncResult asyncResult) {...}
  }
}
```

Calling the Web service is now a matter of creating an instance of the proxy and calling the method you're interested in:

```
localhost.CalcPiService service = new localhost.CalcPiService();

void calcButton_Click(object sender, System.EventArgs e) {
  piTextBox.Text = service.CalcPi((int)digitsUpDown.Value);
}
```

---

5. See the ReadMe.htm file that comes with the book's samples for detailed instructions on setting them up.

Because Web services make calls across machine and often network boundaries, you should assume they'll take a long time, and, if called synchronously, they'll block the UI thread. You can use the standard techniques discussed in this chapter to call Web service methods asynchronously, but as you can tell in the generated proxy code, there's built-in support for asynchronous operations via the BeginXxx/EndXxx method pairs, one for each method on the Web service.

The first step in retrofitting the sample application to use the Web service is to call the Web service proxy's BeginCalcPi method:

```
enum CalcState {
  Pending,
  Calculating,
  Canceled,
}

CalcState state = CalcState.Pending;
localhost.CalcPiService service = new localhost.CalcPiService();

void calcButton_Click(object sender, System.EventArgs e) {
  switch( state ) {
    // Start a new calculation
    case CalcState.Pending:
      // Allow canceling
      state = CalcState.Calculating;
      calcButton.Text = "Cancel";

      // Start Web service request
      service.BeginCalcPi(
        (int)digitsUpDown.Value,
        new AsyncCallback(PiCalculated),
        null);
      break;

    // Cancel a running calculation
    case CalcState.Calculating:
      state = CalcState.Canceled;
      calcButton.Enabled = false;
      service.Abort(); // Fail all outstanding requests
      break;

    // Shouldn't be able to press Calc button while it's canceling
    case CalcState.Canceled:
      Debug.Assert(false);
```

continues

```
      break;
    }
}
```

void PiCalculated(IAsyncResult res) {...}

The BeginCalcPi method takes the method parameters and an instance of an AsyncCallback delegate. The application provides the PiCalculated event handler to match the AsyncCallback signature. The PiCalculated method, which will be called when the Web service returns, is responsible for harvesting results.

Also, even though there is no way to get progress from a Web service (all the more reason to call it asynchronously), calls to a Web service can be canceled by a call to the Abort method. Be careful with this one, however, because it will cancel all outstanding requests, not just a specific one.

When the AsyncCallback event handler is called, it means that the Web service has returned something:

```
void PiCalculated(IAsyncResult res) {
  try {
    ShowPi(service.EndCalcPi(res));
  }
  catch( WebException ex ) {
    ShowPi(ex.Message);
  }
}
```

The call to EndCalcPi, passing in the IAsyncResult parameter, provides any results of calling the Web service. If the Web service call was successful, the return value is pi. If, on the other hand, the Web service call was unsuccessful, because it timed out or was canceled, EndCalcPi will throw a WebException. That's why PiCalculated wraps the call to EndCalcPi in a try-catch block. ShowPi will be called on to show either the digits of pi that were calculated by the Web service or the exception message (the result of a canceled Web service call is shown in Figure 14.7).

The ShowPi method displays the results of the Web service invocation:

```
delegate void ShowPiDelegate(string pi);

void ShowPi(string pi) {
  if( this.InvokeRequired == false ) {
```

FIGURE 14.7: The Result of a Canceled Call to the Pi Web Service

```
    piTextBox.Text = pi;
    state = CalcState.Pending;
    calcButton.Text = "Calc";
    calcButton.Enabled = true;
  }
  else {
    ShowPiDelegate showPi = new ShowPiDelegate(ShowPi);
    this.BeginInvoke(showPi, new object[] {pi});
  }
}
```

Notice that the ShowPi method contains the check to see whether an invoke is required, and it calls Control.BeginInvoke to transfer from the current thread to the UI thread, just as we've been doing for most of this chapter. This is necessary because the Web service completion notification will come in on a thread other than the UI thread.

Where Are We?

The pi calculator example demonstrates how to perform long-running operations while still displaying a progress dialog and keeping the UI responsive to user interaction. Not only does it leverage multiple threads to split the UI from a long-running operation, but also the UI thread communicates further user input back to the worker thread to adjust its behavior. Although it could use shared data, the application uses a message passing scheme between threads to avoid the complications of synchronization.

.NET has extensive threading support, so techniques other than message passing can certainly be used to achieve the same ends. However, whatever method you choose, it's important to remember that a worker thread cannot call methods nor set properties on a control. Only the UI thread can do that. The Control.InvokeRequired property tells you whether you need to transition from a worker thread to a UI thread, and the Control.Invoke and Control.BeginInvoke methods perform the transition for you.

■ 15 ■
Web Deployment

S O FAR, THIS BOOK HAS BEEN targeted at using WinForms to build
applications, forms, and controls. The traditional means of deploying
such code is via a setup application, or more recently, a Microsoft Installer
(MSI) file. The problem is getting the setup executed on the desired client
machines and, after that's done, keeping the clients up-to-date.

Web applications, on the other hand, offer a much more primitive application and control implementation framework, but a much simpler deployment model. All that's needed to keep a Web client user up-to-date is to
keep the files on the Web server itself up-to-date. WinForms supports this
model not only for controls hosted on a Web page but also for WinForms
applications themselves, marrying the simplicity and power of WinForms
development with the simplicity and power of the Web deployment model.

Hosting Controls in Internet Explorer

One way to deploy WinForms code over the Web is to use Internet
Explorer (IE) 5.01+ to host a WinForms control on a Web page. You do this
using an HTML object tag formatted appropriately:

```
<object
  id="iectrl"
  classid="iectrl.dll#iectrl.UserControl1"
  width="100"
  height="100">
```

continues

```
</object>
```

The object tag is very much like the object tag used to pull in a COM control, something we've had for several versions of IE. The ID defines the variable name to be used in script code. The width and height define the dimensions that the control will draw itself into.

Control Creation

The only thing that's different is the classid attribute. Instead of specifying a COM class ID (CLSID), classid specifies the name of the .NET type to create in the form:

```
<dll>#<namespace>.<class>
```

The sample classid attribute shown in Figure 15.1 refers to the User-Control1 class in the iectrl namespace in the iectrl.dll assembly. This classid will cause IE to download the DLL (if it's not already cached), create an instance of the iectrl.UserControl1 class, and show it on the Web page.

The control in Figure 15.1 is a UserControl that looks like Figure 15.2 in the Designer.

As part of the creation process, you can augment the object tag with nested *param* tags that set public properties on the control after a successful creation:

```
<object id="iectrl" ...>
  <param name="somethingPrefix" value="hi! " />
</object>
```

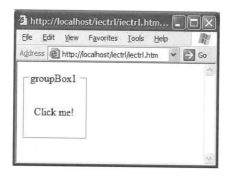

FIGURE 15.1: A WinForms Control Hosted in IE

FIGURE 15.2: The Sample Control Shown in the Designer

This code sets the SomethingPrefix property of the newly created UserControl1 object to the value "hi!". Setting of parameters is pretty loose in that the case doesn't matter, nor do the double quotes around the value (unless you're embedding spaces, as in this example). All reasonable means will be used to find the appropriate property and to convert the value to the appropriate type. If there is no public property named SomethingPrefix, the parameter will be ignored.

Control Interaction

After you've created the object, you can set properties and call methods in client-side script using the same syntax you'd use for the native objects of the scripting language itself:

```
<!-- page.htm -->
...
<input
  type="button"
  value="Say Something"
  onclick="iectrl.saySomething('something')" />
```

This HTML creates a button that, when pressed, calls the SaySomething method of the iectrl object, which just happens to be the WinForms control created earlier in the object tag. Similar HTML can be used to handle the control's events:

```
<!-- page.htm -->
...
<script for="iectrl" event="OuchEvent(degree)">
```

```
   alert("Ouch to the " + degree + "th degree!");
</script>
```

This HTML creates an event handler for the iectrl object that handles the OuchEvent, taking a single argument. Until now, all the interoperability mappings between unmanaged COM objects on the IE side and managed objects on the .NET side have been seamless as far as the control was concerned. To be hosted in IE, a WinForms control merely has to derive ultimately from the Control class, implement a public constructor that takes no arguments, and expose public properties and methods.[1] However, exposing events requires greater work. For example, the UserControl1 class exposes a single public event:

```
// UserControl1.cs
...
namespace iectrl {
  public delegate void OuchCallback(int degree);

  public class UserControl1 : UserControl {
    public event OuchCallback OuchEvent;
    ...
  }
}
```

To expose a control's events to IE requires bundling them into a COM *source* interface, which is a list of methods that constitute events that a COM object will fire. To bundle a set of .NET events into a COM source interface, you must list the events as methods whose names match the names of the events in the .NET control and whose signatures match the delegates of which the methods are instances:

```
// UserControl1.cs
...
 [InterfaceType(ComInterfaceType.InterfaceIsIDispatch)]
public interface IOuchEvents {
  [DispId(1)] void OuchEvent(int degree);
}
```

---

1. Technically, to be hosted in IE, a WinForms control must also set the assembly-side Allow-PartiallyTrustedCallersAttribute, which is discussed in more detail later in this chapter.

In addition to listing each event as a method, you must use the DispID attribute to mark each method in the interface with an interface-unique, positive integer needed by COM. Also, you must use the InterfaceType attribute to mark the interface as a whole as a COM source interface. Both attributes come from the System.Runtime.InteropServices namespace.

After defining the interface, you also must use the ComSourceInterfaces attribute (also from the System.Runtime.InteropServices namespace) to mark the control that fires the events from that interface:

```
// UserControl1.cs
...
[ComSourceInterfaces(typeof(IOuchEvents))]
public class UserControl1 : UserControl {...}
```

This combination of attributes will provide the COM wrapper around your .NET control with enough metadata to perform the mapping needed to expose events to HTML in IE. Unfortunately, exposing events to IE isn't enough to actually fire events. You must do two more things before this will work.

The first additional requirement is that you increase permissions so that code deployed from the Web has permission to make the transition from managed to unmanaged code. This can be accomplished by awarding Full Trust to the assembly that contains the control. For this, you use the Trust An Assembly Wizard available from Start | Settings | Control Panel | Administrative Tools | Microsoft .NET Framework Wizards. This process is discussed at length later in this chapter.

The second requirement for firing events into unmanaged code is that you grant the permission to call unmanaged code to the managed code hosting your WinForms controls. You use the Assert method of the permission object:

```
// UserControl1.cs
...
void label1_Click(object sender, EventArgs e) {
    // Assumes assembly granted unmanaged code permissions
    SecurityPermissionFlag flag = SecurityPermissionFlag.UnmanagedCode;
    SecurityPermission perm = new SecurityPermission(flag);
    perm.Assert();// DANGER! (read on!)
```

continues

```
    if( OuchEvent != null ) OuchEvent(10);
}
```

However, it's very likely that neither of these requirements makes sense unless you're familiar with .NET's security model, which I discuss next.

Code Access Security

.NET brings with it a new security model for deployed code. Instead of an assembly getting the permissions of the process running the code, the .NET Code Access Security (CAS) model grants code permissions based on where the code originates.[2] To view the current permission settings on your machine, use the Microsoft .NET Framework Configuration tool (available in your Administration Tools menu). Drilling into the Permission Sets for the Machine's Runtime Security Policy reveals a number of entries, including FullTrust, LocalIntranet, Internet, and so on. Figure 15.3 shows the set of Internet permissions.

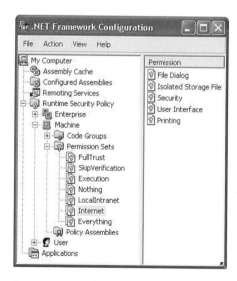

FIGURE 15.3: Default Internet Permission Set

---

2. For a much more detailed discussion of CAS, you'll want to read *Essential .NET* (Addison-Wesley, 2003), by Don Box, with Chris Sells.

Table 15.1 compares the LocalIntranet permission set to the Internet permission set.

Assemblies are associated with a permission set in any number of ways: according to the publisher, the site, the strong name, the security zone, and so on. Most of the default code groups associate code with a zone. For example, the My_Computer_Zone is associated with the FullTrust permission set, and the Local_Intranet_Zone is associated with the LocalIntranet permission set. In release 1.0 of .NET, the Internet_Zone was associated with the Internet permission set, but as of service pack 1 of the .NET runtime, code from the Internet_Zone is associated with the Nothing permission set by

TABLE 15.1: Intranet and Internet CAS Permissions

Permission	Level	LocalIntranet	Internet
FileDialog	Unrestricted	Yes	No
FileDialog	Access=Open	Yes	Yes
IsolatedStorageFile	Allow=AssemblyIsolationByUser	Yes	No
IsolatedStorageFile	Allow=DomainIsolationByUser	Yes	Yes
Printing	Level=DefaultPrinting	Yes	No
Printing	Level=SafePrinting	Yes	Yes
Reflection	Flags=ReflectionEmit	Yes	No
Security	Flags=Assertion	Yes	No
Security	Flags=Execution	Yes	Yes
UI	Unrestricted	Yes	No
UI	Clipboard=OwnClipboard	Yes	Yes
UI	Window=SafeSubWindows	Yes	Yes
UI	Window=SafeTopLevelWindows	Yes	Yes
Web	Connect=http to originating site	Yes	Yes
Web	Connect=https to originating site	Yes	Yes

default. This change in SP1 reflects some doubt that Microsoft had as to the full safety of the .NET Framework Class Library code. As of .NET 1.1, the doubts have been resolved, and the Internet_Zone is again associated with the Internet permission set.

The zone where an assembly originates is determined by the path used to find the assembly, as shown in Table 15.2.

If an assembly needs to know the zone it's running in, it can access the zone via the Zone class in System.Security.Policy:

```
using System.Security;
using System.Security.Policy;
...
string appbase = AppDomain.CurrentDomain.BaseDirectory;
SecurityZone zone = Zone.CreateFromUrl(appbase).SecurityZone;
```

By default, the loaded assembly gets the union of all the permissions from all the code groups to which it belongs and must live within the confines of those permissions. Any attempt to perform an action for which the assembly does not have the corresponding permission will result in a security exception.

Checking for Permissions

Although an application can catch a SecurityException if it violates its set of permissions, it can also check first to see whether it's got the permissions it's after. This allows an application to downgrade its capabilities if appropriate permissions aren't available. Checking for permission is a matter of

TABLE 15.2: How an Assembly's Zone Is Determined

Path	Example	Zone
Local file	c:\ foo\foo.exe	MyComputer
UNC name or non-dotted site URL	\\server\foo\foo.exe or http://server/foo/foo.exe or http://localhost/foo/foo.exe or z:\foo\foo.exe if z is mapped to a network share	LocalIntranet
All numeric IP address or dotted-site URL	http://1115768663/foo/foo.exe or http://www.sellsbrothers.com/foo/foo.exe or http://127.0.0.1/foo/foo.exe	Internet

creating a permission object, demanding that permission, and catching the security exception if the demand fails.

For example, to check whether your control is allowed to fire an event into unmanaged code, you use an instance of the SecurityPermission class from the System.Security.Permissions namespace:

```
using System.Security;
using System.Security.Permissions;

bool HavePermission(IPermission perm) {
    try { perm.Demand(); }
    catch( SecurityException ) { return false; }
    return true;
}

void label1_Click(object sender, EventArgs e) {
  SecurityPermissionFlag flag = SecurityPermissionFlag.UnmanagedCode;
  SecurityPermission perm = new SecurityPermission(flag);
  if( !HavePermission(perm) ) return;
  ... // Fire event
}
```

If you wonder which permission you need for a specific call, you should start with the security exception itself. Unfortunately, unlike most other exceptions in .NET, the security exception provides somewhat terse information. That's to prevent bad people from learning too much about an application's implementation, although it does tend to make debugging security exceptions a bit harder. In these cases, I check the documentation, which is surprisingly good about telling you which permissions are needed and when.[3]

Awarding Permissions

Even if your assembly has permission to perform an action, such as calling unmanaged code, it's not necessarily the case that another assembly calling your assembly has those permissions. CAS is set up so that a request for a permission will be denied unless everyone in the call chain

---

3. To check on all kinds of details, including permissions, for a WinForms control hosted in IE, you might try adjusting the undocumented DebugIEHost Registry setting as discussed at http://discuss.develop.com/archives/wa.exe?A2=ind0109A&L=DOTNET&P=R9256.

has the needed permission. For example, even if an assembly hosted in IE has permission to call into unmanaged code, as of .NET 1.x the managed code hosting that assembly does not have that permission. If the control needs to exercise a permission that the code above it in the call chain doesn't have, the control must grant the permission it has to everyone hosting it. You do this using the Assert method on the permission object:

```
void label1_Click(object sender, EventArgs e) {
  // Make sure we have permission to call unmanaged code
  SecurityPermissionFlag flag = SecurityPermissionFlag.UnmanagedCode;
  SecurityPermission perm = new SecurityPermission(flag);
  if( !HavePermission(perm) ) return;

  // Grant managed hosting code permission to call unmanaged code
  perm.Assert();
  if( OuchEvent != null ) OuchEvent(10);
}
```

In this code, we create a permission object again, but after checking to make sure we have the appropriate permission, we also grant that permission, albeit temporarily, until the method returns. In general, granting permissions in this way is a really bad idea and should be used only in a very narrow scope. The reason that .NET is checking everyone in the call chain is to make sure that bad assemblies don't coerce good assemblies into performing their evil deeds. By asserting permission, you're telling .NET that you'll vouch for everyone in the call chain—a weighty responsibility to take onto your shoulders.

No-Touch Deployment

In addition to letting you deploy WinForms controls, .NET also lets you use IE to deploy entire WinForms applications. This is a completely new feature for the Windows platform. You can best see its value by trying it:

1. Using the New Project dialog, create a new Windows application and call it DeploymentFun.
2. Feel free to drag and drop some controls from the Toolbox, but before going too far, compile your application.

3. In the shell explorer, navigate to your DeploymentFun\bin folder and right-click on the Debug folder, choosing Properties.

4. Choose Web Sharing and turn it on, using DeploymentFun as the name of the share. This will create a new Internet Information Server (IIS) Web application containing DeploymentFun.exe.

5. Now surf to your WinForms app using Start | Run and the following URL: http://localhost/DeploymentFun/DeploymentFun.exe.

6. After basking in the glory of using *no-touch deployment* (NTD) to deploy a real Windows application over the Web without doing any setup, stop playing around and read the rest of this chapter!

Application Download

As a test of the *no-touch deployment model* for WinForms applications, I built a simple game, as shown in Figure 15.4.[4]

On the Web server, deployment of a .NET application is merely a matter of dropping the .exe file into a Web application directory so that the Web server can hand out the bits on demand. The .NET runtime is not required on the server, nor is Microsoft's Internet Information Server nor even Windows itself. On the client side, however, things are a bit more interesting. When you feed Internet Explorer an URL such as http://localhost/wahoo/wahoo.exe, it forms an HTTP request for the wahoo.exe file to be streamed back to the client:

```
GET /wahoo.exe HTTP/1.1
Accept: */*
Accept-Language: en-us
Accept-Encoding: gzip, deflate
User-Agent: Mozilla/4.0 (compatible; MSIE 6.0; Windows NT 5.1; Q312461;
.NET CLR 1.0.3705)
Host: localhost
Connection: Keep-Alive
```

The response from the server is just a stream of bytes:

---

4. Any similarity to any other very popular game that you may already be familiar with is strictly intentional.

FIGURE 15.4: The Game of Wahoo!

```
HTTP/1.1 200 OK
Server: Microsoft-IIS/5.1
Date: Fri, 01 Feb 2002 02:11:29 GMT
Content-Type: application/octet-stream
Accept-Ranges: bytes
Last-Modified: Fri, 01 Feb 2002 01:41:16 GMT
ETag: "50aae089c1aac11:916"
Content-Length: 45056

<<stream of bytes from wahoo.exe>>
```

In addition to the bytes themselves, the last modified date and time are cached by IE on the client side. This is used to form a request each subsequent time that the application is launched using the same URL:

```
GET /wahoo.exe HTTP/1.1
Accept: */*
```

```
Accept-Language: en-us
Accept-Encoding: gzip, deflate
If-Modified-Since: Fri, 01 Feb 2002 01:41:16 GMT
If-None-Match: "50aae089c1aac11:916"
User-Agent: Mozilla/4.0 (compatible; MSIE 6.0; Windows NT 5.1; Q312461;
.NET CLR 1.0.3705)
Host: localhost
Connection: Keep-Alive
```

The If-Modified-Since header is kept in IE's download cache and is sent back with each request. In this way, if the bits on the server haven't changed, the server can respond with a header that indicates that the cache is still good, reducing the payload that needs to be downloaded to the client:

```
HTTP/1.1 304 Not Modified
Server: Microsoft-IIS/5.1
Date: Fri, 01 Feb 2002 02:42:03 GMT
ETag: "a0fa92bc8aac11:916"
Content-Length: 0
```

The bytes themselves are cached in two places: IE's download cache, managed by IE, and the *.NET download cache*, which is a cache for .NET assemblies (both .exe and .dll files) downloaded on demand. The contents of the .NET download cache can be examined using gacutil.exe /ldl and cleared using gacutil.exe /cdl. If, during your testing, you'd like to ensure that a download happens, make sure to clear IE's cache using the Internet control panel and clear .NET's cache using gacutil.

Versioning

While we're talking about caching and downloading the "latest version," you may be curious about how actual versions affect things. As you may know, you can tag a .NET assembly with a specific version using the AssemblyVersionAttribute:[5]

```
// Strong naming is required when versioning
[assembly: AssemblyKeyFileAttribute("wahoo.key")]
[assembly: AssemblyVersionAttribute("1.2.3.4")]
```

---

5. .NET versioning is discussed at length in *Essential .NET* (Addison-Wesley, 2003), by Don Box, with Chris Sells.

With this in mind, you may wonder whether .NET versioning affects caching and downloading. It does—sometimes.

When a request is formed for http://localhost/wahoo/wahoo.exe, the runtime doesn't have any idea which version we'd like, so it simply asks the Web server for the latest *HTTP version* as indicated by the If-Modified-Since header sent along with the HTTP request. If the runtime already has the latest HTTP version, no download needs to happen. However, if the server has a newer binary (based on the date/time stamp on the file)—even if that binary is of a lower *.NET version* (based on the Assembly-VersionAttribute)—the latest HTTP version will be downloaded. In other words, the .NET version plays no role in what constitutes the "latest version" of the application launched with an URL.

On the other hand—and this is the "sometimes" part—any assembly can reference other assemblies, either implicitly as part of the manifest or explicitly via the Assembly.Load method. For example, wahoo.exe references wahooControl.dll. Whatever the .NET version is of wahoo-Control.dll that wahoo.exe compiles against will be the version that the *assembly resolver* (the part of the .NET runtime responsible for finding code) expects to find at run time. If that .NET version of wahooControl.dll is in the cache, the assembly resolver will not send a request to the Web server asking whether it has a newer .NET version. This means that if you'd like the client to have a newer .NET version of a referenced assembly, you must make sure that the Web server is serving up an updated EXE assembly that refers to the referenced assembly.

Related Files

As I just mentioned, assemblies can reference other assemblies. For example, an assembly may already be present in the *Global Assembly Cache* (GAC), the place where systemwide shared assemblies are kept in .NET. If an assembly is in the GAC, such as System.Windows.Forms.dll, then that's where the assembly will be loaded from. If the assembly is not in the GAC, the .NET download cache is checked. If the download cache doesn't contain the assembly, the assembly resolver goes back to the originating server using the *application base (appbase)* of the assembly. The appbase is the "directory" from which the initial assembly was loaded—for example, c:\wahoo or http://localhost/wahoo. The appbase is available using the

GetData function of the currently executing *application domain (appdomain)*, which is the context under which all .NET code runs.[6] The appbase can be obtained for the appdomain in this way:

```
string appbase = AppDomain.CurrentDomain.BaseDirectory;
```

For example, when wahoo.exe needs wahooControls.dll and it's not present in the GAC or the download cache, the assembly resolver will go back to the originating Web server, as you've seen. Referenced assemblies, however, are not the only files that the assembly resolver will look for when an executable is loaded. In fact, on my machine when I surf to the initial version of the signed wahoo.exe after the caches have been cleared, 35 requests are made for files, as shown in Table 15.3.

TABLE 15.3: Files Requested When Surfing to wahoo.exe

Request #	GET Request
1	/wahoo/wahoo.exe
2	/wahoo/wahoo.exe.config
3	/wahoo/WahooControl.DLL
4	/wahoo/en-US/Wahoo.resources.DLL
5	/wahoo/en-US/Wahoo.resources/Wahoo.resources.DLL
6	/wahoo/bin/en-US/Wahoo.resources.DLL
7	/wahoo/bin/en-US/Wahoo.resources/Wahoo.resources.DLL
8	/wahoo/en-US/Wahoo.resources.EXE
9	/wahoo/en-US/Wahoo.resources/Wahoo.resources.EXE
10	/wahoo/bin/en-US/Wahoo.resources.EXE
11	/wahoo/bin/en-US/Wahoo.resources/Wahoo.resources.EXE
12	/wahoo/en/Wahoo.resources.DLL

---

6. For details of appdomains and appbases, you should read *Essential .NET* (Addison-Wesley, 2003), by Don Box, with Chris Sells.

TABLE 15.3:   Files Requested When Surfing to wahoo.exe (continued)

Request #	GET Request
13	/wahoo/en/Wahoo.resources/Wahoo.resources.DLL
14	/wahoo/bin/en/Wahoo.resources.DLL
15	/wahoo/bin/en/Wahoo.resources/Wahoo.resources.DLL
16	/wahoo/en/Wahoo.resources.EXE
17	/wahoo/en/Wahoo.resources/Wahoo.resources.EXE
18	/wahoo/bin/en/Wahoo.resources.EXE
19	/wahoo/bin/en/Wahoo.resources/Wahoo.resources.EXE
20	/wahoo/en-US/Wahoo.resources.DLL
21	/wahoo/en-US/Wahoo.resources/Wahoo.resources.DLL
22	/wahoo/bin/en-US/Wahoo.resources.DLL
23	/wahoo/bin/en-US/Wahoo.resources/Wahoo.resources.DLL
24	/wahoo/en-US/Wahoo.resources.EXE
25	/wahoo/en-US/Wahoo.resources/Wahoo.resources.EXE
26	/wahoo/bin/en-US/Wahoo.resources.EXE
27	/wahoo/bin/en-US/Wahoo.resources/Wahoo.resources.EXE
28	/wahoo/en/Wahoo.resources.DLL
29	/wahoo/en/Wahoo.resources/Wahoo.resources.DLL
30	/wahoo/bin/en/Wahoo.resources.DLL
31	/wahoo/bin/en/Wahoo.resources/Wahoo.resources.DLL
32	/wahoo/en/Wahoo.resources.EXE
33	/wahoo/en/Wahoo.resources/Wahoo.resources.EXE
34	/wahoo/bin/en/Wahoo.resources.EXE
35	/wahoo/bin/en/Wahoo.resources/Wahoo.resources.EXE

The .config File

The first request in Table 15.3 makes sense because it's the assembly we asked for to begin with. The second request is for a .config file, which you may recall from Chapter 11: Applications and Settings. If you're serving your WinForms application from an IIS installation, you'll need to enable anonymous access to your .exe file's Web application. Also, if ASP.NET is installed on the server, you may need to override the default behavior in a virtual directory to disable any .config files being supplied. If you find that your application's .config is available on the server but is not being downloaded to the client, use the following settings in a web.config file at the base of the virtual directory:

```
<configuration>
  <system.web>
    <!--
    Remove the *.config handler so that we can serve up
    *.exe.config files, but make it forbidden to serve up the
    web.config file itself.
    -->
    <httpHandlers>
      <remove verb="*" path="*.config" />
      <add verb="*" path="web.config"
        type="System.Web.HttpForbiddenHandler"/>
    </httpHandlers>
  </system.web>
</configuration>
```

These configuration settings remove the restriction on all .config files and reinstate it for only web.config files, which still need protection from download. Some versions of ASP.NET disable all .config files, whereas others don't, so if the <remove> element causes an error, you shouldn't need these extra settings in your web.config at all.

Resources

The third request in Table 15.3 is for the wahooControl.dll assembly that wahoo.exe references, as we expect. The next request is for a resources assembly called Wahoo.resources. You should recognize this request (and the rest of the requests) as made by the resource manager looking for localized resources, as discussed in Chapter 10: Resources. These requests are being made for the WahooControl object's background image, which is stored in the wahooControl assembly's resources.

On the local machine or a LAN, the localization probe performed by the resource manager is chewy goodness, but that's not necessarily so in a WAN environment. When the latest wahoo.exe and wahooControl.dll are already cached on my machine, I've seen these additional requests take more than 75 percent of the load time. These extra round-trips can make for a very poor user experience, especially when culture-neutral resources are the only resources in your application.

In this case, you have a couple of options. One option is to avoid using WinForms Designer to set properties that use resources. In this way, the Designer-generated code doesn't create a resource manager. Then, to load resources, you write the code yourself in a culture-neutral way:

```
public MainForm() {
  // Let the Designer-generated code run
  InitializeComponent();

  // Init culture-neutral properties
  this.game.BackgroundImage =
    new Bitmap(typeof(MainForm), "sblogo.gif");
}
```

Loading resources manually is handy for resources that you know are culture-neutral and never want to localize, but it does mean giving up WinForms Designer for resource management. If you share my addiction to WYSIWYG form design, the resource manager supports an optimization that often makes this kind of handwritten code unnecessary. Recall NeutralResourcesLanguageAttribute from Chapter 10: Resources. This attribute marks the resources bundled in your assembly as culture-specific so that they will be found first without the round-trips to the Web server when launched from that culture:

```
[assembly: NeutralResourcesLanguageAttribute("en-US")]
```

This attribute reduces the number of requests from 34 to 2 when the assembly is launched from a machine with the culture of the assembly, thereby improving load times considerably. If you'd like to let the Designer generate the code and reduce round-trips for cultures other than the one in which you're writing the application, you can put zero-length files in the first places that the resource manager looks. For example, zero-length files on the server under the following names will be used for the English language and the US:

```
en-US\assemName.resources.dll
en\assemName.resources.dll
```

The presence of zero-length files at the appropriate locations causes the resource manager to find the resource files it's looking for, even if they're empty. When it comes to resolving specific resources, zero-length files will cause an extra lookup by the resource manager for a culture- or language-specific resource, but if it's not found, the culture-neutral resources in the resolving assembly will be used in the normal way.

Working Offline

Of course, the ultimate reduction of requests is to use no requests at all. By putting IE into offline mode (via the File menu), surfing to an NTD application will work completely from the cache. A better model is to use the cache automatically if the client machine was not connected to the Internet or the server was unavailable, but, as of .NET 1.1, that feature is not part of the NTD implementation.

Partially Trusted Assembly Considerations

As I mentioned earlier in this chapter, by default .NET code deployed over the Web will be awarded a smaller set of permissions than code launched directly from the hard drive in the MyComputer zone. Any assembly, whether it's an .exe or a .dll, that's launched from the MyComputer zone will be *fully trusted* by default, and this means that it can do anything that the launching user is allowed to do. Assemblies deployed from the Web, on the other hand, will be *partially trusted*, because they aren't allowed to do everything. If you're building assemblies that are designed to work in a partially trusted environment, you need to take this into account, or else your users will see a lot of security exceptions.

For example, the wahoo and wahooControl assemblies are designed to work within the restricted set of Internet permissions, and this meant that it was difficult to implement the functionality I wanted. The challenging areas I encountered included the following:

- Allowing partially trusted callers
- Remembering and restoring user settings
- Handling keystrokes
- Communicating with Web services
- Reading and writing files
- Parsing command line arguments

Allowing Partially Trusted Callers

The first problem I ran into when deploying my wahoo.exe and wahooControl.dll assemblies was enabling wahoo.exe to make calls into wahooControl.dll. This happened as soon as I signed wahooControl.dll with a public/private key pair (as all .NET assemblies should be signed):

```
[assembly: AssemblyKeyFileAttribute("wahoo.key")]
```

.NET has a giant Frankenstein switch for each signed assembly, and this switch determines whether the assembly is secure enough to be called from partially trusted assemblies. By default, a signed assembly does not allow calls from partially trusted assemblies. This means that after wahooControl.dll is signed, by default it can't be called from a partially trusted assembly, even the one that caused it to be downloaded (in this case, wahoo.exe). To enable an assembly to be called from a partially trusted assembly, you need to set the assemblywide AllowPartiallyTrustedCallersAttribute (APTCA):

```
[assembly: AllowPartiallyTrustedCallersAttribute]
```

Although setting APTCA enables wahooControl.dll to be called from wahoo.exe, it also allows it to be called from any other partially trusted assembly. You should be very careful when you apply APTCA, because now you're on the hook to make sure that your assembly is robust in the face of partially trusted callers. Microsoft itself was cautious in applying this attribute, as you can see in Table 15.4, which shows the major .NET assemblies that allow partially trusted callers as of .NET 1.1.[7]

TABLE 15.4: Major .NET Assemblies and Their APTCA Setting

Assembly	ACPTA Set
Accessibility.dll	Yes
CustomMarshalers.dll	No
Microsoft.JScript.dll	Yes
Microsoft.VisualBasic.dll	Yes
Microsoft.VisualBasic.Vsa.dll	No
Microsoft.VisualC.Dll	No
Microsoft.Vsa.dll	Yes
Microsoft.Vsa.Vb.CodeDOMProcessor.dll	No
mscorcfg.dll	No
mscorlib.dll	Yes
RegCode.dll	No
System.Configuration.Install.dll	No
System.Data.dll	Yes
System.Data.OracleClient.dll	No
System.Design.dll	No
System.DirectoryServices.dll	No
System.dll	Yes
System.Drawing.Design.dll	No

---

7. To generate this list, I used Keith Brown's most excellent FindAPTC utility, available at http://www.develop.com/kbrown/security/samples.htm

TABLE 15.4: Major .NET Assemblies and Their APTCA Setting (continued)

Assembly	ACPTA Set
System.Drawing.dll	Yes
System.EnterpriseServices.dll	No
System.Management.dll	No
System.Messaging.dll	No
System.Runtime.Remoting.dll	No
System.Runtime.Serialization.Formatters.Soap.dll	No
System.Security.dll	No
System.ServiceProcess.dll	No
System.Web.dll	Yes
System.Web.Mobile.dll	Yes
System.Web.RegularExpressions.dll	Yes
System.Web.Services.dll	Yes
System.Windows.Forms.dll	Yes
System.XML.dll	Yes

Any assembly that doesn't have the APTCA setting cannot be used from any partially trusted assembly, even those given the "Everything" permission set. Only fully trusted assemblies can access assemblies that aren't trusted for partially trusted callers. In addition, you must use APTCA to mark assemblies containing WinForms controls to allow the controls to be hosted in IE.

Settings

After an application has been run once, even an NTD application, users expect that any settings that they have changed will be saved for the next time the application is run. Storing and restoring application and user settings is covered in Chapter 11: Applications and Settings, but there are special considerations when you manage settings from partially trusted code.

For example, by default partially trusted code doesn't have permission to access the Registry or permission to access the file system without user interaction. However, isolated storage is explicitly allowed from partial trust, and this makes isolated storage the perfect place for user settings. Recall from Chapter 11: Applications and Settings how isolated storage works:

```
void MainForm_Closing(object sender, CancelEventArgs e) {
  // Save the form's position before it closes
  IsolatedStorageFile store =
    IsolatedStorageFile.GetUserStoreForAssembly();
  using( Stream stream =
          new IsolatedStorageFileStream("MainForm.txt",
          FileMode.Create,
          store) )
  using( StreamWriter writer = new StreamWriter(stream) ) {
    FormWindowState state = this.WindowState;
    this.WindowState = FormWindowState.Normal;
    writer.WriteLine(ToString(this.Location));
    writer.WriteLine(ToString(this.ClientSize));
    writer.WriteLine(ToString(state));
  }
}
```

The ToString method is a helper for converting simple types to strings using a type converter:

```
// Convert an object to a string
string ToString(object obj) {
  TypeConverter converter =
    TypeDescriptor.GetConverter(obj.GetType());
  return converter.ConvertToString(obj);
}
```

Although type converters are easy to use, they're not as full featured as .NET serialization (as covered in detail in Appendix C: Serialization Basics). However, because .NET serialization can be used to set an object's private fields, its use is strictly forbidden from partial trust, making type converters a useful partial trust alternative.

Custom User Input

In addition to saving user settings between runs, most applications need to take user input of some sort. If the user input is going to one of the standard WinForms controls, that's not a problem from partially trusted code. However, if a control needs to handle special keys—WahooControl, for example, needs to handle arrow keys—then as of .NET 1.1, it must take special measures.

Arrow keys, Tab, and Shift+Tab are special keys because of their use in moving between controls in a form. This means that a rogue assembly allowed to consume the arrow keys could easily hijack an entire form. For that reason, a control is not allowed to override ProcessDialogKey or IsInputKey, either of which would allow such an activity. The .NET runtime will throw a security exception whenever it attempts to compile a method that contains code that creates an instance of a type that overrides these or similar methods, protecting the user from a form-jacking. Unfortunately, this means that you can't use these methods to have WahooControl handle the arrow keys.

Another way to handle the arrow keys is to let the parent form retrieve the keys in its own implementation of OnKeyDown (an action that's allowed) and pass them to the control for processing. For a form to handle keystrokes that can be handled by a child control, such as the arrow keys, a form can set its own KeyPreview property to true. All this worked fine until experimentation with .NET 1.x showed that some of the current WinForm controls, such as StatusBar and Button, don't actually let the parent form at these special keys in other controls that allow special keys through aren't on the form, like TextBox. Because the main Wahoo! form contains only a custom control and a status bar, this becomes an "issue." As a workaround, the main Wahoo! form creates an invisible TextBox and adds it to the list of controls that the form is hosting:

```
public MainForm() {
  ...
  // HACK: Add a text box so that we can get the arrow keys
  Controls.Add(new TextBox());
}
```

Frankly, I'm not proud of this technique, but it lets the arrow keys through in a partially trusted environment, and one does what one must while waiting for a new platform to shake out.

Communicating via Web Services

Communicating with the user is not the only job of an NTD application. Very often an application must also communicate to the outside world. In the partially trusted zones, this communication is limited to talking back only to the originating site and only via HTTP requests and Web services. Luckily, the originating site is often what we want to talk to anyway, and Web services are easily flexible enough to handle the majority of our communication needs.

In addition to being flexible, Web services provide a much saner model for the split of server-side and client-side code. Instead of maintaining client state on the server, as a Web application often does, Web services typically provide a stateless end point that receives requests for service. These requests are typically large-grained and atomic in order to reduce requests and to let the client maintain its own state.

Generating the client-side proxy code necessary to talk to a Web service is as easy as adding a Web Reference to your project. You do this by pointing VS.NET at the URL for the Web service's WSDL (as discussed in Chapter 14: Multithreaded User Interfaces). Calling a Web service is a little tricky, however, because partially trusted code isn't allowed to make Web service calls anywhere but back to the originating server. It's up to you to make sure that the URL, which is hard-coded into the generated Web service proxy code, points at the originating server. You can do this by replacing the site in the hard-coded URL with the site that you discover dynamically using the application domain's appbase:

```
// Get a client-side Web service proxy of any type, replacing
// the "localhost" site with the appbase site
static SoapHttpClientProtocol GetServiceForAppBase(Type type) {
  // Create an instance of the service using .NET Reflection
  SoapHttpClientProtocol service = (SoapHttpClientProtocol)
    type.Assembly.CreateInstance(type.FullName);
```

continues

```
  try {
    // Set URL to server where this came from
    string appbase =
      AppDomain.CurrentDomain.BaseDirectory;
    string site =
      System.Security.Policy.Site.CreateFromUrl(appbase).Name;
    service.Url =
      service.Url.Replace("//localhost/", "//" + site + "/");
  }
  // If we can't create a site from the appbase,
  // then we're not an NTD app and there's no reason to
  // adjust the service's URL
  catch( ArgumentException ) {}

  return service;
}

void GetHighScores() {
  // Get scores
  WahooScoresService service = (WahooScoresService)
    GetServiceForAppBase(typeof(WahooScoresService));
  WahooScore[] scores = service.GetScores();

  // Show high scores...
}
```

The GetServiceForAppBase helper creates an instance of any type of client-side Web services proxy and then, if the application is NTD, replaces the "localhost" site with the site indicated by the appbase. This makes it handy not only to test your NTD application on your own machine from the MyComputer zone, but also to get the appropriate site when the NTD application is launched from an URL.

Reading and Writing Files

After I'd gotten the current high scores via the Web service, I found that I wanted to be able to cache them for later access (to savor the brief moment when I was at the top). .NET makes it easy to read and write files and to show the File Save and File Open dialogs. Unfortunately, only a limited subset of that functionality is available in partial trust. Referring again to Table 15.1, notice that the Intranet zone has unrestricted file dialog permissions but no file I/O permissions. This means that files can be read and written, but not without user interaction.

Unrestricted access to the file system is, of course, a security hole on par with buffer overflows and fake password dialogs. To avoid this problem but still allow an application to read and write files, a file can be opened only via the File Save or File Open dialog. Instead of using these dialogs to obtain a file name from the user, we use the dialogs themselves to open the file:

```
SaveFileDialog dlg = new SaveFileDialog();
dlg.DefaultExt = ".txt";
dlg.Filter = "Text Files (*.txt)|*.txt|All files (*.*)|*.*";

// NOTE: Not allowed unless we have FileIOPermission
//dlg.AddExtension = true;
//dlg.FileName = "somefile.txt";

if( dlg.ShowDialog() == DialogResult.OK ) {
  // NOTE: Not allowed to call dlg.FileName
  using( Stream stream = dlg.OpenFile() )
  using( StreamWriter writer = new StreamWriter(stream) ) {
    writer.Write("...");
  }
}
```

Notice that instead of opening a stream using the SaveFileDialog File-Name property after the user has chosen a file, we call the OpenFile method directly. This gives partially trusted code the ability to read from a file, but only with user intervention and providing the code no knowledge of the file system.

Command Line Arguments

One commonly used option when launching an application that doesn't bring to mind security restrictions (but still has them, as we'll see) is passing command line parameters. In a normal application, command line parameters are available from the string array passed to Main:

```
static void Main(string[] args) {
  foreach( string arg in args ) {
    MessageBox.Show(arg);
  }
  ...
}
```

Similarly, URLs have a well-known syntax for passing arguments:

```
http://itweb/hr452.exe?uid=csells&activity=vacation
```

The combination of the two makes it seem natural to be able to pass command line arguments to NTD applications using the special URL syntax. Unfortunately, the support for pulling command line arguments from the launching URL is new to 1.1[8] and underdocumented. Also, because the launching URL is used to create the path to the .config file, full support for command line arguments requires that some code be run on the server side as well.

Client-Side Support for NTD Arguments

To pull the arguments out of the launching URL requires, first, that we have access to the launching URL from within the NTD application. To access the launching URL, .NET 1.1 provides the APP_LAUNCH_URL data variable from the application domain:

```
// Works only for .NET 1.1+
AppDomain domain = AppDomain.CurrentDomain;
object obj = domain.GetData("APP_LAUNCH_URL");
string appLaunchUrl = (obj != null ? obj.ToString() : "");
System.Windows.Forms.MessageBox.Show(appLaunchUrl);
```

The URL used to launch the NTD application, including arguments, is provided in full by APP_LAUNCH_URL. Unfortunately, APP_LAUNCH_URL isn't available in .NET 1.0. However, because the path to an NTD application's .config file is only the URL (including arguments) with ".config" tacked onto the end, we can use that to pull out the equivalent of the APP_LAUNCH_URL in .NET 1.0. For example, suppose we launch an application from this URL:

```
http://foo/foo.exe?foo=bar@quux
```

That yields the following .config file path:

```
http://foo/foo.exe?foo=bar@quux.config
```

---

8. There is a workaround to enable pulling command line arguments from the launching URL that works in .NET 1.0, too, and it's covered later in the chapter.

The application domain provides access to the .config file path, so we can use that and a little string manipulation to get what we need:

```
// Works only for .NET 1.1+
AppDomain domain = AppDomain.CurrentDomain;
object obj = domain.GetData("APP_LAUNCH_URL");
string appLaunchUrl = (obj != null ? obj.ToString() : "");

// Fall-back for .NET 1.0
if( appLaunchUrl == "" ) {
  const string ext = ".config";
  string configFile = domain.SetupInformation.ConfigurationFile;
  appLaunchUrl =
    configFile.Substring(0, configFile.Length - ext.Length);
}

System.Windows.Forms.MessageBox.Show(appLaunchUrl);
```

No matter which way you get the URL used to launch the NTD application, both default Intranet and Internet permissions for .NET 1.x allow access to command line argument information from partially trusted clients. After you've got the full URL, it can be parsed for the arguments. The question mark should be used to pull off the arguments at the end, and the ampersand should be used to separate individual arguments. Unfortunately, although .NET provides classes for easily parsing and decoding query string-like URL command line arguments, partially trusted applications don't have permissions to use them, so parsing must be done by hand.[9]

Server-Side Support for NTD Arguments

The client side is not all there is to handling command line arguments for NTD applications. The URL, including arguments, is used to produce the path to the .config file, so if you want to serve up a .config file, you need some server-side code to deal with requests for .config files formed this way:

```
http://foo/foo.exe?foo=bar&quux.config
```

---

9. The samples that come with this book provide source code for full parsing and decoding of URL arguments.

These requests must be translated into requests like the following, with the arguments stripped away:

```
http://foo/foo.exe.config
```

The ASP.NET code needed to do this is beyond the scope of this book, but the included samples demonstrate one simple handler that does the job.[10]

Debugging NTD Applications

As is certainly obvious by now, debugging and working around security-related issues are the hardest parts of deploying an NTD application. If you launch an NTD application via an URL, you may have noticed that there are no processes running that have that name. Instead, each application launched via an URL is hosted by ieexec.exe, which sets up the appropriate environment before loading the application. To debug an NTD application in the appropriate environment, you must debug against an instance of ieexec.exe started with the appropriate arguments to launch the application. Unfortunately, the usage of ieexec.exe is undocumented, but the reverse-engineered usage for .NET 1.1 is shown here:

```
Usage: ieexec.exe <url>
urlAssembly to launch, e.g. http://localhost/foo.exe
```

Launching ieexec.exe in this way will cause it to pull down the application, if it's not already cached, and launch it according to the permissions granted based on the code group:

```
C:\> ieexec.exe http://127.0.0.1/wahoo/wahoo.exe
```

The benefit of being able to launch ieexec.exe directly like this is that it can be used as the launching application for debugging in VS.NET, as shown in a sample project's settings in Figure 15.5.

Notice that Debug Mode has been set to Program (it defaults to Project) and that Start Application has been set to the full path of ieexec.exe so that

---

10. For more information: "Launching No-Touch Deployment Applications with Command Line Arguments," Chris Sells, MSDN Online, June 2, 2003

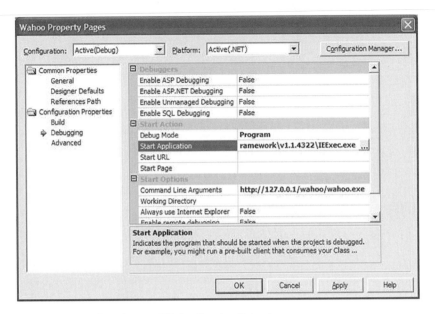

FIGURE 15.5: Debugging an NTD Application Using ieexec.exe

it will be used to host your application. The Command Line Arguments field has been set to the URL used to launch the application. To test default Intranet or Internet permissions when launching NTD applications hosted on the local machine, you use the "localhost" and "127.0.0.1" sites,[11] respectively. With these settings, starting an application under debugging will provide you a normal interactive debugging session, but the permissions will be reduced to match the evidence awarded as if the application were launched with an URL, just as it will be deployed. This is really the only way to catch permissions problems when you target a partially trusted environment, so I encourage you to debug in this manner before shipping your NTD application.

Under .NET 1.0, the ieexec.exe usage was considerably different. However, you can achieve the same results when executing ieexec.exe under .NET 1.0 by tacking a 0 (zero) onto the end of the command line:

---

11. IE looks for a "." in the site to determine the zone that an URL indicates. For example, "itweb" is in the Intranet zone because there's no ".", whereas "google.com" is in the Internet zone because it has a ".".

```
C:\> ieexec.exe http://127.0.0.1/wahoo/wahoo.exe 0
```

Although ieexec.exe is useful for debugging, its usage is undocumented, so future versions of the .NET Framework may well launch NTD applications differently (as demonstrated by the different usages between .NET 1.0 and .NET 1.1). Hopefully, future versions of .NET will provide a much more seamless debugging experience so that we needn't concern ourselves with the ieexec.exe usage.

Increasing Permissions

Although it's certainly possible to build full-featured applications that run within the confines of a reduced permission set, you can easily eliminate these restrictions by allowing well-known assemblies increased or even unrestricted permissions. This is especially useful in a corporate intranet in which client machines are configured by the same staff that deploys the NTD applications.

There are a number of ways to increase permissions for an assembly. For example, if you're unhappy with the changes that were made in .NET 1.0 SP1, you can raise or lower permissions for any zone as a whole using the Adjust .NET Security Wizard (available via the Microsoft .NET Framework Wizards item on the Administration Tools menu), as shown in Figure 15.6.

If you'd like to be a little less sweeping in your security changes (a practice I heartily recommend), you can use the Internet Control Panel to configure your system to trust all assemblies from a specific site, as shown in Figure 15.7.

Any sites listed as trusted in the Internet Control Panel settings are awarded Internet permissions. If this is still too broad, you can be even more restrictive by setting permissions on an assembly-by-assembly basis.

If you'd like to adjust permission for a specific assembly, you can set up a custom code group using the Microsoft .NET Framework Configuration tool, or you can use the Trust an Assembly Wizard. This tool creates a code group named Wizard_N, where the N varies according to the number of times you run the wizard. When you run this tool, you enter the URL to the assembly you'd like to trust:

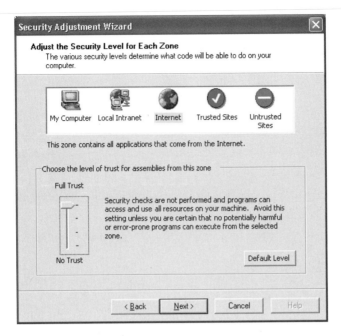

FIGURE 15.6: Adjusting .NET Security

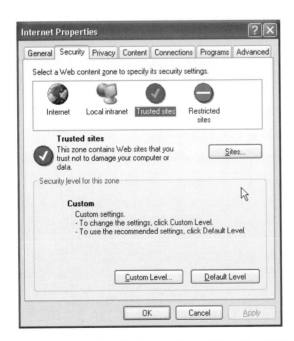

FIGURE 15.7: Using the Internet Control Panel to Add Trusted Sites

```
http://trustedmachine/hr452/hr452.exe
```

Based on that URL, you'll be asked whether you'd like to trust only this assembly, all assemblies from the same publisher, or all of the assemblies having the same public key. To simplify security configuration, it's a good idea to sign all your assemblies with the same public/private key pair. For example, I signed both wahoo.exe and wahooControl.dll and can adjust both of their permissions at once by choosing to trust assemblies having the same key, as shown in Figure 15.8.

Here I've set all assemblies having the same public key, regardless of version, to be trusted. This is a good policy because it allows an entire family of trusted applications to be trusted with a single code group.

After you've specified which assemblies to trust in the Trust an Assembly Wizard, you'll be asked how much trust you'd like them to have on a sliding scale. It's hard to tell from the user interface shown in Figure 15.9, but the tick marks, from bottom to top, assign the permission sets Nothing, Internet, LocalIntranet, and FullTrust.

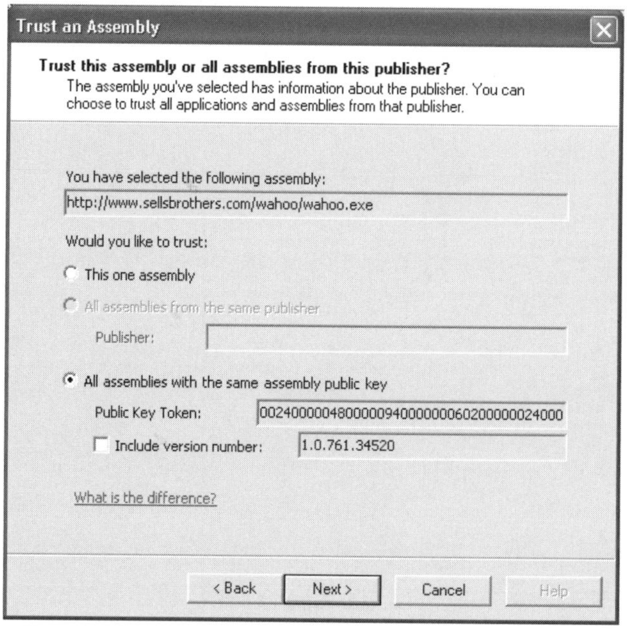

FIGURE 15.8: Trusting All Assemblies Having the Same Public Key

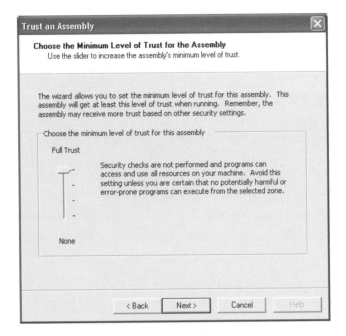

FIGURE 15.9: How Much an Assembly Is Trusted

With the new code group in place, the next time you surf to the URL .NET will match the membership condition to the new code group and will give the assembly the adjusted permissions.

Awarding permissions to your own assemblies is a matter of creating a code group with a membership condition that matches your assemblies—which site it came from, which URL it came from, which key it's signed with, and so on—and matching it to a set of permissions.

Furthermore, you can build your own custom permission set or use one of the default permission sets. Deciding whether to build your own custom permission set is a matter of being familiar with the built-in permission sets, although creating a new one that overlaps with a built-in one won't hurt anyone.

However, if you need access to any assemblies not marked with APTCA, then you'll need to create a code group that awards your assembly the FullTrust permission set. None of the other default named permission sets, even the Everything permission set, can award permissions to access assemblies not marked with APTCA.

Increasing Permissions Programmatically

As facile as you may become with the .NET permission policy administration tools, you never want to wander to each of your clients' machines to create the necessary code groups and permissions sets that they need to run your code, especially if that code is to be deployed across the Internet. Luckily, .NET provides classes to create code groups and permission sets. For example, the following code is used to create a custom code group to award all Internet permission to assemblies signed with a known key:

```
using System.Security;
using System.Security.Permissions;
using System.Security.Policy;

// Generated with 'secutil -c -s wahoo.exe'
byte[] publicKey = { 0, 36, ... };

// Find the machine policy level
PolicyLevel machinePolicyLevel = null;
System.Collections.IEnumerator ph =
  SecurityManager.PolicyHierarchy();

while( ph.MoveNext() ) {
  PolicyLevel pl = (PolicyLevel)ph.Current;
  if( pl.Label == "Machine" ) {
    machinePolicyLevel = pl;
    break;
  }
}

if( machinePolicyLevel == null ) return;

// Create a new code group giving Wahoo! Internet permissions
PermissionSet permSet1 = new NamedPermissionSet("Internet");
StrongNamePublicKeyBlob key = new StrongNamePublicKeyBlob(publicKey);
IMembershipCondition membership1 =
  new StrongNameMembershipCondition(key, null, null);

// Create the code group
PolicyStatement policy1 = new PolicyStatement(permSet1);
CodeGroup codeGroup1 = new UnionCodeGroup(membership1, policy1);
codeGroup1.Description =
  "Internet permissions for Sells Brothers Wahoo!";
codeGroup1.Name = "Sells Brothers Wahoo!";

// Add the code group
machinePolicyLevel.RootCodeGroup.AddChild(codeGroup1);
```

```
// Create a new code group giving all of
// sellsbrothers.com Execute permission
PermissionSet permSet2 = new NamedPermissionSet("Execution");
IMembershipCondition membership2 =
  new SiteMembershipCondition("www.sellsbrothers.com");

// Create the code group
PolicyStatement  policy2 = new PolicyStatement(permSet2);
CodeGroup  codeGroup2 = new UnionCodeGroup(membership2, policy2);
codeGroup2.Description =
  "Minimal execute permissions for sellsbrothers.com";
codeGroup2.Name = "sellsbrothers.com minimal execute";

// Add the code group
machinePolicyLevel.RootCodeGroup.AddChild(codeGroup2);

// Save changes
SecurityManager.SavePolicy();
```

This code actually adds two code groups: one to award Internet permissions to all assemblies signed with a known strong name, and a second one to work around an "issue" that emerged in .NET 1.0 SP1 whereby a site as a whole must have at least Execute permission for any other permissions awarded a strong name to take effect. We start by using SecurityManager to find the top of the Machine runtime policy hierarchy, where we'll add the new code groups. We then grab the Internet NamedPermissionSet and join it with StrongNameMembershipCondition to produce the new code group. We then name the new code group something that'll make sense in the administration tools and add it to the root code group along with all the existing code groups. (If we had wanted to award our assemblies full trust, we'd have passed the string "FullTrust" instead of "Internet" when creating this NamedPermissionSet object.) After creating the first permission set, we do the same thing again with the Execution NamedPermissionSet and the SiteMembershipCondition, naming them and adding them as well.

To commit the changes to the Machine runtime security policy, we ask SecurityManager to save, and that's it. This code is all that's necessary to award permissions from existing permission sets to your assemblies.

If you want to create a custom permission set, the code is similar except that you create an instance of an empty NamedPermissionSet object and add permission objects that derive from CodeAccessPermission, such as FileIOPermission and DirectoryServicesPermission. You then add new permission sets to the machine policy via the AddNamedPermissionSet method:

```
// Create a named, empty permission set
NamedPermissionSet permSet =
  new NamedPermissionSet("My Permission Set", PermissionState.None);

// Add a permission
IPermission perm = new DirectoryServicesPermission();
permSet.AddPermission(perm);
machinePolicyLevel.AddNamedPermissionSet(permSet);
```

Notice the use of PermissionState.None passed to the Named-PermissionSet constructor. Without that, you get a permission set just like FullTrust, with all permissions. Instead, you want an empty permission set that has only those permissions that you explicitly add.

Deploying Permissions

After you've got managed code to award permissions, it needs to run on the machine with FullTrust. Otherwise, it won't have permission to modify the permission policy (it must also be running as a Win32 Administrator). Placing an EXE on a Web server and asking users to click on a link won't do, because then the code will be in a partially trusted environment and we're back where we started.

The easiest way to package managed code for fully trusted execution on the client machine is to use a Microsoft Installer file. MSI files are executed by a runtime engine that downloads the code to the machine before running it, thereby giving us the permissions we need to award other permissions. Also, MSI files have built-in support in the intranet world for deployment tools such as Systems Management Server and Active Directory. In a less sophisticated deployment environment, such as smaller businesses or the Internet, you can provide a link that, after a prompt, executes the MSI file on the user's machine. Even if all your users have to run the MSI themselves, that still requires only one installation to enable the permissions needed for, say, every NTD application deployed from the IT group's internal Web site.

There are many ways to build MSI files, but the most readily available one comes with advanced versions of VS.NET. The trick is to convince a setup project to execute your code during installation. Assuming you've got a VS.NET solution with a setup project and a class library project, you have only two major tasks left to do this convincing.

The first task is to add a class to your class library project that derives from System.Configuration.Install.Installer and is tagged with the RunInstaller(true) attribute. An instance of any such class will be created by the MSI engine during setup, so that's where you put your custom code. The easiest way to get such a class is to right-click on your class library project in Solution Explorer and choose Add New Item | Code | Installer Class. It will create a place for your permission award code in the constructor:

```
[RunInstaller(true)]
public class Installer1 :
  System.Configuration.Install.Installer {
  public Installer1() {
    ...

    // TODO: Add your permission award code here
  }
}
```

Your second task is to add this assembly to the list of custom actions that your setup will perform during installation. To do that, right-click on your setup project in Solution Explorer and choose View | Custom Actions. This will show you a list of the custom actions at each phase of the setup, as shown in Figure 15.10.

To add a custom action to the install phase, right-click on the Install custom action list and choose Add Custom Action. This will show the list of folders to place your custom action code into, as shown in Figure 15.11.

Double-click Application Folder and choose Add Output to choose the output from one of the other projects in the solution. Make sure the class

FIGURE 15.10: Setup Project Custom Actions

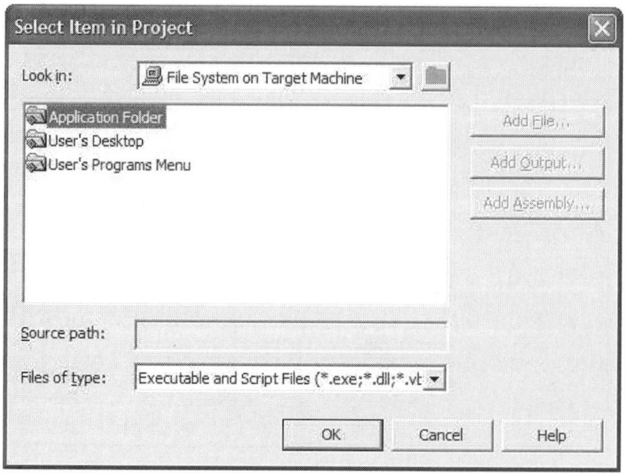

FIGURE 15.11: Choosing a Folder for a Custom Action

library project with your installer class is selected at the top, and choose Primary Output, as shown in Figure 15.12.

These settings will cause the installer classes in your class library assembly to be created during the Install phase of your MSI setup. Now, when you build and execute the MSI file produced by the setup project,

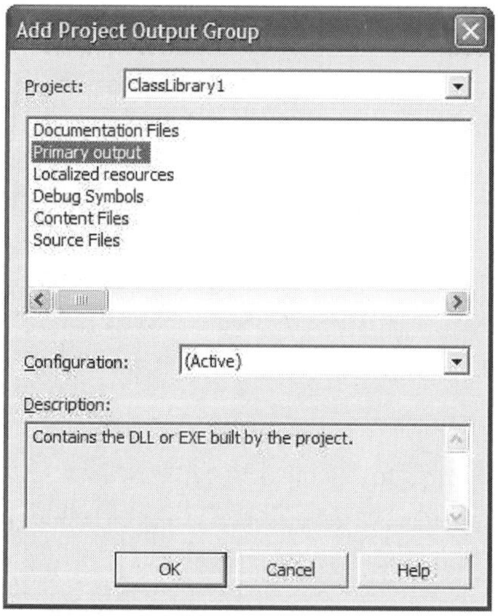

FIGURE 15.12: Choosing the Primary Output of Your Class Library Project to Act as a Custom Action

your code will execute at FullTrust and can award permissions for your assemblies.

Authenticode

One more detail that you may find interesting has nothing to do with code, but with the .NET security settings for NTD applications and WinForms controls downloaded over the Web. In .NET v1.0, assemblies from both the Intranet and the Internet zones were allowed to run, but the Internet permissions were considerably reduced from the Intranet permissions. As of version 1.0 SP1, Microsoft decided that .NET wasn't quite cooked enough to support the rough-and-tumble of the Internet, so it changed the settings to disable code from the Internet altogether (although you could always turn it back on). Now, in version 1.1, Microsoft is confident that it's got a secure platform, and it has turned execution of code from the Internet back on by default, and the Internet permissions themselves have not been reduced. But that's not all. .NET v1.1 also brings the Authenticode model back from COM.

The COM Authenticode model was "punitive." If users OK'd a hunk of code to run, it could do absolutely anything it wanted, subject to the permissions of the users (most of whom, let's face it, run as Administrator). If the code did something bad, a team of experts could track it down, find the certificate, and bring the bad people who wrote the code to hard justice (my understanding is that the A-Team was brought out of retirement at least once to help with this effort).

The .NET CAS model, on the other hand, is "preventive," in that the user is never asked, but the code has only a limited set of permissions if it's from a source other than the local hard drive. In practice, it turns out that both models have their uses. CAS is great, of course, for keeping bad things from happening. Authenticode, on the other hand, is good at letting users know that code from outside their machine is about to execute and asking them if that's OK. Whether or not to ask is determined by the same Internet security settings that determine whether or not to ask for a COM control. Figure 15.13 shows the default settings for code from the Internet zone in .NET 1.1.

FIGURE 15.13: NET 1.1 NTD Security Settings

You'll notice that when code from the Internet zone is executed, by default there are no user prompts. The same is true of the Intranet zone. This is more permission than the default settings for ActiveX/COM controls, which default to Prompt (for signed controls) and Disable (for unsigned controls). Of course, for COM controls, Authenticode is all the security there is, whereas in .NET, there's all of CAS to continue to protect the user.

Authenticode doesn't affect which permissions an NTD application has. Instead, Authenticode is a gate that affects execution permissions based on user settings before anything else happens, as well as providing an optional prompt. However, the permission set is still awarded based on other evidence. Authenticode behavior is as follows:

- **.NET Code Enabled:** permissions awarded silently
- **.NET Code Prompt:** permissions awarded or denied based on user prompt results
- **.NET Code Disabled:** all permissions denied

So, under .NET 1.1, if an NTD application is allowed to run at all (either it's silently enabled or the user says yes to the prompt), it gets whatever permissions it would get in .NET 1.0, where everything was configured like the ".NET Code Enabled" setting.

Where Are We?

Because .NET code can be deployed over the Web, you can host WinForms controls in Internet Explorer as well as launch NTD applications using URLs. NTD applications combine the best of the HTML deployment model and the Windows Forms UI development model, without the baggage of HTML UI limitations. Especially for the Intranet zone, where you get to dictate the client-side configuration, there's no need to restrict yourself to the limitations of the Microsoft HTML runtime (that is, Internet Explorer). Instead, you can move up to the Microsoft .NET runtime, which has been designed to build and deploy your applications in a whole new way.

◾A◾
Moving from MFC

C HANCES ARE THAT IF YOU'RE A C++ programmer with experience in Windows and an interest in client-side applications, you've been an MFC programmer. And whether or not you found that experience wholly pleasurable, you probably expect quite a few things from your client-tier application framework. This appendix briefly explains which of your expectations will be fulfilled (and then some), and which are going to cause you "issues."

A Few Words About MFC

In 1992, Microsoft released MFC 1.0 as part of the Programmer's Workbench. MFC was a set of about 60 classes targeted mainly at wrapping the windowing and drawing parts of the 16-bit Windows API. Its goal was to wrap the implicit and inconsistent object models inherent in the operating system with an explicit, consistent C++ object model, and it did as good a job as could be expected given the state of Microsoft's C++ compiler at the time.[1]

---

1. At the time, Microsoft's C++ compiler was far behind the pack in the implementation of things such as templates, exceptions, and runtime type identification (RTTI). This tardiness caused ripples in the design of MFC, and in the Windows C++ programmer community, that can still be felt to this day.

In 2002, Microsoft released MFC 7.0 as part of Visual Studio .NET 2002. MFC had grown to more than 200 classes, and, along the way, its goal had expanded: to provide a complete C++ object model replacement of the Win32 API. As of version 7.0, MFC grew to be the most feature-rich way to build commercial-quality client-tier applications in Windows.[2] Here's a list of the major features that MFC programmers have grown to rely on:

- Support for dialog-based, SDI, multi-SDI, and MDI applications
- Document-View Architecture
- Printing, print setup, and print preview
- Floating toolbars, status bars, and dialog bars
- Context-sensitive help
- Object Linking and Embedding (both client and object)
- OLE Automation
- COM control hosting
- Active Document servers
- Full integration into VS.NET, including four of the most comprehensive wizards that the IDE provides
- Dynamic Data Exchange and Validation
- Command routing
- Command UI updating
- Windows logo compliance
- Shell integration (icons, drag and drop, DDE, and command line parsing)
- Wrappers for a large percentage of the Win32 API, including windowing, drawing, databases, sockets, Registry access, the file system, threading, and more
- Auto-upgrade from 16 bits to 32 bits[3]
- Tons of third-party and community support

---

2. It also grew on the server side, but MFC has always been firmly grounded on the client.
3. This isn't important now, but man oh man, it was a big deal when we were all busy porting our 16-bit applications to 32 bits.

If you've read the rest of this book, you'll notice that MFC provides a lot of features that I didn't talk about. If you're starting with this appendix as an MFC programmer wondering what WinForms does and doesn't offer, you may be disappointed to hear that I haven't covered all the features in this list (although I certainly have covered a number of them). Either way, the hard, cold truth is that MFC provides more features than WinForms does for building stand-alone, document-based applications.

For example, if you want to build a text editor, you can do that in MFC by running a wizard, choosing the right options, and writing only a few lines of code. By running the wizard, you get an application to start with that includes a status bar, a toolbar (floating), all the File, Edit, and Help menu items implemented (including a most recently used file list, printing, and context-sensitive help), all in a fully logo-compliant SDI, multi-SDI, or MDI application, based on your whim that day. As a document-based application framework, MFC has no peer.

However, in recent years the world seems to have moved away from document-based applications. Relatively few folks seem interested in building text editors or word processors or spreadsheets. Instead, the bulk of the applications are either completely HTML-based or n-client applications talking to network, database, or Web services back ends. It's for this use that .NET as a whole and WinForms specifically have been tailored.

That's not to say that WinForms can't be used to build darn nice document-based applications. In fact, because WinForms is only a small piece of the more than 2,000 public classes provided in .NET, it's likely that if what you're looking for isn't in WinForms, it's found somewhere else in .NET. For example, WinForms itself (the System.Windows.Forms namespace) doesn't provide any custom drawing support at all. Instead, GDI+ (in the System.Drawing namespace) supplies that functionality.

And this is the chief difference between MFC and WinForms. MFC was meant as a replacement for the underlying Win32 API, but that didn't stop the Win32 API from growing. In fact, as much as MFC has grown over the years, the functionality of the underlying OS has increased at least tenfold. WinForms, on the other hand, is meant to be a replacement only for the windowing part of Win32. It's the rest of the .NET Framework classes that are meant to replace the rest of Win32. Of course, .NET will never replace the entire Win32 API, but because most new functionality is slated to be added to .NET in the future, it's clear that betting on the future of .NET is a wise wager.

MFC Versus WinForms

Some folks do need to build document-based applications, and even though WinForms isn't designed to support that as well as MFC is, it's not very hard to build complete document-based applications if you're armed with the knowledge of what WinForms does and doesn't provide as compared with MFC. Table A.1 shows a feature-based summary focused on building document-based applications.

TABLE A.1: MFC Versus WinForms/.NET

Feature	MFC	WinForms/.NET
Application Wizards	Four	Four
IDE Integration	Yes	Yes
Dialog, SDI, MDI Applications	Yes	Yes
Multi-SDI Applications	Yes	No
UI Layout	Yes (dialogs only)	Yes
Docking and Splitting	Yes (simple)	Yes
Anchoring	No	Yes
Toolbars and the like	Yes	Yes (no floating)
Printing, Preview, Setup	Yes	Yes
OLE/Active Documents	Yes	No
COM Control Hosting	Yes	Yes
Automation	Yes	Yes (Remoting)
F1 Help	Yes	Yes
DDX/DDV	Yes	Yes (DDX not needed)

TABLE A.1:   MFC Versus WinForms/.NET (continued)

Feature	MFC	WinForms/.NET
Win32 Wrappers	Yes	Yes
Data Binding	Yes (simple)	Yes
Cross-Language	No	Yes
Cross-Platform	No	Yes
Cross-Bitness	16/32	32/64
Web Deployment	No	Yes
Third-Party Support	Yes (huge)	Yes (growing)
Document-View	Yes	No
Document Management	Yes	No
Shell Integration	Yes	Yes (via installer)
Command Unification	Yes	No
UI Updating	Yes	No
Command Routing	Yes	No
Source Code	Yes	No
Managed Environment	No	Yes

The Differences

Even the features shared by MFC and WinForms/.NET are often implemented differently in the two worlds, so the following is a short discussion of each of the features.

Application Wizards

VS.NET 2003 provides MFC wizards to build applications, DLLs, COM controls, and Internet Server API (ISAPI) extensions. VS.NET 2003 provides WinForms wizards to build applications and controls for each of the four languages that are supported (C#, VB.NET, C++, and J#). VS.NET also gives you wizards for producing class library and ASP.NET server-side applications and libraries. Chapter 1: Hello, Windows Forms and Chapter 8: Controls discuss the WinForms wizards.

IDE Integration

VS.NET provides direct IDE integration for developing MFC and WinForms applications and controls. The WinForms integration is more extensive, mainly because of the strong UI layout environment and data binding, which are discussed as appropriate throughout the book.

Dialog, SDI, and MDI Applications

Both MFC and WinForms provide complete support for dialog-based, Single Document Interface (SDI), and Multiple Document Interface (MDI) applications. However, although MFC comes with a wizard that provides a great deal of functionality to help you get started when you're building SDI and MDI applications, all the WinForms wizards produce empty *forms*, which can serve as dialogs or MFC-style view windows depending on how they're used. This means that you must add all the standard UI and features every time you need an SDI or MDI application in WinForms. Except for the document management features, most of the body of this book is about how to develop applications that include the kinds of features you'd expect to find in an MFC application, with the specifics of MDI applications in Chapter 2: Forms.

Multi-SDI Applications

Multi-SDI applications—applications that have a single instance but multiple top-level windows—are fully supported in MFC. Although WinForms doesn't come out of the box supporting multi-MDI applications, Chapter 11: Applications and Settings fully explains how to build them.

UI Layout

Drag-and-drop design and layout of user interface are supported in MFC only for dialogs. Normal views must be laid out in code. WinForms, on the other hand, treats all windows in a unified manner, so the same drag-and-drop Designer works for any kind of window. What kind of window it is—

modal or modeless, dialog or view—depends on how it's used, not on how it's designed.

Something else that's a bit different in WinForms is that the UI design environment reads and writes code instead of keeping control type and position information in a separate resource file. That code is relegated to a single method, but it is definitely mixed in with the rest of the code of the window, and that is very different from the way MFC dialogs are built. Each scheme has its pros and cons, but MFC programmers will notice the difference right away (and then may let it make them unhappy before letting it grow on them).

The WinForms Designer is discussed as appropriate through the book.

Docking and Splitting

WinForms lets you dock controls to the edges of a window as well as designate a control to take up the remaining space of the window. You can attach docked controls to splitters so that as a splitter is moved, it resizes the appropriate controls. All this is available in the design environment so that you can see what the docking and splitting will look like at design time.

MFC, on the other hand, does docking and splitting in code only. The dialog editor doesn't support this feature. Also, splitting in MFC requires separate window classes, whereas in WinForms all the docked and split controls are easily accessible from within the single container. Docking and splitting are discussed in Chapter 2: Forms.

Anchoring

When a window is resized in MFC, any controls that need to change size with the size of the containing window must be resized by hand in the WM_SIZE message handler. In contrast, WinForms anchoring (combined with docking) allows a control to be resized automatically as the container resizes. Anchoring is discussed in Chapter 2: Forms.

Toolbars and the Like

MFC excels in providing not only industrial-strength window adornments (such as toolbars, status bars, and dialog bars) for building full-featured applications, but also great IDE integration for editing them and a wizard to place initial versions for you. WinForms provides the same industrial-strength controls (as discussed in Chapter 8: Controls), but its support, especially for editing toolbars, is barely adequate, and it has no wizard to get you started. Also, WinForms has no built-in support for "floating" windows, such as floating toolbars.

Printing, Preview, and Setup

Both MFC and WinForms provide similar complete support for printing, print preview, print settings, and page settings.

OLE/Active Documents

Object Linking and Embedding is a technology for exposing and consuming data and the UI from one application into another. MFC provides complete support for this technology. WinForms supports only enough OLE to host COM controls.

Active Documents, another COM-based technology, is rather like a cross between Object Linking and Embedding and controls, but it has never really gained any traction. MFC supports it, but WinForms does not.

COM Control Hosting

Both MFC and WinForms provide complete support for hosting COM controls, and both do it using wrappers that provide an API appropriate to their respective environments. Unfortunately, neither gives you seamless integration. See Chapter 2: Forms for a discussion of how WinForms hosts COM controls.

Automation

Both MFC and WinForms provide complete support for both consuming and producing COM objects for use in application automation. In addition, .NET gives you another way to access objects between processes. Called .NET Remoting, this technology can be used as a means of application automation. Chapter 11: Applications and Settings has a short example of .NET Remoting for use in communicating between instances of the same application.[4]

---

4. Ingo Rammer's *Advanced .NET Remoting* (APress, 2002) provides complete coverage of .NET Remoting.

F1 Help

Both MFC and WinForms support integrating help into an application, although only MFC provides a wizard to get you started. The WinForms support for integrated help is discussed in Chapter 3: Dialogs.

DDX/DDV

Because MFC was developed before Microsoft's C++ compiler supported exceptions, MFC has a two-stage construction model for windows. This means that the C++ object will come into existence before the underlying OS object or any of the contained child controls. Because of this, MFC dialogs need to move data back and forth between member variables to allow clients to provide initial child control data before the child control is created, and to make the final child control data available after the child controls have been destroyed. The mechanism to make this happen is called Dynamic Data Exchange (DDX). Similarly, validating the data as it moves is called Dynamic Data Validation (DDV). Whereas DDX is necessary because of the design of the library, DDV is always necessary.

The WinForms data exchange model is different. Each Windows object is created as an object and is shown when necessary without forcing the developer to be concerned about whether or not the underlying OS handle has been created. This means that child control properties can always be accessed directly at any time during their lifetime. In other words, the DDX is handled transparently by the controls themselves, eliminating the need to think about in it WinForms.

Data validation is still necessary, of course, and is fully supported in WinForms as discussed in Chapter 3: Dialogs.

Win32 Wrappers

Because both MFC and .NET are meant as replacements for the underlying Win32 API, it makes sense that both of them have a large number of wrapper classes to hide that API. And although .NET has MFC beat by about an order of magnitude in terms of APIs wrapped, MFC has the edge in that it's much easier to access unwrapped Win32 APIs in unmanaged C++ than it is in managed code.

Data Binding

MFC has only token support for data binding. The WinForms data binding support takes its cue from Visual Basic and provides extensive data binding support and data provider integration with the IDE. Chapter 12: Data Sets and Designer Support and Chapter 13: Data Binding and Data Grids provide an introduction to this enormous topic.

Cross-Language

MFC is a class library for C++ programmers only. WinForms (and the rest of .NET) is available to Microsoft-provided languages such as Managed C++, Jscript.NET, VB.NET, and J#, as well as dozens of third-party languages (although only Managed C++, J#, C#, and Visual Basic .NET have WinForms Designer support).

Cross-Platform

MFC is supported across all versions of Windows, and is supported across some UNIX variants by third parties. WinForms is supported under the desktop versions of Windows starting with Windows 98, and the latest version Windows CE (although VS.NET 2003 is required for Windows CE support).

Cross-Bitness

MFC was originally built to support 16-bit Windows and, because of the degree of isolation from the underlying OS, made porting to 32 bits largely a recompile in many cases. Currently, WinForms is supported only under 32 bits but will certainly provide a high (and likely seamless) degree of portability when you move your code to 64 bits.

Web Deployment

MFC applications need to be installed or copied to a machine before they can be run (with the exception of executing an application from a network share). WinForms applications support this mode of deployment, of course, but they also support no-touch deployment, which allows a WinForms application to be launched via an URL, downloaded automatically, and launched without an explicit copy or install. This model, covered in depth in Chapter 15: Web Deployment, combines the richness of Windows applications with the deployment of Web applications.

Third-Party Support

MFC programmers have years' worth of books, articles, sample code, FAQs, archives, third-party tools, and general community knowledge at their disposal. However, even though WinForms was first released in February 2002, it has already gained a lot of those assets, and the rate of acquisition is accelerating.

Document-View

MFC 2.0 introduced Document-View, a simplified version of Model-View-Controller that separates a document's data from the view of that data. This model so permeates MFC that it wasn't until relatively recent versions of the IDE that the wizards supported generating non-Document-View code. The central idea of Document-View is a good one, but the MFC specifics of document management, such as serialization and dirty bit management, made it difficult for non-document-based applications to fit the model.

WinForms went the other way. Instead of imposing an application framework model on all applications, WinForms provides only a windowing framework. However, the central idea of separating the data from the view is still a good one and needs no real support beyond what's provided by the .NET runtime itself.

Document Management

Beyond the idea of separating data from view, the major productivity enhancement of Document-View was the document management piece, including dirty bit management, file dialog management, most recently used file lists, change notification, and so on. Those enhancements are sorely missed in .NET when it comes to building document-based applications. Luckily, that support is not very hard to build, and an example is provided with this book.

The core of document management is the ability to serialize an object graph that represents an application's data. .NET provides complete support for that kind of serialization, and a brief introduction can be found in Appendix C: Serialization Basics.

Shell Integration

Another part of the document-based piece provided by MFC is the automatic registration of file extensions with the shell and the handling of file open request operations from the shell. WinForms provides direct support for neither of these operations, but both are discussed in Chapter 11: Applications and Settings.[5]

Command Unification

MFC unifies interaction for multiple kinds of controls to commands that can be handled singly. For example, to the user, choosing File | Open from a menu is the same as clicking on the Open File toolbar button. These activities are unified at the class and IDE level, letting the developer easily handle all ways of invoking the same command in a single spot. WinForms provides no such facility at the class or Designer level. Only manual coding can reduce the duplication (although, to be fair, it's only a couple of lines of code).

UI Updating

Another benefit of command unification in MFC is the ability to enable or disable a command as needed without the explicit need to disable a menu item or a toolbar button separately. WinForms requires that UI elements be enabled or disabled explicitly.

Command Routing

MFC supports routing commands to any interested subscriber. .NET supports this same idea with delegates, as described in Appendix B: Delegates and Events.

---

5. You have to look closely to see the coverage of shell integration in Chapter 11: Applications and Settings, but it's there. Check out the first couple of Registry settings examples, where you'll find the core piece that you'll need to associate a document extension in the shell with your WinForms application.

Source Code

MFC provides full source code that can be read and stepped through in the debugger. The .NET Framework source code is not provided and cannot be stepped through in the debugger. Reading the source code for the .NET Framework requires a disassembler tool and a lot of patience.

Managed Environment

MFC is an *unmanaged* environment in the sense that memory and security must be managed by the developer explicitly. The .NET runtime provides automatic handling of both memory and security, making .NET a *managed* environment. A managed environment can sometimes cause a degradation in performance (although it's surprising how rare that is), but it always results in a more robust application, especially given how hard it is to track down and deal with memory and security problems. My experience is that even given a lack of some application framework features, I'm much more productive in .NET than I ever was in C++ or MFC.

Strategy

If you're moving from MFC as a programmer, this book will help you understand the new WinForms model, especially as focused by the discussion so far in this appendix. The basics are similar, so a typical MFC programmer won't have much difficulty picking up WinForms. However, WinForms is only a piece. I recommend spending some time with the C# language itself as well as the rest of the .NET Framework to fill in what you're going to need outside of WinForms.

If you're moving MFC code to .NET, you need some careful planning. Here are some considerations:

- If you can afford to start over from scratch, that will yield the most maintainable code base, but it will take the longest.
- If the bulk of your MFC code is in COM controls (or can be moved to COM controls), then you can use WinForms as a host for those controls and write new code in .NET.
- If you need to bring the MFC application itself forward, you can flip the Use Managed Extensions bit on your MFC project and gain the

ability to host WinForms controls[6] from your MFC 7.1 code. This also lets you write new code in .NET.

- If the new code you'd like to integrate into your existing MFC code is not a control, you can use COM to interoperate with the .NET code while still keeping your MFC code unmanaged.

Which options apply to you depend on your specific circumstances, but in general, I recommend a strategy that lets you write the bulk of your new code in .NET, even if it means building some of the features for WinForms that you're missing from MFC.

Genghis

Before you decide to rebuild all the MFC features, you'll want to check the Genghis library[7] to see whether that feature has already been rebuilt. Genghis is a set of WinForms components and controls to fill the needs of document-based application development in WinForms. As of this writing, it includes the following features:

- Command line parser
- Completion combo
- Control hosting status bar
- Cursor changer
- Custom check state treeview
- Custom XP theming controls
- File Search Engine
- FileDocument class (doc/dirty bit management)
- FindReplaceDialog
- FolderNameDialog
- HandleCollector for the world

---

6. For a discussion of how to host WinForms controls as COM controls in an MFC application, see "Windows Forms: .NET Framework 1.1 Provides Expanded Namespace, Security, and Language Support for Your Projects," Chris Sells, *MSDN Magazine*, March 2003.
7. The Genghis Group, http://www.genghisgroup.com

- Header group box control
- Image combo
- More robust validation à la WebForms
- Most recently used (MRU) files support
- MSN Messenger-style pop-up window
- Multiple top-level window support
- Multiple-instance detection
- Screen Saver class
- Scrollable PictureBox control
- Sorting listview (including the little triangle thingy)
- Splash Screen class
- Command line helper for no-touch deployment applications (including server-side code)
- Window serializer
- Wizard framework

Figure A.1 shows a sample document-based application built using Genghis.

Genghis is a shared source project, and the license allows you to use the code in your own applications free of charge. And, if you've got anything to contribute, the list of existing features is exceeded only by the list of desired features.

FIGURE A.1: A Sample Document-Based Genghis Application

B
Delegates and Events

THE FOLLOWING STORY is reprinted from my Web site as a more thorough, although less reverent, explanation of delegates and events. The characters in this story are fictional, and any similarity to real persons or events is unintentional.

Delegates

Once upon a time, in a strange land south of here, lived Peter. Peter was a diligent worker who would readily accept requests from his boss. However, his boss was a mean, untrusting man who insisted on steady progress reports. Because Peter did not want his boss standing in his office looking over his shoulder, Peter promised to notify his boss whenever his work progressed. Peter implemented this promise by periodically calling his boss back via a typed reference like so:

```
class Worker {
  public void Advise(Boss boss) { this.boss = boss; }
  public void DoWork() {
    Console.WriteLine("Worker: work started");
    if( boss != null ) boss.WorkStarted();

    Console.WriteLine("Worker: work progressing");
    if( boss != null ) boss.WorkProgressing();
```

continues

607

```
        Console.WriteLine("Worker: work completed");
        if( boss != null ) {
          int grade = boss.WorkCompleted();
          Console.WriteLine("Worker grade= " + grade);
        }
      }
      Boss boss;
    }

    class Boss {
      public void WorkStarted() { /* boss doesn't care. */ }
      public void WorkProgressing() { /* boss doesn't care. */ }
      public int WorkCompleted() {
        Console.WriteLine("It's about time!");
        return 2; /* out of 10 */
      }
    }

    class Universe {
      static void Main() {
        Worker peter = new Worker();
        Boss boss = new Boss();
        peter.Advise(boss);
        peter.DoWork();

        Console.WriteLine("Main: worker completed work");
        Console.ReadLine();
      }
    }
```

Interfaces

Now Peter was a special person. Not only was he able to put up with his mean-spirited boss, but he also had a deep connection with the universe around him. So much so that he felt that the universe was interested in his progress. Unfortunately, there was no way for Peter to advise the universe of his progress unless he added a special Advise method and special callbacks just for the universe, in addition to keeping his boss informed. What Peter really wanted to do was to separate the list of potential notifications from the implementation of those notification methods. And so he decided to split the methods into an interface:

```
interface IWorkerEvents {
  void WorkStarted();
  void WorkProgressing();
```

```
    int WorkCompleted();
}

class Worker {
  public void Advise(IWorkerEvents events) { this.events = events; }
  public void DoWork() {
    Console.WriteLine("Worker: work started");
    if( events != null ) events.WorkStarted();

    Console.WriteLine("Worker: work progressing");
    if(events != null ) events.WorkProgressing();

    Console.WriteLine("Worker: work completed");
    if(events != null ) {
      int grade = events.WorkCompleted();
      Console.WriteLine("Worker grade= " + grade);
    }
  }
  IWorkerEvents events;
}

class Boss : IWorkerEvents {
  public void WorkStarted() { /* boss doesn't care. */ }
  public void WorkProgressing() { /* boss doesn't care. */ }
  public int WorkCompleted() {
    Console.WriteLine("It's about time!");
    return 3; /* out of 10 */
  }
}
```

Delegates

Unfortunately, Peter was so busy talking his boss into implementing this interface that he didn't get around to notifying the universe, but he planned to get to that as soon as possible. At least he'd abstracted the reference of his boss far away from him so that others who implemented the IWorkerEvents interface could be notified of his work progress.

Still, his boss complained bitterly. "Peter!" his boss fumed. "Why are you bothering to notify me when you start your work or when your work is progressing?!? I don't care about those events. Not only do you force me to implement those methods, but you're wasting valuable work time waiting for me to return from the event, which is further expanded when I am far away! Can't you figure out a way to stop bothering me?"

And so, Peter decided that even though interfaces were useful for many things, when it came to events, their granularity was not fine enough. He wished to be able to notify interested parties only of the events that matched their hearts' desires. Toward that end, Peter decided to break the methods out of the interface into separate delegate functions, each of which acted like a little tiny interface of one method each:

```csharp
delegate void WorkStarted();
delegate void WorkProgressing();
delegate int WorkCompleted();

class Worker {
  public void DoWork() {
    Console.WriteLine("Worker: work started");
    if( started != null ) started();

    Console.WriteLine("Worker: work progressing");
    if( progressing != null ) progressing();

    Console.WriteLine("Worker: work completed");
    if( completed != null ) {
      int grade = completed();
      Console.WriteLine("Worker grade= " + grade);
    }
  }
  public WorkStarted started;
  public WorkProgressing progressing;
  public WorkCompleted completed;
}

class Boss {
  public int WorkCompleted() {
    Console.WriteLine("Better...");
    return 4; /* out of 10 */
  }
}

class Universe {
  static void Main() {
    Worker peter = new Worker();
    Boss boss = new Boss();

    // NOTE: We've replaced the Advise method with the
    //       assignment operation
    peter.completed = new WorkCompleted(boss.WorkCompleted);
    peter.DoWork();
```

```
    Console.WriteLine("Main: worker completed work");
    Console.ReadLine();
  }
}
```

Static Subscribers

Delegates accomplished the goal of not bothering Peter's boss with events that he didn't want, but still Peter had not managed to get the universe on his list of subscribers. Since the universe is an all-compassing entity, it didn't seem right to hook delegates to instance members (imagine how many resources multiple instances of the universe would need...). Instead, Peter needed to hook delegates to static members, which delegates support fully:

```
class Universe {
  static void WorkerStartedWork() {
    Console.WriteLine("Universe notices worker starting work");
  }

  static int WorkerCompletedWork() {
    Console.WriteLine("Universe pleased with worker's work");
    return 7;
  }

  static void Main() {
    Worker peter = new Worker();
    Boss boss = new Boss();

    // NOTE: the use of the assignment operator is *not* good
    //       practice in the following 3 lines of code.
    //       Keep reading for the right way to add a delegate
    peter.completed = new WorkCompleted(boss.WorkCompleted);
    peter.started = new WorkStarted(Universe.WorkerStartedWork);
    peter.completed = new WorkCompleted(Universe.WorkerCompletedWork);
    peter.DoWork();

    Console.WriteLine("Main: worker completed work");
    Console.ReadLine();
  }
}
```

Events

Unfortunately, the universe, being very busy and unaccustomed to paying attention to individuals, had managed to replace Peter's boss's delegate with its own. This was an unintended side effect of making the delegate fields public in Peter's Worker class. Likewise, if Peter's boss got impatient, he could decide to fire Peter's delegates himself (which is just the kind of rude thing that Peter's boss was apt to do):

```
// Peter's boss taking matters into his own hands
if( peter.completed != null ) peter.completed();
```

Peter wanted to make sure that neither of these could happen. He realized that he needed to add registration and unregistration functions for each delegate so that subscribers could add or remove themselves but couldn't clear the entire list or fire his events. Instead of implementing these functions himself, Peter used the event keyword to make the C# compiler build these methods for him:

```
class Worker {
  ...
  public event WorkStarted started;
  public event WorkProgressing progressing;
  public event WorkCompleted completed;
}
```

Peter knew that the event keyword erected a property around a delegate, allowing only clients to add or remove themselves (using the += and -= operators, if the client was written in C#), forcing his boss and the universe to play nicely:

```
static void Main() {
  Worker peter = new Worker();
  Boss boss = new Boss();
  peter.completed += new WorkCompleted(boss.WorkCompleted);
  peter.started += new WorkStarted(Universe.WorkerStartedWork);
  peter.completed += new WorkCompleted(Universe.WorkerCompletedWork);
  peter.DoWork();

  Console.WriteLine("Main: worker completed work");
  Console.ReadLine();
}
```

Harvesting All Results

At this point, Peter breathed a sigh of relief. He had managed to satisfy the requirements of all his subscribers without having to be closely coupled with the specific implementations. However, he noticed that although both his boss and the universe provided grades of his work, Peter was receiving only one of the grades. In the face of multiple subscribers, he really wanted to harvest all of their results. So, he reached into his delegate and pulled out the list of subscribers so that he could call each of them manually:

```
public void DoWork() {
  ...
  Console.WriteLine("Worker: work completed");
  if( completed != null ) {
    foreach( WorkCompleted wc in completed.GetInvocationList() ) {
      int grade = wc();
      Console.WriteLine("Worker grade= " + grade);
    }
  }
}
```

Asynchronous Notification: Fire and Forget

In the meantime, his boss and the universe had been distracted with other things, and this meant that the time it took them to grade Peter's work had been greatly expanded:

```
class Boss {
  public int WorkCompleted() {
    System.Threading.Thread.Sleep(3000);
    Console.WriteLine("Better..."); return 6; /* out of 10 */
  }
}

class Universe {
  static int WorkerCompletedWork() {
    System.Threading.Thread.Sleep(4000);
    Console.WriteLine("Universe is pleased with worker's work");
    return 7;
  }
  ...
}
```

Unfortunately, because Peter was notifying each subscriber one at a time, waiting for each to grade him, these notifications now took up quite a bit of his time when he should have been working. So, he decided to forget the grade and just fire the event asynchronously:

```
public void DoWork() {
  ...
  Console.WriteLine("Worker: work completed");
  if( completed != null ) {
    foreach( WorkCompleted wc in completed.GetInvocationList() ) {
      wc.BeginInvoke(null, null);
    }
  }
}
```

Asynchronous Notification: Polling

This clever trick allowed Peter to notify the subscribers while letting him get back to work immediately, letting the process thread pool invoke the delegate. Over time, however, Peter found that he missed the feedback on his work. He knew that he did a good job and appreciated the praise of the universe as a whole (if not his boss specifically). So, he fired the event asynchronously but polled periodically, looking for the grade to be available:

```
public void DoWork() {
  ...
  Console.WriteLine("Worker: work completed");
  if( completed != null ) {
    foreach( WorkCompleted wc in completed.GetInvocationList() ) {
      IAsyncResult res = wc.BeginInvoke(null, null);
      while( !res.IsCompleted ) System.Threading.Thread.Sleep(1);
      int grade = wc.EndInvoke(res);
      Console.WriteLine("Worker grade= " + grade);
    }
  }
}
```

Asynchronous Notification: Delegates

Unfortunately, Peter was back to the very thing he wanted his boss to avoid with him in the beginning: looking over the shoulder of the entity doing the work. So, he decided to employ another delegate as a means of notification when the asynchronous work was completed, allowing him to get back to work immediately but still be notified when his work had been graded:

```
public void DoWork() {
  ...
  Console.WriteLine("Worker: work completed");
  if( completed != null ) {
    foreach( WorkCompleted wc in completed.GetInvocationList() ) {
      wc.BeginInvoke(new AsyncCallback(WorkGraded), wc);
    }
  }
}

void WorkGraded(IAsyncResult res) {
  WorkCompleted wc = (WorkCompleted)res.AsyncState;
  int grade = wc.EndInvoke(res);
  Console.WriteLine("Worker grade= " + grade);
}
```

Happiness in the Universe

Peter, his boss, and the universe were finally satisfied. Peter's boss and the universe were allowed to be notified of the events that interested them, reducing the burden of implementation and the cost of unnecessary round-trips. Peter could notify each of them, ignoring how long it took them to return from their target methods while still getting his results asynchronously. The result was the following complete solution:

```
delegate void WorkStarted();
delegate void WorkProgressing();
delegate int WorkCompleted();

class Worker {
  public void DoWork() {
    Console.WriteLine("Worker: work started");
    if( started != null ) started();

    Console.WriteLine("Worker: work progressing");
    if( progressing != null ) progressing();

    Console.WriteLine("Worker: work completed");
    if( completed != null ) {
```

continues

```csharp
        foreach( WorkCompleted wc in completed.GetInvocationList() ) {
          wc.BeginInvoke(new AsyncCallback(WorkGraded), wc);
        }
      }
    }

    void WorkGraded(IAsyncResult res) {
      WorkCompleted wc = (WorkCompleted)res.AsyncState;
      int grade = wc.EndInvoke(res);
      Console.WriteLine("Worker grade= " + grade);
    }

    public event WorkStarted started;
    public event WorkProgressing progressing;
    public event WorkCompleted completed;
}

class Boss {
  public int WorkCompleted() {
    System.Threading.Thread.Sleep(3000);
    Console.WriteLine("Better..."); return 6; /* out of 10 */
  }
}

class Universe {
  static void WorkerStartedWork() {
    Console.WriteLine("Universe notices worker starting work");
  }

  static int WorkerCompletedWork() {
    System.Threading.Thread.Sleep(4000);
    Console.WriteLine("Universe is pleased with worker's work");
    return 7;
  }

  static void Main() {
    Worker peter = new Worker();
    Boss boss = new Boss();
    peter.completed += new WorkCompleted(boss.WorkCompleted);
    peter.started += new WorkStarted(Universe.WorkerStartedWork);
    peter.completed += new WorkCompleted(Universe.WorkerCompletedWork);
    peter.DoWork();

    Console.WriteLine("Main: worker completed work");
    Console.ReadLine();
  }
}
```

Peter knew that getting results asynchronously came with issues, because as soon as he fired events asynchronously, the target methods were likely to be executed on another thread, as was Peter's notification of when the target method has completed. However, Peter was familiar with Chapter 14: Multithreaded User Interfaces, so he understood how to manage such issues when building WinForms applications.

And they all lived happily ever after. The end.

■ C ■
Serialization Basics

T HE .NET FRAMEWORK is a many-splendored thing. Parts of this book
have explored sections of the framework that are completely outside
the System.Windows.Forms namespace because you need that knowledge
to build real WinForms applications. A similar topic is serialization. The
need for serialization can be found in any number of places, but for applications developers, serialization is used to save and restore settings data and
document data. It's in that narrow view that we explore this topic.

Streams

Serialization is the ability to read and write an arbitrary object graph (reading is sometimes called *deserialization*). Before we can talk about serializing
objects, we need to talk about where they're going serialized to.

Whenever an object is serialized, it must go somewhere. It may go into
memory, a file, a database record, or a socket. Generally, where the data is
actually written doesn't matter to the object itself. It needs to store the same
data regardless of where it goes. All the object generally cares about is that
bytes can be written and read, and sometimes we'd like to skip around
among the bytes. To satisfy these desires, .NET provides the abstract base
class Stream from the System.IO namespace:

```
abstract class Stream : MarshalByRefObject, IDisposable {
  // Fields
```

continues

```
    public static readonly System.IO.Stream Null;

    // Properties
    public bool CanRead { virtual get; }
    public bool CanSeek { virtual get; }
    public bool CanWrite { virtual get; }
    public long Length { virtual get; }
    public long Position { virtual get; virtual set; }

    // Methods
    public virtual IAsyncResult BeginRead(...);
    public virtual IAsyncResult BeginWrite(...);
    public virtual void Close();
    public virtual int EndRead(IAsyncResult asyncResult);
    public virtual void EndWrite(IAsyncResult asyncResult);
    public virtual void Flush();
    public virtual int Read(byte[] buffer, int offset, int count);
    public virtual int ReadByte();
    public virtual long Seek(long offset, System.IO.SeekOrigin origin);
    public virtual void SetLength(long value);
    public virtual void Write(byte[] buffer, int offset, int count);
    public virtual void WriteByte(byte value);
}
```

.NET provides several classes that derive from Stream, including MemoryStream, FileStream, and IsolatedStorageFileStream. The MemoryStream class is fun to play with because it has no permanent side effects:

```
using System.IO;
...
string s = "Wahoo!";
int n = 452;
using( Stream stream = new MemoryStream() ) {
  // Write to the stream
  byte[] bytes1 = UnicodeEncoding.Unicode.GetBytes(s);
  byte[] bytes2 = BitConverter.GetBytes(n);
  stream.Write(bytes1, 0, bytes1.Length);
  stream.Write(bytes2, 0, bytes2.Length);

  // Reset the stream to the beginning
  stream.Seek(0, SeekOrigin.Begin);

  // Read from the stream
  byte[] bytes3 = new byte[stream.Length - 4];
  byte[] bytes4 = new byte[4];
  stream.Read(bytes3, 0, bytes3.Length);
  stream.Read(bytes4, 0, bytes4.Length);
```

```
    // Do something with the data
    MessageBox.Show(UnicodeEncoding.Unicode.GetString(bytes3) + " " +
        BitConverter.ToInt32(bytes4, 0));
}
```

This code creates a specific implementation of the abstract Stream class, making sure to close it (even in the face of exceptions). The code then uses the stream for writing and reading bytes, being careful to seek back to the beginning of the stream in between these actions. We could have written exactly the same code for any stream.

However, the manual conversion of the string object back and forth between the bytes is kind of a pain. To avoid writing that code, we've got the StreamWriter and StreamReader classes:

```
string s = "Wahoo!";
int n = 452;
using( Stream stream = new MemoryStream() ) {

    // Write to the stream
    StreamWriter writer = new StreamWriter(stream);
    writer.WriteLine(s);
    writer.WriteLine(n);
    writer.Flush(); // Flush the buffer

    // Reset the stream to the beginning
    stream.Seek(0, SeekOrigin.Begin);

    // Read from the stream
    StreamReader reader = new StreamReader(stream);
    string s2 = reader.ReadLine();
    int n2 = int.Parse(reader.ReadLine());

    // Do something with the data
    MessageBox.Show(s2 + " " + n2);
}
```

This code is considerably simpler because the conversion to bytes is managed by the stream writer and readers as they work on the stream. However, the stream writer and readers are oriented toward text only, and that's why we wrote each piece of data on its own line and why we had to parse the integer back out of the string when reading. To avoid the conversion to and from strings, we can write the data in its native binary format using the BinaryWriter and BinaryReader classes:

```
string s = "Wahoo!";
int n = 452;
using( Stream stream = new MemoryStream() ) {

    // Write to the stream
    BinaryWriter writer = new BinaryWriter(stream);
    writer.Write(s);
    writer.Write(n);
    writer.Flush(); // Flush the buffer

    // Reset the stream to the beginning
    stream.Seek(0, SeekOrigin.Begin);

    // Read from the stream
    BinaryReader reader = new BinaryReader(stream);
    string s2 = reader.ReadString();
    int n2 = reader.ReadInt32();

    // Do something with the data
    MessageBox.Show(s2 + " " + n2);
}
```

Using BinaryWriter and BinaryReader eliminates the need for string conversion, but our code still must keep track of the types of the objects we are writing and the order in which they must be read. We can group the data into a custom class and read it all at once, but BinaryWriter and BinaryReader don't support custom classes, only built-in simple types. To read and write arbitrary objects, we need a formatter.

Formatters

A *formatter* is an object that knows how to write arbitrary objects to a stream. A formatter exposes this functionality by implementing the IFormatter information from the System.Runtime.Serialization namespace:

```
interface IFormatter {
  // Properties
  SerializationBinder Binder { get; set; }
  StreamingContext Context { get; set; }
  ISurrogateSelector SurrogateSelector { get; set; }

  // Methods
  object Deserialize(Stream serializationStream);
  void Serialize(Stream serializationStream, object graph);
}
```

A formatter has two jobs. The first is to serialize arbitrary objects, specifically their fields, including nested objects.[1] The formatter knows which fields to serialize using Reflection,[2] which is the .NET API for finding out type information about a type at run time. An object is written to a stream via the Serialize method and is read from a stream via the Deserialize method.

The second job of a formatter is to translate the data into some format at the byte level. The .NET Framework provides two formatters: BinaryFormatter and the SoapFormatter.

Just like BinaryWriter, the BinaryFormatter class, from the System.Runtime.Serialization.Formatters.Binary namespace, writes the data in a binary format. SoapFormatter, from the System.Runtime.Serialization.Formatters.Soap namespace,[3] writes data in XML according to the Simple Object Access Protocol (SOAP) specification. Although SOAP is the core protocol of Web services, using the SOAP formatter for the purposes of serializing settings or document data has nothing to do with Web services or even the Web. However, it is a handy format for a human to read.

There is one stipulation on any type that a formatter is to serialize: It must be marked with SerializableAttribute, or else the formatter will throw a run-time exception. After the type (and the type of any contained field) is marked as serializable, serializing an object is a matter of creating a formatter and asking it to serialize the object:

```
using System.Runtime.Serialization;
using System.Runtime.Serialization.Formatters;
using System.Runtime.Serialization.Formatters.Soap;
...
[SerializableAttribute]
class MyData {
  // NOTE: Public fields should be avoided in general,
  //       but are useful to simplify the code in this case
  public string s = "Wahoo!";
```

---

1. Formatters even make sure that cyclic data structures are handled properly, allowing you to serialize entire object graphs.
2. For a thorough explanation of .NET Reflection, see *Essential .NET* (Addison-Wesley, 2003), by Don Box, with Chris Sells.
3. To access this namespace you must add a reference to the System.Runtime.Serialization.Formatters.Soap assembly.

```
    public int n = 452;
}


static void DoSerialize() {
  MyData data = new MyData();
  using( Stream stream =
          new FileStream(@"c:\temp\mydata.xml", FileMode.Create) ) {
    // Write to the stream
    IFormatter formatter = new SoapFormatter();
    formatter.Serialize(stream, data);

    // Reset the stream to the beginning
    stream.Seek(0, SeekOrigin.Begin);

    // Read from the stream
    MyData data2 = (MyData)formatter.Deserialize(stream);

    // Do something with the data
    MessageBox.Show(data2.s + " " + data2.n);
  }
}
```

After creating the formatter, the code makes a call to Serialize, which writes the type information for the MyData object and then recursively writes all the data for the fields of the object. To read the object, we call Deserialize and make a cast to the top-level object, which reads all fields recursively.

Because we chose the text-based SOAP formatter and a FileStream, we can examine the data that the formatter wrote:

```
<SOAP-ENV:Envelope ...>
<SOAP-ENV:Body>
<a1:Form1_x002B_MyData id="ref-1" ...>
<s id="ref-3">Wahoo!</s>
<n>452</n>
</a1:Form1_x002B_MyData>
</SOAP-ENV:Body>
</SOAP-ENV:Envelope>
```

Here we can see that an instance of Form1.MyData was written and that it contains two fields: one (called s) with the value "Wahoo!", and a second one (called n) with the value "452." This was just what the code meant to write.

Skipping a Nonserialized Field

We have some control over what the formatter writes, although probably not in the way you'd expect. For example, if we decide that we want to serialize the MyData class but not the n field, we can't stop the formatter by marking the field as protected or private. To be consistent at deserialization, an object will need the protected and private fields just as much as it needs the public ones (in fact, fields shouldn't be public at all!). However, if we apply NonSerializedAttribute to a field, it will be skipped by the formatter:

```
[SerializableAttribute]
class MyData {
  public string s = "Wahoo!";
  [NonSerializedAttribute] public int n = 452;
}
```

Serializing an instance of this type shows that the formatter is skipping the nonserialized field:

```
<SOAP-ENV:Envelope ...>
<SOAP-ENV:Body>
<a1:Form1_x002B_MyData id="ref-1" ...>
<s id="ref-3">Wahoo!</s>
</a1:Form1_x002B_MyData>
</SOAP-ENV:Body>
</SOAP-ENV:Envelope>
```

IDeserializationCallback

Good candidates for the nonserialized attribute are fields that are calculated, cached, or transient, because they don't need to be stored. However, when an object is deserialized, the nonserialized fields may need to be recalculated to put the object into a valid state. For example, if we expand the duties of the n field of the MyData type to be a cache of the s field's length, there's no need to persist n, because it can be recalculated at any time.

However, to keep n valid, the MyData object must be notified when s changes. Using properties keeps the n and s fields controlled. However, when an instance of MyData is deserialized, only the s field is set, and not the n field (recall that the n field is nonserialized). To cache the length of the s field in n after deserialization, we must implement the IDeserialization-Callback interface:

```
interface IDeserializationCallback {
  void OnDeserialization(object sender);
}
```

The single method, OnDeserialization, will be called after the formatter has deserialized all the fields. This is the time to make sure that the nonserialized fields of the object have the appropriate state:

```
[SerializableAttribute]
class MyData : IDeserializationCallback {
  string s = "Wahoo!";
  [NonSerializedAttribute] int n = 6;

  public string String {
    get { return s; }
    set { value = s; n = s.Length; }
  }

  public int Length {
    get { return n; }
  }

  #region Implementation of IDeserializationCallback
  public void OnDeserialization(object sender) {
    // Cache the string's length
    n = s.Length;
  }
  #endregion
}
```

If you've got any fields marked as nonserialized, chances are you should be handling IDeserializationCallback to set those fields at deserialization time.

ISerializable

To gain even more control over the serialization process, you can implement the ISerializable interface and a special constructor:

```
[SerializableAttribute]
class MyData : ISerializable {
```

```
  string s = "Wahoo!";
  int n = 6;

  public string String {
    get { return s; }
    set { value = s; n = s.Length; }
  }

  public int Length {
    get { return n; }
  }

  public MyData() {}

  #region Implementation of ISerializable
  public MyData(
    SerializationInfo info, StreamingContext context) {
    // Get value from name/value pairs
    s = info.GetString("MyString");

    // Cache the string's length
    n = s.Length;
  }

  public void GetObjectData(
    SerializationInfo info, StreamingContext context) {
    // Add value to name/value pairs
    info.AddValue("MyString", s);
  }
  #endregion
}
```

Implementing ISerializable.GetObjectData puts your class on the hook to populate the name/value pairs that the formatter is using to fill the stream during serialization. GetObjectData is provided with two pieces of information: a place to put the fields to serialize (called the *serialization information*) and the location where the object is going (called the *context state*). GetObjectData must add all the fields to the serialization information that it would like to have serialized, naming each one. The formatter uses these names to write the data:

```
<SOAP-ENV:Envelope ...>
<SOAP-ENV:Body>
<a1:Form1_x002B_MyData id="ref-1" ...>
<MyString id="ref-3">Wahoo!</s>
</a1:Form1_x002B_MyData>
```

continues

```
</SOAP-ENV:Body>
</SOAP-ENV:Envelope>
```

Deserialization happens with the special constructor, which also takes serialization info and a context state, this time to pull out the data. The SerializationInfo class provides several methods for pulling out typed data. For built-in types, you can use the specific method, such as GetString. For general types, you can use the GetValue method. For example, the following two lines of code are equivalent, with the latter the only choice for custom types:

```
s = info.GetString("MyString");
s = (string)info.GetValue("MyString", typeof(string));
```

Data Versioning

The types that hold the data are always subject to the .NET rules of versioning,[4] but that doesn't really help you when it comes to reading and writing old versions of the data using new versions of the object. One way to support versioned data formats is to write a version ID into the stream as part of a custom implementation of ISerializable:

```
[SerializableAttribute]
class MyData : ISerializable {
  string s = "Wahoo!";
  int n = 6;
  ArrayList oldStrings = new ArrayList(); // v2.0 addition
  static string currentVersion = "2.0";
  ...
#region Implementation of ISerializable
  public MyData(
    SerializationInfo info, StreamingContext context) {
    // Read the data based on the version
    string streamVersion = info.GetString("Version");
    switch( streamVersion ) {
      case "1.0":
        s = info.GetString("MyString");
        n = s.Length;
        break;
```

---

4. The details of .NET type versioning are covered in *Essential .NET* (Addison-Wesley, 2003), by Don Box, with Chris Sells.

```
      case "2.0":
        s = info.GetString("MyString");
        n = s.Length;
        oldStrings =
          (ArrayList)info.GetValue("OldStrings", typeof(ArrayList));
        break;

      // Version is not supported
      default:
        string message =
          string.Format("Version {0} is not supported.", streamVersion);
        throw new SerializationException(message);
    }
  }

  public void GetObjectData(
    SerializationInfo info, StreamingContext context) {
    // Tag the data with a version
    info.AddValue("Version", currentVersion);
    info.AddValue("MyString", s);
    info.AddValue("OldStrings", oldStrings);
  }
#endregion
}
```

This implementation writes a Version string on all the data it writes, and then it uses that string to decide which data to read back in at run time. As the data in a class changes, marking it with a version gives you a way to migrate old data forward (or to save old versions, if you'd like).

Notice also that the new hunk of data added is an ArrayList. Just like the simple types, the collection classes (along with a large number of other classes in the .NET Framework) can be serialized, making this model useful for all kinds of things, from storing user settings (as discussed in Chapter 11: Applications and Settings) to saving document state.

▎D
Standard WinForms Components and Controls

WINFORMS PROVIDES SEVERAL CLASSES meant to be composed to build applications. How (and whether) instances of these classes need to interact with the user determines whether they are components or controls. The technical distinction isn't important unless you're building one (as covered in Chapter 8: Controls and Chapter 9: Design-Time Integration). What is important is knowing what's available out of the box for your use, as listed in Table D.1. This appendix briefly covers all these except for the print-related components, which are discussed in Chapter 7: Printing.

TABLE D.1: Standard WinForms Components and Controls

Components	Controls
ColorDialog (page 634)	Button (page 644)
ContextMenu (page 641)	CheckBox (page 645)
ErrorProvider (page 642)	CheckedListBox (page 647)
FontDialog (page 635)	ComboBox (page 647)
HelpProvider (page 642)	DataGrid (page 649)
ImageList (page 640)	DateTimePicker (page 651)

TABLE D.1: Standard WinForms Components and Controls (continued)

Components	Controls
MainMenu (page 641)	DomainUpDown (page 652)
OpenFileDialog (page 635)	GroupBox (page 657)
PageSetupDialog (Chapter 7: Printing)	HScrollBox (page 651)
PrintDialog (Chapter 7: Printing)	Label (page 643)
PrintDocument (Chapter 7: Printing)	LinkLabel (page 644)
PrintPreviewDialog (Chapter 7: Printing)	ListBox (page 646)
SaveFileDialog (page 636)	ListView (page 648)
Timer (page 639)	MonthCalendar (page 650)
ToolTip (page 643)	NumericUpDown (page 653)
	Panel (page 657)
	PictureBox (page 646)
	PrintPreviewControl (page 654)
	ProgressBar (page 653)
	RadioButton (page 645)
	RichTextBox (page 654)
	Splitter (page 655)
	TextBox (page 644)
	StatusBar (page 656)
	TabControl (page 658)
	ToolBar (page 655)
	TrackBar (page 653)
	TreeView (page 649)
	VScrollBar (page 652)

The WinForms documentation does a really good job of providing the details of each standard component and control. This appendix is a quick look at each of them to give you an idea of what you have to choose from.

Components and Controls Defined

A *component* is a class that implements the IComponent interface from the System.ComponentModel namespace. How to implement IComponent is covered in Chapter 9: Design-Time Integration, but any class that implements IComponent becomes a component and can thereafter be integrated with a component hosting environment, such as VS.NET. In VS.NET this integration means that the component can show up on the Toolbar, can be dropped onto a design surface (such as a Form), and can have public properties set and public events consumed in the Property Browser.

The chief difference between a control and a component is the location where the interaction with the user occurs (if there is an interaction with the user). A control draws in a container-provided region and takes input from the user. For example, a TextBox is a control. On the other hand, a component may show a UI and take some input from the user, but it doesn't do so in a container-provided region. For example, the OpenFileDialog class is a component that interacts with the user, but in a separate window and not in a region on the form that creates the dialog.

The distinction between a component and a control is further evident on a VS.NET design surface itself, as shown in Figure D.1.

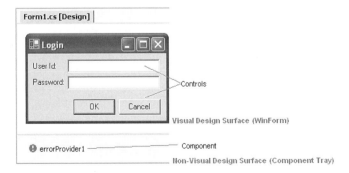

Figure D.1: Components Versus Controls

Standard Components

The following is a quick survey of the components immediately available in the Windows Forms Toolbox by default.[1]

Standard Dialogs

WinForms provides several standard dialog components that act as wrappers on the standard dialogs in the Windows shell.[2] All the standard print-related components—PageSetupDialog, PrintDialog, PrintPreviewDialog, and PrintDocument—are covered in Chapter 7: Printing.

Figures D.2, D.3, D.4, D.5, and D.6 show the four remaining standard dialogs as provided by the ColorDialog, FontDialog, OpenFileDialog, SaveFileDialog, and FolderBrowserDialog components.

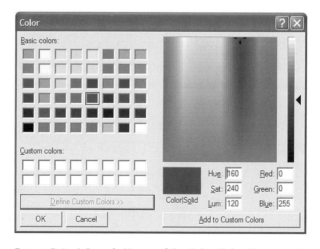

FIGURE D.2: A Sample Usage of the ColorDialog Component

---

1. .NET provides many more components that can be used with WinForms applications, but a survey of all those is beyond the scope of this book.
2. Because the need for previewing print output is prevalent, WinForms provides a standard PrintPreviewDialog even though the Windows shell does not.

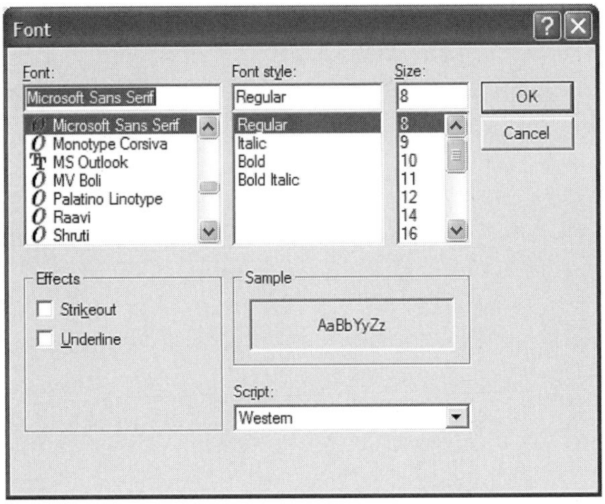

FIGURE D.3: A Sample Usage of the FontDialog Component

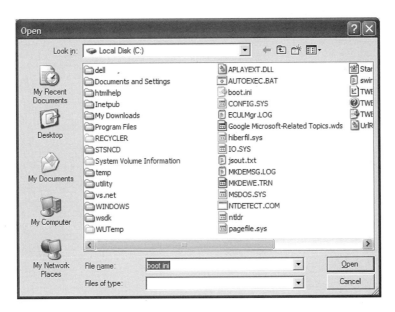

FIGURE D.4: A Sample Usage of the OpenFileDialog Component

FIGURE D.5: A Sample Usage of the SaveFileDialog Component

FIGURE D.6: A Sample Usage of the FolderBrowserDialog Component

Generally, you're most concerned with the Color property of Color-Dialog, the Font property of FontDialog, and the FileName property of OpenFileDialog and SaveFileDialog. However, all the dialogs provide other properties you'll want to examine, including the DefaultExt and Filter properties of OpenFileDialog and SaveFileDialog. Here's an example of the standard dialog components assuming that each of the components was created by dropping it onto a design surface:

```
// Use the ColorDialog
void chooseColor_Click(object sender, EventArgs e) {
  // Set initial color
  this.colorDialog1.Color = this.BackColor;

  // Ask the user to pick a color
  if( this.colorDialog1.ShowDialog() == DialogResult.OK ) {
    // Pull out the user's choice
    this.BackColor = this.colorDialog1.Color;
  }
}

// Use the FontDialog
void chooseFont_Click(object sender, EventArgs e) {
  // Set initial font
  this.fontDialog1.Font = this.Font;

  // Ask the user to pick a font
  if( this.fontDialog1.ShowDialog() == DialogResult.OK ) {
    // Pull out the user's choice
    this.Font = this.fontDialog1.Font;
  }
}

// Use the OpenFileDialog (used just like the SaveFileDialog)
void chooseFileToOpen_Click(object sender, EventArgs e) {
  // Set initial file name
  this.openFileDialog1.FileName = this.fileNameTextBox.Text;

  // Ask the user to pick a file
  if( this.openFileDialog1.ShowDialog() == DialogResult.OK ) {
    // Pull out the user's choice
    this.fileNameTextBox.Text = this.openFileDialog1.FileName;
  }
}
```

All the standard dialogs, including the print-related dialogs (except for PrintPreviewDialog), are limited to only modal operation via ShowDialog because that's what the shell dialogs support. Only PrintPreviewDialog, which is provided in WinForms but not provided in the shell, supports the modeless Show method.

Notify Icons

Another service provided by the Windows shell is the notification tray, where applications can put their own icons to interact with the user, as shown in Figure D.7. The NotifyIcon component has the following interesting properties and events:

- **Visible property:** whether or not the icon is shown on the tray
- **Icon property:** the icon to show
- **Text property:** the tooltip over the icon
- **ContextMenu property:** the menu to show when the user right-clicks on the icon
- **Click event:** when the user clicks on the icon or selects from the context menu
- **Double-Click event:** when the user double-clicks on the icon
- **MouseDown, MouseMove, and MouseUp events:** custom interaction with the user

Figure D.7 shows a notify icon implemented with the following code. It sets the tooltip text and icon at run time based on the user clicking and choosing menu items from a context menu:

```
// Icons
Icon northIcon = new Icon(@"C:\...\ARW02UP.ICO");
Icon eastIcon = new Icon(@"C:\...\ARW02RT.ICO");
Icon southIcon = new Icon(@"C:\...\ARW02DN.ICO");
Icon westIcon = new Icon(@"C:\...\ARW02LT.ICO");

// Helper
void SetDirection(string direction) {
  // Set the tooltip
  compassNotifyIcon.Text = direction;
```

FIGURE D.7: A Sample Usage of the NotifyIcon Component (See Plate 26)

```
  // Set the icon
  switch( direction ) {
    case "North": compassNotifyIcon.Icon = northIcon; break;
    case "East": compassNotifyIcon.Icon = eastIcon; break;
    case "South": compassNotifyIcon.Icon = southIcon; break;
    case "West": compassNotifyIcon.Icon = westIcon; break;
  }
}


// Context menu item: North
void northMenuItem_Click(object sender, EventArgs e) {
  SetDirection("North");
}


// Context menu item: East, South, and West elided


// Click handler
void compassNotifyIcon_Click(object sender, EventArgs e) {
  switch( compassNotifyIcon.Text ) {
    case "North": SetDirection("East"); break;
    case "East": SetDirection("South"); break;
    case "South": SetDirection("West"); break;
    case "West": SetDirection("North"); break;
  }
}
```

Timer

The example in Figure D.7 uses mouse clicks to do some primitive animation of the notify icon, but a more fun implementation would do animation itself. Because animation is simply a matter of changing an image after a certain amount of time has elapsed, our code to change the image is halfway there. All that's needed is a way to be notified when a certain amount of time has elapsed, a perfect job for the Timer component.

The Timer component notifies a listener via the Tick event based on two properties. The Enabled property must be set to true for the Tick event to fire. The Interval property is the number of milliseconds to wait between Tick events. The following example uses a timer to animate the notify icon:

```
// Notify icon click handler
void compassNotifyIcon_Click(object sender, EventArgs e) {
  // Toggle animation
  timer1.Enabled = !timer1.Enabled;
  timer1.Interval = 1000; // Animate once/second
}
```

continues

```
// Timer Tick event handler
void timer1_Tick(object sender, EventArgs e) {
  switch( compassNotifyIcon.Text ) {
    case "North": SetDirection("East"); break;
    case "East": SetDirection("South"); break;
    case "South": SetDirection("West"); break;
    case "West": SetDirection("North"); break;
  }
}
```

Image List

All this animation brings to mind the task of managing images, and that's what the ImageList component is for. An *image list* is a collection of images of the same size, color depth, and transparency color (as determined by the Size, ColorDepth, and TransparencyColor properties). The images themselves are in the Images collection and can contain any number of Image objects. You can edit the Images collection directly using Image Collection Editor, as shown in Figure D.8.

To use the ImageList after the images have been populated in the collection editor, you pull them by index from the Images collection property:

```
void SetDirection(string direction) {
  int index = -1;
  switch( direction ) {
    case "North": index = 0; break;
    case "East": index = 1; break;
```

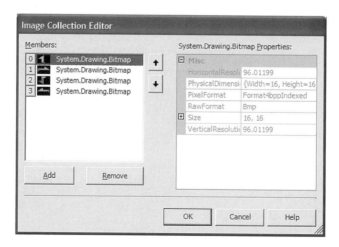

FIGURE D.8: Image Collection Editor

```
    case "South": index = 2; break;
    case "West": index = 3; break;
  }

  // Set background from the image list
  this.BackgroundImage = backgroundImageList.Images[index];
}
```

What's nice about this code is that all the related images come from a single place. However, the ImageList component has some limitations:

- You can't edit an image after it's been added; you must remove the old image and add the edited image.
- You can have only a fixed size of up to 256 pixels in either dimension.
- Image Collection Editor is difficult to use for images larger than 16 pixels in either direction.
- You must access images by index; you can't access them by name.
- Images are available only as type Image and not directly as type Icon, so if you need the Icon type you must convert it from Image.

These limitations, however, don't stop the image list from being useful. Chapter 8: Controls explains how to use image lists to set the images for toolbars and other controls that need small, fixed-size, related images.

Main Menus and Context Menus

The MainMenu component shows the menu at the top of a form and provides events when the user selects an item. The ContextMenu component, shown in Figure D.9, provides a menu to be associated with a control and invoked using the context mouse button (most often the right mouse button). Both the MainMenu and the ContextMenu components are covered in Chapter 2: Forms.

FIGURE D.9: A Sample Usage of the ContextMenu Component

Error Provider, Help Provider, and Tooltips

The ErrorProvider component gives you a way to notify users that a control has invalid data currently entered, as shown in Figure D.10.

HelpProvider supports the handling of the F1 key and ? button on a dialog. Figure D.11 shows an example of the pop-up help supported by the help provider.

As yet another way to show pop-up information, Figure D.12 shows the ToolTip component, which pops up when a user hovers the mouse over a control.

The error provider, the help provider, and the tooltip component are especially useful when you're building forms to be used as dialogs, so these components are discussed in detail in Chapter 3: Dialogs.

Standard Controls

The basic unit of the user interface in WinForms is the control. Everything that interacts directly with the user in a region defined by a container is an

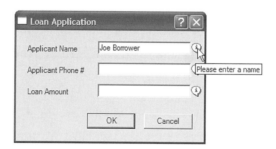

FIGURE D.10: A Sample Usage of the ErrorProvider Component

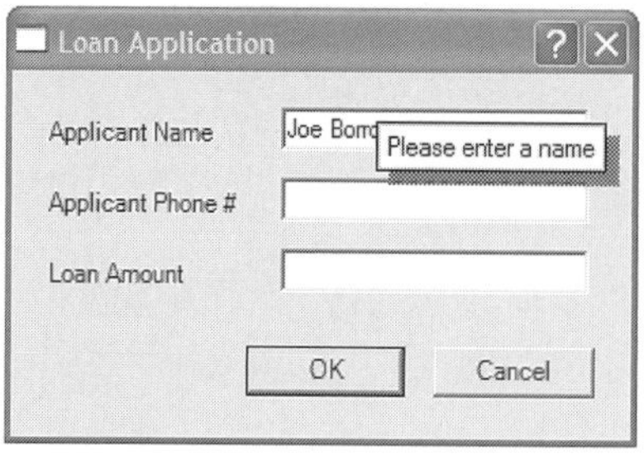

FIGURE D.11: A Sample Usage of the HelpProvider Component

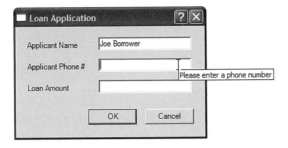

FIGURE D.12: A Sample Usage of the ToolTip Component

instance of an object that derives, directly or indirectly, from the System.Windows.Forms.Control class.

Non-Container Controls

Non-container controls are those that don't contain other controls.

Label

The Label control, shown in Figure D.13, holds literal text that is meant to be informative to the user. For example, in a typical application, labels are displayed near text boxes to inform the user what the text box contains. Text inside a label wraps to the width of the label. The label text can be aligned to any side or corner of the control.

```
// Label
label1.Text = "This is some test text...";
label1.TextAlign = ContentAlignment.TopCenter;
```

LinkLabel

LinkLabel objects, shown in Figure D.14, are just like labels but allow for one or more links to be embedded into the label. These links are clickable elements that trigger events.

FIGURE D.13: A Label Control in Action

This control is commonly used to allow users to click on links to Web sites from Windows Forms applications. You can add text to the link label in the same way as any other label:

```
// Will automatically parse common URLs
linkLabel1.Text = "http://sellsbrothers.com";
```

To make the link work, you must handle the LinkClicked event:

```
void linkLabel1_LinkClicked(
  object sender, LinkLabelLinkClickedEventArgs e) {
  // Start IE with the URL
  System.Diagnostics.Process.Start(e.Link.LinkData as string);
}
```

TextBox

TextBox objects, shown in Figure D.15, are used to display user-editable text. The text box allows for either single or multiline display and editing of text. The most common thing you'll do with a text box is retrieve the text within it:

```
MessageBox.Show(textBox1.Text);
```

Button

Button objects, shown in Figure D.16, are used to trigger actions on forms. When a button is pressed, the Click event is triggered:

```
void button1_Click(object sender, System.EventArgs e) {
  MessageBox.Show("Ouch!");
}
```

Click here to continue...

FIGURE D.14: A LinkLabel Control in Action

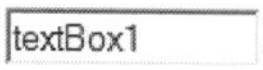

textBox1

FIGURE D.15: A TextBox Control in Action

button1

FIGURE D.16: A Button Control in Action

In addition, buttons can be designated as a form's AcceptButton or CancelButton. These designations specify that the button is automatically clicked when the user presses the Enter key (AcceptButton) or the ESC key (CancelButton).

CheckBox

CheckBox objects, shown in Figure D.17, are most often used to indicate the answer to a yes/no question. Check boxes normally have two states: checked or unchecked. Testing the state of the check box is as simple as retrieving the value of the Checked property:

```
if( checkBox1.Checked ) MessageBox.Show("Check box checked!");
```

Check boxes also support a mode in which they have three states: checked, unchecked, and indeterminate. When this mode is enabled, a check box starts in an indeterminate state and reacts to user input to toggle between checked and unchecked.

RadioButton

RadioButton controls, shown in Figure D.18, are similar to check boxes in that they can have a checked and an unchecked state, but RadioButton controls are normally used in a series to indicate one of a range of options. When more than one radio button is placed in a container (a form or one of the container controls listed later), the radio buttons allow only one button at a time to be selected. You can test radio buttons in the same way you check check boxes:

```
if( radioButton1.Checked ) MessageBox.Show("Radio button checked");
```

□ checkBox1

FIGURE D.17: A CheckBox Control in Action

○ radioButton1

FIGURE D.18: A RadioButton Control in Action

PictureBox

The PictureBox control's one and only function is to display images to the user, as shown in Figure D.19. The picture box supports most bitmap formats (.bmp, .jpg, .gif, and so on) and some vector formats (.emf and wmf). Here is an example of setting an image into a PictureBox control:

```
pictureBox1.Image = new Bitmap(@"c:\windows\zapotec.bmp");
```

ListBox

ListBox, shown in Figure D.20, holds multiple items that can be selected by a user. You manipulate items in a ListBox using the Items collection property. A list box supports selection of one or more items in the list by the traditional Ctrl-clicking of items. You can find out the selected item by using the SelectedItem property:

```
MessageBox.Show("Selected Item is: " +
  listBox1.SelectedItem.ToString()));
```

In addition, you can handle the SelectedIndexChange event whenever the selection changes:

```
void listBox1_SelectedIndexChanged(object sender, EventArgs e) {
  // Item changed, so let the user know which one is selected
  MessageBox.Show("Selected Item is: " +
    listBox1.SelectedItem.ToString()));
}
```

FIGURE D.19: A PictureBox Control in Action

FIGURE D.20: A ListBox Control in Action

CheckedListBox

A checked list box, shown in Figure D.21, is an extension of the list box that allows selection of multiple items in the list by checking boxes. In all other ways the checked list box is identical to the standard list box.

ComboBox

The ComboBox control, shown in Figure D.22, is a hybrid of a list box and a text box. The text box part of the control allows you to enter data directly into the control. When the user clicks on the down button, a list of items is shown, and users can pick items from this list. Like a text box, a combo box can be configured to allow free-form entry of information or to allow users to select only items that are in the list of items within the control. Because the control is part text box and part list box, it's not surprising that it can do a little of both. As with the text control, the most common task is usually retrieving the text:

```
MessageBox.Show(comboBox1.Text);
```

As with the list box, you can handle the event when the selected index changes:

```
void comboBox1_SelectedIndexChanged(object sender, EventArgs e) {
  // Item changed, so let the user know which one is selected
```

continues

FIGURE D.21: A CheckedListBox Control in Action

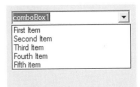

FIGURE D.22: A ComboBox Control in Action

```
    MessageBox.Show("Selected Item is: " +
      comboBox1.SelectedItem.ToString()));
}
```

ListView

The ListView control, shown in Figure D.23, is similar to the list box in that it shows multiple items that can be selected either individually or as multiple selections. The chief difference is that the list view supports views much like Windows Explorer's view of files. ListView supports a large icon view, a small icon view, a list view, or a details view. The details view supports more than one piece of information per item and allows you to define columns to show for the list of items. You can change the view by changing the View property:

```
listView1.View = View.SmallIcon;
```

As with the list box, you can trap the change in the selected index:

```
void listView1_SelectedIndexChanged(object sender, EventArgs e) {
  // Show the first of the selected items
  MessageBox.Show("Selected Item is: " +
    listView1.SelectedItems[0].ToString()));
}
```

TreeView

The TreeView control, shown in Figure D.24, is used to show hierarchies. The tree is made up of nodes. Each node can contain a nested list as exposed via the Node property collection, which is what provides the hierarchy. To create nodes in the tree view, you use code such as this:

FIGURE D.23: A ListView Control in Action

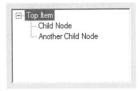

FIGURE D.24: A TreeView Control in Action

```
// Create Tree Items
TreeNode topNode = treeView1.Nodes.Add("Top Item");

// Add child nodes in the top node
topNode.Nodes.Add("Child Node");
topNode.Nodes.Add("Another Child Node");
```

In addition, the control supports events for expanding nodes, something that allows you to lazily load the tree view as the user looks down the hierarchy.

DataGrid

The primary function of the DataGrid control, shown in Figure D.25, is to allow binding to data sets and other multidimensional data sources. It allows you to store three dimensions of data. Although grids are often thought of as containing two-dimensional data (rows and columns), the data grid also allows the display of multiple tables, and that provides the third dimension. Chapter 13: Data Binding and Data Grids explains data grids and data binding in detail.

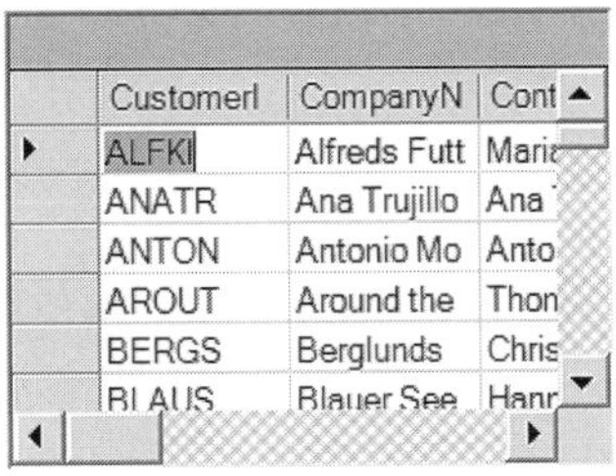

	CustomerI	CompanyN	Cont ▲
▶	ALFKI	Alfreds Futt	Marie
	ANATR	Ana Trujillo	Ana
	ANTON	Antonio Mo	Anto
	AROUT	Around the	Thon
	BERGS	Berglunds	Chris
	BLAUS	Blauer See	Hanr ▼

FIGURE D.25: A DataGrid Control in Action

MonthCalendar

The MonthCalendar control, shown in Figure D.26, is used to show or select specific dates. You can retrieve the selected date this way:

```
// Get all the Dates chosen
// SelectionStart is beginning Date
// SelectionEnd is last date
// SelectionRange will return all the dates
MessageBox.Show(string.Format("Date(s): {0} - {1}",
  monthCalendar1.SelectionStart.ToShortDateString(),
  monthCalendar1.SelectionEnd.ToShortDateString()));
```

The look and feel of the calendar can be changed to blend in with your applications. In addition, you can show multiple months simultaneously by specifying the CalendarDimensions of the control. You can also add bold-face to an array of specific dates or yearly dates on the calendar. This is especially useful for creating holiday and vacation calendar applications. The user can select multiple dates or a range of dates, although the maximum number of days selected is limited by the MaxSelectionCount property.

DateTimePicker

The purpose of the DateTimePicker control, shown in Figure D.27, is to display a user-editable date or time or both. To help control the dates and times that are displayed, the control allows for specifying a minimum and maximum date and time. To specify whether you want a date or a time, you choose a format for the text in the control. Short and long specify different date formats, and time specifies a time format. The drop-down

FIGURE D.26: A MonthCalendar Control in Action

FIGURE D.27: A DateTimePicker Control in Action

arrow on the control shows a calendar control to let users pick specific dates. Usually, if you are using the control for times, you will want to enable the up and down buttons by specifying true for ShowUpDown, as shown in Figure D.28.

To retrieve the date or time from the control, you get the Value of the control:

```
// Show the Date (or time) picked
MessageBox.Show(dateTimePicker1.Value.ToShortDateString());
```

HScrollBar

The HScrollBar control, shown in Figure D.29, is a horizontal scrollbar. Although most controls that use a scrollbar do so automatically, you can use this control to specify a scrollbar for subtle uses such as specifying a range of large values. You can specify the minimum and maximum range using the Minimum and Maximum properties:

```
hScrollBar1.Minimum = 0;
hScrollBar1.Maximum = 10;
```

FIGURE D.28: A DateTimePicker with ShowUpDown Enabled

FIGURE D.29: An HScrollBar Control in Action

The ValueChanged event communicates when the value has changed, and the Value property exposes the current scroll value:

```
void hScrollBar1_ValueChanged(object sender, EventArgs e) {
  MessageBox.Show("Current scroll value: " +
    hScrollBar1.Value.ToString());
}
```

VScrollBar

The VScrollBar control, shown in Figure D.30, is a vertical scrollbar. It is just like the HScrollBar but is drawn vertically instead of horizontally.

DomainUpDown

The DomainUpDown control, shown in Figure D.31, allows you to specify a list of items that the arrow buttons will switch between. The functionality is much like that of the combo box, but this control does not support showing the entire list at once. This control is ultimately a text box with the up/down control added so that the user can still type any desired text. Retrieving data from the control is identical to retrieving data from a text box:

```
MessageBox.Show(domainUpDown1.Text);
```

NumericUpDown

Functionally the NumericUpDown control is much like the DomainUpDown control, but the intention of this control is to allow the user to specify a numeric value. The control, shown in Figure D.32, supports minimum

FIGURE D.30: A VScrollBar Control in Action

domainUpDown1

FIGURE D.31: A DomainUpDown Control in Action

FIGURE D.32: A NumericUpDown Control in Action

value, maximum value, and a step value to allow you to control which number can be selected. You can select the numeric value of the control using the Value property:

```
MessageBox.Show(numericUpDown1.Value.ToString());
```

TrackBar

The track bar, shown in Figure D.33, allows the user to specify a numeric value with a maximum and a minimum value. The control captures the arrow, Page Up, and Page Down keys to control how the values are moved on the track bar. You can specify the number of positions in the bar, the number of values between each visible tick, and the number of ticks to move on an arrow key move or on the Page Up and Page Down key moves. You can catch the changed event of the track bar this way:

```
void trackBar1_ValueChanged(object sender, System.EventArgs e) {
  MessageBox.Show(trackBar1.Value.ToString());
}
```

ProgressBar

The progress bar, shown in Figure D.34, is simply a user feedback control that displays a level of completion. The control allows you to specify the minimum and maximum values, although the control continues to show the blocks shown here. You call the increment method with a number for the amount to move the progress bar. There is no decrement method, but incrementing with a negative value will cause the progress bar to back up:

FIGURE D.33: A TrackBar Control in Action

FIGURE D.34: A ProgressBar Control in Action

```
// Advance the Progress bar
progressBar1.Increment(1);

// Decrement the Progress bar
progressBar1.Increment(-1);
```

RichTextBox

The RichTextBox control, shown in Figure D.35, is used for input and display of text formatted in the rich text format. The control lets you set ranges of text with various fonts, colors, and sizes. You can save the document in the rich text edit control using the SaveFile method:

```
// Save the file
richTextBox1.SaveFile("myfile.rtf", RichTextBoxStreamType.RichText);
```

PrintPreviewControl

The PrintPreviewControl, shown in Figure D.36, is used in creating a print preview window, as discussed in Chapter 7: Printing.

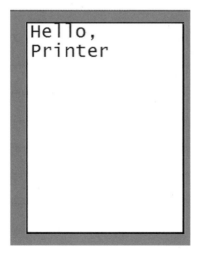

This is a rich text box. This format
was created by Microsoft
(http://www.microsoft.com).

FIGURE D.35: A RichTextBox Control in Action

FIGURE D.36: A PrintPreviewControl Control in Action

Splitter

The Splitter control, shown in Figure D.37, is used to allow dynamic resizing of a docked control within a form. Docking and splitting are discussed in detail in Chapter 2: Forms.

ToolBar

A ToolBar, shown in Figure D.38, is similar to a main menu except that toolbars usually are used to specify buttons to press for quicker access to specific functionality. The toolbar is made up of a collection of buttons

FIGURE D.37: A Splitter Control in Action

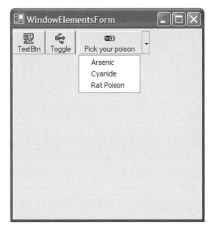

FIGURE D.38: A ToolBar Control in Action

exposed by the Buttons property. The supported button styles are standard, toggle, separator, and drop-down. The drop-down button allows you to specify a menu to show when the down button is pushed. You can handle toolbar button clicks by handling the ButtonClick event on the toolbar itself and checking the sender to see which button was clicked:

```
void toolBar1_ButtonClick(
  object sender, ToolBarButtonClickEventArgs e) {

  if( sender == toolBarButton1 ) { ... }
  else if( sender == toolBarButton2 ) { ... }
}
```

StatusBar

The StatusBar control, shown in Figure D.39, is used to show the standard status bar on the bottom of a form. The status bar can either show a simple piece of text or show a series of panels, each of which can be either a text panel or an owner-drawn panel. You can change the text in a panel on a status bar like so:

```
// Set the text in one of the panels
statusBar1.Panels[0].Text = "Working...";
```

FIGURE D.39: A StatusBar Control in Action

Container Controls

Container controls are used to hold other controls. These are commonly used to break complicated forms into manageable sizes or for creating logical groups.

Panel

The Panel control, shown in Figure D.40, is a flat container for other controls to be placed within. The panel can have its frame style changed to suit the design of a particular form.

GroupBox

A GroupBox, shown in Figure D.41, is a Panel control that has a label and a frame.

TabControl

The TabControl control, shown in Figure D.42, is a hybrid of a container and a control. The tabs on the top of the control are buttons that switch between pages. Each of the pages is a separate container for controls. When using a tab control, you design each page's content by dragging and dropping controls onto the tab control's surface as you would if each tab page

FIGURE D.40: A Panel Control in Action

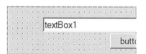

FIGURE D.41: A GroupBox Control in Action

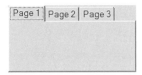

FIGURE D.42: A TabControl Control in Action

were a separate dialog. You can programmatically switch tabs by setting the SelectedIndex or SelectedTab property:

```
// Change the index to the third page (2 = 3rd page)
// Both lines do the same thing, select the page by index
// or page control name
tabControl1.SelectedIndex = 2;
tabControl1.SelectedTab = tabPage3; // Name of page control
```

Bibliography

The following resources either were used to prepare this book or are good resources for more information.

Ballinger, Keith. *.NET Web Services: Architecture and Implementation with .NET*, Boston, MA: Addison-Wesley, 2003.

Box, Don, with Chris Sells. *Essential .NET, Volume 1: The Common Language Runtime*, Boston, MA: Addison-Wesley, 2003.

Celko, Joe. *Instant SQL Programming*, Birmingham [Eng.]: Wrox Press, 1995.

Chiu, Peter. ntcopyres.exe, http://www.codeguru.com/cpp_mfc/rsrc-simple.html, October 2001.

"Finding and Fixing Slammer Vulnerabilities," http://www.microsoft.com/security/slammer.asp, February 2003.

Microsoft Developer Network, http://msdn.microsoft.com

Newcomer, Joseph. "Avoiding Multiple Instances of an Application," http://flounder.com/nomultiples.htm, March 2003.

Onion, Fritz. *Essential ASP.NET*, Boston, MA: Addison-Wesley, 2003.

Rammer, Ingo. *Advanced .NET Remoting*, Berkeley, CA: APress, 2002.

Richter, Jeffrey. *Applied Microsoft .NET Framework Programming*, Redmond, WA: Microsoft Press, 2002.

Sells, Chris. ".NET Delegates: A C# Bedtime Story,"
http://www.sellsbrothers.com/writing/delegates.htm, 2001.

Sells, Chris. ".NET Image Re-Coloring," *Windows Developer Magazine Online*,
http://www.sellsbrothers.com/writing/DotNetImageReColoring.htm,
November 2002.

Sells, Chris. ".NET Zero Deployment: Security and Versioning Models in the
Windows Forms Engine Help You Create and Deploy Smart Clients," *MSDN
Magazine*, July 2002.

Sells, Chris. "A Second Look at Windows Forms Multithreading," *MSDN Online*,
September 2002.

Sells, Chris. "Components Are Not Just For GUIs," *Windows Developer Magazine
Online*, http://www.windevnet.com/documents/s=7481/win1027981809543/,
July 2002.

Sells, Chris. "Creating Non-Rectangular Windows," *Windows Developer Magazine
Online*, http://www.windevnet.com/documents/s=7535/win1034118484572/
1003cso.html, October 2002.

Sells, Chris. "Increasing Permissions for Web-Deployed WinForms Applications,"
MSDN Online, November 2002.

Sells, Chris. "Launching No-Touch Deployment Applications with Command Line
Arguments," *MSDN Online*, June 2, 2003.

Sells, Chris. "Microsoft .NET Framework Resource Basics," *MSDN Online*,
February 2003.

Sells, Chris. "Printer Margins, Part 1," *Windows Developer Magazine Online*,
http://www.windevnet.com/documents/s=7481/win1048094898724/,
March 2003.

Sells, Chris. "Printer Margins, Part 2," *Windows Developer Magazine Online*,
http://www.windevnet.com/documents/s=7481/win1049396577703/,
April 2003.

Sells, Chris. "Resources and WinForms," *Windows Developer Magazine Online*,
http://www.sellsbrothers.com/writing/ResourcesAndWinForms.htm,
September 2002.

Sells, Chris. "Safe, Simple Multithreading in Windows Forms, Part 3," *MSDN
Online*, January 2003.

Sells, Chris. "Safe, Simple Multithreading in Windows Forms," *MSDN Online*, June 2002.

Sells, Chris. "Serialization Basics, Part 1," *Windows Developer Magazine Online*, http://www.windevnet.com/documents/s=7481/win1044571786904/, February 2003.

Sells, Chris. "Serialization Basics, Part 2," *Windows Developer Magazine Online*, http://www.windevnet.com/documents/s=7481/win1045093344162/, February 2003.

Sells, Chris. "Serialization Basics, Part 3," *Windows Developer Magazine Online*, http://www.windevnet.com/documents/s=7481/win1046801931106/, March 2003.

Sells, Chris. "Windows Forms Layout," *MSDN Online*, December 2002.

Sells, Chris. "Windows Forms: .NET Framework 1.1 Provides Expanded Namespace, Security, and Language Support for Your Projects," *MSDN Magazine*, March 2003.

Sells, Chris. "WinForms Auto-Scaling," *Windows Developer Magazine Online*, http://www.sellsbrothers.com/writing/winformsAutoScaling.htm, November 2002.

Sells, Chris. "WinForms Data Validation," *Windows Developer Magazine Online*, http://www.sellsbrothers.com/writing/winformsDataValidation.htm, November 2002.

Sells, Chris, et al. Genghis class library, http://www.genghisgroup.com.

Skinner, Morgan. DebugIEHost Registry setting, http://discuss.develop.com/archives/wa.exe?A2=ind0109A&L=DOTNET&P=R9256&I=-3, September 2001.

Weinhardt, Michael, and Chris Sells. "Building Windows Forms Controls and Components with Rich Design-Time Features, Part 1," *MSDN Magazine*, April 2003.

Weinhardt, Michael, and Chris Sells. "Building Windows Forms Controls and Components with Rich Design-Time Features, Part 2," *MSDN Magazine*, May 2003.

Weinhardt, Michael, and Chris Sells. "Regular Expressions in .NET," *Windows Developer Magazine*, http://www.wd-mag.com/documents/s=7547/win0212d/, November 2002.

Wildermuth, Shawn. *Pragmatic ADO.NET*, Boston, MA: Addison-Wesley, 2003.

The material from the following *MSDN Magazine* articles served as the base for Chapter 9: Design-Time Integration, and Chapter 15: Web Deployment:

Sells, Chris. ".NET Zero Deployment: Security and Versioning Models in the Windows Forms Engine Help You Create and Deploy Smart Clients," *MSDN Magazine*, July 2002.

Weinhardt, Michael, and Chris Sells. "Building Windows Forms Controls and Components with Rich Design-Time Features, Part 1," *MSDN Magazine*, April 2003.

Weinhardt, Michael, and Chris Sells. "Building Windows Forms Controls and Components with Rich Design-Time Features, Part 2," *MSDN Magazine*, May 2003.

Index

Microsoft .NET Development Series

.NET Framework
Standard Library
Annotated Reference
Volume 1:

Microsoft .NET Framework
Class Libraries Team
Brad Abrams, Editor

0321154894

.NET Web Services
Architecture and Implementation

Keith Ballinger

0321113594

Essential .NET
Volume 1
The Common Language Runtime

Don Box
with Chris Sells

0201734117

Graphics
Programming
with GDI+

Mahesh Chand

0321160770

The C#
Programming
Language

Anders Hejlsberg
Scott Wiltamuth
Peter Golde

0321154916

A First Look at
ADO.NET and
System Xml v 2.0

Alex Homer
Dave Sussman
Mark Fussell

0321228391

A First Look at
ASP.NET v.2.0

Alex Homer
Dave Sussman
Rob Howard

0321228960

The
Common Language
Infrastructure
Annotated Standard

James S. Miller
Susann Ragsdale

0321154932

Essential ASP.NET
with Examples in C#

Fritz Onion

0201760401

Essential ASP.NET
with Examples in Visual Basic .NET

Fritz Onion

0201760398

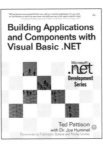

Building Applications
and Components with
Visual Basic .NET

Ted Pattison
with Dr. Joe Hummel

0201734958

Windows Forms
Programming in C#

Chris Sells

0321116208

Windows Forms
Programming in
Visual Basic .NET

Chris Sells
Justin Gehtland

0321125193

The Visual Basic
.NET Programming
Language

Paul Vick

0321169514

Programming
in the .NET
Environment

Damien Watkins
Mark Hammond
Brad Abrams

0201770180

Pragmatic ADO.NET
Data Access for the Internet World

Shawn Wildermuth

0201745682

For more information go to www.awprofessional.com/msdotnetseries/

informIT

YOUR GUIDE TO IT REFERENCE

Articles

Keep your edge with thousands of free articles, in-depth features, interviews, and IT reference recommendations – all written by experts you know and trust.

Online Books

Answers in an instant from **InformIT Online Book's** 600+ fully searchable on line books. For a limited time, you can get your first 14 days **free**.

POWERED BY
Safari
TECH BOOKS ONLINE

Catalog

Review online sample chapters, author biographies and customer rankings and choose exactly the right book from a selection of over 5,000 titles.